The Berkeley Co-op Food Book

Eat Better and Spend Less

The Berkeley Co-op Food Book

edited by Helen Black

Eat Better and Spend Less

 Bull Publishing Company

Design: Mary Sheppard

© Copyright 1980
Bull Publishing Co.
P.O. Box 208
Palo Alto, California 94302

ISBN 0-915950-43-X
Library of Congress
Catalog No. 80-65492

Table of Contents

Foreword

This book climaxes more than twenty-five years of daily, dedicated labor by the staff of professional home economists who are part of the Education Department of the Berkeley Co-op, a member-owned, member-controlled consumers cooperative that operates twelve supermarkets and several non-food facilities in the San Francisco Bay Area, California.

It was labor — but it was a labor of love. Day after day, week after week, the home economists turned out, and continue to turn out, articles, information sheets, graphic displays, store shelf signs, recipes, suggested menus, and many other materials, all revolving around the central theme of helping consumers to buy more wisely and more economically, and to prepare and serve what they buy in the most nutritious, most tasteful way.

It can truly be said that the Berkeley Co-op's home economists pioneered in making practical, reliable consumer information available to all. The program was started by Mary Gullberg and Betsy Wood. They broke the ground that has become, in more recent years, a fertile field for many institutions — serving the consumer. They were largely responsible for the Berkeley Co-op's participation in a number of major consumer breakthroughs, both in California and in the nation as a whole, including:

- enactment of a bread enrichment law (1970) in California
- sale of nitrite-free hotdogs (1971) at Berkeley Co-op
- enactment of nutritional labeling by the Federal Food and Drug Administration (1971-72)
- enactment of a compulsory dairy product ingredient labeling law (1972) in California

These things might never have happened except in a consumers co-op. The reason is simple: a consumer co-op is organized differently from other businesses. No member, no matter how many shares he or she owns, has more than one vote. One member, one vote! The result is an organization very responsive to its membership rather than to its largest shareholder. The Berkeley Co-op membership has always vigorously supported the efforts of its home economists to seek solutions to consumer problems.

Helen Black, who selected, refined and organized the materials in this book from thousands of pages produced over the years by her colleagues and herself, has been a Co-op home economist for fifteen years. She is also a registered dietitian, and a skilled and entertaining writer.

Some of the home economists represented in this book are no longer with the Berkeley Co-op. But each, no matter how long she was employed, made an important contribution to the operation of the Co-op and, through that medium, to the welfare of consumers.

Lee Awner
Education Director
Berkeley Co-op
December 1979

Introduction

This book is not a cookbook.

It is true that the Berkeley Co-op's staff of home economists have been engrossed in the subject of food and cooking over the years. Our identification with food is such that if some shopper hollers "Hello, food lady" from across the store we respond at once. We know who's being addressed.

But our fascination with food extends far beyond the mere pleasure of eating. Aided and abetted by the wide-ranging curiosity of Co-op shoppers, we have gathered information on nutrition, food labeling, food costs, food preparation, additives, toxins, safe storage and handling, meal planning, and — very important — legislation and administrative regulations involving food. We are indebted to all the knowledgeable people who helped us, including our suppliers and many persons in government agencies, cooperative extension services and the University of California.

This information has been relayed to our members through Buy Word, a column appearing in the *Co-op News*, the Berkeley Co-op's weekly publication which goes to all members; through information sheets distributed in the stores; through special exhibits displayed in the stores. It also is relayed through unique point-of-purchase cards posted on the shelves in the stores, depicted as boxed items "from your Co-op home economist" in this book, and, of course, through direct answers to questions asked by shoppers in person or by phone or letter. It seems to us that shoppers have taken from these writings whatever was practical and appropriate for them and used it in varying degrees to better their eating.

This book has been drawn from these materials.

Some of the articles selected for the book are updated. Others have been left as originally written, either because it was impractical to update and reprice them, or because the points made were valid without updating. (Besides, one gains a certain melancholy perspective at the spectacle of yesterday's prices.) The date of original publication has been included on articles which have not been updated. Names of authors appear on Buy Word articles but not on other materials.

Most of the writings come from Co-op home economists, past and present. They are Trudy Ascher, Helen Black, Nancy Bratt, Wendy Gardner, Mary Gullberg, Judy Heckman, Marion Hildebrandt, June Kadish, Mary Ruth Nelson, Thelma Phipps, Julia Robinson, Catherine Sinnott, Joan Taylor, Jean Tuggle, and Betsy Wood. However, some articles were written for us by others, including the late Jim Hardcastle of Capricorn Coffee Company, Dr. Korel Popper, chemist (now retired) with the U.S. Department of Agriculture, and Adolph Kamil, pharmacist with the Consumers Co-op of Berkeley. We much appreciate their expert and well-written contributions.

Finally, we are most grateful to Ann Norberg for her painstaking work of classifying our materials for us; and to Max Awner, veteran Co-op journalist, for his help in editing and polishing the selected materials, and for making many suggestions which improved the final product.

Helen Black
December 1979

How to be an Active, Informed Consumer

A short history of the consumer movement

A Play * by Betsy Wood
Scene: Morning, University Avenue Co-op Coffee Bar
Characters: George, a Co-op member
Sally, Coffee Bar Manager

George: Morning, Sally.
Sally: Morning, George. What'll it be?
George: (Reading menu) Breakfast Special looks good!
Sally: (Calling over shoulder) O.J., two eggs, bacon, toast, hashbrowns, coffee.
George: Sally, hold the orange juice. I don't like what Anita Bryant is doing.
Sally: (Calling) No O.J.!
George: And skip the eggs. Been told to cut my cholesterol.
Sally: Hold the eggs!
George: Better forget the bacon. They say nitrites cause cancer.
Sally: No bacon on that order!
George: And leave off the hash browns. (Patting his stomach) All that fat and additives, you know.
Sally: (Calling still) Forget that special. (To George) Toast and jelly coming up!
George: No jelly please. I'm told it's 55% sugar. And no butter. Saturated fat, you know.
Sally: (Forever cheerful) Dry toast then?
George: Better not toast it. I just read about high temperatures and the damage it does.
Sally: Here's your bread.
George: (Glancing behind counter) I see it's Wonder Bread. Sally, you know about IT&T.
Sally: Sugar and cream?
George: No. Not me! Not good for me.
Sally: Here's your coffee, friend.
George: Don't bother, Sally. I've heard caffeine causes heart problems . . .
Sally: We've got oatmeal. Ready in a minute. I just add hot water.
George: N'mind. That stuff is over-processed.
Sally: Nice seeing you, George.
George: Thanks, Sally. I'll just sit here and smoke a cigarette.

*Opened to wild audiences at University Avenue in May, bombed in Washington in June, was a rave at the Co-op family camp at Camp Sierra.

Sept. 18, 1978

Big four monopoly *by Betsy Wood*

In 1972 the Federal Trade Commission (FTC) issued a complaint that the "Big Four" ready-to-eat cereal manufacturers have illegally monopolized the market. FTC alleged that for 30 years these companies have maintained a highly concentrated, non-competitive market structure by proliferation of brands, trademark promotion, unfair advertising, restrictive retail shelf space programs and acquisition of competitors.

The BIG FOUR	Dollar Volume of Ready-to-Eat Cereals	Market Share
Kellogg's	300 million	45 percent
General Mills	141 million	21 percent
General Foods	92 million	16 percent
Quaker Oats	56 million	9 percent

The complaint said the companies failed to challenge each other's price increases and by their actions:

. . . obtained excessive profits

. . . blockaded entry into the market

. . . forced consumers to pay higher prices than they would have had to pay in a competitive market.

Does this all surprise you?

We rather doubt it. This is still in the talking stage. It's called pre-trial discovery.

Five years later, September 24, 1979 the "Big Four" cereal companies still have 87% of the ready-to-eat cereal market. The charges brought against them by the Federal Trade Commission went to trial in 1976.

This case has been in trial since April, 1976. Since then, Quaker has been dismissed from the case; they claimed that they did not share in the monopoly profits, among other things, and the judge agreed with them. Kellogg began presenting their defense in April, 1978; General Mills followed. At this point, the administrative judge hearing this case retired, and an interval elapsed before a new judge, Alvin Berman, was appointed. The trial will begin again in Washington, D.C., October 2, 1979, with General Foods presenting their defense.

According to the Federal Trade Commission, the trial may end around the end of 1979. There are already some 36,000 pages of testimony. When the trial ends, the various parties must submit their proposed "findings of fact" for the judges to consider. This could take an additional year! When a decision is made, the parties then can appeal the decision. More time will elapse.

What will happen if the decision is made against the cereal companies? Certain remedies have been proposed by FTC, including divestiture of plants by the cereal companies, making some five new cereal companies out of existing plants; licensing of trade marks so that other companies could produce these brand name cereals; and prohibiting Kellogg or other companies from offering shelf space plans to retailers, in which case the cereal company makes a computerized plan for arranging the various brands of cereal in the shelf space alloted for cereal by the retailer.

A little bitty breakfast cereal company
by Mary Gullberg

Skinner's Raisin Bran has managed to capture 3 percent of the raisin bran market with very little money spent on advertising and in competition with cereal giants such as Kellogg's and General Foods. The latter have imitated Skinner's Raisin Bran, spent an estimated $8 million yearly on advertising and now have the lion's share of the $140 million raisin bran market. Skinner's product sells for a little less than the competition. U.S. Mills, Inc., who makes Skinner's, is proud of its high quality standards and feels that this is reason they have been able to keep a toehold in the face of enormous competition. It was first produced in 1926 and apparently has a loyal following among breakfast cereal fanciers.

Most new cereals these days are formulated and advertised to appeal to children. They have contrived names, like Kellogg's latest "Corny Snaps," they have sugar as a principal ingredient, and they are heavily fortified with vitamins and minerals to compensate for the fact that they are made of refined cereal flours.

The battle for shelf space in the cereal section of the supermarket is a really tough one. Slow sellers tend to get pushed to the end of the top shelf while the giants, by adding new products to their existing lines, expand the space they require on the shelves. Kellogg offers to revamp the cereal section for the retailer using its computer program to allocate space according to sales. Testimony by grocers at the FTC hearings, which seek to determine if there are oligopolistic practices in the cereal industry, estimated that 80 percent of the nation's supermarkets have used such help from Kellogg at one time or another. Kellogg accounts for 45 percent of the cereal sales, General Mills has 21 percent and General Foods 16 percent. No wonder it's difficult for a small company to hold its small share of sales let alone increase them. **5/25/77**

On banning and education *by Betsy Wood*

"Co-op is two-faced," one shopper says. "You tell us not to buy light meat tuna to save the porpoises. Then why does Co-op sell the darned stuff?" The more we urge shoppers not to buy something, the more we get this criticism. But another member says, "Ban things from our shelves? Never! I want freedom of choice. Let's handle it all by education."

Both "sides" are equally vociferous. To both I've said, "Banning of major items is a matter for committees to study and for the board to decide. And besides, education often makes a big difference."

Does education work? Yes. Often.

People from Project Jonah, a group working to save porpoises and whales, approached the Co-op on the tuna issue. The Consumer Protection Committee studied it, and the majority recommended that this be handled by education. The board agreed.

Through a few articles, shelf cards, exhibits, we've urged switching from light meat tuna (the big seller), which may kill porpoises when the tuna is caught, to white tuna or bonito. Our ads have featured white tuna (expensive) or bonito

(a tuna-like fish, but cheap). Other groups stressed the issue too.

Sales show these changes in 2 years.
Light meat tuna............down 34%
White meat tuna.............up 40%
Bonito.....................up 300%

By the end of 1976, bonito, still unknown to many shoppers elsewhere, was selling as much as all five kinds of Co-op tuna combined. Hooray! (Meanwhile, light meat tuna fishermen have developed ways to cut the number of porpoise killed).

Yes, other shopping patterns change

High sugar breakfast cereals sales are down by about one half (see Sept. 20, 1976, Co-op News) after an extensive education and merchandizing campaign. Banning the baddies was suggested by individuals but was never brought to a committee.

Ban? Sometimes.

Grapes and iceberg lettuce not picked by United Farm Workers have been "banned" by the Co-op board for years. So have high hazard pesticides. And aerosols with fluorocarbon propellant were banned after extensive committee research concluding that continued use not only endangered the user but the rest of us as well. Along with the banning went extensive education, and most people found they could get along fine without any aerosols.

3/16/77

Why not buy as advertised?

by Catherine Sinnott

"There's an adventure in every bite"

I am sure you have noticed that commercials for foods on television use mostly slogans and very little useful information. "Honey Combs has a big bite," "Hershey, the great American chocolate bar." Food, especially breakfast and snack food, is advertised as crunchy, munchy, fun and even American. Some ads promise prizes, excitement, friends, action and tingle for your mouth. Many have entertaining presentations with song, color and great imagination. Ad-writers must search hard for gimmicks such as cereal that can be formed into words, like Alpha Bits, or that makes sounds when you add milk. Ad campaigns are like election campaigns. Slogans just say, "Vote for Smith" and if they say it often enough, we do. GOOD and FUN become synonymous with sugar.

The high sugar monster is still on the prowl

Some parents seem to think that sugared cereals are more nutritious than candy and cookies. They don't know that some cereals contain more sugar than candy does. Adding a few vitamins and advertising the food as healthy seems to make parents feel safe about high sugar cereals. They may even feel safe enough not to bother providing the vegetables, fruits, whole wheat, etc. needed for good nutrition.

You're on your own

At this point in time there doesn't seem to be much hope that advertisers will change and just push good food, good nutrition and good toys. Manufacturers don't care about you. They care about profits. As long as relatively cheap products such as wheat and sugar can be changed in shape, color, etc., to make them highly profitable, this will be done. YOU ARE ON YOUR OWN to learn to select foods for good food value rather than jazzy advertising. By now we know that brain washing is possible. Don't let it happen to you.

Food, expecially breakfast and snack food, is advertised as crunchy, munchy, fun and even American. Some ads promise prizes, excitement, friends, action and tingle for your mouth.

Advertisers: curious about consumers *by Helen Black*

If you've got a creepy feeling that someone's watching — you're right! Only it's not Big Brother, it's just another advertising agency surveying us consumers.

Advertisers have this morbid curiosity about us. After all, they spend a lot of money to influence our buying! It's only natural that they should scrutinize us up and down, probing for our soft, weak underbellies.

Any parent can tell you that love for the kids is expressed (in part) by giving them good, wholesome food. Betty Crocker did a survey and discovered this basic, pure motive of parents everywhere. Then she twisted it, ever so slightly, for her own purpose: a new campaign to sell cookie, cake and frosting mixes. "Desserts are a way to show others you care . . . associated with strong family values and emotions . . . to nourish the spirit," a spokesman says. Don't be surprised at her new slogan for selling desserts: "Bake someone happy."

Advertisers get panicky when consumers get restive. When beef prices skyrocket, or we worry about wasteful use of land, or health problems from eating too much fat, sales of beef drop off. So it's time for an ad blitz! Time for billboards showing succulent steaks! Time for magazine ads, with glowing accounts of the nutrients in beef!

And advertisers sure worry about us, too. Such as, are the kids learning to read and write? From Advertising Age a few weeks back:

". . . we all have a tremendous stake in whether people can read and write in this country. There is little point to writing a novel, creating an advertising campaign, or designing an attractive cereal box if nobody out there can read the message."

We consumers have a little morbid curiosity of our own. Such as, what does it cost to influence our buying? Checking this out, I found that Wrigley has reformulated its gum, Orbit, and endowed it with a budget for one month of $500,000. Morton's has a new dessert line with a media budget of $6,000,000 for the first year. For a grand total, the expected advertising expense in the U.S. for 1979 is $49 billion up from $44 billion in 1978.

July 9, 1979

To heck with pesticides, let's harvest the pests! *by Helen Black*

Well, we all know everybody's worried about high meat prices and the shortage of protein foods in the world. At the same time, we've got these horrid pesticide excesses. It's about time we put these two problems together and came up with one solution. Such as, why not harvest these crawling or flying friends and use them for food? If other countries can do it, so can we! Personally, I have a LOT of faith in the advertising of the U.S. food industry. I just KNOW they could get us to eat these strange foods. After all, look at what they've got us eating already!

But you're probably thinking, nobody knows the nutritive value of these critters. Wrong! I have a United Nations publication which gives this information on insects eaten in other parts of the world. Under the section titled MEAT, POULTRY AND INSECTS, the following comes to light:

. . . The protein content of flying ants (carebera sp.) varies remarkably with the sex! The male is 10 percent protein and 1 percent fat, while the female is 3 percent protein and 10 percent fat, which nearly doubles the caloric value. True, dieters would have to limit their intake of high calorie females. On the other hand, we could package the males as a low calorie snack.

. . . caterpillars, palm-weevils and other larvae are available raw, dried, fried, and smoked in some countries. The dried form is a whopping 53 percent protein! Why wouldn't these be great, with Hamburger Helper?

. . . Lake Fly Cake (Chaoborus edulis) also has a high protein content — 49 percent. If it's cake, Americans will love it. Actually, it's probably a dry product called cake, but there's no reason we couldn't sweeten it. Then it'll go over big.

. . . Grasshoppers (Acridium, Zonocerus) are available raw, or as a flour. The protein is a more modest percentage, but it's still twice that of wheat flour. As an added benefit, grasshoppers are high in iron. One serving would provide more than the Recommended Dietary Intake for men.

. . . Termites, too, are available raw, dried, smoked, fried. Their protein is about 35 percent, and they are high in fat. So high in fat that my thought is that we should extract the fat and use it for frying.

It's clear that we've been missing a bet! What are we waiting for?

5/14/73

TV — a sugar pusher *by Wendy Gardner*

Your 3 and 5 year old darlings are constantly asking for "Apple Jacks - Apple Jacks" . . . and you feel like a monster as you pass by the HoHo's, Twinkies and soda pop to the chorus of "I wanna, I wanna."

Don't give in, parents . . . the real monster is TV.

Children watch TV approximately 7 hours per day. By the age of 16 children have spent 13,000 hours in school and 22,000 hours watching television. Each year, 200 hours is spent by most children watching advertisements for mostly high sugar products.

So, what's a parent to do?

Sure, turn off the tube more often . . . also

1. Watch television with your kids. Look at how the advertisers appeal. Note the lack of programming with positive health messages.

2. Say no! . . . but more than no. At a recent workshop sponsored by the Committee on Children's Television (CCT) guidelines for parents were created including the suggestion that parents explain to young children that the people who make sugary foods make lots of money when children buy the products which they sell. Discuss with your children the clever ways the advertiser sells a product. Also express your concern to your child that he or she have a healthy body by eating good basic foods rather than such junk as high sugar snacks. Remind them of good tasting foods other than sweets, such as crispy apples, cold milk or whatever.

3. Praise or complain to the companies which advertise. Just use the address required by law to be on the package.

4. Boycott the sugar products.

5. Praise or complain to popular programs where characters are models for children. Perhaps the Six Million Dollar Man or Wonder Woman should eat raw vegetables. Should Cookie Monster become Salad Monster? Find the address and telephone number of the TV station and broadcasting company in the yellow pages of your phone book. Send a copy of your letter to the Federal Communications Commission, 1919 M. Street, N.W., Washington, D.C. 20554.

> **Parents could explain to young children that the people who make sugary foods make lots of money when children buy the products which they sell.**

J.H.

How to become a school lunch activist
by Wendy Gardner

Hooray parents!

You're still working on that uphill battle to use basic foods. But your efforts are being wiped out by your child's school lunch experience.

A junk food nightmare

There are vending machines enticing your child to divert school lunch money to buy soft drinks, potato chips and candy. The lunchroom atmosphere is chaotic, and children's bag lunches with candy and cakes are swapped between youngsters.

The lunch menus seem to reflect the high salt, high fat, high sugar diets which the U.S. Senate Committee on Nutrition & Human Needs warns may contribute to obesity, high blood pressure, heart problems, and certain kinds of cancer. For example, there are frequent appearances of salty, high fat pizzas, hot dogs, gravies, ham and sausage on luncheon menus. There is white bread, sweet desserts, and your child selects the sweet chocolate milk or whole milk. (Assuming your child was accustomed to nonfat milk at home.)

Start where the action is

April is a month when budgets and menus for the next school year are being planned. Although school lunch programs are federally and state regulated, they are run on the local level and are sensitive to local pressure. Anytime is right to get the action started.

1) Send for: *School Food Action Packet,* Center for Science in the Public Interest, P.O. Box 7226, Washington, D.C. 20044. Cost is $1.50.

This book outlines problem areas to look at and suggests how to go about getting solutions.

2) Arrange a visit to your child's school.

Ask about vending machines, school lunch menus, additives in foods, frequency that very sweet or salty foods are served, etc.

3) Talk up your ideas. Call a meeting, organize a committee, do some research. Set some goals and priorities. Negotiate with staff.

Involve older children in the process.

After doing research and sharing your concerns with parents and staff, you may discover that requiring vending machines to carry more nutritious foods is a priority. Or you may find that attending the board of education budget meetings is the way to start to make certain the business aspects of serving a school lunch do not overrun the nutritional welfare of your children. Or you might write letters to the board of education or the food processors involved. Getting the message to them is very important.

Look, John! Look, Mary! See the UPC
by Helen Black

See the UPC on food labels! See the stripes, broad and narrow! See the numbers underneath! See the UPC on more and more foods! What's it all about? What is UPC?

UPC means Universal Product Code, that's what. The stripes identify the manufacturer, brand, size, etc. of an item. With UPC on food labels a store can use a scanning device to read the code and match it up with the price, fed into a computer. With UPC and the necessary equipment stores can eliminate "ringing up" of groceries in the old familiar way. And stores can save the expense of putting prices on each item sold. And that's PROGRESS, we're told.

Already I'm getting nervous

Already it's very hard to compare prices of foods. Without a price on the item, even if it's well-marked on the shelf, it'll be even harder.

What if I want to compare the price of canned kidney beans, stocked in one part of the store, with dried beans stocked in another section? What if I want to compare nonfat dry milk with fresh milk? It's going to mean more running back and forth to check the shelf price. And I've got to remember the shelf prices, at the checkstand, to be sure I'm being charged the right price.

Can shelf pricing meet the challenge?

Supermarkets have been known to be a little sloppy about shelf prices. With UPC and automatic pricing, the shelf system will have to get a lot better. Most frightening is the ease with which prices can be changed in a computer. How can shelf pricing keep up?

At the checkstand: moment of truth

Electronic checkstands, when scanners are used, will be faster and that's all to the good. But this speed will also make it harder for shoppers to see what prices are being charged. Even though the new cash register tape will better identify the item and price charged for it, by that time it'll be an extra hassle to change your mind or corrrect mistakes. If a mistake is suspected, someone will have to go back to check the shelf price to be sure.

Saved . . . by a government agency?

We've seen some effective consumer surveillance on prices charged. Shoppers have looked at the price in the ad, on the can, on the shelf, and finally at the price rung up at the checkstand. The sharp-eyed shopper now picks up discrepancies. Some people wonder if a government agency, the Bureau of Weights and Measures, for example, could equal such surveillance on the accuracy of scanned prices. If so, we'll pay a pretty penny for it in necessary taxes.

On crowded labels

Already Co-op faces extra expense when the UPC will not fit on an otherwise satisfactory label. A new label for an item can cost several thousand dollars. The UPC may take up space we'd like to use for consumer information. Sadly, the extra expenses of changing labels are roughest on small companies. Some of them, as such new expenses become necessary to compete, will go out of business.

How much money will stores save?

Scanning will save an estimated 2% gross sales, or more; the savings from elimination of item pricing is estimated to be from 0.3-0.6% of gross sales. It will still be cost effective to item price with scanning. We should point out that in the supermarket industry such savings will go to shareholders in the form of increased profits. In the Co-op, on the other hand, any savings will be returned to the members.

11/4/74

Modern Mythology

or where did all the money go?

by Betsy Wood

You're broke. You sure would like to hobnob with money, but somehow it's always out. It's flown the coop by the time you get through the checkstand. Frustrated and angry, you think things should be better by now. Maybe you're suffering from a chronic case of Modern Mythology brought on in part by these modern myths:

Everything is getting better.

Well maybe some things are. But for the average working person real earnings haven't changed since 1967.

Surely there are fewer poor people as time goes on.

Dead wrong. During 1975 there were 2½ million new people "at poverty level"* for a grand total of 26 million or 11 percent of our population.

The rich pay 75 percent of their income in taxes.

Wrong again. The richest 10 percent of our people pay roughly 20 percent of their income in taxes, while the poorest 10 percent still pay about 11 percent in taxes. Sixty percent of the people pay a steady 16-17 percent.

The Department of Agriculture says people spend under 20 percent of their income for food.

Maybe true for rich people. But if you're in the lowest fifth, incomewise, it would take 53 percent of your income to buy the "Low Cost Plan" diet worked out by the Agriculture Dept.

Food stamps go mostly to students and strikers.

Not so. Two recent studies show that only 1.3 percent of food stamp participants are students and less than one-tenth of 1 percent are strikers. Less than one percent of the food stamp households have incomes over 1½ times the poverty level.

Well, modern myths or not, you're still broke and need help just to buy food. You might in-vestigate these programs:

Food stamps — Call your local welfare office for information.

WIC — (Women, Infants and Children) provides food vouchers for pregnant and nursing women, and children up to 5 years. Check with your local health department.

*The "poverty level" was defined in 1975 as $5050 yearly income for a family of four; in 1979, that level is defined at $6700. (Note: Part of the material for this article came from The Christian Science Monitor, September 28, 1976.)

11/10/76

How to get by on Food Stamps

by Betsy Wood

To get by on food stamps, you need to follow all these DO's and DON'Ts.

DON'T have teenagers, cause they eat too much. Food stamp allotments are based on families with school-age children. It takes 30 percent more money to feed a teenager than the "average child."

Especially, **DON'T have teenage boys,** because they take 45 percent more money than the average child.

DON'T have a big family, because after eight people each additional person is only allowed $22 per month for food.

DON'T be old or have diabetes or allergies. Special diets take MONEY, which you don't have.

DO have all day to spend. (This means you can't be a full-time worker, getting the minimum wage, trying to stay off welfare and support your kids). You need time: to take the bus, to stand in line at the welfare office to get certified, to wait to pounce on the mailman on the 1st and 15th, to wait in line to cash your check, to wait if the cashier runs out of money, to wait in line to buy your stamps, to get to the office before it closes at 5:15, and of course to wait at the checkstand on the busiest days of the month. And you need time to cook everything from scratch and grow your own vegetables.

DO forget what you've learned about cheap food. Right now, for sheer calories, cake mix is cheaper than bread or beans or rice or potatoes.

DON'T live in a time of inflation, because food stamp allotments are always 6 to 12 months behind actual costs.

DON'T be poor, because poor people's food has gone up a lot more than rich people's food.

DON'T be Oriental or Chicano or anything else with a cultural eating pattern. If you grow up without a cultural eating pattern, maybe you won't be accustomed to rice or beans. (Rice costs double what it did a year ago and beans cost five times as much.)

DON'T be too interested in nutrition, because you might think you should have lots of fresh fruits and vegetables or whole wheat bread — and you can't buy these often. (The U.S. Department of Agriculture says that the Economy Plan on which food stamp allotments are based is "designed for temporary use" and "does not provide as nutritious a diet as other plans." It suggests "less milk, meat, poultry, fish, eggs, fruits, and vegetables than other plans.")

DO have a rich aunt so you can eat there often.

DO have lots of extra cash around to pay the cash required to get stamps and to supplement your stamp food with goodies like meat and fresh milk.

DO be thankful that on July 1st your allotment went up. If you are in a family of four, you now get stamps valued at $1.25 per day per person, maximum.

But, you say, you've been making it without my advice? Let me know how you do it.

Note: This is a historical piece. In 1974, the price of beans and rice shot up out of sight. Food stamps are distributed on a completely different basis now and the allotment is now up to $1.67 per day, as of July 1979.

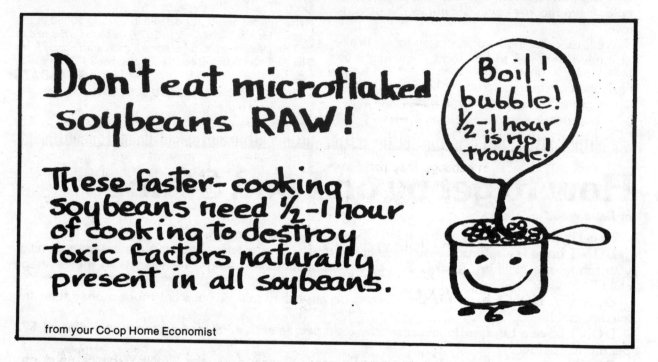

from your Co-op Home Economist

It's really not all that simple *

by Mary Gullberg

The total chemical environment and the vast variety of foods available to humankind make any attempt to pinpoint a cause-and-effect in cases of food-related illnesses very difficult. The exception is cases of poisoning due to microorganisms or accidental contamination of the food by grower, processor or consumer.

Foods are probably the most complex part of our total environment, since they contain toxic substances as part of their normal composition, and furthermore, chemicals such as pesticides and food additives may be applied to them during growth, storage or processing. Many chemicals naturally present in foods are the same ones used in efforts to produce, process, distribute and cook them. Most food additives also occur naturally in foods — vitamins, protein components, organic salts of many minerals, spices, flavorings and natural coloring materials.

Only a relatively few additives have been completely made by man. Toxic metals (lead, mercury, cadmium, arsenic, zinc) that may contaminate foods by environmental pollution or processing vessels also are normally present in foods because they occur in soil and water and thus get "built into" the growing plant. Other chemical compounds are generated by the heating, drying, freezing and pickling of foods.

We are able to control quite rigidly what we put into foods during processing, but the natural composition of foods is mostly beyond the pale of regulatory control. Take the potato — 150 distinct chemical substances have been found including solanine, alkaloids, oxalic acid, arsenic, tannins, nitrate, and over 100 more, all with no recognized nutritional value. Orange oil has at least 42 chemical entities, and all vegetables, fruits and other natural foods are similarly complex.

How do we survive the impact of myriads of potentially toxic substances in natural foods? First, the concentrations are so low that, except when grossly exaggerated quantities are eaten over an extended period of time, the levels that cause toxicity are never reached. If cabbage constitutes a large part of the diet for a long time, the goitrogenic substances in cabbage may produce goiters in persons eating the cabbage. It is the diversity of foods in our diets that protects us from these hazards.

Secondly, our bodies can handle small amounts of many different chemical substances in spite of the fact that larger amounts of any one of them perhaps could not be tolerated.

Lastly, there are natural antagonisms among these trace elements that reduce their toxicity. For example, a toxic level of cadmium in the diet is reduced by an accompanying high level of zinc. High manganese content interferes with iron absorption but can be offset by additional iron in the diet. Copper antagonizes molybdenum, selenium cancels out mercury, cobalt antagonizes iron.

This principle of "safety in numbers" in a wide variety of foods eaten has been recognized as applying to food additives and pesticides as well by the joint FAO/WHO Expert Committee on Food Additives. An increase in the number of additives on a permissible list doesn't necessarily mean that the amount used has increased but rather that these are alternate choices which reduce the chances of cumulative levels of any one. Pesticides also have a lower hazard when many different ones are alternately used for a single purpose.

*Summarized from "Natural Food Toxicants — A Perspective" by Julius M. Coon, Ph.D., NUTRITION REVIEWS, Vol. 32, No. 11, November 1974.

Food plants . . .

sometimes are unfriendly

Of course most plants seem friendly enough. In appearance they have a certain non-aggressiveness, a disarming passivity. But do not be too trusting. Plants, including food plants, do not grow themselves purely for our pleasure. Rather they grow for the survival of their species! Perhaps they increase their chances of survival by being indigestible, or by causing disagreeable bloating, or even by being truly toxic. The food person in each household should know of these crafty ways of plants.

More about naturally occurring toxicants in foods

by Mary Gullberg

In the last article I outlined some of the natural poisons in foods and discussed the reasons why we seldom have problems with them. These were that they occur in small amounts, and we eat a wide variety of foods generally and so get very low exposures to the toxic materials. Also, some of them when eaten together cancel each other out.

There are other ways that we are protected. Certain processing methods render the foods safer. Heating removes the cyanogenetic glycosides and some of the goitrogens. Refrigeration, canning, freezing, drying and even packaging suppress contamination by harmful microorganisms and chemical changes in the foods that could produce toxins. The worldwide food distribution system dilutes potential hazards caused by local imbalances or environmental factors.

Some safety in numbers

A short summary of some further examples of toxic materials in foods will underline the safety factor provided by a wide variety of food choices. Favism, a form of hemolytic anemia, is caused by a toxin in the fava bean. Buckwheat contains a factor that produces fagopyrism, a photosensitization to sunlight resulting in inflamed eyes, nose and ears in cattle. Similar photosensitizing agents occur in parsnips, carrots, parsley, dill and limes.

Lycopene, which is related to carotene, the vegetable form of vitamin A, can cause illness when it accumulates in the livers of persons who chronically consume large amounts of tomato products.

Nitrates may reach harmful levels in vegetables and forage plants grown in soils high in nitrates. A severe anemia similar to that caused by carbon monoxide, was produced in children who ate leftover spinach that was not refrigerated. Bacteria growing in the spinach changed the nitrates to nitrites, the chemical form that destroys the hemoglobin in the red blood cells.

Honey poisoning has occurred in both Europe and the United States. It becomes poisonous when bees collect nectar from mountain laurel, rhododendron, azalea and oleander, which contain potent heart stimulants.

Many plants used as food by both people and animals contain glycosides that produce hydrocyanic acid, an extremely toxic chemical, in the stomach. Some of the foods that contain these glycosides are bitter almonds; seeds of peach, plum, apricot, cherry and pear; lima beans and tapioca. Some 180 plant species are known to contain them and many of these are used for cattle feed.

Health Department's role

So the public health agencies are charged with protecting us from many hazardous foods and monitoring the sanitation of all foods offered for sale. We protect ourselves by eating a wide variety of foods and by handling the foods we intend to eat in safe and sanitary ways. And lastly, we should be wary of collecting and eating wild plants, berries, nuts and fruits unless we are quite sure they are safe to eat.

On being choosy about food additives

by Helen Black

For those who wish to be selective in their anxiety about food additives, help is at hand. Why worry collectively, if you can single out those chemicals which are most worrisome? EATER'S DIGEST, by Michael Jacobson, is an easy reference on the food additives in greatest use. Published first in 1972 by Anchor, it was updated in 1976 and costs $2.95.

The first chapter discusses the possible dangers of additives, gives some basic classification of additives, plus fascinating bits about the functioning of the Food and Drug Administration.

The second chapter is the most interesting and useful to me. Food additives are listed in alphabetical order. Dr. Jacobson gives for each a speedy run-down on the ways the additive is used in food processing; describes the knowledge, or lack of knowledge, of its safety or danger as used in food; and winds it all up with references.

The last chapter looks at standards for foods, including information on optional ingredients and labeling requirements or lack of requirements for additives.

There are four appendices, including a list of banned additives, a partial list of Generally Recognized As Safe (GRAS) substances with their functions, the chemical formulas of some additives, and a glossary. Plus a bibliography, plus an index.

Dr. Jacobson graduated from the University of Chicago in chemistry and received his PhD in microbiology from Massachusetts Institute of Technology in 1969. He has worked as a consultant to the Center for the Study of Responsive Law and is one of the founders of the Center for Science in the Public Interest. The Salk Institute of San Diego provided him with financial support while he wrote this book. He is also a co-author of the pamphlet, *The Chemical Additives in Booze*, as well as "Chemical Cuisine," a large wall chart on food additives.

'Chemical Cuisine'
by Mary Gullberg

Nutrition Action, a project of the Center for Science in the Public Interest, 1755 S. St., N.W., Washington, D.C. 20009, has prepared a large wall chart titled CHEMICAL CUISINE. It lists what the center's experts consider to be the degree of hazard for a large number of food additives. Here are a few examples from the much longer lists in the chart:

Safe. Ascorbic acid, carotene, calcium propionate, carregeenan, casein, citric acid, EDTA, glycerin, vegetable gums, hydrolyzed vegetable protein, lactic acid, lactose, mono- and diglycerides, polysorbate, sodium benzoate, sorbitol. Many of these are naturally occurring components of foods.

Caution — may be unsafe or is used in food we eat too much of, such as soft drinks and beer, fats and fat-containing foods, cereals and desserts: BHA, MSG, phosphoric acid, phosphates, propyl gallate, sulfur dioxide, sodium bisulfite.

Avoid — either unsafe or inadequately tested: Artificial colors, BHT, brominated vegetable oil, caffeine, quinine, saccharin, sodium nitrite and nitrate. In this group sugar and salt are listed, not because they pose any hazard if one does not overuse, but because many of us do consume too much for good health.

This listing seems to the Co-op home economists to be based on fairly good evidence. We thought we should share it with you since many of you have asked for such information.

February 6, 1978

Those rat facts about saccharin
by Helen Black

Are you familiar with the Bronx Cheer? Lately it's been widely used to ridicule the rat studies which showed that saccharin could cause rat cancer. Some people are hooting over reports that the fateful doses given the rats was about equivalent to the saccharin in 800 cans of diet soda. Not even a highly motivated teenager drinks that much soda in one day.

But this kind of rat test is NOT being questioned by sober scientific types. It is a bonafide method of identifying the weak cancer-causing chemicals whose effects show up 20-40 years later in humans. In contrast, highly potent chemicals do not usually require the same type of tests before their harm is recognized.

Why large doses must be used

The problem in identifying weak cancer-causing chemicals is that only one out of 20,000 Americans may be susceptible, yet that means that 10,000 people could develop the disease because of the chemical. There is not enough money nor trained people to study 20,000 rats to see if only one will develop cancer. Instead fewer animals are used with correspondingly higher doses. Such dosage identifies the tumor-producing capacity with meaningful, consistent and reproducible results. This system has been studied using chemicals known to produce cancer in humans and has been found to be reliable. It is now well known that if a large dose of a chemical causes cancer in animals, a low dose will probably cause cancer in some humans.

Do large doses of anything cause cancer? No!

This is another misconception floating about. The fact is that while extremely high levels of most substances can be harmful or even fatal, only a few cause cancer. For example, of 120 pesticides and industrial chemicals chosen for study because of evidence of toxic effects in humans, only 11 were shown to cause cancer in mice.

July 20, 1977

ARTIFICIALLY SWEETENED SOFTDRINKS:
ARE THEY WORTH IT?

Serious doubts have been raised about the safety of saccharin, the artificial sweetener used in many low calorie soft drinks.

Why not try a sparkling glass of ice water?

from your Co-op Home Economist

Nitrites and nitrosamines

by Mary Gullberg

Last report on nitrosamines was a Buy Word in the Co-op News of 4/20/77. How about an update?

Nitrosamines are known carcinogens formed when nitrite combines with amines from protein either when the nitrite-containing cured meat, poultry or fish is cooked or in the mouth or stomach when both components are present.

The U.S. Department of Agriculture on May 16, 1978 lowered the level of nitrite that can be added to bacon. There is increasing concern about nitrites since the recent MIT study showed that nitrites can induce cancer in laboratory animals.

The reason for the retention of preservatives in cured meat products is that in the past, nitrite has functioned to prevent botulism. Industry, FDA and USDA are now forced to develop new methods for controlling these competing health problems. The responsibility for regulating nitrites in our food is shared by two agencies and involves three different laws.

The MIT nitrite study has now been reviewed by FDA scientists who concluded that doses of nitrite fed to rats ranging from 250 to 2,000 ppm did increase the cancer risk from 7.9% in those fed no nitrite to 12.5% in the combined test groups. FDA and USDA have formed an Interagency Working Group for Nitrite Research to review all research in nitrite and nitrosamines, identify gaps in our knowledge and recommend research to fill these gaps. 11/6/78

The above information is from the Joint Statement of Carol Tucker Foreman, Assistant Secretary for Food and Consumer Services and Donald Kennedy, Commissioner of Food and Drugs on behalf of the USDA and the Public Health Service, Department of HEW before the Subcommittee on Agricultural Research and General Legislation, Committee on Agriculture, U.S. Senate, 9/25/78.

Nitrites in food
by Mary Gullberg

Are nitrites only in cured meat products?

No way! While the figures available for nitrites from foods other than cured meats are estimates, the indication is that only about 2% of the total dietary nitrites we are exposed to come from cured meats. The remaining 98% comes from other foods, drinking water and saliva. Even smog makes a contribution on days when it is heavy.

Saliva accounts for about three-fourths of the daily nitrite ingestion. An appreciable part of this is believed to come from the digestion of food and the action of bacteria upon it in the small intestine. The remainder comes from nitrates in the saliva reduced to nitrites by the bacteria in the mouth. The human body is exposed to an average of 33 milligrams per day of nitrite of which only 0.7 milligrams comes from cured meats.

Drinking water in the United States very **seldom** exceeds the standard set by the U.S. Department of Public Health of ten milligrams per liter (about one quart) of water. Water from private wells, however, may be higher in nitrate, especially water from shallow wells where the soil is impermeable. This nitrate can come from sewage pollution of the water, or from runoff from agricultural land.

Adults tolerate considerable dietary nitrate/nitrite but infants are more sensitive. Nitrite reacts with the hemoglobin in the red blood cells transforming it into methemoglobin which cannot be used to transport oxygen. The body rapidly replaces the defective methemoglobin except in the infant who has such a small amount of blood that a large amount of hemoglobin could be tied up at one time causing an oxygen deficit. This hazard to infants has only been found where well water high in nitrate was used to prepare their formulas.

(This information is from recently published material from both the National Research Council-National Academy of Sciences and the American Meat Institute. Both base their tentative conclusions on a rather limited amount of published scientific research from such as MIT and Iowa State University.)

10/16/78

What is GRAS?

by Mary Gullberg

GRAS (Generally Recognized As Safe) is a catchall. Into it were dumped all the food additives the Food and Drug Administration thought didn't need to be tested for safety at the time the Food Additive Amendment went into effect in 1958. Since 1972 a team of outside scientific experts has been taking a second look at these additives to make sure they are safe by today's standards. So far they have examined about half the 400 GRAS items and found only a few they considered questionable. Some of these are:

Caffeine not only occurs naturally in coffee, tea and cocoa but is added to cola-type beverages. The experts could not agree on the hazard but recommended additional studies in animals, human adults and children to check for birth defects and effect on behavior.

MSG has been alleged to be a possible hazard to infants under 12 months. The committee felt there was no hazard to adults at the present level of use, although a few suffer from "Chinese restaurant syndrome." Baby food manufacturers no longer add it to their products.

Protein hydrolysates are okay if derived from casein (a milk protein) but further studies are recommended for those from other sources. They should not be added to infant formulas or baby foods.

Licorice, licorice extracts, and ammoniated glycyrrhizin can cause temporary high blood pressure if used heavily. There is no hazard with normal use.

Regular sugar or corn sugar products are involved in tooth decay but pose no other known hazard. Recommendation is for further studies on the effects of increased consumption.

Nutmeg, mace, and their essential oils are recommended for further studies although there is no evidence of hazard at present.

FDA is committed to review all food additives and currently is reviewing GRAS and non GRAS flavors and colors. Here are some of the actions FDA has taken:

Placed **mannitol** on an interim status until more study is done on thymus gland growth in female rats.

Sorbitol was affirmed as GRAS, also **Dill** and **Garlic**.

Proposed that **BHT** be placed on interim status while checking effects on rat livers. **BHA** is also on interim status, though there is less urgency that for **BHT**.

The following are proposed for affirmation as GRAS: beeswax, clove oil, licorice, mustard as a flavor; gelatin as a thickener; iodine and sorbose (a source of vitamin C) as dietary supplements.

(This information was abstracted from "The GRAS list Revisited" which appeared in the May, 1978 issue of the magazine *FDA Consumer*.)

Nov. 27, 1978

How natural are those 'natural' vitamins?

by Adolf Kamil, Co-op Pharmacist

The idea that "natural" vitamins provide special benefits for our bodies has been raging around the Co-op. This has occurred despite repeated assertions by our home economists and pharmacists that vitamins have the same properties whether they are called "natural" or "synthetic." We know of no advantages to justify the higher prices that "natural" labels often command.

Co-op does stock "natural" vitamins for the many shoppers who prefer the products so labeled. In addition to our natural food stores, the pharmacies have been offering an expanded selection, and now our regular food stores have them, too.

Spurred by our growing sales, we have been trying to find out more about these products. A few weeks ago I visited two manufacturers of "natural" vitamins in Southern California. These companies make capsules, tablets, and other dosage forms sold under some of the most famous brand names found in "health food" stores, as well as our Co-op stores.

During the visits it became clear that many vitamin products labeled "natural" or "organic" are not really what I had imagined those terms to mean.

For example, their "Rose Hips Vitamin C Tablets" are made from natural rose hips combined with chemical ascorbic acid, the same vitamin C used in standard pharmaceutical tablets. Natural rose hips contain only about 2 percent vitamin C, and we were told that if no vitamin C were added, the tablet "would have to be as big as a golf ball." A huge stock barrel containing raw material for tablet manufacture was labeled "Rose Hips — Adjusted to contain 50 percent Ascorbic Acid". Nevertheless, the labels on the bottles read by the consumer were titled simply "Rose Hips Vitamin C." Would you have guessed that the amount of vitamin C coming from rose hips was but a tiny fraction of the amount added as a chemical?

Similarly, the B vitamins turned out to be mostly synthetic chemicals added to yeast and other natural bases.

Vitamin E products are indeed derived from natural sources — mainly vegetable oils such as wheat germ, soy bean, and corn. These are sold as cheaply as the synthetic variety. But in order to concentrate the vitamin in a capsule small enough to swallow, various chemical solvents must be used for extraction and separation. The vegetable material is grown with use of the usual insecticides and chemical fertilizers. Even the gelatin capsule must contain a preservative so that it won't turn rancid.

Again, the labels on the finished products say "natural" and "organic" without qualification. Here the terms are used quite differently from the way I had thought of them before.

Apparently, these words can be used freely, because there are no legal definitions of "natural" or "organic." In fact, since the vitamins themselves are identical, no one can tell them apart, either in a test tube or in an animal. A legal distinction could hardly be enforced when no way can be devised to test the difference.

3/6/72

FDA will regulate OTC vitamin and mineral drugs

by Mary Gullberg

The Food and Drug Administration (FDA), for the first time in its history, is engaged in a massive review of safety and effectiveness of all over-the-counter (OTC) drugs. This project is now in its eighth year and only about 40% completed. Seventeen "expert panels" are charged with recommending changes in product formulations and their labeling. Improvements in areas such as OTC laxatives, cough and cold remedies, dental and sleep aids, etc., are expected to save the consumer money as well as improve the products' usefulness. It is certain that consumer education by FDA, pharmacists, physicians, and the drug industry itself is a key requirement to the success of this undertaking.

The most recent panel to submit its recommendations[1] to FDA is the one dealing with therapeutic vitamin-mineral formulas[2] that make claims on their labels for treating certain conditions. Three-fourths of all vitamin-mineral products make no such label claims and are classified as food supplements. They fall under the regulations applying to foods. It is expected that no changes will be made in these products. According to the panel recommendations, products classified as OTC drugs involve some hazard to consumers and should therefore be regulated as to the amount and types of ingredients permitted as well as to dosage and contraindications.

Here are some examples of the panel's comments:

1) Calcium, iron and zinc are effective as single-mineral pills. Magnesium, phosphorus and potassium are not because deficiencies are rare. Copper, iodine, fluoride and manganese are dangerous in high doses.

2) Over a hundred miscellaneous ingredients that make no contribution to the effectiveness of the formula are considered inappropriate. Among them are apricots, brewer's yeast, buckwheat, comfrey root, hesperidin, kelp, lecithin, rose hips and wheat germ.

3) Combinations of the fat-soluble vitamins (A, D, E and K) should not be permitted, since such combinations are neither safe nor rational.

4) Elderly persons do not need so-called "geriatric" formulas, since their requirements are the same as other persons. Women do not need those labeled "for women taking oral contraceptives," because there is no evidence that these persons need additional folic acid.

5) Vitamins A, D and C are toxic in large amounts over various periods of time. Labels should warn of this toxicity.

1) Federal Register, March 16, 1979 and FDA Consumer, April 1979.

2) This particular "expert panel" was the Advisory Review Panel on Over-The-Counter Vitamin, Mineral and Hematinic Drugs. Like all the seventeen expert panels, it was chosen from nominations that came from consumer and other organized groups all over the country. The final panel had representatives from minorities, from health and other food groups, from the medical, pharmaceutical and nutritional professions, and one person who represented the general public.

June 25, 1979

Vitamin and other pills

may contain ingredients NOT REQUIRED TO BE ON THE LABEL including sugars, colors, flavors, binders, fillers, coatings, preservatives.

from your Co-op Home Economist

The cost of food labels *by Mary Gullberg*

Who pays? We have received a number of protests from members because we have pointed out that label changes cost **money.** The food business is one of such low margins that increasing the cost of doing business is a serious matter, not to be jumped into lightly. Ultimately, the consumers will have to pay for label changes as a part of the price they spend for food.

What do consumers want on labels? The recent **FDA, USDA** and **FTC** hearings held across the country revealed that consumers want:

1. All ingredients listed on food labels.
2. Total sodium and total sugars on labels.
3. Percentage of major ingredients on labels.
4. Open dating on food products.
5. Nutritional information that is understandable.
6. Better government regulation of fortified foods.
7. Education on how to use all this information.

What's the cost of getting this information on labels? There's a **labor cost** to gather the information and to redesign the label so it is both legible and legal. There are **analytical laboratory costs** to get the needed information. **FDA** insists it must be accurate. Changing **printing plates** for the new labels and losing money when **present label inventory** is discarded add up to additional costs.

Just suppose FDA makes nutritional labeling mandatory! Or suppose **FDA** decides to require some type of declaration of the sodium and various sugars in the products? Universal Cooperatives, which is ultimately responsible for all Co-op labels, estimates that such major changes for our 600 Co-op label products would cost:

$53,000 to rearrange the labels (new designs, printing, inventory loss, etc.)

$28,000 staff time

$105,000 at least for analytical laboratory tests

This breaks down to an average of $320 per product which, even if spread over ten years, is still a yearly cost of $32 per product.

It's not that we are dragging our feet on this matter. We are as keen for informative labels as anyone in the business. We just think you consumers should know approximate costs and that all of us make sure that when we do change labels we have researched all the problems first.

2/19/79

Speak up if you don't like it

by Mary Gullberg

A while ago, I talked to a group of fifty women — all employed as consumer advisors by major food processing companies. These women handle consumer complaints about their companies' products and services. I described how we handle consumer education and quality control problems at the Co-op. They were flabbergasted to learn how we do things and how many shoppers bring products back when something is wrong with them. They said they get very little feedback from consumers and very few complaints about the products their companies make. So I said I would tell you how to complain about national brand products . . . those sold under names such as Del Monte, Best Foods, General Foods, General Mills, Purina et al.

Write a letter! The address is on the label. The company's name, the city and state, and the zip code are all you need. Type your letter if possible and keep a copy. Address the letter to "Department of Consumer Complaints" or "Department of Public Relations." Be polite. Be brief. Be objective. Be confident.

Describe the problem including the exact name and size and any code number and/ or dates on the package.

Keep the evidence if it is not perishable. Do not send it with your letter. Keep the cash register slip with the purchase date and the price paid for the product.

Three things may happen:
1. Your letter may be ignored.
2. You may receive a form letter with an apology from the company's public relation department.
3. Or, you may hit the jackpot and receive a letter and one or more free samples of the product.

Before You Shop

Being smart about shopping

How to pick a good supermarket

by Mary Gullberg

Suppose you move to a new town or a different area in a metropolitan district and you're lost without your dear old Co-op, what to do? Case the joints in the new place, take notes as you go, record prices of frequently purchased items, then sit down and rate the various stores you visited. Try your first and second choices to see how they stack up under actual shopping conditions before you decide.

Here are some things (besides prices) to observe as you cruise the unfamiliar markets. These are not listed in order of importance — only you can know if a particular practice is important to you.

1. **Pricing.** Are most items singly priced or are they, for example, 3 for 57¢? Do the shelf tags carry unit prices (price per pint, pound or count)? Are the items individually price marked even if the cash registrers use a scanning device for ringing up the sale?

2. **Frozen foods.** Are the foods solidly frozen? Is the temperature of the box near zero degrees? Are frozen foods piled near front of the freezer where temperatures may not be low enough for long storage? Are stacks of products left in the aisle thawing while clerk is checking out customers or is out to lunch?

3. **Dairy and egg boxes.** Are the eggs refrigerated? Is the temperature of these boxes 42° F. or lower? Are they clean? Do the meat labels give the species, primal cut and retail name (like "Beef Chuck Steak")?

5. **Produce.** Is it wilted, poorly trimmed, dirty, or untidily thrown into the case? Is there adequate variety for your needs? Are there too many impulse items such as salad dressing, croutons, salad seasonings, salad bowls, etc.?

6. **Grocery.** Are there too many "out of stocks" on the shelves? Are marked down items in such poor condition (dented on seams, swollen or badly rusted) that they ·should not be sold?

7. **General appearance of the store.** Is the store cluttered with advertising posters, banners and other gimmicks? Is there a directory to help you find things? Are the front end aisle displays filled with junk foods and impulse items?

8. **Checkstand area.** Is the service good? Are checkers friendly and efficient? Are the checkstands cluttered with impulse items? Do you leave with a feeling that you would like to return because the store really cares about pleasing you?

The worst bargains in the supermarket

by Helen Black

Until those guys up front figure out how to be the winning supermarket with the lowest prices, the highest quality and STILL stay in business, I'll just keep saying the same old thing. Which is, the best way to save money is by making careful choices when you shop. No matter where you shop. Here are a few of the worst choices you can make, in terms of what you get for your money.

Bacon, hotdogs and spareribs because . . . you get less meat, more fat or bone than in most other cuts.

Honeydews, cantaloupes and strawberries in early Spring because it's too early in the season and the price is high. Such fruits come a long way at this time of year, and melons especially are apt to be small and not very good.

3¼ oz. size 'Chicken of the Sea' tuna because the price per can may be low but the price per pound is the highest of any size can of tuna.

Hamburger Helper because you're paying a lot for a pinch of herbs, some dried tomato sauce, about 1½ cups of macaroni! And you still have to buy the meat! That's a high price for convenience.

Del Monte individual pudding cups because that's a lot of packaging for a little bit to eat, and what you eat is a product of many additives, artificial color and flavor.

Birdseye frozen vegetables in sauces because with all that sauce there's less vegetable. That means less of the nutrients which are hard to get, and more nutrients (fat and calories!) which are too easy to get! Plus, a high price for convenience.

Don't forget! Almost any food you prepare at home will be more nutritious than a highly processed convenience food.

Secrets of a smart shopper

Prices going up, up, up and away? What to do? Here are some ideas from your home economists. Give them a try.

Before you go to the store

★ Establish a rough limit on what a certain type of food should cost for your family of four. For example, not more than $2.50 (or whatever you decide) for the main dish for dinner; 45¢-60¢ for breakfast fruit, or vegetables for dinner or dessert, etc.

★ Certain foods are good buys all year 'round. Use them frequently. For example, your list might include frozen orange juice, canned tomatoes, regular or low-fat milk and/or nonfat dry milk, or several bulk grains. Each family will have its own favorites.

★ Keep a shopping list in your kitchen. As you finish an item that you use regularly, put it on the list. As you think of ideas for upcoming meals, put the needed items on the list.

★ Plan to do a major shopping once a week. Plan your menus ahead for one week, if possible. Check supplies on hand and complete your shopping list accordingly. The less often you go to the store, the fewer opportunities you will have for impulse buying, although you may want to pick up fresh food at least twice a week.

★ When planning menus, consider the cost of convenience foods. If you buy "built-in maid service," you usually pay for it. There are exceptions (frozen orange juice, frozen peas) but they are rare. While a convenience food can be a blessing on occasion, regular use can skyrocket the budget. For instance, macaroni and cheese "made from scratch" is much less expensive, almost as easy to prepare, and usually more nutritious than the packaged or frozen products.

★ Plan to buy "store" brands of canned and frozen foods, paper products, health and beauty aids, etc. Usually the quality is comparable to nationally advertised brands while the cost is less. A case in point is laundry bleach. Co-op bleach and Clorox are identical in compositon but Co-op costs less.

★ Check ads for seasonal low prices on meat, poultry, fish, fresh produce and grocery items. Alter your menu when you find a good buy. Buy only amounts you can use before storage time lapses. Compare prices of fresh, frozen and canned versions of the same item. Also compare prices of bulk products with the packaged versions. Sometimes there is considerable price difference, while the nutritive value may be the same. Flavor, of course, may differ considerably.

★ Save shopping time by organizing your shopping list according to categories as stocked in the store so that you do not retrace your steps. Plan to buy frozen and refrigerated items last so that they will not warm up too much.

★ If you shop for specials at several stores, be aware of impulse purchases, extra transportation, and shopping time which may negate savings.

★ Eat before you shop! Research has shown that a hungry shopper is more likely to indulge in impulse buying.

★ Leave the kids home if you can't say "NO" and mean it.

★ Buying larger sizes? Use Unit Pricing information to see if it's worth doing. Small sizes on sale may be a better bargain. Beware of optical illusions in packaging. Sometimes a larger bottle, for example a salad oil bottle, contains fewer ounces than one that looks smaller.

★ Avoid or choose with care items displayed on center or end aisles or at the front of the store. In some stores these may be "impulse purchases" and poor values. Sometimes they are "in and outs" — products not regularly stocked which may or may not be poor buys.

★ Don't buy a product just because a demonstrator offers you a sample. Consider if this is really something you want at a price you can afford.

★ Ask the checker to call the prices as he/she rings up your order. No one can remember all prices accurately. Special prices may not be marked on the package; clerks may ring up the regular price.

After you shop

★ Don't stop on the way home to do errands. Many foods deteriorate rapidly in quality if unrefrigerated for an hour or more.

★ Check your purchases against the cash register tag to see that you paid only for what you received and that the prices charged were correct. If you find inaccuracies or discrepancies, report them to the manager the next time you shop.

★ Keep track of your food costs. Separate costs of non-foods and pet foods from "people foods." Compare what you are spending with the guidelines in the Appendix.

★ Check if you are wasting food by preparing too much or serving foods your family doesn't like. Either prepare quantities that will just feed your family for one meal without leftovers, or plan to have enough leftovers for another meal.

Make a shopping list

by Wendy Gardner

Tired of extra shopping trips and wasting money on impulse items?

Instead . . . .
1. Plan your menus for a week ahead.
2. Use up perishable items on hand.
3. Look at the recipes used for your menus and note what ingredients you need to buy.
4. MAKE A SHOPPING LIST

Try Wise's Method or Use Your Own

Co-op member Tamar Wise suggests that you shop by grocery categories. Add any product you buy regularly to the list below and eliminate items you do not buy. Arrange the rest in the order found in your store. Plan your shopping route to BUY COLD AND FROZEN ITEMS LAST.

Make a permanent list and xerox it or enter it in a notebook. Use the list as a reminder or place it next to the paper on which you write your shopping list. If you use a full-size paper, you may have space for brand, size, price, or other comments.

GROCERIES (Staples)

Tip: Compare *price per pound or quart, etc.* (unit prices) before choosing.

soft drinks, beer
coffee, tea, cocoa
dry, evaporated milk
cereal
salad dressings, mayonnaise
catsup, pickles
tomato sauce, other
rice, noodles, beans

Mexican food
Oriental food
gourmet food
crackers, cookies
bread, muffins
peanut butter
jams, honey, syrup
baking supplies

spices
oil
pudding mixes, gelatin
canned meat, fish
soups & prepared foods
canned vegetables
canned fruit
fruit juices

NONFOODS

paper products
shampoo, toothpaste
pet food
drug items
soap and detergents
cleaning supplies
housewares

PRODUCE

Tip: Stroll around to look at ALL the oranges, apples or potatoes before choosing. Sometimes they're not stocked together; you may miss the best buy.

bulk foods
dried fruits
salad makings
fruits, citrus
potatoes, carrots
vegetables

MEAT DEPARTMENT

Tip: Look at the bone and fat as well as price per pound. Compare price *per serving*

meat
poultry
fish

DELI

Tip: Luncheon meats can be very expensive per pound. Cheeses can be a good buy. One pound of cheese has as much protein as 1⅓ pounds of ground beef.

cheese
luncheon meats
tortillas
pickles

DAIRY FOODS

milk, yogurt, cottage cheese
margarine, butter
eggs

FROZEN FOOD

ice cream
vegetables, juices

Confessions of a weekly shopper

by Helen Black

february

S	M	T	W	T	F	S
					1	2
3	4	5	6	7	8	9
10	11	12	13	14	15	16
17	18	19	20	21	22	23
24	25	26	27	28	29	

I had fallen into deplorable ways. Every night or so, after work, I was shopping for food. It was awful! Trying to organize my thoughts, hurrying to decide what to buy, waiting in line feeling cranky and mean! Finally I gave up and went back to the One Big Weekly Shopping Trip. It's worked just dandy, now that I'm used to it. Here's what's good about it.

Get thee behind me, decisions!

I should be at the store at 10 minutes to six to face the most important decision of the day . . . dinner? No, thanks! No longer do I attempt this decision during my precarious late-afternoon mental state. Instead, I do it on my Weekly Shopping Trip. Having decided in advance what's for dinner, I fix it more or less automatically. Thus my brain is free to relax and socialize so that dinner can be the glorious end to a hard day, rather than the final trauma!

Admitted, food shopping isn't getting any easier.

But it's always been hard work. Now, I allocate prime time for shopping. Nobody does a good job in a rush, tired out, worried about something else, or hungry. Instead I try to choose a time when I can give the job the attention and judgment it deserves. It takes at least an hour in the store, plus another half hour at home to put the food away. Getting to the store when it first opens, or shopping in the early evening when other people are still eating, may be worth the effort because the stores are relatively uncrowded. However, all items may not be available.

Food costs a lot of your income

Maybe one fourth or more. Should you work 10 hours to pay for food grabbed in a few thoughtless, frenzied minutes? No! I say. Shopping once a week has some money "smarts." First, I find I have a better idea what I'm really spending for food. (I can easily subtract the total amount for non-food when I get home. It's one lump sum, instead of a few bucks here and a few bucks there which somehow I never get around to totaling up.) Second, I know about how much of various foods we use per week, how often I need staples, so I take better advantage of specials. Of course, those who have the time and gas can maybe make a killing driving from one store to another, skimming off only the specials.

Cracking the storage barrier

Admittedly, this is a challenge. Shopping once a week means for me that we have fresh fish or liver or ground beef or some such perishable food the night that I shop. If this seems too limiting, it's still worth it! It also means using fresh vegetables like asparagus as soon as possible, while buying carrots, winter squash, oranges and grapefruits and other produce which will stand a week's storage. For big milk users, it may mean falling back on fresh concentrated milk or nonfat dry milk after a few days.

Tomorrow's dinner, started tonight

When I am very well organized, which isn't always, I may start tomorrow night's dinner while fixing tonight's. Just a small start can be a big help, such as getting out a recipe, or digging out an inconveniently stored casserole. I may even cut up a chicken, mix up a marinade or salad dressing, or trim the fresh string beans for tomorrow night. Whatever little thing it is, I'm grateful that it's already done, when tomorrow night rolls around.

Supermarket pie-in-the-sky

by Helen Black   *May 24, 1976*

Where, oh where, is that supermarket in the sky with the very cheapest prices?

Is it Safeway, which recently has increased sales by 11 percent while profits plunged 28 percent? If so, it will not stay cheap long.

Some of us cynical old Co-op hands are doubtful that shopping the cheapest supermarket . . . if there REALLY is one . . . is the best way to save money on food. We've seen price wars before. And we've looked at price comparison between competitive supermarket chains over the years, where long lists of **typical** foods of **equal** quality are priced on the same day. We've seen the differences of 5-10 percent **at most**. That's peanuts, compared to the savings which can be made by skillful "trading down," meaning choosing a cheaper version of a product usually bought. Trading down may mean buying a different menu item at lower price, or a less convenient, or less fancy, or lower quality item. According to Sylvia Porter, trading down can save 27-30 percent on grocery bills.

Trading down takes some effort. It takes a sharp eye for unit prices; willingness to change a planned menu when prices are higher than expected, as well as a good backup of recipes to substitute; and practice. But it's sure great for survival, especially during sudden food price rises, or sudden loss of income, or sudden increase of mouths to feed, or inflation squeeze. For example:

Look for cheaper packaging. Lasagne in a box costs more than lasagne in a plastic bag. The 27 percent saved by buying Co-op's lasagne instead of Golden Grain's in a box is partly due to packaging cost.

Or change your menu. Now try changing from lasagne to spaghetti, both Co-op brands. You'll save 34 percent on that trade down. But a switch from pastas generally to rice will result in additional savings. Rice is cheaper and of similar nutritional value. Buy Co-op rice instead of Co-op spaghetti and save 8 percent on that trade down. If you make a grand sweep and trade down all the way from Golden Grain lasagne to Co-op rice you save a whopping 55 percent!

Try a more nutritious meat. For example, beef heart has more iron and B vitamins than ground beef. Sometimes it is also cheaper, $1.25 per pound compared to $1.59.

Is this high quality necessary? Maybe jack cheese at 1.89 per pound does as well as sharp cheddar at 2.35 or more. Savings are 19 percent.

Watch that convenience! It's usually high priced. Hamburger Helpers range from $1.70-2.09 per pound, more than you may wish to pay for meat.

Prices updated Aug. '79.

Photo by Jane Scherr

There's useful information on milk cartons, as store home economist explains to young shoppers.

Using the units

by Judy Heckman   *August 11, 1975*

Every so often we like to remind you about that great shopper's friend — **the unit price.** It's a little sticker on the edge of the shelf that makes it all possible. No need to worry about the size of the container — you can compare the 8-ounce can for 49¢ with the 6-ounce can for 35¢. Complicated figuring or gadgets aren't necessary because all the work has been done by our computer. **All shoppers have to do is know about it and use it.**

How it works:

The Units Symbol on the tag	Unit	Example of item listed on that unit
OZ	Ounce	Instant coffee
PT	Pint	Salad dressing
LB	Pound	Breakfast cereal
QT	Quart	Infant formula
E	Each	Cigars
100	100 Count	Paper plates
10	10 Count	Lawn leaf bags
100SF	100 Square Feet	Aluminum foil
1000	1000 Count	Toothpicks
MXD QT	Mixed Quart	Canned soup
MXD PT	Mixed Pint	Frozen juices

It's the **unit price** that gives the important information. Unless we've made a mistake, the units are always the same within any one group of foods. All you need to do is compare the unit price and you know immediately which is the better buy in terms of cost. (Of course, you may not always want to buy the least expensive item but unit pricing can help you decide whether the extra cost is worth it to you.) The unit price even helps you compare all those odd numbers and sizes of facial tissues, toilet paper and paper towels by giving the cost per 100 square feet.

There are still many items that aren't on unit pricing. These may be things like spices that are so tightly shelved that there just isn't room for the tag. Or they might be "outside vendor" items, such as crackers, or health and beauty aids where the "units" are not all the same.

We hope you use unit pricing. When trying to stretch dollars it can be one of the best friends you've got.

Read the label

THE LAW SAYS THAT ingredients must be listed in order of decreasing amount. If the label says "Gravy & Meat Slices" it means there is more gravy than meat.
from your Co-op Home Economist

What you can find on a label

by Joan Taylor

More and more people are becoming concerned about what they are eating and what is added to their food such as sugar, fat, salt and chemicals. Labels can help you. If more than one ingredient is used there must be a list of ingredients. The ingredients will be listed in order of decreasing weight. The largest amount is listed first.

Sugar

You may find sugar in products listed in different forms of sugar. *They are still sugar.*

sucrose   corn syrup
dextrose   honey
lactose   invert sugar
molasses   fructose

Nutrient Label

If nutritional information is on the label you will find the serving size, servings per container, and nutrients found in the product.

Weight

Don't forget to look at the weight of containers. Sometimes packaging can fool the eye when you want to compare size.

For information and complaints

There is a company name and address which consumers can write to for information or to make product complaints.

Nutrition labeling *by Mary Ruth Nelson*

The something new on food labels

Take a good look at food labels when you shop. You will find that the labels of some foods now show the amounts of certain nutrients per serving. The new nutrients labeling regulations, adopted by the Food and Drug Administration in March of 1973, have made it possible for manufacturers to label the nutrient content of their products. These regulations require that the nutrients be labeled as a percentage of the U.S. Recommended Daily Allowances (U.S. RDA). The U.S. RDA, a liberal daily nutrient allowance, REPLACES the now outdated Minimum Daily Requirements (MDR) which we may particularly remember from the labels of ready-to-eat cereals and special dietary foods.

What is a nutrient?

A nutrient is a substance that is required for nourishment of the body. There are over 40 nutrients that are known to be essential for humans. Protein, fat, carbohydrate, calories and the numerous vitamins and minerals are among the nutrients shown on the Nutrition Information Panel of the label. You can now learn what goodies are present in various foods so labeled. You may also discover that some snack "foods" really contain so few nutrients that they may not be worth the calories they add to the daily diet!

Labeling is voluntary except . . .

for foods that are enriched or fortified with added nutrients such as dry cereals, bread, flour, rice, macaroni, noodles, milk and margarine. Additionally, if a manufacturer makes a claim mentioning calories, protein, vitamins, minerals or any other nutrient, then that food MUST have nutrition labeling.

What's required?

The following information is required on all nutrition labels and in the order as listed:

Nutrition Information Per Serving
Serving Size
Servings Per Container
Calories
Protein
Carbohydrate
Fat

Percentage of U.S. Recommended
Daily Allowances (U.S.RDA)

Protein	Riboflavin
Vitamin A	Niacin
Vitamin C	Calcium
Thiamine	Iron

The serving size is established by the manufacturer. TAKE CARE when figuring daily nutrient intake based on the serving size; it may be MORE than is normally eaten at a time.

The servings per container vary with the size of the container and the type of food.

Calories per serving will help us make food choices depending upon whether we need more or fewer calories. For example, two foods might provide similar amounts of vitamin A per serving, but the caloric content could vary greatly.

The protein, carbohydrate and fat per serving is stated to the nearest gram. (Think of a level teaspoon of sugar as weighing about 5 grams.) This information will be useful to those on special diets.

Nutrition information as a Percentage of the U.S. Recommended Daily Allowances (U.S. RDA) is mandatory for only eight of the forty plus nutrients needed by humans. The U.S. RDA is a liberal allowance set about 40% above the amounts needed to prevent symptoms of deficiency in most of the population. However, if you select naturally occurring foods that supply adequate amounts of these eight nutrients, it is very likely you will get enough of all of the other needed nutrients.

A few hints on how to use the label information

1. Learn the names of the eight nutrients for which a % U.S. RDA must appear on the label. (Check closely. Some products will not have the standard list of eight, but will refer to the missing ones in a footnote.) You will discover that only certain foods contribute sizeable amounts of these nutrients. One needs to eat a variety of foods to meet these allowances.

2. When planning meals, always compare the nutrient and caloric content of foods that may be substituted for a similar type food in the meal, such as vegetables for other vegetables, milk products for milk, and so on.

Additionally, plan meals in terms of the four basic food groups: 1) milk and milk products; 2) meats, poultry, fish, eggs, cheese and dry beans or peas; 3) vegetables and fruits; and 4) bread and cereals. Each group makes a different contribution to the diet and each should be included in every meal.

3. Warning! Don't buy foods solely on their high vitamin and mineral content. Many fabricated foods, such as the highly processed cereals, may contain 100% of the eight nutrients. However, these foods probably are lacking in many nutrients that are present only in naturally occurring foods. The constant use of highly processed foods could result in a deficiency of some nutrients not included in the mandatory U.S. RDA.

4. Don't fret if every member of your household is not getting 100% of the eight mandatory nutrients. Almost without exception, the levels for each of these nutrients represent the highest values for all the various age-sex groups and probably not everyone needs those amounts.

5. Do not expect your family to eat foods just because they are "good for you." Nutrients are wasted if foods are not eaten. Therefore, choose wisely the foods you KNOW your family likes to eat.

The Way Things Are

by Helen Black

Some companies have chosen to put nutritional information on their labels, including Co-op, Del Monte, Green Giant and Campbell's Soup. One by one the products with these labels are appearing on our shelves. Even with those few available so far, marvelous truths are revealed!

The awful truth about pears and peaches

A glance at the labels of Co-op Canned Pears and Del Monte Canned Peaches tells it: peaches have significant amounts of vitamins A and C, while pears are low in both.* And NEITHER have much else of importance. This is no criticism of Co-op! Far from it! It is a matter of the way things are, with peaches and pears.

Amazing difference in bean types

Del Monte nutrition labels show that one cup of Italian Green Beans provides 15 percent of the USRDA for vitamin A, 40 percent of the vitamin C, and even 10 percent of the riboflavin. As for Blue Lake Green Beans, vitamin A is 26 percent and vitamin C is 15 percent of the USRDA.

Knotty knowledge of mixed foods

Here's a tough one. Even if you know about peas, beans, corn and rice, how can you figure out the nutritional value of mixtures of the same, or of creamed vegetables? Well, Green Giant figures it out for you. Their nutritional label information will provide you with fascinating tidbits. Particularly, it is interesting to see the way caloric value, protein and fat vary in the different combinations.

Much, much more? Maybe

Shoppers should register their approval by writing companies to request this labeling, or by buying products which have this labeling already. When the time comes to order a new batch of labels, food companies will decide whether the expense is worth it to them. For your sake and mine, the decision should be in favor of this real buyer's boon, nutrition information on the label.

*Remember, figures given are percentages of the U.S. Recommended Dietary Allowances (USRDA) adapted for label use by the FDA. When those figures are lower than 10 percent, consider the amount of that nutrient to be on the low side, usually.

INGREDIENTS: GREEN BEANS, WATER, SALT.

NUTRITION INFORMATION—PER ONE CUP SERVING
SERVINGS PER CONTAINER—APPROX. 2

CALORIES	35	CARBOHYDRATE	7g
PROTEIN	2g	FAT	0g

PERCENTAGE OF U.S. RECOMMENDED DAILY
ALLOWANCES (U.S. RDA) PER ONE CUP SERVING

PROTEIN	2	NIACIN	2
VITAMIN A	15	CALCIUM	6
VITAMIN C	6	IRON	8
THIAMINE (VIT. B_1)	2	PHOSPHORUS	2
RIBOFLAVIN (VIT. B_2)	4	MAGNESIUM	6

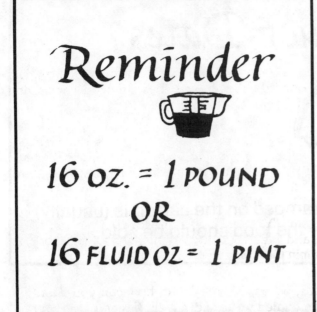

Reminder

16 OZ. = 1 POUND
OR
16 FLUID OZ = 1 PINT

from your Co-op Home Economist

Photo by Jane Scherr

*It's never too soon to start teaching kids
to read labels.*

How to take your kids shopping for breakfast cereals

by Helen Black

When vacation is upon us it means taking the kids along when you shop. Your crochety old Co-op Home Economist suggests that it is never too soon to start teaching kids to read labels! They can practice on something exciting, like breakfast cereals.

First and second graders can read the net weight. Don't tell them to pick out the big box — let them hunt for the 18 oz. or whatever size you need. Maybe they'll find out how many ounces in a pound, too.

Third and fourth graders can look for sugar. It'll take them a little time to find "ingredients" in that small print. But it's worth it. Tell them to skip any cereal that lists sugar as the first ingredient. Tell them the first ingredient is the most, the last ingredient listed is the least. Then let them hunt the cereals with your least sugar.

Fifth graders can check added vitamins. Fifth graders are old enough to face such hot controversies! Are vitamins A and D added? How much? Many authorities think that these vitamins, known to be toxic in large amounts, should not be added to breakfast cereals.

Sixth graders can figure the best buy. With paper and pencil, some sixth graders have fun figuring out price-per-pound of different sizes and brands. Others call that cruel and unusual! So let them check the unit price shelf labels instead.

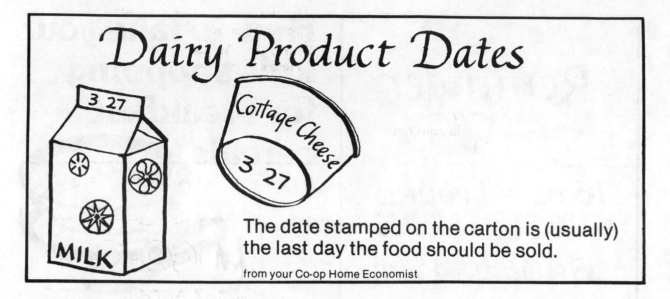

Dairy Product Dates

3 27

Cottage Cheese
3 27

MILK

The date stamped on the carton is (usually) the last day the food should be sold.

from your Co-op Home Economist

Let's hear it for open dating! *by Helen Black*

Let us all observe one minute of praise for open dating! Here we are taking for granted this great boon to food buyers, when just yesterday, it seems, we bought milk, eggs, luncheon meats, etc., without the faintest idea when the food was packed or how long it should keep.

This is NOT to say the battle is won! Not on your tintype! For one reason, still with us is the scarcely legible date. What good is a date you can't read? Second, there's still confusion among food packers as to when to use pull dates rather than pack dates, or whether to use an expiration date. A date needs those few words of explanation which clearly indicate whether it's pull, pack or expiration. Third, sad to say, there are still plenty of mavericks such as the canning companies, holding on for dear life to their secret codes. And last, even well-dated products seldom describe the temperature and storage conditions under which the product will stay safe. So we aren't exactly hurtling towards Grade A perfection! But making progress, anyway.

Just so you could see how they're going, I thought I'd pass out a few "grades" on food dates.

Kellogg's and Skinner's breakfast cereals rate A

Hurray for these clearly visible dates! And they tell us what it is, right on top, "Better if used before 6 Dec. '80." Post cereals get only B; they've got a date, but no explanation. General Mills, Quaker, Ralston Purina and Nabisco all get F for using indecipherable codes, such as G310Z.

I wish I could give Oroweat an A . . .

. . . Because Oroweat is a bread company using a date rather than a color coded twist. Alas, the pull date is obliterated in the packaging, and there are no words of explanation. So mark Oroweat down to B.

Calumet gets A

What a delight to have an expiration date on baking powder! Right on the top are the words, "Use before date on bottom."

Co-op flour has climbed to B

For a while we had a sticky situation where the supplier of one kind of flour was using a pack date, while another was using a pull date. Now they're both using a pull date but with, alas, no explanation. I'm sorry to say that Gold Medal (General Mills) gets an F on flour, too, as well as on breakfast cereal; they're using a code.

Campbell's soups, bless 'em!

Most canners have made no move towards open dating their products. Campbell's has taken the plunge, with a legible date embossed on the end of the can. Alas, there's nothing to tell us it's a pull date, not a pack date.

Too bad, Co-op Margarine gets C . . .

. . . Because sometimes it has a date, sometimes, a code. Not really puzzling! We have TWO suppliers of Co-op Margarine. One provides this service, the other doesn't, yet. Nice to see that Parkay and Saffola both have dates,

with the words clearly visible, "Best when purchased before . . ."

Thank you, Asumaya Tofu!

Here's a date we've really needed. Tofu has climbed up from no information at all, to a date which we've been told over the phone is a pull date. When they get those few extra words on the label, we'll give 'em an A.

FRESH MEAT CODES

The number stamped on the package is the day of the month the meat was wrapped.

POUNDS NET. WT. 0.00 — TOTAL PRICE $0.00 — PRICE PER POUND .00

WHOLE BODY FRYER 07———

from your Co-op Home Economist

PULL DATE:

the date after which a product should not be sold. If properly stored, the product is good for a certain period after the date.

PACK DATE:

the date when the product was packaged.

EXPIRATION DATE:

date after which the product may not be good.

How much are you willing to pay for the word "HEALTH" on your tomato sauce?

by Betsy Wood

Consider two 15 oz. cans of tomato sauce, available side by side at the Co-op Natural Food Store:

HEALTH VALLEY	CO-OP
85¢	29¢

The label says:
"No citric acid"...........................
"No sugars".............................
"No preservatives"......................
"No artificial colors or flavors"..............

Health Valley Ingredients:

Tomatoes, (water, tomato paste), sea salt, natural spices and herbs, tamari soy sauce (water, soy beans, wheat, sea salt).

But Co-op:
Contains no citric acid
Has no sugar
Also has no preservatives (canned foods are preserved by the heat of the canning process). Likewise has no artificial color or flavor (These additives are almost never in canned food. One exception: maraschino cherries).

Co-op Ingredients:

Tomatoes, salt, dehydrated onion, dehydrated garlic, spices, natural flavors.

Co-op is fairly typical of other "commercial" tomato sauces. We have a second "natural" brand, Gerardi, also costing 85¢, containing "tomatoes, salt, pepper, spices."

Co-op News, December 11, 1978

What's Natural

by June Kadish

What's natural? A simple definition is "existing in or produced by nature." I like that. It's uncomplicated.

So, what's it mean when we talk about natural foods? Once the processors change the vegetable, grain and meat shapes by puffing, compressing, grinding, reforming or extending, we've left natural and are into processed.

Some labels take liberties

Have you read the ingredient label on Daisy Fresh Natural Mango Flavored Juice Drink? It says "water, juice, citric acid, potassium alginate (stabilizer), natural flavors and artificial colors." What's so natural about that?

Quaker's 100% Natural Cereal with Apples and Cinnamon is "naturally sweetened with brown sugar and honey." At least it's not "unnaturally" sweetened. That's a plus.

Don't be misled by the word "natural" on a label. Read the ingredient list. Stick to basics as often as possible.

Labels that say

"NO Preservatives," "NO Cholesterol," "NO Artificial Color or Flavor" may imply falsely that other similar products do contain these things.

OIL labels that do not list preservatives do not contain them.

The Food & Drug Administration requires that preservatives be listed on all labels.

No vegetable oil contains preformed cholesterol. It is found only in animal fats.

from your Co-op Home Economist

What it costs to eat

Coping with high food prices

by Mary Gullberg

If a family of four (2 adults and 2 school age kids) is taken as a model family, this family spent $62.60 weekly for food in July, 1979, compared to $29.90 in September, 1969.* That's a whopping 109% increase. If, on the other hand, this same family had had more income available to spend for food and had followed the U.S. Department of Agriculture's "Liberal Food Plan," they would have spent $94.50 a week in 1979 compared to $47.10 in 1969, an increase of 101%. This seems to point up the fact that inflation hits the lower income groups harder, forcing them to spend more of their income on food, housing and other fixed costs of living than those with higher incomes.

One way for people to increase the mileage from their food dollars is to buy more milk products, vegetables and fruits, and bread and cereal products. We could spend less for the higher priced foods such as animal protein foods (meat, poultry, fish and cheese) and fats, oils, high sugar foods, coffee, tea and soft drinks, all of which take larger bites out of the food dollar. In place of animal protein foods, we could use more dry beans, legumes, and nuts. Another inflation-fighting tip is to use more home-prepared foods and fewer ready-to-eat ones. This may mean that if the cook's time is limited, he or she may need to get the rest of the family involved in food preparation. It may also be necessary to stick to dishes and menus that can be prepared in a minimum amount of time.

A survey reported by Sylvia Porter recently and conducted each year by pollsters Yankelovich, Skelly and White said people were coping with inflated prices by:

Buying lower-priced house brands rather than name brands

Buying just the amount they need

Buying in quantity if it is cheaper and can be stored until used.

These trends are heavily influenced by the attitudes and habits of the working women. Forty-three percent of the women who shop in supermarkets work full or part-time.

*Figures from the Consumer and Food Economics Institute of the U.S. Department of Agriculture. These figures are for their "Low Cost Food Plan" for one week's food eaten at home.

The cost of feeding babies

by Betsy Wood

Most of us know that breast feeding a baby is best — psychologically, nutritionally, for health and economy. Breast milk provides substances which help protect a baby from various diseases, as well as allergies and skin problems.

But if you are feeding your baby a bottle, what does it cost? There are many choices. This table gives the ranges of costs. We've omitted some brands.

Cost of Milk and Infant Formulas

		Cost per quart
FRESH	Whole Milk, Valley Gold	.37
CANNED Concentrated	*Evaporated Milk, Co-op	.48
POWDERS Concentrated	Similac	.66
LIQUIDS	*Isoylac	.70
READY TO FEED	*Enfamil	.82
	Isomil (soy)	.98
	Similac, qt. cans	1.02
	Enfamil, 8 oz. cans	1.50
	Similac, 8 oz. bottles	2.10

* Add one part liquid

You can see that formula in 8 oz. cans costs three times as much as formula made from evaporated milk — $547 a year versus $175 a year. Sugar in some form is usually added to formula made with fresh or canned milk. In addition, an iron supplement must be given. So the cost would be slightly higher than indicated.

Fresh milk should not be used for babies under 6 months without boiling, because there is evidence of slight internal bleeding from feeding fresh milk.

Co-op News, 11/27/78

What it costs to eat
at home for one week October, 1979

	Low Cost	Liberal Cost
Woman, 20-54 years	$15.20	$22.60
55 years and over	$13.70	$20.00
Man, 20-54 years	$18.70	$28.40
55 years and over	$16.50	$24.70
Family of 4 with 2 preschoolers	$51.90	$77.80

Both low cost and liberal cost plans are nutritious but low cost plan has less meat, eggs, fruits and vegetables, convenience foods and more potatoes, dry beans and peas, flour, cereals and baked goods.

By making such more economical choices one person can save from $350-$500 per year.

Note: These figures are based on food plans developed by the U.S. Department of Agriculture, priced every three months and reported in the Family Economic Review. It is assumed that all food is purchased in stores and prepared at home. The figures above assume a 4 person living group. Persons living alone should add 20%.

Your liquid dollar

Is this the way you want to spend it?

by Betsy Wood

We pour many liquids down our gullets: beer, liquor, coffee, soft drinks, juices, water. But how much does all this cost?

Here's how we spend our billions for liquids (not counting milk):

	Cost per year* billions	% of "liquid dollar"
Beer	$11.1 ⎫	
Liquor	9.2 ⎬	56%
Wine	2.0 ⎭	
Coffee	7.6 ⎫	
Tea & other beverages	1.3 ⎭	22%
Soft drinks	6.6	16%
Juices, canned, frozen, chilled	2.2	5%
Fruit drinks	.4	1%
Spent on liquids	40.4	100%

Only 5% For All Juices?

Yes, and that's really very little. (If we added citrus *fruit* it would still be only 8% of the total). Juices provide some vitamins, minerals, the delight of real food, as well as calories. Beer has a few B vitamins and calories. The others provide just calories or nothing except goodies like alcohol, caffeine, artificial flavors, colors, additives.

We know that lots of alcohol, caffeine and sugar aren't good for us. Besides, if we get too many of our calories from low-nutrition sources, it's hard to fill in our nutrient needs from the rest of our diet. If you want to adjust your drink dollar, the possibilities are wide open.

Our Family's Solution

- To practically stop drinking coffee and substitute herb teas, black tea, even hot water.
- To shun all soft drinks; to take juice on outings; to dilute juices with water to make fruit drinks.
- Not to buy hard liquor but still drink beer and wine, in moderate amounts.
- To drink that revolutionary beverage, water.

> **Secret Fruit-Drink Recipe Revealed!**
> ½ glass grapefruit juice
> ½ glass water
> 1 ice cube

Keeping track of your food costs

by Helen Black

Question: I made this GREAT New Year's resolution to keep track of all my food costs this year. Only I never got started. Can I start now or should I wait until January 1?

Answer: We urge you to start *now*. After all, if you are over-spending on food now, just think how much you'll be over spent by next January 1.

You don't need to keep track for the whole year — just for a typical week (or month), now and then. From this, figure your food costs per month and year and modify your spending accordingly.

Follow these easy rules:

1. Save all your grocery sales slips. Add them up at the end of the period.

2. Subtract 20% of the total for nonfood items. This is a low average figure for non-food purchases in supermarkets. To be more accurate you can add up the tax on your sales slips and figure

back from this the actual amount spend on non-foods. (This works, of course, only in states where there is no tax on food.) If tax in your state is 5%, multiply the tax by 20; if it's 6%, multiply by 17; if it's 7%, multiply by 14 to get the approximate cost of your nonfoods.

3. Add in the amount of money spent for food eaten away from home.

Question: But how can I tell if I'm spending too much?

Answer: One way is to use your cost for food for one week as a base with which you can make comparisons in six months or a year.

Another way is to compare to what others spend. A family of 4 can get by on $271 per month or $62.60 per week.* How do I know? Because the U.S. Department of Agriculture tells us so. Every three months the USDA publishes the cost of food needed to feed people old or young, male or female. The USDA uses four food plans at four cost levels. Each plan consists of a nutritionally balanced list of food. The low-cost food plan includes nonfat dry milk instead of fresh, more beans and less meat, cabbage more often as a source of vitamin C, etc.

Question: One more thing I'm embarrassed to mention. I can't seem to keep food prices in my head. How can I keep my food costs down if I can't remember prices?

Answer: Why not try carrying a little price book? In it, write down the items you regularly buy with the regular price. Most people have 20-40 items which they regularly buy: a certain size, of a certain brand, at a certain price. Use one page for fresh meats, one for produce, one for pet foods, one for milk and deli, etc. When you forget a price, look in your book to find out what you paid before. Did the price go up? If so, this is the moment of truth! Decide if you want to take that price rise or choose an alternative product, another brand, or whatever. I thought this was a dumb idea till I tried it. It works for me and it can for you.

*A man and woman between 20 and 54 years, with children between 6 and 8, and 9 and 11, Low Cost Food Plan, July 1979.

When times are tough *by Catherine Sinnott*

What would you do if you found yourself with three days to go, three kids to feed, and down to only a few dollars to buy food for your family? Emergencies do come up in all families. Even though there are ways to get free food in such emergencies, they can be temporarily out of reach.

Three Days — Three Kids — Three Dollars?

A Cornell University publication in 1967 said that to be nutritionally well-fed for a whole day, one pound of enriched flour, ⅔ cup skim milk powder, one (four-ounce) sweet potato, three ounces of cabbage and ¼ pound of margarine are more than enough food for a 25-year-old man. These five foods would provide most the the nutrients he needs and he would not be hungry.

Bored, maybe, but not hungry! The 2700-plus calories from these foods might have cost about 35¢ back then; they cost 63¢ in 1979, but that is still very cheap. This combination would be hard to put together in an appetizing way and is mentioned here to show that these particular foods are adequate (they provide enough protein and calories and good amounts of most vitamins and minerals) as well as inexpensive. Our expensive tastes, customs, likes, dislikes and shopping habits finally determine how much more than 63¢ a day we spend.

The calories needed by a mother with three young children all under ten years old could be as much as 8700 a day to meet the Recommended Daily Allowance. Today, even this "bare bones" list of foods suggested by Cornell in the amounts needed for this family of four could not be bought for $3 but would cost about $6.

Menus May Be a Bit Dull

If you really have three kids and three days to go, you will be looking for something inexpensive that your family will eat, that will keep them from being extremely hungry, and that will nourish them as well as possible. Hopefully there will be something at home to go with what you buy. Dry beans or peas may be 50¢ per pound. By adding an onion or carrots and other vegetables and seasonings you can design a hearty main dish. If you have the other ingredients at home, you can make six loaves of bread (or lots of biscuits or tortillas) with a five-pound bag of flour (89¢ on September 26, 1979). A two-pound bag of rice will make about 15 cups of cooked rice. Combined with raisins and milk, rice is good for breakfast. Rice with small amounts of vegetables or meat or beans might be served for lunch or dinner. Some reconstituted dry milk should be used too.

How to eat meat and save "bread"

by Catherine Sinnott

Everybody talks about it, but no one does anything about it. The "it" in this case is the high cost of meat. You can't "beat the price of meat" but some families can re-adjust their menus so that it doesn't hurt so much.

Co-op Home Economists have worked out some low-cost meals that have actually been prepared for their families.

Be Your Own Meat Artist — and Save

One easy way to save money on meat is to buy large cuts of meat and cut them into various shapes suitable for stew, dinner steaks, breakfast steaks, goulash, oriental dishes, stroganoff and countless other recipes.

Chuck roast is a versatile, fairly inexpensive cut of meat that lends itself to all kinds of recipes. When you finish cutting all these interesting shapes, you still have the bones to make soup.

A stroganoff recipe that often results from chuck roast surgery in my house (and when there's no sour cream handy) goes as follows:

About 1 pound of chuck roast cut the size of
*   french fried potatoes*
2 tablespoons flour
1 teaspoon salt
1 cup evaporated milk, undiluted
1 tablespoon lemon juice (or vinegar)
A few small or sliced mushrooms
2 onions, sliced
Oil (2 or 3 tablespoons)

Assemble all the ingredients (and two frying pans) so you can work quickly. Add the lemon juice to the milk. Start the onions frying slowly in a little oil. Stir them occasionally until the onions are lightly browned. In the other frying pan heat a tablespoon or two of oil to a high heat and brown the meat quickly. Stir in the mushrooms. Lower the heat and stir in flour and salt. Add evaporated milk, lemon juice mixture and fried onions. Cook only until ingredients are blended, a minute or two. Serve on hot, freshly cooked noodles or rice. Dark Rye bread and Russian salad could complete this meal.

To make one version of Russian salad, marinate several cooked vegetables (carrots, potatoes, beets, green beans and peas) for about an hour in french dressing. Pour off the dressing and toss vegetables with a bit of mayonnaise. Serve on shredded lettuce.

Meat Loaf Plus

by Nancy Bratt

I used to feel I could afford to buy ground beef and not have to extend it. No more!

Now, with one pound of ground beef, I get a meat loaf for five or six people, adding:

2 eggs, beaten
1 cup milk, or canned tomatoes, or other
*   liquid*
1 cup bread crumbs (dry or instant cereals
*   can be substituted)*
leftover vegetables
1 medium chopped onion
salt and herbs

Mix all together and bake in a loaf pan for about an hour at 350 degrees. Baked potatoes are good with this, but start them about 15 minutes before the meat loaf. (I put in extra potatoes because we like baked potatoes sliced and fried for breakfast with bacon and eggs.)

For this dinner: summer squash, cooked until just tender with a touch of garlic and a sprinkle of Romano cheese, crisp lettuce for a salad, and wedges of the least expensive melon for dessert. Makes an inexpensive meal.

How a family of six managed on a food stamp budget *Catherine Sinnott*

Once I asked my family (three adults and three children) to join me in a few weeks of extra careful budgeting. The amount of money allowed for these weeks was the amount a family of six would get if they were receiving food stamps.

At the time we tried this in 1974 this was $204 per month, or $46.20 per week. (In 1979 it would be $306 per month). The shopping for this period was done just as if the payment was actually stamps, so of course no pet food, cleaning products, paper products, liquor or other non-food items could be included.

The reaction of the family was fairly positive, though it was impossible to cater to individual tastes as much as usual. Craving for steaks, off-season fruits or fancy baked goods could not be satisfied. Everyone had to help with the cooking since it took extra time to cook and bake. Because we worked with basic foodstuffs, extra time was needed for preparation.

Extra time was also needed for planning and shopping. I wrote out the menus quite completely for the morning and evening meals. Lunches were planned in a more general way, allowing plenty of materials for soups, sandwiches and salads. Lunch was the time to use leftovers, also. Shopping was done once a week. Some bargains were found because of store specials and seasonally plentiful fruits and vegetables. Luckily, we had a few apples and plums from our own trees.

We used some very old ways of saving, but which take a little work. We saved everything. All the vegetable and meat juices went into soups and gravies. Fruit juices went into gelatin desserts. Fats were saved for baking or frying. Leftover meat loaf went into sandwiches, and the crumbs of the meat loaf went into the soyburgers.

I think our meals were nutritious and fairly attractive. But this is not much money for a family of six. The amount is adequate ONLY if the family uses strict discipline in food selection and preparation.

The menus were planned as follows:

Breakfasts:
Fruit or fruit juices, cereal and milk, hot cakes or eggs and toast except Sunday when we had an old family favorite — corn oysters. (See recipe below).

Lunches: Sandwiches, soup or salads

Dinners:

SUNDAY
Fish Sticks
Cabbage salad
Applesauce

MONDAY
Meat Loaf
Corn on the cob
Baked potato
Green salad

TUESDAY
Mackerel fish pie
Romaine salad
Fresh bread

WEDNESDAY
Lasagne
French bread
Tossed green salad

THURSDAY
Cheese and onion pie
Broccoli
Whole wheat rolls

FRIDAY
Tacos with everything
Fruit salad
Refried beans

SATURDAY
Soyburgers
Carrots
Mashed potatoes
Muffins

Snacks —

Tapioca pudding - gelatin salad - Homemade cookies - Homemade breads - Crackers (lg. pkg. saltines) - Apples - Plums - Applesauce - Dill Pickles - Cheese - Tortillas - Dried prunes - Celery - Carrots

Recipe for Corn "Oysters"

⅓ cup crushed corn flakes
⅓ cup old-fashioned rolled oats
⅓ cup white cracker crumbs
¼ cup flour
½ tsp. baking powder
½ tsp. salt
4 eggs (separated)
1 cup cream style corn

Mix dry ingredients together and stir in corn and egg yolks. Carefully fold in egg whites that have been stiffly beaten. Drop oyster-shaped tablespoons onto buttered, medium-hot frying pan or griddle. Serve with butter or margarine.
2-4 servings.

Waste not — want not

by Catherine Sinnott

A penny's worth saved is better than a penny earned because you don't have to pay tax on it. Food waste is a good place to save a penny's worth.

Don't Throw It Out!

A recent study (1973 and 1974) by the University of Arizona showed that the average household in Tucson wasted nearly $2 worth of edible food per week. About $100 per year went into the garbage can alone. Not counted was the garbage that went down the garbage disposals (21 percent of the families had garbage disposals in good working order). Also not counted were leftovers fed to pets, food waste going into compost piles and all beverages spilled or thrown out, so actual food waste was considerably more than was actually measured. The average garbage can food waste in the two-year study was 9 percent of the total food brought into the family home.

It Can Be Done!

Perhaps we could learn something from Michigan State University about avoiding food waste at home. In 1972 MSU started a "Food Ecology" project to cut down on waste in the cafeterias where MSU dispensed 65,000 meals each day. When the actual plate waste was weighed, the startling figure was approximately four tons of food waste a day. A campaign was started to cut waste. Cafeteria servers wore signs saying, "If you want less, tell me." Theme posters featured such messages as "Stop Food Waste" and "Complete Your Meal." Food waste monitoring continued as did the publicity, and the number of tons wasted was significantly reduced. Indiana U. followed the method used at MSU and reduced their cafeteria's waste 33 percent in only one month, a potential saving of $230,000 a year.

Watch It!

If you are responsible for serving the food in your family, how about starting out by serving smaller portions or stressing the take-only-what-you-eat theme? Encourage eating fruits and vegetables with their skins on. Buy cups or glasses with wide bases so less milk is spilled. Save outer vegetable leaves and cooking water for soup. Save fruit juices to use in making bread or muffins. Examine your own food waste and determine where the worst waste problems are at your home. Maybe it would mean putting the leftovers in a labeled container in the refrigerator or freezer where they will not be forgotten.

It's Rewarding!

Cutting down food waste is a satisfying project because we get an immediate reward right at home. By small changes in our habits collectively, we can save enormous amounts of food that might have been wasted. We can thereby save billions of dollars nationally, as well as a tidy sum for ourselves.

Diary of a cheap cook

by Helen Black

I have a confession to make. All along, I've been a cheap cook. NOT just since the great rise in food prices. NOT just since the great inflation. NOT just since the oil crisis. Before it was chic. I got some secret glee from a food bargain. Way back, I was a closet scrimper . . .

September, 1944. "Conspicuous waste"! What a cute idea! Veblen thinks of wasting food as a way of showing off to your friends. Sets you up as superior. Shows that you can afford to waste. I never thought of it that way. That's why the neighbors look down on me for my economies.

January, 1954. Beans are cheap, but so low in status. Should never have served them at my last dinner party. Loud cries of indignation from the men, the trouble-makers. They feel affronted when confronted with cheap food, no matter how delicious.

March, 1964. Shopped today, thirsting for a bargain. Slathered over the ten-pound bags of potatoes, so cheap, such a saving in that size. But, can I use 10 pounds, before some spoil? A terrible risk! What a challenge! I triumphed with baked potatoes, scooping out the hot potato and mashing with added cottage cheese, oregano, margarine, salt and pepper to taste and returning it to the shells. Made lots; they froze nicely.

August, 1974. These days people are more tolerant of greedy bargain hunters like me. Times have changed. Nobody noticed my cry of joy at the meat counter over the turkey drumsticks at 39¢ per pound. I had realized I could simmer them, use the meat for turkey enchiladas, and so avoid serving the drumsticks intact with their aggravating bony tendons! Worked beautifully! Cooked the drumsticks in some leftover carrot cooking water! When they were tender, I removed about 30 tendon fragments easily, and cut up the meat.

And January, 1984? EVERYBODY WILL BE DOING IT! Thrift will become our way of life, as waste was before. Even men will learn to relish leftovers, remembrances of meals past. Old experienced scrimpers will be respected. "Conspicuous economy" will become the new way of showing off! What a prospect! How I hope it happens.

Everbody's talking about nutrition, but . . .

But what are they doing about it? *by Mary Gullberg*

Woman's Day magazine conducted a survey ("Family Food Study" by Yankelovich, Skelly and White) recently which turned up some interesting findings from the 1,188 persons surveyed. Sixty percent of those questioned would settle for fewer children's TV programs in exchange for a ban on advertising directed at children under 12. Fifty percent wanted pesticides banned even though it might mean fruits and vegetables would cost more. Further, seventy-one percent worry about pesticides, sixty-two percent are concerned about food

Photo by Jane Scherr

Questions on nutrition are among those most often asked Co-op home economists in the stores.

additives, and sixty-eight percent think natural foods are healthier than processed ones.

People think physical fitness and nutrition go hand in hand, according to survey findings. However, almost half those surveyed felt that the whole day's food should be balanced but it's not necessary to eat three meals a day nor are there special foods for breakfast, lunch or dinner. These people seem more relaxed, less rigid in their lifestyles.

Interest in nutrition is high, with 77 percent admitting to recently activated interest in this subject. Fifty-one percent want more information on how to choose better foods, 40 per-

cent want to avoid harmful ingredients. One out of five was on a diet and 44 percent of the families had one or more members overweight.

But has all this interest changed eating habits? Three out of four said they eat what they like. Seventeen percent of them don't worry about this behavior, while 59 percent try for a balanced diet but not too hard. Only 14 percent feel strongly about "eating what's good for you" and 10 percent are watching their calories. Major barriers to good nutrition were felt to be snacking (45 percent), no time to cook (51 percent of the employed women) and television advertising to children (36 percent of the parents).

June 19, 1978

Who's in charge? Nobody

by Helen Black

Everybody knows the right thing to do is to eat right! There is no disagreement on this point. The problem is, who's in charge of eating right?

Not me, said the eater

I eat what I like! I eat the doughnut, because it's sweeter than plain bread. I load up on soft drinks, because they go down easy. It's not MY fault that all these things are so handy when I'm hungry, at vending machines in schools, at coffee shops, at doughnut shops, at end-aisles in supermarkets . . . it's not my fault that I eat the way I do!

Not me, said the cook

I fix what they like to eat! If it's not too much trouble, that is. It's not MY fault that they're finicky eaters!

Not me, said the shopper

I buy what I know they'll eat. Besides, I can buy only what's in the store. It's not MY fault that there are so many too-sweet, too-fattening, easy-to-fix products in the stores!

Not me, said the supermarket

I sell what I know people will buy. And I put it where they can't miss it when they shop! It's not MY fault that I have to sell what's on the market, what's been advertised, what people ask for.

Not me, said the manufacturer

I only make what people want. And I have to scream, to rave, to advertise! Otherwise, people wouldn't KNOW they want our sweet, spicy, over-seasoned, easy-to-eat products!

So nobody's in charge!

Instead, maybe it's EVERYBODY'S responsibility. The manufacturer could choose to scream about some more nutritious products. The supermarket could choose to put them where people couldn't miss them. The shopper could choose to find them. The cook could choose to learn to cook them. And the eaters? They could solve the whole problem — they could choose to eat right!

The great American diet and how to change it

This time, it's a committee of the U.S. Senate recommending that we change our diets.*

This is not the first semi-authoritative body of recent years to issue stiff warnings about the excesses of the American diet. Others have offered similar advice. One reason for concern is that death rates from heart disease, diabetes and certain kinds of cancer in various countries, when compared to food eaten, seem to indicate a possible relationship with excess calories and high dietary fat, sugar or salt.

The Senate committee's seven goals have the support of some very eminent authorities. Most nutritionists will agree with most of the goals but will restaurant operators and food processors cut down salty, sugary and fatty foods? Others may wonder why limits on alcohol were not suggested. But can we wait until EVERYBODY agrees before taking steps to attain these goals?

My opinion is that these goals represent at least the direction in which we need to go.

The Senate committee's seven goals:

1. Avoid overweight. Do this by avoiding excess calories AND by increasing energy expenditure. Reducing food intake below 1200-1400 calories is not recommended for average sized people because that amount of food will not provide adequate vitamins and minerals.

2. Eat less fat. Presently, we're getting about 40 percent of calories from fat; the goal is to reduce it to 30%. To meet this goal a person who needs about 2000 calories per day can cut out about 2 tablespoons of butter or margarine or other fat.

3. Eat less saturated fats. They recommend that 10 percent of our calories come from saturated fat, plus 10 percent each from polyunsaturated and monounsaturated fat. This means choosing some oils and margarines to replace butter, lard and hydrogenated fats; choosing poultry and fish to replace some beef, pork and lamb; choosing lowfat or nonfat milk in place of some whole milk.

4. Eat more starchy foods. Eat more complex carbohydrates, such as are in bread and potatoes, and more natural sugars as in vegetables and fruits. The goal is to increase this section from a mere 28% up to 48% of calories.

5. Eat less sugar. Reduce refined sugar intake from the current 18% of calories to 10. On a 2000-calorie diet, this would be equal to about 4 tablespoons sugar per day. Note: one 12 oz. can of soda has about 3 tablespoons sugar!

6. Eat less cholesterol. From an average intake of 600 milligrams of cholesterol, the recommendation is for 300 mg. per day. By reducing total fat and saturated fat, cholesterol tends to be reduced too. Though eggs are very high in cholesterol, an egg every other day can be included at this level.

7. Eat less salt. Americans eat from 6 to 18 grams of salt a day; the goal is to reduce this level to 5 grams (2000 mg. sodium). This would mean not adding salt at the table, and avoiding highly salted foods such as potato chips, soy sauce, etc.

*U.S. Senate Select Committee on Nutrition and Human Needs, December, 1977.

Fight the fat

How to eat less fat

Lately, we're being advised to eat for health and longevity. The most staggering advice is the suggestion that we reduce calories that come from fat in food to 30% of the total calories eaten each day.

This recommendation, from the Senate Select Committee on Nutrition and Human Needs, assumes we all know that calories also come from protein, carbohydrates and alcohol in the diet as well as fat. It comes at a time when Americans are reported to be weighing more for their age than a few years ago: the average weight for height of adults has increased by four pounds since 1962. This seems like a worrisome trend towards more obesity, but the advice is not aimed only at people who are overweight. Instead, it is said that even normal weight people would derive health benefits by cutting down fat calories and making up the deficit with starchy foods such as potatoes, bread or rice.

Great! But how on earth does one translate the 30%-calories-from-fat diet into real food? Where does the bacon and eggs breakfast, the hamburger-milkshake lunch, the beef stroganoff dinner fit into such a diet? I set about figuring this out and as a result of my diligent calculations I can now report which typical combinations of foods are on the unhappy side of 30% fat calories, and vice versa.

The cereal-milk breakfast makes it, bacon and eggs don't

Shredded wheat, whole milk and orange juice are an 18% fat calorie breakfast. With low fat milk, the same breakfast is only 15% fat calories and with nonfat milk, it's down to 7%. On the other hand, pour half and half on your cereal and the fat calories shoot up to 44%. The bacon and eggs breakfast, even with a poached egg (no added fat) and a skimpy ½ teaspoon of butter or margarine on toast does not make it either. It is, alas, 55% fat calories.

What's for lunch?

The peanut butter sandwich, whole milk and apple lunch scandalized me with fat calories reaching 48%. A cheese sandwich in place of peanut butter is even worse, at 56% fat calories.

However, switching to nonfat milk dropped fat calories down to 34% and 38% respectively. The hamburger, milkshake and French fries luncheon came out at 43% fat calories.

Dinner — the biggest challenge

For dinner, I calculated a recipe from the Co-op Low Cost Cookbook, Hamburger Stroganoff. Assuming that one-fourth of the recipe was eaten with 1 cup cooked rice, the fat calories are, sob, 44%. This is based on using lean ground beef, 15% fat. (With higher fat ground beef, some but not all of the extra fat would cook out and probably be discarded). All is not lost, however! Yogurt can easily be substituted for the sour cream in this Stroganoff recipe, dropping the fat calories down to 30%. Eureka! We made the recommendation!

Of course it matters what else is eaten. So I checked out the fat calories in some vegetable combinations, as follows:

	Calories from fat
1 cup peas with 1 teaspoon butter	32%
Green Giant Sweet Peas in Butter Sauce	36%
Birds Eye Green Peas with Cream Sauce	53%

Do not look to salad to help lower your overall percent calories from fat. Since the caloric value of salad greens are low, the fat in salad dressing is high, the percent of calories from fat is always high.

Dessert can be dangerous, with cookies, pies, cakes or ice cream — or very safe, with fruit, ice milk or yogurt:

Fresh fruit	4%
Ice milk	30%
Oatmeal cookies	30%
Devils Food Cake	33%
Apple pie	39%
Ice cream	50%
Brownies	58%

Snacks may be dangerous or just dandy:

Raw vegetables (carrots)	4%
Pretzels	10%
Bread, no butter	12%
Saltines	24%
Butter crackers	35%
Snack crackers (Ritz)	51%
Potato chips	63%

A palatability fight?

These calculations have been sobering. Perhaps we are caught in a "palatibility fight" with fat, hence the Ritz crackers instead of sodas, the Peas in Cream Sauce instead of plain peas. I think we need to consider what else is pleasurable in eating — the chewing, the subtle flavors, the sourness or bitterness of foods — and not be led astray by the all-too-easy sensory satisfaction of high fat foods.

—Helen Black, Co-op Home Economist

The complete report of the Senate Select Committee on Nutrition and Human Needs entitled "Dietary Goals for the United States, Second Edition" may be purchased by mail for $2.30 from the U.S. Government Bookstore, 450 Golden Gate Ave., Room 1023, San Francisco 94102. Checks or money orders should be made payable to the Superintendent of Documents.

Is pizza junk food? *by Mary Gullberg*

The answer is no if you indulge only occasionally, but pizza is a high calorie, high fat food and nutritionists are telling us that we shouldn't overeat on calories or fat, particularly animal fat. We took a recipe for pizza from *Joy of Cooking* and made some calculations. The recipe was for 4 or 8 servings. One-eighth of the pizza had 408 calories, a quarter supplied 815 calories. Forty percent of the calories were from fat.

The Senate's Select Committee on Nutrition and Human Needs recommends eating less fat — according to the committee, no more than 30% of our total calories should come from fat. Another goal recommended that no more than 10% of our calories should come from animal fats, the remaining 20% should be divided equally between mono- and polyunsaturated fats.

So, getting back to our hypothetical pizza, too frequent consumption of pizza gives us too many calories in one serving making it hard to fit in the other foods we need during the other meals of the day. Secondly, the olive oil in pizza is largely monounsaturated and the cheeses and pepperoni contain only animal fats. Therefore, this pizza missed the goal of 30 percent calories from fats as well as 10 percent of the day's calories from unsaturated fat. However, low fat foods with pizza would help lower fat calories for that meal.

Other goals recommended by the Senate Select Committee are eat more starchy food, eat less cholesterol, eat less sugar and far less salt. If you think about these goals a little, you will realize that true junk foods (soft drinks, candy, most desserts, cookies, potato chips and other chips) are ruled out for regular eating if you are trying to improve your food choices along the lines recommended by the committee.

The calorie needs of a teenager go way up, but the protein requirements don't climb proportionately. Even athletes or people doing heavy work need protein in proportion to their size rather than in proportion to their activity.

When a home economist comes to supper *by Betsy Wood*

I sang for my supper last week. I had invited myself to a friend's home and was pumped with questions. There are four kids in the family and my friends are bewildered about prices and food shopping like the rest of us. Here's a somewhat organized version of what we said:

Does Anthony need extra protein, more than Fred?
(Anthony is tall and lean and fifteen. Fred is his tall and lean father).

Just a little. The calorie needs of a teenager go way up, but the protein requirements don't climb proportionately. Even athletes or people doing heavy work need protein in proportion to their size rather that in proportion to their activity.

Is it OK for Anthony to fill up on carbohydrate?

YES, IF . . . **If** he gets his basic nutrient needs first and **if** the carbohydrate food is a reasonably good one that contributes other nutrients besides calories. Everyone should eat daily at least two servings of protein food, four servings of vegetables and fruits (one high in vitamin C such as citrus, one high in vitamin A such as carrots or greens), and four servings of breads or cereals. A teenager should have a quart of milk or its equivalent in cheese.

To fill in the calories it's okay to have thirds on spaghetti, fourths on potatoes, or five pieces of toast. But try to discourage filling up on soda pop, cupcakes, candy and other high-sugar foods. If possible many of the "starches" should be whole grain — brown rice, whole wheat bread, plain oatmeal. Co-op Special Formula bread is a nutritious white bread with extra soy flour, dry milk and wheat germ.

Potatoes, especially baked or steamed, contribute vitamin C and iron. And of course all kinds of beans provide protein, B vitamins and iron as well as carbohydrate.

How much protein do we each need?

You say in the Co-op News that the average adult needs from 45 to 55 grams a day. How about the kids?

The following amounts allow for a margin of safety to cover a wide variety of people.

Recommended Daily Allowances — Protein

Adult male, 154 lbs.	56 grams	**Boys,** 11-14 years	45 grams
Adult female, 120 lbs.	44 grams	15-18	56 grams
Pregnant	+ 30 grams	**Girls,** 11-14	46 grams
Lactating	+ 20 grams	15-18	46 grams
Children, 1-3 years	23 grams		
4-6	30 grams		
7-10	34 grams		

Isn't it hard to get that much protein?

Actually, no. Studies show that the average American eats about twice as much protein as he needs. Protein is the nutrient (besides calories and fat) that is best provided for in American diets. We keep talking about protein, maybe because we're obsessed with meat and meat prices, but it's very hard for Americans not to get enough protein.

However, because the vitamins and minerals that occur in protein foods are NOT easy to get in recommended amounts, nutritionists advise eating 2 or 3 servings of meat, fish, eggs, or beans and 2 servings of milk or milk products per day.

In the Co-op News (August 6) you list cost of 20 grams of protein. I can't visualize it.

If you divide a pound of ground beef and make four patties, each one will yield about 3 ounces of cooked meat. Three ounces of cooked meat yields about 20 grams of protein.

Some people don't realize that meat is not all protein. Beef is roughly 60 percent water, 20 percent fat and 20 percent protein.

How does a vegetarian manage?

(She didn't ask this but I thought you would want to know).

This takes more thought and planning but it's not hard. Protein foods should be spread through all three meals. Also, either small amounts of animal foods (milk, eggs, etc.) should be eaten at the same meal with plant foods, or combinations that enhance protein quality, such as beans and grains, should be used. The recommended allowance might be met with these foods eaten in one day:

1 cup beans, cooked	15
2 eggs	12
1 cup milk	9
1½ ounce cheese	11
4 servings fruits and vegetables	8
4 servings bread or cereal	9
Total	64

Frankly, if I were a vegetarian I would be more concerned about getting enough iron and other vitamins and minerals than getting enough protein.

I was rewarded with a banquet: a stew made with shank meat from the freezer (two pounds to serve eight, cooked long and slow, then cut up), lots of vegetables and a rich gravy. Shell noodles were cooked and added to stretch it all. We had sautéed zucchini slices from the garden topped with grated cheese, lettuce salad from my garden, and whole wheat blackberry muffins for dessert. Great!

I'm gonna lose 20 pounds . . . if it kills me!!!

by Wendy Gardner

So . . . how are you going to do it?

Impulse I: By eating only grapefruit juice and bananas until I've reached my goal?

Impulse II: By eating one meal a day until I've lost 20 pounds?

Impulse III: By eliminating all breads and starchy foods until I've reached my goal?

Impulse IV: By cutting out rich desserts, junk foods, and eating smaller portions forever and ever?

On the positive side . . .

Becoming motivated to lose excess weight, making a plan and sticking to it is more than half the battle. But a plan which totals you out in the process will be short-lived. A good diet stresses basic nutritional foods during and after the period of dieting. Besides, who wants to make the same resolution next year?

On the other hand . . .

Impulse I: This diet is composed mostly of carbohydrates. You might lose weight on it, but a larger portion than normal of weight lost will be lean body tissue. Your own muscle protein will be wasted because your body needs a certain amount of circulating proteins which in this case is not available in the diet. This type of fad diet is deficient in most of the major nutrients and should never be followed more than a day or two.

Impulse II: There are two arguments against eating one meal a day. 1) Eating one meal does not necessarily mean you are eating fewer calories. It is possible to eat a day's supply of calories in one meal. In order to lose one pound a person must — over a period of time — eat 3500 calories less than his body burns up.

2) In animal studies one-meal eaters become more efficient in the use of food and have an increased capacity for fat synthesis. A correlation is made that an infrequent intake of large meals may predispose humans to obesity, elevate their cholesterol levels, and interfere with their metabolism of sugar. *

Impulse III: One slice of bread and ½ cup of rice or oatmeal contain about 70-80 calories. It is the fatty spreads we put over them that ruin our waistlines. A well-balanced diet will have three to four servings of enriched bread or cereal. The spreads are expendable. Breads and cereals are good sources of the B Vitamins, iron and other essential nutrients.

Impulse IV: You guessed it. This solution is most logical if you were eating protein foods, fruits, and vegetables. Do not forget a good source of calcium such as milk or cheese. *

*Gilbert A. Leveille, *Lipogenic Adaptations Related to Pattern of Food Intake*, Nutrition Reviews, Vol. 30, No. 7, July, 1972, p. 151.

Warning: Driving a car may be more 'fattening' than eating potatoes!

by Mary Ruth Nelson

Ridiculous? Not really. Potatoes and some other very nutritious but starchy foods are often "put down" by labeling them "fattening." But have you ever heard of an automobile or an electric typewriter that was labeled as "fattening"? Think about it.

'Fattening' makes a negative impression

That word is vague but we get the feeling that it means something bad. We should avoid things so labeled. But, if we do give in and eat such foods, it's often done in grand style — we double or treble the calories by adding butter or other fat. This thoroughly convinces us that potatoes are "fattening."

It all has to balance out

To maintain a constant body weight, the number of calories TAKEN IN must equal the number of calories USED UP. For every pound of weight GAIN, we must TAKE IN 3500 MORE calories than our body uses; for every pound of weight LOSS, there must be 3500 fewer calories in our diet than our bodies require.

What you do does matter

Suppose you used to walk to and from work but recently you decided to drive the 1¼ mile — about 10 to 12 city blocks — both ways. Driving would use less than 20 calories, walking about 250.

If you don't change any other activity and eat the same amount of food as before, you would gain about 17 pounds a year. However, if you continued walking to and from work, your other activities remained the same, and you ate the same amount of food except for ADDING a cup of boiled potatoes daily, you would gain only 12 pounds in a year. That's what I mean when I say driving a car may be more "fattening" than eating potatoes.

You decided to replace your manual typewriter with an electric one. If you usually typed 6 hours/day, 5 days a week and everything else remained constant, you would USE 360 FEWER calories/week. This would amount to over 5 pounds weight gain per year from using the electric typewriter instead of the manual one.

What you add to a food is important

You can increase the caloric content many-fold by adding varying amounts of fats:

	Calories/cup
Boiled potatoes, salt added	118
Mashed potatoes, using some milk & fat	197
Boiled potatoes with 1 tablespoon of fat	220
Potato salad with salad dressing	248
Scalloped potatoes with milk & butter	255
Fried potatoes	456
Potato chips (4 ounces)	644

(Dancing, the "body language," for an hour would use up most of the calories in the potato chips. Is it worth it?)

Name calling does matter

We are the losers if we eliminate a nutritious food such as potatoes from our diet because it's "fattening." A cup of boiled potatoes contains iron, B vitamins, almost no fat and furnishes almost half of the daily allowance for vitamin C. And all that for a little over 100 calories. Is that too great a price to pay for a 20 minute walk?

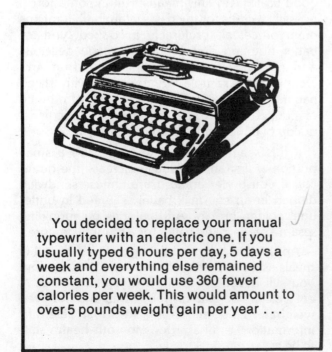

You decided to replace your manual typewriter with an electric one. If you usually typed 6 hours per day, 5 days a week and everything else remained constant, you would use 360 fewer calories per week. This would amount to over 5 pounds weight gain per year . . .

Unwanted calories, ugh!

by Helen Black

Ever since water went out of style as a thirst-quencher we've had this awful problem of getting ugly calories with our beverages. Because wine, soft drinks, fruit drinks and even fruit juice are high calorie in the amount drunk to quench thirst. Water, of course, is calorie-free.

The wine flows like water

In our new enlightened state we drink wine with dinner in long-stemmed glasses. It is the American Way of Life! But alas, from a nutritional standpoint wine is just another junk food and the calories are substantial. Switching from water to 2 small glasses of wine (that's about 200 calories) could result in a weight gain of more than 2 pounds per month, a whopping 28 pounds a year!

. . . And soft drinks are higher

That fruit soda is a horrid source of calories. One 12 oz. fruit soda with its 11 teaspoons of sugar has about 170 calories; a couple of those a day are even worse caloric hazard than wine. Gingerale, colas, quinine water, etc. are slightly lower.

. . . And fruit drinks are highest

Koolade, Hawaiian Punch, Cranberry Juice Cocktail, Tang are yet higher in sugar and calories. They range from 160 to 200 calories or as much as 12 teaspoons of sugar in a 12 oz. portion. Perhaps these drinks are not consumed as thirst quenchers, only as rare treats? I hope so.

. . . And good old fruit juice

Even apple juice, that lovable old standby, is a high calorie beverage too. If you drink 12 oz. of apple or orange juice instead of fruit soda, you get 180 calories. Orange juice is a good source of vitamin C, but apple juice is distressingly low in vitamins and minerals. Think of it as a wholesome treat, not as a substitute for water.

Jack Sprat could eat no fat
His wife could eat no lean
And so betwixt them both, you see
They licked the platter clean.

(Nursery rhyme. Author unknown)

by June Kadish

Somewhere out there among our Co-op shoppers are those who identify with Jack Sprat and want to gain weight, not lose it. Loud groans from most of us! But, indeed, it's true, and it strikes me that we're constantly suggesting ways to cut calories and hardly ever addressing ourselves to the thin ones who would like to pad their bones.

Calories and Calm

Weight gain or loss can be equated to calories taken in vs. calories expended. If you eat more calories than your body can use, you will gain weight. If you eat more frequently you may be able to increase your calorie intake. The atmosphere in which you have your meals may be as important as what you eat. Try to eat in a calm, relaxed manner. This may mean eating before or after the family for a while if meal time is a bit hectic. In all this, we assume you are choosing foods from the Basic Four food groups which have been discussed frequently in a variety of ways through our consumer information.

What's all the fuss about, you may ask? Just eat more and you will gain weight. Not so easy, say the thin ones. We already eat as much quantity as we can manage and never seem to put on an ounce. Well, there's hope. First of all, we assume that you've had a recent physical exam and there's no medical reason behind your inability to gain. The calorie additions suggested below are generally high in fat so be sure your doctor says it's o.k. to make these dietary changes. Next step is to take a hard look at your eating habits, the quality of your diet as well as the quantity.

Regular meals and snacks

Basic eating patterns of Americans emphasize three meals a day. Certainly if you're trying to gain weight, don't skip a meal. In fact, you may be able to up your calorie intake by eating several smaller meals. Have a snack in mid-morning: a peanut butter sandwich with a glass of milk, a cheese omelet, or sliced fresh fruit with half and half. Have you acquired the habit of a good breakfast? This means fruit in some form, possibly a citrus for the day's vitamin C. It means grain or cereal (preferably a cooked type for better nutrition and economy) made delicious and caloric with extra toppings of fruit and cream. For example, try oatmeal with sliced bananas, heavy cream and a dusting of nutmeg or cooked brown rice with stewed apricots, a dollop of butter and cinnamon.

If this seems like a lot to tackle, try a small portion at first and gradually increase the quantity. If you prefer bread, try a cheese sandwich dipped in an egg-milk batter, sautéed in butter until golden brown. Add calories by sprinkling sesame seeds in the batter for a crunchy texture.

Apply these kinds of suggestions to other meals as well. If after a few months of this effort, you still haven't gained an ounce, continue to eat well and be grateful you're thin and not overweight which, according to most scientific information, is a hazardous-to-your-health state to be in.

Beating the sweets: how much is too much? *by Helen Black*

Once I ate a doughnut at the Co-op coffee bar to cries of "Shame! Shame!" from Co-op checkers, shoppers and other shocked spectators.

Their reasoning was that Co-op Home Economists keep telling other people to cut down on sweets and therefore should never ever themselves eat sweets, especially in public. Now this is downright mean. Like anyone else, if it's there, I may eat it. Let me hurry to say that Co-op home economists do not counsel abstinence, anyway. Instead, following Nature's Law that things are always more complicated than we humans wish, we say, "Don't eat too many sweets!" And how much is too much? Well, that's the part that's complicated.

Sweets . . . why not?

Because they replace nutritious foods, because they're terrible on teeth, because they add excessive calories, because they may be related to health problems in later life.

Eight sweets a day . . . good grief!

A typical American diet has been described as including a sugared cereal, two soft drinks, a candy bar, cookies, a sweet dessert, sugar in coffee and jam on toast. Do you eat that much? More? It may be later than you think.

How sweet is sweet?

By most charitable estimates, the above diet includes about 13 tablespoons of sugar or some 700 calories **just from the sugar alone.** A sweet-sweet, such as a serving of frosted cake has 3 or more tablespoons of sugar; the sweetened cereal has 1; soft drinks 2 or 3. Custard or ice cream has about 1 tablespoon, a slice of cinnamon toast has only 1 teaspoon sugar.

A matter of love, expectations and rewards.

They say our parents started it all using sweets as rewards, confusing them with love. Somehow sweets came to be prized above all other foods. Now some parents do things differently. They do not offer sweets to their young children. They let those eager appetites be rewarded with better foods. When the children are older and exposed to sweets, limits are put on them. It takes determined parents to do this!

Honey, artificial sweeteners, even juices are not the answer.

If the problem is one of expecting and wanting all foods to be sweet, then sweet substitutes are no real solution.

For teenagers, danger ahead.

Teenagers or others with urgent caloric needs, may stow away rich sweet-sweets with no noticeable over-weight. But the very big danger is the HABIT. It may persist long after the teen years.

We think one moderate sweet per day is plenty.

Most diet plans do not cope with the problem of sweets, or they simply include none or minimal sweets. It is discouraging, accustomed as many are to 8 sweets a day, to try for the ideal of no sweets. So we think 1 a day is a good compromise though even this is too much for some people who are sedentary, or for small children. Why not try to:

. . . **Put more distance between sweet-sweets!** Eating 2 a day? Work towards 1. Eating 1 a day? Try 1 every other day.

. . . **Try less-sweet desserts.** Try puddings, lightly sweetened fruits in place of candy, cake and cookies.

. . . **Learn to love attractive non-sweets.** Reach for the nuts, seeds, fruits, cheese, vegetables with dips instead of a sweet.

Hypertension and a Black cultural perspective

by Julia B. Robinson, R.D.

What is it?

Hypertension, commonly known as high blood pressure, is the result of an abnormal increase of pressure against the walls of the blood vessels which transport blood from the heart to all parts of the body. It strikes men, women, and children of all races. About 23 million Americans have it but only 10 percent of them know it.

Is it dangerous?

High blood pressure is the major health problem in America today. It is the greatest single cause of death. Hypertension can induce stroke, heart attacks, heart failure, kidney failure, and other perils such as hardening of the arteries in the heart, brain and limbs, permanent loss of vision, and the senility of old age. It is a disease one can have and feel absolutely healthy. It is often unnoticed, painless, and symptomless. For these reasons, this disease is as dangerous as an assassin's bullet and two million Americans unnecessarily risk premature death because the incidence of the diseases associated with it is three to five times greater among hypertension victims than among normal individuals. It kills mainly because it is not detected and controlled.

What causes it?

The actual cause of hypertension is obscure. However, researchers have shown that high blood pressure is caused by a number of factors: fear, anxiety, tension, stress, obesity, diet, and certain other psychological and physiological disorders.

How does it affect Black people and why?

Among Black people, the incidence of hypertension is not only more frequent but also it develops earlier in life, is often more severe and causes higher mortality at younger ages. Studies have shown prevalence of high blood pressure among Blacks at a ratio twice as high as in the White population.

One authority states that there is a mosaic of causes for the higher rate of hypertension among Blacks in America. Another suggested that "the United States itself may be taking its unhappy hypertensive toll on Black people. Sociological rage, sustained emotional stress, economic worries, the daily psychic battles for self respect . . . . may all have induced high blood pressure in the Black person." (Ebony Magazine, June 1973)

Obesity and diet also play overwhelmingly important roles in controlling or triggering hypertension in Blacks. For example, if a person is obese and Black there is a good chance he has hypertension. Also, there is a positive correlation between salt intake and high blood pressure; therefore, a heavy or exclusive diet of soul food could be a major contributing factor since such foods as spicy barbecue sauces, heavily salted greens and beans, bacon, salt pork, ham and ham hocks (all of which are among soul food specialties) would not be restricted or limited. A selective diet consisting of a variety of foods as well as restricting the above foods considerably is recommended.

What should you do about it?

Individuals who feel perfectly well should visit a doctor regularly or a health or hypertension screening clinic to determine if they have high blood pressure. Campaigns to find people with hypertension are now being conducted — contact your local heart association or health department for information.

If you are already aware that you have the disease, follow your doctor's orders. No matter how good you feel. The measures the doctor takes to control your high blood pressure may include drugs, diet, or changes in living habits. Obese persons are often placed on a reduction type diet in which a normal amount of meat, chicken, fish, eggs and skim milk is eaten to supply protein. Fats, starches, sugar, cereals, cream, and foods made from these fat-producing substances are restricted. Often, the blood pressure comes down as the pounds go off.

A person with serious hypertension may be required to follow a sodium-restricted diet. No one should undertake a low-salt diet, however, except on the advice of a physician. The doctor will decide what type of diet is required, if any, and will see that the individual is instructed on how the diet should be followed. For the person on a low-sodium (low-salt) diet there are more and more foods on the market that are prepared without salt. These include bread, canned vegetables, soups and meat.

Salt: on loving it less
by Helen Black

And when did YOU learn to love salt? Not yesterday, I'll bet. More likely, when you were very young. Humankind learned to love it, and we mined it, fought over it, used it as money, and treasured it, starting at least 3000 years ago. The taste for salt is an acquired one. Primitive people who have never had it available dislike it at first, but quickly overcome their dislike. In complex societies, the prestige value of salty, highly seasoned foods may be part of the reason such food is preferred.

The lovableness of salt is a worry

For many years high blood pressure has been treated with low salt diets. Now, doctors are suggesting that excessive salt in the diet, maybe from infancy, is the cause of high blood pressure in susceptible people.

Into the mouths of babes?

Do babies need added salt? No. They get plenty of sodium as it naturally occurs in milk, eggs, meat, vegetables. Furthermore, babies do not have an inborn taste for salt, as they do for sugar. So it is practical to avoid salt in baby food. Let them learn to like it later. Baby food manufacturers have eliminated salt in their products in recent years. Parents who go the cheaper route of making their own baby food can leave the salt out too. When the baby is fed from the table, the food can be salted after the baby's portion has been removed.

Salted, saltier, saltiest

Adults may be eating more salt today because more of our food is processed and preseasoned. About the only processed foods not salted are canned, dried or frozen fruits and juices, jams and jellies, and some frozen vegetables.

Most people know that salt is added to bread, even though it doesn't taste salty. We taste the salt in butter, margarine, canned vegetables, and it's listed on the label, anyway. But would you suspect salt in cottage cheese? It's there, and in buttermilk too. Such foods should be required to state all ingredients on the label.

Much saltier are catsup, pickles, prepared mustard, olives, potato chips, salted popcorn, soda crackers, corned beef, bacon, salt pork and ham. Some of these foods, used as seasonings, are not used in large amounts. Others, used as snacks, may be eaten in large amounts and may be adding much salt to the diet.

Some foods are much saltier in one form than in another. For example, processed cheese spreads are about twice as salty as natural cheddar cheese; prepared French or Italian salad dressing may be as much as four times as salty as mayonnaise; very thin stick pretzels may be twice as salty as thicker pretzels.

Among the very saltiest of foods are bouillon cubes and soy sauce. Soy sauce has 4-6 times the salt as the same amount of catsup.

First line of defense: the supermarket

When you shop, choose less salty foods. Buy unsalted peanuts in the shell, for snacks. At home, try easing up on the salt. You may be adding more than necessary. In becoming unaccustomed to salt, you will notice flavors frequently masked by saltiness. This is a very big PLUS for those who get along without, or with less, salt!

Fiber: indigestible and indispensible *by Mary Gullberg*

What's fiber? Fiber is material that humans lack the enzymes to digest although the bacteria in the large intestine may break down some fiber. Most fiber passes through the body unchanged. It takes up water on this trip making a very soft stool that is easy to evacuate. The time it takes for the food to pass through the gut is also speeded up.

Beneficial effects? Most of the evidence for benefits from fiber is based on the incidence of a given disorder in a relatively uniform population that, in this case, is consuming a low amount of fiber and relatively high amounts of fat and protein. Conditions known to be associated with low-fiber diets are constipation, diverticular disease of the colon, hemorrhoids and varicose veins. Unfortunately ownership of transistor radios is also . . . statistically . . . related to these diseases! So much for epidemiological evidence.

Cancer of the colon has not been found to be correlated with low-fiber diets. However, fiber from pectin, rolled oats or wheat bran is known to lower the blood cholesterol. Overweight can be helped by fiber since a high-fiber diet will contain fewer calories. Pectin and guar gum are thought to aid diabetics by reducing their need for insulin.

African diets very high in fiber are correlated with the absence of the disease conditions listed above. However, these people didn't live long enough to develop the diseases of old age which is essentially what we are talking about.

Vegetables and fruits contain fiber but they are so high in water that they can't compete with wheat bran, shredded whole wheat, whole wheat bread, wheaties or grapenuts. It takes 7 pounds of celery to equal the fiber contained in 7 tablespoons of bran.

A word of caution to fiber enthusiasts. High fiber foods have a lowered digestibility for the protein they contain. For example, the protein in white bread is 91 percent digestible, that in whole wheat bread is 87 percent and the protein in high fiber breakfast cereals is 81 percent digestible.

Should cellulose from wood be added to foods? Some scientists in Germany found that eating a bread which contains wood cellulose allows the cellulose to get into the blood and to be excreted in the urine. The Canadian Food and Drug has banned the use of wood cellulose, in Canadian foods. Branola bread contains bran, not cellulose, but we don't know whether the other nutrients in the bran (some vitamins and minerals) are actually capable of being absorbed from the human gut.

February 23, 1977

Eating for two *by Judy Heckman*

Pregnant and want a healthy baby? EAT! The health of you and your unborn baby depends upon a well-balanced and nutritious diet every day.

Beware of friendly advice because new knowledge has changed many of the traditional ideas of what and how much to eat when you're pregnant. Weight gain used to be a big issue. Women were scolded and given low-calorie diets if they gained beyond a certain magic number. **A gradual and steady pattern of weight gain is the important factor, not whether the individual exceeds some established weight limit.** A minimum weight gain of 24 pounds is now considered necessary for all pregnant women. This figure reflects the weight of the baby as well as the necessary weight increases of certain body tissues. Dieting to lose weight has no place during pregnancy because nutrient needs can't be met by low-calorie diets.

Ideas have also changed about salt restrictions and the use of diuretics. A certain amount of fluid retention is normal. It's called physiological edema and it's the body's way of dealing with the demands of pregnancy. Restricted salt intake and diuretics only interfere with delicate mechanisms for regulating fluids. Food should be lightly salted to taste (notice we're talking about **lightly salted** since many of us use too much salt) and diuretics reserved for other medical conditions.

What two need. While we usually don't recommend vitamin and mineral supplements, pregnancy is a special time when a well-balanced diet can't supply adequate amounts of certain nutrients. Iron is one such nutrient. Most women don't get enough in normal times, let alone when they are pregnant. Because the iron requirement is so high, the pregnant woman needs an iron supplement in addition to the iron obtained from a well-balanced diet. FOLIC ACID supplements should also be prescribed as well as FLUORIDE in areas where the water is not fluoridated. A well-balanced diet of nutritious foods can supply all the other important nutrients needed for a successful pregnancy and a healthy baby.

A well-balanced diet during pregnancy includes: *

Food Group	Serving Size	Number of Servings/day
Protein Foods		
Animal	2-3 ounces	4
Vegetable	1 cup cooked	
Milk, Vit. D fortified, and milk products	1 cup	4
Grain products, preferably whole grain	1 slice bread or ½ cup cooked cereal	3
Vitamin C rich fruits and vegetables	½ cup orange or grapefruit juice (size varies with item)	1
Leafy green vegetables	1 cup raw or ¾ cup cooked	1
Other fruits and vegetables	½ cup	1
Oils and margarines	1 tablespoon	2

*This is a suggested food guide as discussed in the recently revised booklet *Nutrition During Pregnancy and Lactation*, developed by the California Department of Health, Maternal and Child Health Unit, 1975.

Who wants to be pregnant?

by Helen Black

If it's YOU who wants to be pregnant, whether this year or next, look to your food and drink today. Certainly, pregnancy is an enchanted state that will transform you! But it won't necessarily transform your food habits. It takes time and effort to do that. NOW is not too soon to get psyched up, take charge and control those habits that are hard on babies.

Alcohol: An old wives' tale?

No. The old wives were right. Alcohol passes through the placental barrier so that when the mother is drunk, so is the baby. Heavy drinking* has been linked to a serious growth and nervous problem of infants, including a type of hyperactivity called Fetal Alcohol Syndrome.

So how much alcohol is safe? Some authorities recommend that pregnant women avoid alcohol entirely, or if they cannot, limit it to 2 drinks per day. Unfortunately, it is not known whether a single drinking episode in the first month, before pregnancy is suspected, will cause some symptoms of Fetal Alcohol Syndrome. Women who hope for pregnancy should start limiting their drinking now.

Caffeine

Like alcohol, caffeine readily passes the placental barrier. Caffeine causes birth defects in animals, but its effect on human embryos has not yet been established. Some experts advise eliminating caffeine during the first three months of pregnancy. Caffeine is present in coffee, tea and cocoa, as well as non-prescription drugs such as cold tablets, headache pills, stay-awake pills, etc.

Don't fool around with junk food

The woman in good nutritional condition before pregnancy as well as throughout pregnancy has a better chance of having a full term, full-size baby. Difficulties related to smaller-than-normal babies can result from inadequate diets. NOW is the time to start eating the good diet. Now is the time to reach your proper weight, not

after pregnancy. Learn to appreciate whole grains, milk or cheese, beans as well as meats, dark green leafy vegetables. If you start learning to fix and eat these foods now, you can drastically improve your diet by the time you're pregnant.

*Heavy drinking is defined by the National Institute on Alcohol Abuse and Alcoholism as 6 drinks per day, each containing one ounce of whiskey or equivalent.
The information on Fetal Alcohol Syndrome is from "Alcohol and Birth Defects," by Fritz P. Witti, FDA Consumer, May 1978.

Twiggy was no fat baby *by Wendy Gardner*

Research indicates that the number of fat cells which a person has throughout life may be determined during the first year of life. An overfed infant may become an obese adult. According to Dr. Derrick Jelliffe, professor in the UCLA School of Public Health, overfeeding of infants is an increasing problem due to 1) bottle feeding, 2) early introduction of solid foods, and 3) social pressure to "grow" a large child.

Breast or the bottle?

Breast milk is easier for baby to digest and since mother cannot see how much milk her baby is getting, she is less likely to overfeed. Human milk has antibodies which are passed by mother to child to protect baby against infections. There are psychological advantages for both members of the nursing pair also.

Bottle-fed babies may be "pressured" to finish the bottle, and this insult may be compounded by feeding solid foods as early as the first few weeks of life by proud but misguided parents. It is important that the parents be able to "read the child's signals and not answer all discomfort signals with food." According to Dr. Hilde Bruch, professor of psychiatry at Baylor College of Medicine, overeating, as a way of life, may be taught the child who is fed by parents in response to his or her every cry of distress. So, love, burp, and play with baby as well as feed the little dear.

Mothers who choose to use a bottle to feed their babies may wish to check that the formulas are not more concentrated than the doctor ordered (a little more is not better). Respect the baby's right to decide when enough is enough.

For the first three months

Unless your baby was premature or had a low birth weight, breast milk contains all the nutrients your baby needs except vitamin D, iron and fluoride. During the first three months, baby uses the iron stored in his or her body before birth. Babies on formulas may require a vitamin C supplement unless the formula has added ascorbic acid.

Solid foods

There is no nutritional reason to introduce solid foods sooner than three to six months after birth. After the first three months, an iron supplement should be started, usually a cereal fortified with iron. Pureed baby foods can be prepared at home, (or see page 91 "Grandma Did It!") and by six to eight months foods from the family meals may simply be modified to suit baby.

Usually the first solids are cereals and fruit

These foods are best fed to baby with a spoon rather than diluted with milk in a bottle. Baby may not eat much the first times they are offered but he or she will soon learn that solid foods are to be eaten with a spoon and this is fun. Spoon feeding usually leads to faster chewing and self-feeding by baby. It is unwise to allow baby to take a bottle to bed. Sleeping while sucking on a bottle prolongs the period of time the food is in contact with the teeth and thus can increase the possibility of dental caries.

And in conclusion

Studies on obesity show that infancy may be the critical time in the formation of the fat cells, both in size and numbers. Once acquired, fat cells are with us for life. A person with a large number of fat cells has a very difficult time controlling his or her weight. So, parents, give baby a head start and let baby "tell" you when enough is enough.

Breast feeding baby: a lost art?

by Wendy Gardner

A rekindling of interest is taking place among new mothers today in an ancient ritual called breast feeding the baby. Although this ritual has been successful for thousands of years, in only about two generations, a nourishment called formula has replaced breast milk as the prime food for infants and is considered the modern method. Yet, mothers and scientists are now learning from grandmothers and animal experiments that although a commercial formula allows an infant to grow, there are advantages to breast feeding that cannot be duplicated.

. . . Breast feeding is the least expensive method if moderately priced foods are chosen for the extra 500 calories per day needed by a mother. For about 43¢ a peanut butter and banana sandwich and a glass of whole milk will provide 500 calories and 20 grams of protein. This compares favorably with the commercial formulas which cost between 68¢ and $2.10 per day. Formula made at home from evaporated milk would cost 48¢ a day. Special equipment costs extra.

. . . Breast feeding is convenient. No special shopping is necessary and there is no need for special sterilized equipment.

Bottle makes bigger, but not better

. . . Bottle fed babies do gain weight faster than breast fed babies. Scientists are now concerned that bottle fed babies may be accumulating extra fat cells that cannot be reduced in number later in life. A baby fed a bottle often is encouraged to finish it, while a baby nursing at the breast regulates the amount eaten.

. . . Human milk contains antibodies which protect against allergy and infections.

Ironically — if breast milk had nutrient labeling, it would not sell

. . . True, the protein, calcium, phosphorus

and sodium are much lower, while lactose, cholesterol, and essential fatty acids are much higher in human milk. The protein in human milk has a higher biological value and is better utilized than cow's milk. An excess of nutrients at an early stage in life may actually be harmful. A high calcium intake soon after birth may lead to greater loss of calcium later in life. High salt diets (sodium) are thought to contribute to hypertension. Therefore, the high mineral and protein content of cows' milk may not be beneficial at all.

Isn't cholesterol a dirty word?

No, cholesterol is a type of fat available in food and made by the body which is distributed in all cells of the body. Adults prone to heart disease may have high blood levels of cholesterol and may be directed to follow low cholesterol diets. Human milk has 6 to 13 times as much cholesterol as the three most widely used formulas. However, laboratory studies indicate that a moderate amount of cholesterol may be important in early life to establish body mechanisms for using cholesterol and preventing atherosclerosis. More studies have to be done to verify these theories, but enough is known to reassure mothers to breast feed.

So wouldn't it be nice if

. . . hospitals gave new mothers fruit rather than formula in the advertising "gift" package?

. . . health clinics promoted breast feeding, rather than formula making?

. . . government and doctors educated the public through television, radio, and pamphlets on the advantages of breast feeding?

. . . employers allowed nursing breaks (liberate babies from bottles)?

Nutrition of pre-schoolers

Preschoolers require the *same nutrients* as other children and adults in the household, but in *varying amounts*. Furthermore, the difference in needs between two children of the same age may be quite large as may be differences between the needs of two children of the same size.

The growth rate of preschoolers drops dramatically compared to the growth rate during the first year of life; the former rate is about one-fourth that of the latter. A two to five-year-old child will grow 2 to 3 inches and gain about four pounds a year. About one-half of the total weight gain goes to muscle development. The growth of bone is slowed during this time, but deposits of minerals in the bone are high. The bones are becoming stronger to keep pace with muscle development and increases in activity.

Nutritional needs

The amounts of nutrients listed below are given as a guide (allowance), not as an absolute need. These allowances are generous for most healthy young children. So, parents, do not fret. Your child may eat fewer nutrients than those in the "allowance" yet be in perfect health.

Calories: The calorie needs of a preschooler may range between 1,000 and 1,500 calories per day. Calorie needs are very much related to activity. During periods of low activity the preschooler's calorie needs may be quite low.

Protein: The protein allowance for 1 to 3 year olds is 23 grams; 4 to 6 year olds, 30 grams. Some of this allowance should be from high quality protein such as milk, cheese, eggs, fish, poultry or meat. This will insure adequate amounts and kinds of amino acids needed to build new tissues, especially muscles.

Calcium: The calcium allowance for preschoolers is 800 milligrams (mg). This mineral as well as phosphorus, strengthens the bones. Although milk is an excellent source of calcium, milk should generally be limited to three 6-ounce glasses per day. Drinking too much milk could lead to low blood iron (anemia) if iron-containing proteins are not included in the diet.

Iron: The iron allowance for 1 to 3 year olds is 15 milligrams; 4 to 6 year olds, 10 milligrams. The larger allowance for the young toddler is most economically obtained from iron-enriched cereals, liver and eggs.

Vitamins and other minerals: The child should eat a variety of basic foods including fruits, vegetables, breads and cereals to meet these needs. Healthy children do not need to take vitamin or mineral supplements.

Food struggles

In the family group, toddlers struggle to be individuals. They are willing to take chances, yet at the same time they want and need approval. Parents need to realize that children may use food in various ways in this struggle. The less importance the parent places on eating, at meal time, the less chance that there will be eating and nutritional problems then and in later life. After all, it's highly unlikely that the small child will waste away from skipping meals or from eating only tiny nibbles of bread and milk. However, for the 3 to 6 year olds, this period is one of increased imitation of parents and peers at the dinner table. It is a "prime" time for parents to set good examples of eating.

Lifetime food habits

The incidence of specific diseases such as heart disease and certain kinds of cancer in various countries, when compared to the food eaten, seems to indicate a relationship with high fat, sugar or salt in the diet. Therefore, to develop good habits during these early years, it is recommended that foods high in sugars, fats, and salt be limited.

Use *more* starchy foods such as whole grain breads and cereals, dried beans and peas, and vegetables.

Use *more* fruits, fresh or lightly sweetened instead of "sweet" treats.

Use *more* fish, poultry, dried beans and peas; use less pork, lamb, veal and beef.

Use *more* low-fat dairy products; use less cream, butter and full-fat milk.

Do not put the sugar bowl or salt shaker on the table at mealtime. (This would require cooperation from both parents as well as older children.)

The age between 3 and 6 years is one of increased imitation of parents and peers at the dinner table. It is a "prime" time for parents to set good examples of eating.

Food plan for preschoolers

(Remember that appetite and calorie needs will vary with activity.)

Protein foods providing calcium: Choose 3 servings per day.

¾ cup	milk, yogurt, tofu
1 slice or ounce	cheddar or other firm cheese
1 cup	ice cream occasionally

Protein foods providing iron: Choose 2 servings per day

2 ounces	chicken, fish, beef, lamb
2	eggs
⅔ cup	cooked beans
4 tablespoons	nut butter

Fruits and Vegetables: Choose 3 or 4 servings, two of which should be from A and B lists because these contain more vitamins and minerals

½ cup	**A**	Citrus juices, berries, tomato, cabbage, cantaloupe, for vitamin C
¼ cup - ½ cup	**B**	Dark green or deep yellow fruits and vegetables, such as winter squash, carrots, apricots, spinach or other greens, for vitamin A and iron
¼ cup - ½ cup	**C**	Other vegetables such as potatoes, beets, cauliflower, etc. Other fruits such as apple, banana, pear, etc.

Bread and cereal group: Choose 3 or 4 servings. Try to use the highly enriched iron cereals occasionally.

¼ cup	Cooked cereal, highly enriched with iron
½ slice	Bread, whole grain preferred
½ cup	Enriched rice, macaroni, spaghetti
1	Tortilla, piece of cornbread

Fats and oils: Choose 1 or 2 servings of vegetable oil, margarine or mayonnaise. One teaspoon is a serving. Limit use of butter, hydrogenated fat or coconut and palm oils.

How to tell the truth about nutrition *by Helen Black*

The air is blue!

It's filled with words about nutrition flying at us from all sides! Words that are knowledge, words that are near-knowledge, and words that are downright doubtful. Pity us all, trying to tell the truth from the fiction. After these many years I have some thoughts about how to recognize A FACT.

Personal experience is not it

"I cured my hangnails by eating green cheese!" Very interesting. It may be a fact that the hangnails did clear up. The non-fact is that the green cheese was responsible. This does not prove that green cheese was *not* involved, either. It simply proves nothing. That's why personal experiences are at the low end of the totem pole for credibility. But sometimes a shrewd personal observation FOLLOWED BY CAREFUL RESEARCH does indeed lead to real facts.

Clinical experience is not it

"My doctor cured my warts with garlic!" Doctors may seem successful with nutritional treatment, often combined with drugs and other therapy. Clinical experiences of doctors are important indications of areas which deserve follow-up in careful research. But until this research is done, forget it. Here are possibilities. Not facts.

Newspaper reports are not it

Clinical studies or experiments reported in newspapers are exciting! The newspaper may even sell better if the reports are sensational! But wait. Think. Be skeptical. Often such reports are premature conclusions of preliminary studies. Alas, too often such research cannot be duplicated in another laboratory!

Population studies are not it

Researchers see different disease rates in different countries, and tie them statistically to eating habits. This points the way to promising areas for research. But until the research clarifies and confirms such relationships, we've got possibilities again. Not facts!

Money, money everywhere, and hardly a cent for nutrition

Well, that's not quite true. But it's vital to know who pays. Did the sugar industry pay for research on the safety of artificial sweeteners? Are such sweeteners competing with sugar on the market? That research needs repeating in another laboratory NOT funded by the sugar industry.

Controlled studies are it, sometimes

In a controlled study, part of the subjects received a nutritional factor while others do not. All other factors are kept exactly the same! Even so, a well-controlled study may be possible only in limited aspects of the nutritional problems. In humans, with our complex emotional responses, great care must be taken that the researchers themselves do not influence the results. Double-blind studies are necessary, in which neither the subject nor the researcher giving the pill knows who gets the vitamin C!

Duplication in another lab . . . Eureka!

Sometimes after painstaking, carefully designed studies done by conscientious people, their results cannot be duplicated in other laboratories. Why? Perhaps some inadvertent bias had crept in. Perhaps the subject is more complex than originally thought. When research is duplicated, a giant step towards establishing fact has been taken.

But we've got plenty of areas of non-fact

Nutritional studies of humans are hard to do, require great skill, scientific acumen, piles of non-suspect money, and the most cautious interpretation. From us, the public, a little patience is required.

Our dilemmas *by Betsy Wood*

We nutrition types may give the impression we're know-it-alls. We speak in certain tones. But nutrition education is fraught with many dilemmas. Here are just a few:

How much should we push, scare, cajole people to get them to improve their diets? Does instilling guilt make people less sure they are in charge of their own eating? Or, on the other hand, are our messages too wishy washy?

How does our mental attitude interact with metabolism? Here we know next to nothing. But I'd like to know how our psyches affect the way our bodies make use of food — beyond the strict vitamin-mineral-protein content.

How do we balance ecology and a good diet? Advocating eating less meat and using less packaging is easy. But what about our urging people to eat an abundance of fresh vegetables and fruits when some of these take lots of energy and land to produce? (For most fruits and vegetables it takes more than a calorie of energy to produce a calorie of food).

Should we demand fresh tomatoes in January? Do we expect too much of a "good" fresh diet year round? What responsibility do we have toward the people of Mexico whose economy and lives are being turned topsy turvy by large-scale production of produce for the U.S. in winter?

Are fresh fruits and vegetables much superior to processed? We have assumed so. But some "fresh" food such as the tomatoes mass-produced in Florida are engineered way beyond anyone's conception of a garden tomato.

How much do we muddy the waters of our nutrition messages by telling all we don't know? How many "ifs," "ands" and "buts" can people take before they're completely confused?

Oct. 2, 1978

Planning for eating

Eat low on the pyramid not high on the hog

The consumer cooperatives in both Norway (NKL) and Sweden (KF) are concerned with the rapid increase in the cost of food in their countries during the past six years. In order to help their members shop economically and still select a nutritious diet, the nutritionists at KF devised a "food pyramid" (see illustration) consisting of three layers of foods.

The base or bottom layer consists of the basic foods. For an adult the following foods in these amounts will provide a good nutritional balance, although they are low in some vitamins and minerals:

Food	Calories	Cost
6 slices bread	390	11c
2 ounces cereal products		
(flour, oatmeal, shredded wheat)	150-200	2, 6, or 10¢ (average 6c)
1 ounce cheese, cheddar or jack	114	10¢
1 tablespoon margarine	100	3¢
3-8 ounce glasses of low fat milk	363	26¢
4 potatoes	360	8¢
	——	——
Total	1,527	64¢

These are all staple foods in the Scandinavian diet and choices and amounts were worked out by nutrition experts. They supply most of the essential nutrients, about two-thirds of the needed calories, and a day's supply in the United States costs 64 cents. The protein in the milk, cheese, bread and potatoes adds up to 50 grams and is of high quality. According to international standards set by the Food & Agriculture Organization and the World Health Organization, this amount of protein is clearly above the safe level.

Scandinavians, like Americans, eat less bread, less potatoes and less cereals than the portions recommended as basic. They also consume considerably more fat and protein. These basic foods, if used as recommended, will change dietary patterns radically. We don't need so much fat with its high calorie count and, in adults, protein over and above the daily 50 grams or so is burned as calories since the body cannot store it. Children under ten, persons with weight problems and old people can reduce the portions a little. Persons doing heavy work will need to increase them.

The Middle Section of the pyramid includes fruits and green and yellow vegetables.

No portions are specified because one can eat as much as desired of these low calorie foods. The basic foods are a bit low in vitamin C, folacin, iron and perhaps other nutrients. Therefore, it is important to choose fruits and vegetables that will supply these nutrients in sufficient amounts. Dried beans and legumes are also in this middle group. They supply good quality protein when eaten with cereal foods at a cost per gram of protein that is one-fourth to one-third that of meat and fish.

The Top Section of the pyramid consists of animal foods rich in protein, of which we need far less than most Americans eat. Unfortunately, even though we don't need these foods for complete nutrition, our eating habits are such that many people eat large amounts. Meat is a high status food, but just one steak can cost as much as all the basic foods. In 1977 on the average each person in the U.S. ate 95 pounds of beef and all meat eaten accounted for about 40% of the total fat in the U.S. diet. From a nutrition point of view, most of us would be better off eating less meat.

Fish and Poultry are not high fat foods. However, the fish crop is limited. If over-fished, any particular species could be endangered. (At present, it is estimated that we are harvesting fish at about the maximum amount possible without over-fishing).

Raising poultry directly for food uses substantial amounts of grain. Egg production is lower down on the grain usage scale, so the more efficient method would be to use chickens for egg production and the old laying hens for human food.

Beef is not acceptable to most of us unless it has been grain fed before slaughter to "finish" it with a layer of fat. Any animal fed on grains before slaughter will be expensive in terms of total calories from grains available to us as food. Milk can be produced by herds grazing on grasses only, but heavy buying can raise the price of both milk and cheese because of the time needed to increase production and the limiting factor of the amount of pasture land available. In general, it is very inefficient from the point of view of both total calories and total protein to process grains through animals.

The Emphasis in the nutrition education put out by both the Danish and Swedish consumer co-ops (both have test kitchens and staff home economists) is now aimed at encouraging people to eat more of the basic foods and less of the expensive animal proteins. The object is not to eliminate animal foods totally as strict vegetarians do but to aim for a lacto-vegetarian eating pattern. Because of the high cost of food in these countries, people are more easily persuaded now than in 1974 when the food pyramid was first introduced in Sweden. Here at home it is easier now to persuade our Co-op's

food merchandisers to feature basic foods in ads and in the food stores.

Gunnar Myrdal in his 1975 Nobel speech said, "In particular, people in the rich countries should be challenged to bring down their lavish food consumption." The Scandinavian food pyramid is an excellent educational tool for helping to achieve this goal.

Most of the information in this report came from a speech by Anna-Britt Agnsater, head of the test kitchen in the Swedish Cooperative, KF, to a meeting of the International Cooperative Alliance in October 1977. I also discussed the use of the food pyramid with Ann Aandaven from NKL's test kitchen when she visited our Co-op recently. Three well-known books which expand further on the general theme of efficient use of the world food supply are "Diet for a Small Planet" by Frances Moore Lappe, "Food First: Beyond the Myth of Scarcity" by Francis Moore Lappe and Joseph Collins, and "Laurel's Kitchen" by Laurel Robertson, Carol Flinders and Bronwen Godfrey. by Mary Gullberg
Co-op News 5/22/78

Calorie needs

Recommended by Food & Nutrition Board. National Research Council. National Academy of Sciences 1979.

FEMALES
120 lbs. - 5'4"

15 to 22 years	2100 calories
23 to 50 years	2000 calories
51 to 75	1800 calories
76 and over	1600 calories

MALES
154 lbs. - 5'10"

15 to 22 years	2900 calories
23 to 50 years	2700 calories
51 to 75	2400 calories
76 and over	2050 calories

The easy way to be sure that one is obtaining all the necessary nutrients is by following a *food guide*. A food guide groups together foods of similar nutrient content and figures out how many servings of each group must be chosen each day to meet nutrient needs. Single meals or whole-day menus may be planned around the food guide. It is a simple solution to an everyday head-ache.

The food guide in most common use in the United States is quite old and many consider it out-dated and inadequate to meet nutritional needs. While nutrition authorities work on a new and better guide, Co-op home economists have worked out an interim food guide which should meet nutrient needs of most people.

Interim Food Guide

The list below has been enlarged from older food guides to allow for nutrients about which more is known today. A variety of choices within food groups helps insure balanced nutrient intake.

Eat these foods every day:

MILK PRODUCTS (protein foods providing calcium) . . . . **2 SERVINGS**
One serving is a cup of milk, yogurt or tofu; 1½ ounces of cheddar-type cheese or 1½ cups ice cream. CALORIC RANGE: 80 (nonfat milk) to 375 (ice cream).

MEATS, EGGS, BEANS, NUTS (protein foods providing iron) . . . . **2 or 3 SERVINGS**
One serving is 2 or 3 ounces cooked (4 or 5 oz. raw) lean, boneless meat, fish or poultry; 2 eggs; 1 cup cooked dry beans, lentils, or tofu; 4 tablespoons peanut butter; ½ cup tuna or nuts. CALORIC RANGE: 140 (2 eggs) to 400 (peanut butter).

GRAIN PRODUCTS (breads, rice, cereals) . . . . **4 to 6 SERVINGS**
One serving is one slice of bread or ½ cup cooked cereal, noodles, rice; ¾ cup dry cereal; 4 crackers; 1 pancake; 1 roll. *Whole* grain cereals are preferred because of higher levels of trace nutrients. CALORIC VALUE: 70 calories.

VITAMIN C RICH VEGETABLE OR FRUIT . . . . **1 SERVING**
One serving is one orange, ½ grapefruit or ½ cup orange or grapefruit juice, 2 tomatoes, 1½ cups tomato or pineapple juice, one stalk broccoli, ½ cup green or red pepper, ¾ cup raw cabbage, greens or chili peppers. CALORIC VALUE: 40 calories.

DARK GREEN VEGETABLE . . . . **1 SERVING**
One serving is 1 cup cooked broccoli, cabbage, greens, brussels sprouts, asparagus; or 1½ to 2 cups raw dark green lettuce, spinach, or scallions (including tops). CALORIC VALUE: 40 calories.

POTATO OR OTHER VEGETABLE OR FRUIT . . . . **1 or 2 SERVINGS**
One serving is ½ cup corn, beets, potato, yams, peas, onion squash, green beans; ¼ cup raisins; one peach, apple, small banana, pear or 4 prunes. CALORIC RANGE: 40 (fruits) to 70 (starchy vegetables).

FATS . . . . **1 SERVING**
One serving is 1 tablespoon oil, margarine, mayonnaise. CALORIC RANGE: 100 calories (margarine or mayonnaise) to 120 (oils).

PLUS OTHER FOODS . . . . **IN LIMITED AMOUNTS**
Use limited amounts of SWEETS (candy, cookies, cake, sweet rolls, presweetened cereals, soft drinks, etc.); FATTY FOODS (fat crackers, potato chips, sauces, gravies, butter, margarine, sour cream, etc.); and alcoholic beverages (beer, wines, hard liquors).

NOTE: The food list above provides between 1100 and 2200 calories per day, depending on the choices within food groups. Persons who need more calories should choose more or larger servings. Persons who need fewer calories should consider increasing caloric expenditure through increased activity, rather than reducing food intake.

Some menu examples

The menus below are based on the Interim Food Guide. They are planned with a small family or single person in mind. Wasting of leftovers is avoided by repeating certain items. For example, tortillas are used in three different ways on three different days.

BREAKFAST	LUNCH	DINNER	SNACK

orange juice
corn tortillas with
   melted cheese
	tuna sandwich on
	   whole wheat bread
	apple
	tomato
	milk
		tofu stir fry with car-
		   rots and broccoli
		brown rice
		pineapple chunks
		   with bananas
			snack of mixed:
			   peanuts
			   sunflower seeds
			   raisins
			milk
			crackers

whole orange, sec-
   tioned
split pea soup made
   with milk
whole wheat toast
   with margarine
	cottage cheese with
	   chopped green
	   onion tops and
	   parsley on
	   romaine
	bran muffin
		tacos with romaine,
		   ground beef,
		   grated cheese
		cold cooked broccoli
		   with French dress-
		   ing
		pineapple with yo-
		   gurt
			tuna with mayon-
			   naise on crackers
			orange juice

sliced bananas with
   milk
cooked egg
whole wheat toast
   with margarine
	split pea soup made
	   with milk
	raw cauliflower and
	   carrots
	crackers
		enchiladas made
		   with tortillas,
		   cheese, ground
		   beef or cooked
		   beans, tomato
		   sauce
		spinach salad with
		   oil and vinegar
		baked apple
			bran muffin
			milk

orange juice
whole wheat French
   toast with mar-
   garine and syrup
milk
	broth with tofu and
	   green onions
	brown rice sauteed
	   with chopped ve-
	   getables and egg
	fresh peach or pear
		sauteed chicken
		   livers in oil
		cooked greens
		noodles
		fruit yogurt
			applesauce
			bran muffin

½ grapefruit
whole grain hot
   cereal with mar-
   garine and sugar
milk
	chopped chicken
	   liver on whole
	   wheat bread with
	   mayonnaise
	sliced green peppers
	   and raw cauli-
	   flower
		scrambled eggs with
		   cheese
		bulgur or brown rice
		corn with margarine
		romaine salad with
		   oil and vinegar
		   dressing
		baked banana with
		   lemon and sugar
			raisins and nuts
			whole wheat toast
			   with margarine
			milk

Abolish dry cereal!
by Nancy Bratt

"But Nancy, I like my kids to be able to get up and get their own breakfast."

What ever happened to the old custom of somebody fixing breakfast and then a family sitting in a group and celebrating the beginning of a new day over some kind of nutritious fuel?

I See Two Tragic Things Happening in Our Culture:

1) To feed a family is becoming just a way of satisfying taste buds and appetites as quickly and painlessly as possible. People aren't thinking of eating food as a way to grow and maintain and regulate healthy bodies.

2) Meal time is becoming extinct. Besides being a time to keep in touch with the people we live with, it's probably healthier to sit down for meals rather than to eat on the run.

Do Your Kids Have to Make Their Own Breakfast?

The least we can do, as adults, is to have foods available from each of the four food groups. Not only people are interdependent; so are nutrients. That's why we keep encouraging GROUPS of foods instead of just a bowl of cereal.

For Each Meal, Have at Least Three of the Following:

Fruits and/or vegetables
Grains
Protein foods (Meat, eggs, legumes)
Milk or milk products

There are Lots of Quickie Breakfasts That Are Okay:

Tomato, cheese and bread
Hardboiled egg, orange juice and milk
Peanuts, grapefruit juice and cheese
Yogurt, bananas, toast

Lots of Children Enjoy Cooking

Wheathearts or Zoom take only a few minutes to cook. Add milk and a glass of juice and you have an okay meal. Or a blender breakfast — milk, fruit, egg whirled in a blender — can be fun and quick.

Start the day with breakfast

If you could help all the members of your family attain better health, be more efficient in their daily activities (including school studies and work projects), and be more relaxed as well just by preparing a meal, wouldn't you do it? On the assumption that many of you would, we are suggesting an emphasis on better breakfasts.

Many nutritionists consider breakfast the most important meal of the day. Since twelve hours, or more, have passed since the previous meal, the body's need for calories and nutrients is great.

Among reasons given for not eating breakfast, the two most often heard are "not enough time" and "can't face food the first thing in the morning." The lack of time is a feeble excuse. A few minutes spent the previous evening in setting the table, getting out any necessary dishes and utensils, and planning the menu can be a tremendous help in slowing down the morning "rush hour." The actual preparation and eating time can be as little as fifteen or twenty minutes for many of the following breakfast suggestions.

Overcoming the "can't face food in the morning" hurdle may be a bit difficult at first, but why not start with a simple menu such as fruit, toast and beverage, and then gradually add to it as morning appetites improve, as they will for many? Incidentally, omitting breakfast as a means of losing weight, rarely, if ever, works. Evidence shows that the calories not eaten in the morning are almost inevitably made up later in the day or at other meals or with snacks.

For some, the solution is to forget so called breakfast foods such as eggs and cereal and think "lunch." Why not a grilled cheese sandwich? Why not a fruit and cottage cheese salad plate? Why not a mug of hot tomato soup and peanut butter on raisin bread? Try these or similar foods to see whether they appeal to your family.

A good breakfast is *not* a doughnut or sweet roll with a cup of coffee. A good breakfast includes fruit or juice rich in vitamin C such as orange, pinapple fortified with vitamin C, tomato juice, berries or melons; it includes a protein food such as eggs, meat, fish or milk; it includes whole grain or fortified cereal products such as bread or breakfast cereals.

Listed below are breakfast ideas, some ordinary, some off-beat.

Mostly Eggs
French toast made from almost any kind of bread: white, whole wheat, raisin, French. Serve with fresh or canned fruit and syrup, honey or jam.
Scrambled eggs flavored with herbs, sautéed mushrooms or onions.
Scrambled eggs covered with cottage cheese, creamed tuna or other fish.
Corned beef hash topped with a poached or boiled egg.
Fruit Frappe: 1 cup milk, 1 egg (wash egg shell before cracking), 1 piece of fruit like banana or peach, blended thoroughly in electric blender. Using Co-op non-fat dry milk powder, one serving would cost as little as 20-25¢.

Mostly Fruit
Fruit fritters made from apples, bananas or peaches or any combination of these, topped with sour cream.
Corn fritters - good with applesauce.
Sliced bananas topped with flavored yogurt and cottage cheese.
Fried mush with jam or maple syrup. Serve with fresh or canned fruit.

An apple and a wedge of cheese, such as Swiss, Jack or Cheddar.

Mostly Bread and Meat
Bacon and tomato sandwiches — try Canadian bacon or ham, more protein, less fat.
Hamburger on toasted English muffin.
Any sliced cheese and luncheon meat with crackers.
Waffles or pancakes with sausage, bacon or ham.
Kippered Snacks (Kippered herring fillets) with lemon juice and mayonnaise on toast or crackers.
Sauteed mushrooms and/or chicken livers on toast.
Tortilla, fried lightly, spread with a bit of green taco sauce and fried onions then folded in half over sliced Monterey jack cheese.

Quickie meals for one *by Joan Taylor*

Do you eat alone?

Do you often go to fast food restaurants to get a quick meal?

From my experiences with working, going to school and social activities, stopping for a fast meal becomes very tempting. I've learned not to give in to temptation. I have discovered some tasty, quick, low-cost, nutritious meals. Here are a few keys to quickie meals.

Plan ahead — cook in advance — have on hand

With a little advance planning, one trip per week to your friendly neighborhood Co-op, plus 15 minutes cooking per evening, can do the trick. In the same amount of time that you spend ordering and waiting for a "yucky" hamburger, greasy fries or chicken, sugary sodas, or stale commercial pies you can prepare yourself a nutritious, low-cost, delicious meal!

Cook in advance, once a week, a few things that can be used in a variety of interesting ways. Things which can be done while cleaning house or watching television. Bake or boil 2 turkey legs, hard-boil ½ dozen eggs, make a pot of brown rice.

Have on hand: (1) 4 or 5 vegetables (broccoli, carrots, bell pepper, green onions, zucchini, green beans, lettuce, tomatoes), (2) cans of cream soups that can double as sauces, such as cream of chicken, celery or mushroom, (3) bread.

Quickies with hard-cooked eggs

Prepare a salad with raw vegetables or left-over cooked ones. Top with sliced eggs and favorite dressing. Good with bread or crackers.

Egg salad sandwich: Finely dice 2 eggs, adding mayonnaise, salt and pepper to taste. If you like, add a small amount of finely diced celery, green onion or bell pepper. Serve with sliced tomatoes.

Turkey delights

Heat ½ can (undiluted) cream soup and add ½ to ⅔ cup of diced turkey. Serve over whole-wheat bread or reheated rice. Lightly cook a single or combination of vegetables. Serve these with, or drain and mix into, the creamed turkey.

Sliced turkey sandwich served with lightly cooked vegetables on the side. Stir ½ teaspoon curry powder into ¼ cup sour cream or plain yogurt and pour this over your vegetables just before serving.

The lonesome eater *by Helen Black*

Old Ms. Nature has designed us to crave company while we eat. Eating goes well with conversation, conviviality, chortling and jollity. Also with grousing, grouching, blowing off steam and other necessary evils. Some people would rather go hungry than eat alone!

Unfortunately, there are people who must eat alone. Too many of them grab a doughnut here, crackers and soda pop there, or any easy-to-eat calories. As for the other nutrients, everybody figures on making it up at dinner or tomorrow or sometime, whenever that is. It happens over and over. It is the stuff of poor nutrition.

Who Eats Alone?

Well, there's the teenager, facing breakfast alone, the parents having gone to work early. There's the housewife, eating lunch alone. There's the single office worker, eating dinner alone. And the elderly retired? They may eat every meal alone.

The Most Awful Crimes

The lone eaters' frequent offenses include:

. . .skipping fruits and vegetables, so they don't get enough vitamins A and C or enough roughage;

. . . skipping milk or cheese, so they don't get enough calcium or that B vitamin, riboflavin;

. . . glutting on sweets or fat foods, so they get too many calories.

A Cunning Plot

Eating alone seems to bring out the worst food habits. Therefore, one must outwit nature with a clever plot: PLANNING! To plan is to decide in advance what to eat.

For example, you decide on Wednesday (or even before!) to eat 1/2 chicken breast baked with lemon juice and herbs, for Thursday's dinner. And you decide on Wednesday to have some French bread and stir-fried broccoli to go with the chicken on Thursday. And you decide on Wednesday to have a ripe d'anjou pear with cottage cheese for dessert. Then on Thursday afternoon, you experience a curious exultation, just knowing the decisions are already made. Just thinking about dinner whets your appetite.

Indulge Your Whims

A young shopper gave me this charming idea: She relishes her dinner alone eating each food in sequence as it finishes cooking. The potato bakes, the artichoke boils, the meat patty fries, while she eats a tossed salad. Next, she enjoys the meat patty. Next, a leisurely session with the artichoke. Finally, the potato, in all its buttery glory. For all these courses she provides herself with fascinating company: some good reading, or an absorbing program on radio or TV.

Space your meals

. . . that is, do not skip one meal and eat twice as much at another. Don't skip breakfast. (A sweet roll and tea is NOT breakfast). If the usual breakfast foods turn you off, try the foods you feel like having . . . chicken and salad? Or . . . "Instant breakfast" of mashed banana and 3 tablespoons of frozen orange juice concentrate blended into a glass of milk. Or . . . vegetable soup and grilled cheese sandwich. Any kind of cheese will do.

Minimum equipment for cooking

Equipment need not be new. Check the second hand stores, flea markets and garage sales. To start, we would suggest this minimum:

1 Frying Pan 8″ or 10″ with cover. Cast iron is excellent
1 Paring Knife
1 Pancake Turner or Spatula
1 Glass Pitcher or Jar (with lid) for mixing juice or milk powder
Measuring Cup and Measuring Spoons
Mixing Bowl
Grater
1 Saucepan (1 quart) with cover
1 Baking Dish of 1 or 2 Qt. Size with cover
1 Long Knife
1 Can Opener
1 Coffee Pot or Teakettle
2 Pot Holders
Cutting Board (an odd piece of plywood can be used)

Cooking with minimum equipment

Consider Irish stew, New England boiled dinner, fish chowder, etc. A series of dishes can be prepared on one burner. If you have a heavy cast aluminum or cast iron pot, it can keep one food hot while another is cooking.

A double boiler is useful for preparing a meal on one burner. Foods such as creamed fish can be kept warm in the upper section while a vegetable cooks in the lower. Or boil a potato, ear of corn or an egg in the lower pot and warm a roll or heat leftover meat in the upper.

If your budget will stretch that far, you might think about buying a toaster-broiler oven which sells for 25 to 35 dollars. It's quite versatile. Or, it is possible to buy a used stove from such outlets as the Salvation Army or Goodwill for about the same price. Be sure it's in good condition and that your landlord will allow you to install it.

Fast and simple for singles

Does the thought of a two or three course lunch or dinner loom as an impossibility? It needn't. There are many easy ways in which to prepare tasty one pot meals.

Rice-Chicken

Sauté 1 or 5 pcs. chicken in a little oil or margarine until brown. Add sliced onion, green pepper or celery. Stir in ⅓ cup long grain brown rice. Add ⅔ cup water plus 1 bouillon cube. Cover and steam slowly for 45-50 mins. During last 5 mins. add spinach leaves, swiss chard or other greens. One serving.

Fish Dish with Peas

Fry 1 strip bacon, cut in pieces. Add some chopped onion, cook until tender. Cut in pieces and add 1 potato and ⅓ lb. fresh fish fillet. Add about ¼ cup water, cover closely, cook over low heat 15 minutes. (Add more water if needed.) Add 1 cup milk and handful of frozen peas; salt and pepper to taste. Reheat: do not boil. One serving.

Split peas make a filling soup for about a dime, without the soaking that dried beans need. Most recipes for pea soup call for ham hocks or bacon, which are not really necessary for protein if some bread is eaten with it. To season, add salt, pepper, a carrot and part of an onion plus herbs, such as thyme, marjoram and/or oregano.

Ramen is good for making an Oriental-style meal out of leftovers (cold meat, raw or cooked vegetables) at less than a quarter per package. (It is a very salty product.)

Occasionally have a meal requiring no cooking at all!

Salad meals

Combine diced leftover cooked meat, fish, poultry, hard cooked eggs, tuna, sardines, canned mackerel with canned garbanzos or other cooked beans. Add raw or cooked vegetables, such as spinach, mushrooms, jicama, turnips or rutabaga. Or add fruit, such as diced pears, apples, mandarin oranges and water chestnuts to add an Oriental touch. Toss the salad with any preferred dressing. Serve with whole wheat, rye or pumpernickel bread. Add milk and an oatmeal cookie; you have a nutritious, delicious meal.

Alternatively, a no-cook meal can be based on two or three pieces of raw or stewed fruit topped with plain yogurt. Raisin bread spread with peanut butter is a delicious accompaniment. With the meal have nonfat milk or cappuccino (half hot coffee and half hot milk).

Have fun with your meals

Create many different atmospheres or settings. Candlelight dinners are always nice; fresh cut flowers on your table or tray add a happy touch. Eat in different places; breakfast in bed, picnic style meal on the floor, in the park or in your backyard.

Enjoy!

Eating habits when you're older

by June Kadish

Senior citizen? Mature person? Golden years? Whatever the euphemism, when we enter the 5th, 6th, 7th or 8th decade of life, many of us tend to eat more poorly than we did when we were younger. That's too bad. It really is important to eat well all your life. Older people, for example, often neglect to eat calcium-rich foods, like milk. Food requirements are about the same no matter your age, with the exception of calorie intake. As one becomes more sedentary, the body's need for fuel decreases — and calories are the body's fuel source.

This message came across to me loudly and clearly recently. For about three months, I had not been spending two active days a week at the El Cerrito Co-op as home economist. In that period of time, I gained three pounds. It may not sound like much, but it is. Had I continued at that rate, the year's accumulation could have been twelve pounds! Happily, I'm back on schedule determined to shed the three pounds.

Problem #1

Perhaps the biggest problem is consumption of empty calories. As we need fewer, the necessity for making sure that each calorie provides important nutrients becomes more important. If you "breakfast" on a two ounce doughnut and black coffee, you've consumed 225 calories and few nutrients. Substitute one slice of whole wheat bread spread with one tablespoon of peanut butter and a cup of skim milk. Caloric intake? 250 calories plus a good start on the day's need for protein, calcium, vitamins and minerals.

Problem #2

An older person often shops for one, which presents the problem of quantities. However, produce items can be bought by the each. Dairy products come in small containers. Frozen foods are in single serving size or can easily be divided. If the packages of meat are too large, ask the meat department for less. They will package one or two chops, or a smaller amount of ground beef if needed.

There are juices in 6 ounce cans, vegetables in buffet sizes. Of course, it's an expensive way to go. Try to use the large sizes in two days or share with a friend.

Problem #3

Most serious for last. Lack of motivation to prepare a meal. Many older people tell us that they just don't feel like bothering. All we can do is urge you to try. Invite a friend. Put a flower on the table. Light a candle and dine by its light. Turn on the radio or play a record. Other ideas? Let us know.

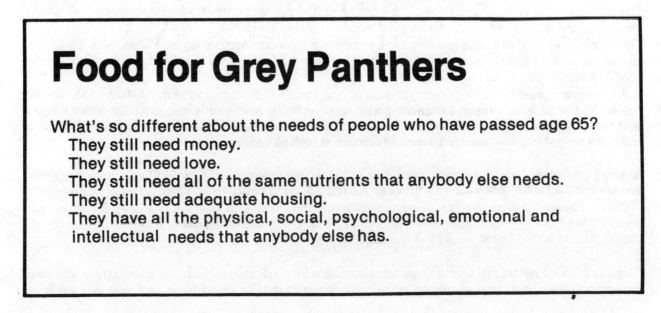

Food for Grey Panthers

What's so different about the needs of people who have passed age 65?
    They still need money.
    They still need love.
    They still need all of the same nutrients that anybody else needs.
    They still need adequate housing.
    They have all the physical, social, psychological, emotional and intellectual needs that anybody else has.

Foods for Backpacking

by Mary Ruth Nelson

How to package

Backpackers need lots of food but remember, it's the cook's vacation also! The time required for meal preparation in camp can be greatly reduced if the food is prepackaged at home. This may save weight in many instances as much of the bulky packaging can be removed.

It is important to group the food by some system such as a day's supply or by meals. This will prevent the supplies from running low in the latter part of the trip when appetites have greatly increased.

Plastic bags, jars and bottles can be used in place of the original packaging for nearly all items. Canned goods such as meat must be kept sterile in the unopened can and freeze-dried foods should be kept in the foil-wrapped packages. Soft or liquid items such as peanut butter, jam, honey or lotion can be transferred to plastic jars or bottles. Dry supplies and foods such as cereals, mixes, coffee and sugar can be placed in plastic bags and secured with rubber bands. Insert a small paper label in each food bag to identify it and to indicate the amount of water to be added or any other important instructions. Place the individual food bags in a larger and stronger plastic bag to minimize punctures and food losses.

Foods to take

Foods for backpacking should be light, relatively moisture-free and of high caloric and nutritive value. Before shopping it's a good idea to make menus for all the meals to insure that *enough* food, but *not too much,* will be available on the trip. It's worth trying to plan well-balanced meals but even so the diet will probably be low in vitamin C (ascorbic acid). Take ascorbic acid tablets (50 mg./day) if you might worry about your daily intake or if the trip will be longer than two weeks.

MOST OF THE FOOD CAN BE REGULAR FOODS, not special backpack foods. Some freeze-dried meats, vegetables and fruits will help round out the menu and lighten the load for the backpacker taking a long trip. Individually-wrapped hard candies may relieve dry throats on the hot dusty trail and will enthrall the little ones.

Include foods from the following groups in each day's menu:

Breads and Cereals: Breads should be dense (buffet rye or pumpernickel) to reduce bulk in the pack, and crackers, hard (rye crisp or pilot bread) to lessen breakage.

Dry mixes prepared at home are often less expensive than commercial ones. Master Mix (p. 222) is useful for making pancakes or biscuits. Make your own trail mix or for breakfast, prepare the home-made Granola-type cereal (p. 145).

Take the precooked or quick-cooking cereals or rice if you will be camping at 8,000 to 10,000 feet altitude. Water boils at a much lower temperature at high altitudes and whole grain breakfast cereals and rices may never get tender due to insufficient heat. However, spaghetti, macaroni and noodles will cook tender but may take 5-10 minutes longer at high altitudes.

Dairy Products: Nonfat dry milk, premeasured in usable amounts, can be used as a beverage either alone or mixed with flavorings. Dry milk can also be added to pancake and biscuit mixes or puddings. Natural cheeses such as cheddar, Swiss, provolone and other firm cheeses will keep for about two weeks if kept cool. Where temperatures are very hot, use processed cheese foods which mold less readily and in which fats separate less quickly.

Vegetables - Fruits: Fruits and vegetables available for pack trips include instant mashed and hash brown potatoes, dehydrated onions, dried mushrooms, regular dried fruits and freeze-dried fruits and vegetables. On the whole, the freeze-dried fruits are very good. They are available either with sugar (RichMoor) or without (Mountain House). It is a good idea to try the freeze-dried vegetables at home before the pack trip as some may not cook to a desired tender stage.

Meats, Nuts and Eggs: Freeze-dried meats such as beef patties, pork chops, sausage, diced beef or chicken are *expensive,* but very lightweight and relatively well-flavored.

Dried egg powder may be used in pudding and pancake mixes for color, flavor and additional protein. Two tablespoons of the powder is equivalent in food value to one fresh egg. Dried egg powder may be re-hydrated, lightly salted, and served as scrambled eggs. (For variation, season with dried spinach, dried chives or other herbs). Mix the egg powder with a small amount of water to make a smooth paste, then add the remaining water. Cook over low heat with constant stirring; remove from heat before eggs are set. *Don't overcook!!* Serve immediately.

Peanut butter and nuts are valuable additions to the menu for variety and their high protein and caloric content.

Fats: Don't forget margarine or canned butter as fats provide twice the calories per ounce when compared with protein or carbohydrate. 1,000 to 2,000 *additional* calories per day may be needed when hiking is strenuous.

Dishes to take

Most menus require only a couple of cooking pots since backpackers usually eat by "courses." A pot may be re-used once or twice to prepare food that will be eaten later in the meal. Check the menus to determine the utensils needed to prepare each meal. The only eating utensils needed are a large cup and a spoon per person.

Dishwashing

NEVER, NEVER wash dishes (or anything) in streams or lakes as it will pollute the water supply. Use a *clean* pot to gather water and wash some distance from source.

Carefully scrape food from dishes and cooking pots. (A metal scratcher hastens the process and can be cleaned by soaking in the hot dish water). Separate cooking pots may be used to heat wash and rinse water. Soap or detergent will make dishwashing easier, rinsing afterward in hot water. (If soap or detergent is not used, rinse the dishes in *boiling* water to remove grease). Allow dishes to air-dry.

Leave a clean camp

Burn all burnables. PACK OUT all non-burnable materials such as glass, cans and any foil or foil-wrap packaging.

Shopping list for backpacking trips

BREAD AND CEREALS
Quick-cooking rice, wheat and oat cereals
Pancake, biscuit, cornbread or gingerbread
  mixes
Spaghetti, macaroni, noodles
Rye Hardtack, Ry Krisp, Swede Krisp
Pumpernickel, Norwegian Flat Bread, Finn Krisp
Granola

FRUITS AND VEGETABLES
Freeze-dried fruits and vegetables
Dried fruits
Dehydrated onions
Instant mashed and hash brown potatoes
Dried mushrooms
Trail Mix (make your own)

DAIRY PRODUCTS
Dry milk powder (nonfat or buttermilk)
Cheddar, Swiss, Provolone or other firm cheese
Grated Parmesan or Romano cheese
Processed cheese food

MEATS, NUTS AND EGGS
Freeze-dried meats
Canned hams requiring NO refrigeration
Canned liver paste or Vienna sausage
Sardines or kippered snacks
Canned chicken and tuna
Dry salami chubs
Beef jerky
Dried egg powder or omelet or other egg mixes
Peanut butter
Canned shelled nuts
Roasted soy beans
Miso
Nutritional Yeast

SWEETS
Honey
Sugar, white or brown
Chocolate bars (no milk chocolate)
Hard candies, individually wrapped
Cookies (dry types and fruit bars)
Marshmallows

MISCELLANEOUS
Margarine or canned butter, oil
Non-dairy powdered cream substitute
Salt and pepper
Herbs and spices
Bouillon cubes
Dehydrated soups
Instant pudding mixes
Fruit gelatin
Instant coffee or tea
Flavored instant drinks
Tang or Wylers drinks
Popcorn

OTHER SUPPLIES
Powdered detergent or soap flakes
Hot pad or heavy glove
Small wire beater
Aluminum foil
Metal dish scratcher
Plastic quart measure
Matches
Cooking spoons, forks or pancake turner. as
  needed

PERSONAL ITEMS
Soap
Toothbrush and powder
Toilet paper
Pocket knife
Flashlight, extra batteries
Chapstick and hand lotion or cream
First aid kit including moleskin
Aspirin
Dark glasses
Sunburn cream or lotion
Hat
Insect repellent

Further ideas can be gained from the *Sierra Club
Wilderness Handbook.*

The perfect hostess Thanksgiving countdown

by Helen Black

7 DAYS BEFORE . . .
Serious housecleaners should complete all major waxing and polishing before today. As for the rest of you, Co-op home economists DO NOT RECOMMEND taking a swipe at the windows on Thanksgiving morning.

6 DAYS BEFORE . . .
Count your dishes, silver, tables and chairs. Will you be using your fine china from Richfield or decorator colored paper plates? Figure your turkey size: allow ¾ to 1 lb. per serving for birds under 12 pounds, and ½ to ¾ lb. per serving for larger birds. Do you have a big enough roasting pan?

5 DAYS BEFORE . . .
Buy your staples. Don't forget such trifles as salt or paper towels! Have you ever run out of coffee on Thanksgiving? Beginners, pick up some canned cranberry sauce or ask Aunt Rosie to bring it. No need to make EVERYTHING from scratch.

4 DAYS BEFORE . . .
Dream of your centerpiece . . . something gorgeous with persimmons, perhaps? Are you getting the refrigerator ready, by using up (or throwing out) leftovers?

3 DAYS BEFORE . . .
Let it thaw, let it thaw! IN THE REFRIGERATOR, NOT ON THE KITCHEN COUNTER. Turkeys over 12 pounds may take 3 days to thaw.

2 DAYS BEFORE . . .
Shop for perishable groceries. By now, your frig is empty and waiting for all the Thanksgiving goodies. And when you've done this 20 times, dear, you'll agree that tonight's dinner can come out of cans.

1 DAY BEFORE . . .
Make the pies, wash the lettuce, make the salad dressing, fix the ingredients for the stuffing . . . BUT DON'T STUFF THE TURKEY 'TIL TOMORROW! YOU WANT TO POISON YOUR MOTHER-IN-LAW?? Fix the centerpiece instead.

THANKSGIVING, THE DAY . . .
Stuff the turkey and throw it in the oven. Let your guests help with the rest of the work . . . it's such a good time to pick up tips from the relatives! But most of the work is already done, anyhow. So here's to your fun, food and family on Thanksgiving!

Contemplating calamities

All of you with emergency food and water supplies at home may now stop reading. The remaining 99 percent of us should consider this lugubrious topic. Because if it's awful to think of earthquakes, fire or flood, it's much worse to be unprepared for them.

Water is More Important than Food

You can last a long time without food, but water you must have. Usually one half gallon per day per person is considered a minimum. Include more for washing or food preparation if you like. In an emergency, water in hot water tanks and toilet tanks is safe to use, though intakes may have to be closed to protect such water.

Choose Canned Foods, Mostly

Partly because of water problems, plan foods which are ready-to-eat such as canned foods which already contain water. Don't store dried foods unless you plan to store extra water for them. Use canned milk, single strength canned juices and soups.

Forget the Leftovers

Can sizes should be right for one meal; you don't want leftovers that you can't store safely.

Expect to be Power-less

Emergency foods should be foods which can safely be eaten cold or with little heating . . . power and gas may be unavailable. Your camp stove and supplies could be invaluable, including fuel, matches, candles, can opener, flashlight . . .! Certainly you can cook over a hibachi with charcoal, too. Just remember it isn't safe to use in a closed room.

Make it Nutritious and Tasty

Plan your food stores around the Four Basic Food Groups, including protein foods; fruits and vegetables; crackers, prepared cereals or breads; canned milk. Snacks are nice, preferably not salty ones which will increase your need for water. Essential for morale are coffee or tea.

How Much and For How Long?

They used to say, store a two week supply of food for each member of your household, against an atom bomb attack. That could be a strain on your storage capacity AND your organizational capacity. Because you've got to use up and replace this food supply every six months to keep it from getting too old! So my advice is to keep your supply at a reasonable size, and make it foods you like well enough to use for unexpected company. That's an emergency that can happen to anyone!

In 1978 we ate standing up

by Helen Black

Certainly, we did a lot of eating in 1978. More than ever, it seems, we did a lot of eating while standing up, even moving around. Everywhere I look I see people walking along, eating.

Mostly people walk along eating doughnuts, or popcorn, or potato chips, or hamburgers, or drinking secretly out of paper bags. But not always. Once I watched a man pawing through the green beans in the produce department. He picked out a couple that pleased him and walked off munching the beans, appearing gratified.

Margaret Mead would be fascinated by this specter of the single, mobile eater: using, but not participating in and oblivious to the vast human ingenuity that produced horticulture, food preservation, cooking and baking, menu planning, graceful table settings and food serving, and innumerable vivacious and elegant mealtime conversations.

What does the stand-up eater think about? Does he laugh over some comic happening? Does he sigh with satisfaction? With hunger satisfied, does his mind turn to wondering? Or to planning the next stand-up feeding?

As children, we had to sit down to eat. Walking while eating could cause us to choke! Fall blue-faced onto the floor, in mortal agony! But of the walking eaters I've seen, none have choked. All seem unconcerned about such hazards.

There's an aimlessness about this type of eating.

There's no plan to it, no combining of foods to meet nutritional needs. It's a matter of eating what's handy; a sort of adaptation, thousands of years later, of our early days as food gatherers before agriculture existed. Perhaps we're completing some dimly discernable cycle of food habits.

We could eat sitting down. Have meals, sometimes with others. Give ourselves the value and beauty of combining foods to compliment and complement each other. Relish that moment of relaxation, that building of anticipation, that musing over which food to taste first. Have that blessed unwinding of the mind, that putting aside of vexation, the laughter, the arguments that are part of eating together with people.

In 1979, let us give ourselves the pleasure of eating sitting down.

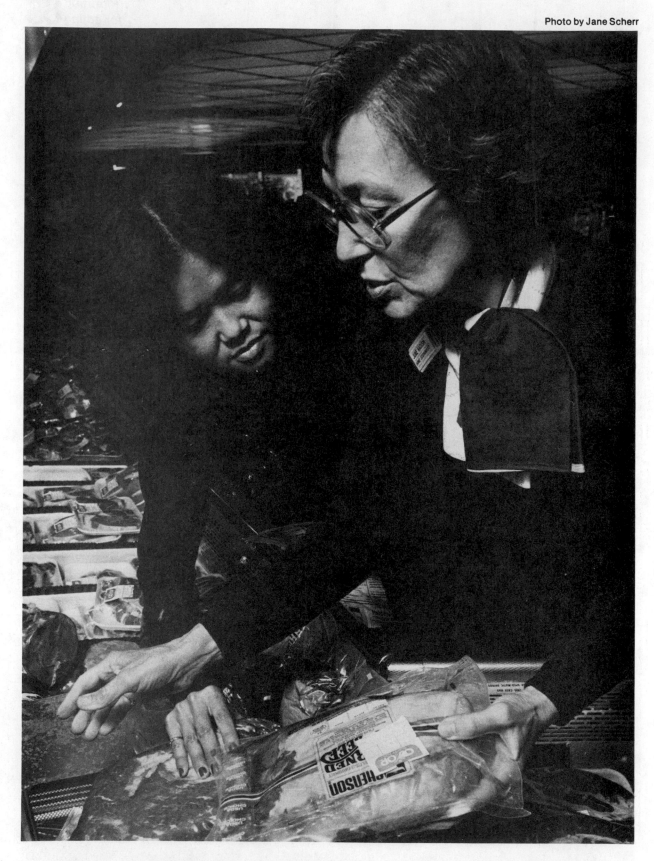

Meat net weights expressed as TENTHS or HUNDREDTHS of a pound are sometimes confusing to shoppers who are more used to ounces, say Co-op home economists.

Start with the children *by Catherine Sinnott*

According to the American Heart Association, 54% of **ALL deaths** in the U.S. are due to heart or blood vessel disease. The expected cost of these diseases in 1978 is $28.5 billion (not counting pain and grief). Good nutrition plays a large part in preventing these diseases. Basically, we need more fruits and vegetables and whole grains and a sharp reduction of fat and sugar in the American diet.

Middle age is a little late

We must start with the children, perhaps by offering alternatives to junk food snacks (candy, chips or soft drinks). The average child gets as much as ¼ to ⅓ of the day's calories from snacks. So it's very important to see that snacks have food value other than fat or sugar.

Beat the hunger alarm

When the child comes in hungry, it's too late. If nothing better is handy, the hungry child succumbs to junk food. So the first rule is to plan and prepare alternatives that **are ready when the child is ready.**

Vegetable or fruit ideas

Prepare a tray of favorite raw vegetables cut in finger-sized pieces to eat with cottage cheese dip (carrots, jicama, broccoli stems, etc.) Fruit is good as is, but try freezing some so it can be eaten frozen (seedless grapes, pieces of melon, apricot halves, peach quarters, strawberries). These frozen fruits can also be blended with milk for a tasty drink (about ½ cup fruit to ¾ cup low fat or nonfat milk).

The measured snack

Control over-eating by putting snacks up in measured amounts — offering a whole bowl of even a nutritious snack may encourage the child to eat too much.

When you shop, plan leftovers

Leftovers make good snacks. Think about it when you shop. Cold pizza or quiche makes a delicious snack. Cold beans (perhaps sprinkled with vinegar) or even cold potatoes taste good to some people.

Children's snacks

THERE'S A FUNNY THING ABOUT FOOD. Everyone must learn to enjoy plenty of different nutritious foods, but eat sparingly of very enjoyable non-nutritious (junk) foods. The trick is to get children to see this . . .

Why use snacks?

When children reject important and needed foods at mealtime, snacks may help to solve the problem. They can be the means of adding vitamin C to the diet of the child who refuses juice for breakfast. Or they can add protein for the child who refuses meat or beans at dinnertime.

A new food may be accepted eagerly when offered as a snack, but rejected in favor of familiar foods when offered as part of a meal.

Some children eat poorly at meals because they are too excited by the gathering of the whole family. Yet, at more relaxed times, when food may safely be picked up by the fingers, when they are not overtired, children will eat the same food they might reject later. If Johnny eats tuna chunks and carrot sticks at 3 o'clock, who cares if he eats only potatoes, milk and fruit for dinner?

Make the most of hunger!

Children who experience acute hunger within two or three hours after eating, as when they are growing fast, may satisfy their hunger with soft drinks or candy. Hunger can be a powerful motive. Use it to your advantage by making good foods available. Satisfying hunger with nutritious food will leave a pleasant memory which will help to establish preference for good foods. Timing is important. The snack must be offered at the time of hunger but not so late that the appetite is spoiled for the next meal.

A reminder: snacking should not replace meals

Though snacks can be useful, there are good reasons for eating meals. Some nutrients may be absorbed better when several foods are eaten at once. Calories are used more efficiently when food is eaten in a few meals instead of in many snacks. But also, a child learns about the society in which he or she lives, through the social give and take at mealtime.

Make a snack plan

First, decide what your family needs. Which foods should be added to their diets by means of snacks? When is the best time to offer them? How much of your limited time are you willing to spend on snacks in addition to meals? If fixing something special which is not eaten makes you frustrated and angry, why not stick to simple foods which may be put away if not eaten? Perhaps a "snack spot" in the refrigerator may be the answer.

Some suggestions for snacks which supplement meals

TO ADD PROTEIN: Offer some hardcooked eggs, chunks of tuna, pieces of cheese, slices of leftover roast. Let them use their fingers. Or stuff celery sticks with peanut butter or with tuna and mayonnaise. Offer nuts, seeds, toasted soybeans or a peanut butter log (see recipe).

TO ADD VITAMIN C: Strawberries, melons, tomatoes, citrus fruits are the best sources; other berries, mangos, nectarines, papayas, raw pineapple are good sources. Serve as is or skewer on a bamboo stick. Try cherry tomatoes, cold cooked potato or sliced jicama. Cut the rind off melon and serve wedges that may be picked up with the fingers. A squeeze of lime adds flavor. Make frozen juice bars.

TO ADD VITAMIN A: Dark green or bright yellow fruits and vegetables add vitamin A. Arrange carrot sticks, green pepper rings, chunks of broccoli or dark green lettuce leaves (dark green veggies also may add vitamin C) on a plate. Serve plain with a dip made from cottage cheese mixed with onion salt, celery salt and chives. Or try cottage cheese mixed with drained crushed pineapple, or tuna and mayonnaise. Put cheese and carrot spread (see recipe) upon whole wheat bread or crackers.

Many children prefer raw vegetables to cooked, and they may particularly resist cooked vegetables at dinner. If these youngsters will eat raw vegetables at snack time then they need not be served cooked vegetables at dinner. Besides the raw ones mentioned above, you might try raw green beans, turnips, broccoli, Brussels sprouts, spinach, chard, green peas or zucchini.

TO ADD CALCIUM: Dairy products are well-known sources of calcium. Try frozen yogurt sticks, cheese chunks, custard, or cottage cheese and fruit. Tofu (soybean curd) is also a good source of calcium and children may enjoy cold cubes of tofu that have been dipped in an egg batter and fried in margarine or butter.

TO ADD B VITAMINS AND MINERALS: Use whole grain and enriched breads and cereals, dairy products, nuts. Put out a big bowl of unshelled mixed nuts and let them crack their own. Warm tortillas with butter or cheese.

Homemade cookies, especially when they contain oatmeal, raisins and nuts may be more nutritious than store-bought cookies. For extra measure, try substituting whole wheat flour for part of the white in your favorite cookie recipe and decrease the sugar.

SNACKS TO LIMIT: Candies, very sweet or rich desserts, commercially prepared cookies, cakes, doughnuts, soft drinks, potato and corn chips, pretzels and crackers are foods to limit. Usually it is difficult if not impossible to restrict these foods entirely; keep them in their place by making rules about when and how often they may be eaten. Or don't buy them.

Snacks to try

Quesadillas   Place ¼ cup of grated cheddar or Monterey jack cheese on top of a whole wheat flour or corn tortilla. Place on a cookie sheet and put in a 350-degree oven until cheese bubbles. Roll up to eat.

Cheese Carrot Spread
½ cup grated raw carrots
½ cup grated cheddar cheese
salad dressing or mayonnaise
salt, pepper, lemon juice to taste

Mix together grated cheese and carrots. Add enough salad dressing or mayonnaise to moisten. Season with salt and pepper and lemon juice. Spread on bread or crackers.

Peanut Butter Log
½ cup peanut butter
4 tablespoons nonfat dry milk powder
½ cup raisins
carob powder and cinnamon (optional)

Blend peanut butter and dry milk until mixture is pretty stiff. (Amount of dry milk you need depends on type of peanut butter you use.) Add raisins and mix with your hands. Roll into a 1 inch thick and 10 inch long log. (Roll in powdered carob and sprinkle with cinnamon.) Wrap in wax paper and chill. Slice or pull apart.

Snack on the run

by Wendy Gardner

Bother!

You have to return the shirt you bought in haste last Saturday. And you have some other things to pick up. So you pile the kids into the car and off you go.

First, Susie's thirsty so you stop for a soft drink, then you buy a snack for Kevin and Michael at the candy counter as you pass through the next store. At one o'clock you have still one more stop to make and everyone's hungry. You zip into the nearest fast food outlet and load up on hamburgers, fries, cola and shakes.

You don't gather moss, just fat

Your fast-paced life-style is what McDonald's, Colonel Sanders and the rest appeal to. Now you are out $10 for high-calorie, refined snacks. Does this contribute to ⅓ of Americans being overweight? Do you need that kind of help? You don't need them to "do it all for you."

Next time:

Grab yourself before going out the door and assemble some easy traveling snacks. Fill a thermos with water or fruit juice. Take raisins, nuts and fruit. Throw in some crackers and cheese or peanut butter or canned sardines and a knife. Some relatively nutritious cookies that travel well are oatmeal-raisin cookies, fig bars or peanut butter cookies. If you have leftover chicken or salad which needs to be cold take a couple containers (i.e. coffee can or leftover margarine or cottage cheese container) of ice to keep things cold. As it melts you have extra drinking water.

If you think ahead

Slice vegetables the night before for dinner and put the remainder in a plastic container with water. For extra crispiness put a couple of ice cubes in before you leave.

Make a mixed bag:

½ cup cold cereal such as Spoon Size Shredded Wheat, wheat squares or oat circles
½ cup peanuts
handful pretzel sticks
½ cup raisins

Stop at a park

Enjoy your lunch. Listen to the birds. Then finish your shopping with a clearer mind and as you pass give old Mac a wink for me.

Babies, Like Everyone Else, Need a Well Balanced Diet

One of the advantages of preparing baby's food at home is that parents should be motivated to give more attention to well chosen and well prepared foods for the whole family. Vegetables should not be drowned in water or overcooked; nutritious foods should be emphasized, desserts (except for fruits) and other low nutrient foods, such as doughnuts, cookies and most crackers, should be kept to a minimum.

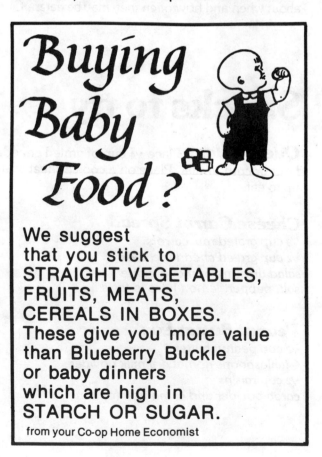

Buying Baby Food?

We suggest that you stick to STRAIGHT VEGETABLES, FRUITS, MEATS, CEREALS IN BOXES. These give you more value than Blueberry Buckle or baby dinners which are high in STARCH OR SUGAR.

from your Co-op Home Economist

Grandma did it

Feeding Baby Using Foods Prepared at Home

Co-op home economists get questions about feeding babies without using commercial baby foods. It isn't difficult. We think many people may want to prepare their baby's food at home, possibly for reasons of economy, for better flavored food, and to be able to feed baby foods which contain the amount of salt, sugar and other seasonings or thickeners you *choose* to add.

The suggestions which follow as to when to introduce new foods to children, as well as amounts to give, are made as general guides and will normally vary from child to child, and even from day to day.

Baby Foods for the First Nine Months of Life

New Born to About Three Months:

Breast fed infants need a vitamin D supplement; formula fed babies need a vitamin C supplement if evaporated milk is used. (Some breast fed babies need extra vitamin C if the mother's diet is not adequate in this vitamin). All infants and children need fluoride, which must be prescribed by a physician if it is not available in the water supply. Phone your water company to find out if your water is fluoridated. **No additional foods are needed.**

Three to Four Months:

This is soon enough to start supplemental foods, beginning usually with cereal. Use iron-enriched baby cereals (Gerber or Pablum brands of oat and barley are best), Instant or Quick Cream of Wheat, or Quick Malto-Meal, twice daily. Other regular cereals do not contain enough iron. Then add cooked fruits pureed or put in a blender; fresh fruits such as apple, pear, banana or peaches can be scraped, mashed or strained. If you want to use commercially prepared fruits as desserts, stick to the straight fruits. Avoid the elaborate combinations such as Blueberry Buckle and Peach Cobbler, since they are more likely to contain additives, including sugar, you may want to avoid.

Four to Six Months:

Any fairly lean meat, fish or poultry plus vegetables can be cooked and put in a blender, the resulting puree put into an ice cube tray, sandwich or ziplock bag, and frozen. When ready to use, place frozen pureed food in a 4 oz. pyrex custard cup, set cup in pan of water, and heat slowly until food is thawed and warm enough to serve. Or you may use a blender or baby food grinder to make small amounts using the foods the family will be served.

If you do not have a blender or grinder, cooked meat can be cut *very fine* and cooked vegetables rubbed through a sieve. Cook in small amount of water and save any excess cooking liquid (though not for more than two days) to use for diluting the pureed vegetables and meats since the water contains dissolved nutrients.

Six to Seven Months:

The transition to finger-fed table food is confusing for the Gerber or Heinz-dependent parent. Ease off on pureed foods and substitute finger foods as baby is able to handle them. Babies often like ground beef (cooked medium), tuna, liverwurst, cheese, and tiny avocado or creamy peanut butter sandwiches. Also, many like a chicken drumstick with a little bit of meat left on, scrambled eggs, breadsticks and graham crackers or zweibach. Some like peeled fruits and vegetables, such as cooked string beans or cooked carrot strips, slightly cooked apple or pear plus other foods from the basic food groups.

Nine to Ten Months:

Baby is usually able to eat foods served to the rest of the family.

Raw Carrots, Nuts and Popcorn are Really Hazardous Finger Foods for babies and small children because they may not chew them thoroughly. Bits of them may get inhaled into the lungs.

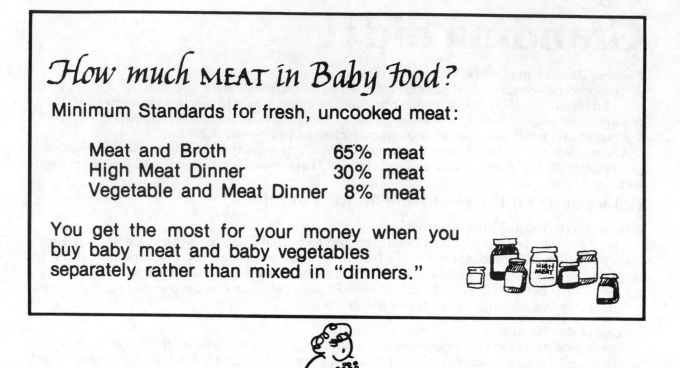

How much MEAT in Baby Food?

Minimum Standards for fresh, uncooked meat:

Meat and Broth	65% meat
High Meat Dinner	30% meat
Vegetable and Meat Dinner	8% meat

You get the most for your money when you buy baby meat and baby vegetables separately rather than mixed in "dinners."

PEA SHELLER

MUSHER UPPER

New ideas on food for pre-schoolers

Your two-year-old dawdles at the table, mixes the noodles with the broccoli, takes one bite of noodles, pushes the plate away and says, "What's for dessert?"

Your four-year-old eats everything on the plate after skipping lunch, but insists that no two foods touch each other on the plate and crumbles into tears when the broccoli falls off the fork on the floor.

Preschoolers vary tremendously in their food habits. Some children will be messy; some will be finicky. There will be cycles of rigorous activity and passive thoughtfulness. Yet their nutritional needs are high in relation to the calories they require. Because children's requirements fluctuate, parents need to be creative in introducing new foods to a child. Preschoolers may not eagerly try new foods.

They may only like the foods most familiar to them.

Hints for Successful Food Acceptance: Be Models

. . . Try to get an agreement with the adults in your family that all will try a new food. If one parent eats greens and carrots, but the other does not, the message that greens and carrots are questionable food comes across loud and clear.

. . . If you shop with the kids avoid pacifying your own hunger with candy, doughnuts, soft drinks or other high sweet foods. Plan ahead for hungry children: Bring snacks from home such as vegetable sticks, cut up fruit or a peanut butter and banana sandwich.

The setting

. . . Children need a time for rest before the

evening meal. Overly excited children find it difficult to settle down to eating.

. . . Keep junk foods (foods which offer little nutrition other than calories) out of the house so that they do not become a point for argument.

. . . Children are influenced by other children in group eating situations. Urge your child's pre-school to offer nutritious foods, if food is part of the program.

. . . Keep the TV off while eating. It is distracting enough to the young child to try to join a dinner conversation with adults who may have been away all day and to manipulate eating utensils at the same time.

Involve Preschoolers

. . . Preschoolers want to be boss, so let them . . .

. . . GROW IT: A garden plot of fast-growing vegetables such as lettuce, peas, radishes, carrots, and even onions may become a snack center for preschoolers.

. . . PREPARE IT: Let children peel or grate carrots, assemble sandwiches, tear lettuce into a salad, or decide what vegetables to put into a vegetable soup.

. . . PLAY WITH IT: Sometimes when children are not very hungry, they may play with their food . . . they are learning more about the texture of broccoli or fish . . . be patient.

. . . OFFER OPINIONS: Do not coax, force, or bribe your child into trying new foods. Treat your child as you do other family members without letting him or her be the center of attention. Children have food preferences, too. Continue to offer different foods even when they have been rejected before. Show no disappointment when they are not eaten. Be sure to reward your child with a compliment if one bite of a new food is taken.

Other Approaches

. . . Serve one of your child's favorite foods at the meal with a new food or recipe. Try only one new food at a time.

. . . Children have a keen sense of taste, and strong or spicy flavors such as onions, cabbage, curry, garlic, ginger may be disliked. A plainer version of a spicy recipe may be served to children.

. . . Portions need to be small. Some children get fat because they are taught to eat more than they need. A teaspoon of various foods is reasonable. A child can always ask for more. Bite-sized pieces and finger foods are suitable for small hands.

. . . If practically no vegetables are eaten, but starch is eaten, use vegetable cooking water to cook rice and macaroni.

. . . TAKE ADVANTAGE OF TIMING: When children are the hungriest (often just before dinner), offer raw vegetable sticks or finger foods from dinner.

GARDENER

Vegetables for pre-schoolers

If the only green food your child has eaten lately is artificially colored (jello) . . . take heart! It takes a while to get used to a new food. And vegetables are worth getting to know.

A variety of vegetables provides small children with vitamins A, C, E, B_6, folacin, potassium, and calcium, as well as traces of many other vitamins and minerals. Adequate vitamin A is supplied by ¼ cup of a dark green or yellow vegetable every other day.

"Mom, Dad, I have nothing to do!"

Let's conduct a poll. Ask a random sample of parents which problem looms largest when children are not in school, and by far the largest group will probably answer with a question, "How can I keep them happily occupied?" One answer is to let boys and girls use the kitchen to prepare a meal, snack or dessert. Food preparation can involve creative experiences with basic foods that let a young child explore, touch, smell, and try new tastes.

Younger children will need supervision if measuring or cooking is required. Stress safety rules with children near a heat source. Keep long hair tied back, arms free of loose clothing and combustible items a safe distance from the flame.

So put on aprons, wash hands and happy creating.

Vegetable Puppets

whole green peppers
potatoes
onions
radishes
summer squash

carrots
leaves of kale
parsley
other vegetables
sticks and toothpicks

Assemble vegetables on a tray. You may wish to chop some vegetables into smaller units, for example carrot coins and wedges of squash, which can be used for facial features. Put an onion, potato, or green pepper on a stick. Use toothpicks to fix features to the "face." Puppets may later be recycled into salads and cooking meals.

Bunny Salad

1 lettuce leaf
1 canned pear half, cut side down
2 raisins for eyes

1 piece of red apple for nose
cottage cheese ball for tail

Assemble all ingredients to form a bunny rabbit sitting on the lettuce leaf. This makes one portion and may, of course, be multiplied many times.

Wormy Bread

6 cups unbleached white flour
½ cup wheat germ
1½ cups scalded milk
2 tablespoons sugar
1 teaspoon salt
2 tablespoons oil
2 eggs

1 package dried yeast
¼ cup warm (105°-110°F) water
1 beaten egg
sesame seeds
poppyseeds
raw peanuts
  (last 3 ingredients optional)

Cool milk to lukewarm. Add sugar, salt, oil, eggs to cooled milk. Stir. Dissolve yeast in warm water. Add milk mixture and stir. Mix in flour and wheat germ. Add more flour if necessary until dough easily pulls away from the side of the bowl. Knead dough on a floured surface 10 to 15 minutes. Put dough in a greased bowl and let it rise covered until double in volume—about 2 hours. Punch down and form into rolls. Roll a handful of dough on a floured surface, making shapes if desired. Brush with egg and roll in sesame seeds or poppyseeds and/or raw peanuts. Put on greased baking pan. Cover with a cloth and let rise 1-1½ hours. Bake in 350°F oven for 15 minutes. Makes about 2 dozen small individual rolls.

Burger-in-a-biscuit

½ pound ground beef, moderately lean
1 green onion, finely minced
1 teaspoon soy sauce or catsup
1 teaspoon cornstarch

¼ teaspoon salt
dash of pepper
8 ounce package refrigerator biscuits

Preheat oven to 375°F. In a mixing bowl, combine ground beef, onion, soy sauce, cornstarch, salt and pepper; mix well. Divide the meat mixture into 5 equal parts and shape each portion into a ball. Remove the biscuits from the package. Place 2 biscuits together, one on top of another, and press together, to make a flat "pancake" shape about 4 inches in diameter. Work quickly so that the dough does not become sticky. Place a meat ball in the center of the dough and stretch dough around meat, pinching the dough closed at the bottom so that the meat is completely enclosed. When the meat is properly wrapped in the dough, it will not pop out during baking. Place on ungreased cookie sheet with the sealed edge down. Bake at 375°F. for 15 to 20 minutes until brown. Serve hot or cold, eating it like a sandwich. These 5 burgers-in-a-biscuit serve 2 or more people depending on appetites!

Hyde Park Co-op

Here is a list of "quickie" ideas

1. Buy a pound of fresh peas and let the children shell and eat them for a snack.

2. Wash apples, remove core and cut them into fourths and spread with peanut butter. Do the same with celery stalks.

3. Cut cheese such as American, Jack or Swiss into bite-sized cubes. Do the same with lunch meat and thread them on toothpicks or pretzel sticks. Serve with juice for a children's afternoon tea party.

4. Wash radishes, celery and carrots. Use a paring knife and potato peeler to make radish roses, celery and carrot curls. Place finished creations in a bowl of ice water so that they will curl and be crisp.

5. Make pizza on English muffin halves or pieces of bread cut out with a cookie cutter. (Use leftover bread and crusts in bread pudding.) Brush bread with tomato paste. Top with choice of grated cheese, luncheon meat, sliced vegetables, olives. Sprinkle top with grated cheese. Bake on cookie sheet at 350° F. until cheese bubbles.

6. Don't forget deviled eggs. Hard cook several of them. Cool quickly. Cut in half. Remove and mash yolk with enough salad dressing for desired consistency, salt and pepper, and possible onion powder, or marjoram, or celery seed. Refill whites with the yolk and decorate with bits of celery, radishes, olives, carrots, green peppers, to make funny faces. Children love these.

7. On the subject of eggs — scrambling them is fun and this method lends itself to variations the children can improvise with. A few ideas to get you started: crisp bacon, minced chives, one or two herbs such as oregano or rosemary, shredded cheese such as jack or cheddar, or a spoonful of cottage cheese added at the last moment and blended in just to heat through.

References using basic foods

1. Center for Science in the Public Interest, 1779 Church St., N.W., Washington D.C. 20036
Creative Food Experiences for Children, (ages 2-12) Mary T. Goodwin and Gerry Pollen, C.S.P.I., 191p., $4.00.
Excellent resource for adults who work with children. Book includes games, activity plans, recipes, resources.
2. Berkeley Health Department, 2180 Milvia, Berkeley, Ca. 94704. *Food for Little People*, (ages 2-7). 30 p., $3.00 plus 5% tax.
Snack and activity guide for adults working with children. Includes recipes and resources.
3. Karen B. Croft, 741 Maplewood Place, Palo Alto, Ca. 94303.
The Good for Me Cookbook (ages 3-12), Karen B. Croft, R&E Research Associates, 70p.
Good recipes, although glossary is misleading.
4. Vicki Cobb, *Science Experiments You Can Eat,* (ages 8-16) J.B. Lippincott Co., 127p., $4.82.
The kitchen becomes a laboratory. Excellent for the young scientist or teachers of science to young children.

For a safer Halloween *by Mary Gullberg*

Hallowe'en, unfortunately, has become a festival involving more risks than formerly. Most of these risks can be reduced or eliminated by following a few simple rules. Some of these suggestions are undoubtedly familiar while others have been developed to meet the newer threats.

Small children visiting neighbors on Hallowe'en should be accompanied by a responsible older child or an adult. If this is not possible, the children should be carefully instructed before leaving home as to how to avoid any possible hazards. If they do not understand or can not be trusted to remember certain rules, they should not go out.

1. Make sure they will not dash across the street in the middle of the block and that they will only cross at intersections after checking that no cars are coming.
2. Costumes should not be so long as to trip children. Shoes should be safe for night walking. Children should stay clear of candles and open flames that might ignite clothes since many fabrics burn readily. Costumes should be visible in dim light. If walking conditions are especially poorly lighted, the children should carry a lighted flashlight.
3. Instruct children as to what kinds of treats to avoid. Tell them not to sample the treats until they return home. You might also want to rule certain houses "off limits" if you feel uncertain about the occupants' intentions toward children.

Plan the route with your child in advance. Set limits as to crossing streets or covering more than an area of one or two square blocks.

Select carefully the group your child will be traveling with. Small groups of three or four are best. Provide suitable chaperonage if you have the slightest doubts about the children's ability to follow the agreed upon rules.

Children should avoid houses with dogs known to be nervous or "good watch dogs." Children should not go into any house.

Agree upon a time for the children to return home and perhaps plan a short party when they do come back.

Bags for treats should not be so large that they are difficult to carry or might cause the child to trip. Insist that the treats be brought home for inspection before any of them are eaten. If anything suspicious is found, report it to the police.

FINALLY, a courteous child who isn't pushy and who remembers to say "thank you" makes for friendlier relationships in your neighborhood. Here's wishing everyone a safe and fun Halloween!

Look Ma, no candy! *by Helen Black*

How'd you like to hear THAT on Hallowe'en, when the kids come home and dump their treasures on the nice clean rug? But most of them would be frightfully disappointed if they didn't get candy when Trick or Treating October 31. And if they expect it only for such SPECIAL OCCASIONS, not as a regular part of the daily diet, it shouldn't be a problem.

Here is a list of substitutes for Hallowe'en candy:

Non-foods don't cause tooth decay
BALLOONS . . . if you've got a powerful set of lungs (Don't give balloons that aren't blown up to young children).
PENCILS, CRAYONS, SMALL PADS OF PAPER . . . won't cost any more than most sweet treats
DIMESTORE JEWELRY . . . the flashier the ring the better! Or if you have the time, money and equipment present a personal Polaroid snapshot to each young goblin.

Non-sweet sweets are treats too
APPLE JUICE . . . for hot and thirsty goblins
SMALL RED APPLES . . . easy for you, too
POPCORN HORRIBLES . . . popcorn balls on sticks with raisin eyes and prune mouth.
SCRAMBLE . . . salty cereal and nut mix.

Remember to keep a supply of pennies or bigger change for Unicef collectors

How to treat children's teeth

What's the problem?

Tooth decay or dental caries is a disease predominantly afflicting children and young adults. Resistance of teeth to decay depends on hereditary and nutritional influences during tooth development. Once the teeth have erupted, conditions in the mouth (saliva, bacteria, food particles, smoothness of tooth enamel, etc.) as well as nutritional status affect susceptibility to caries.

Over 95% of the U.S. population suffers from dental disease. The number of cavities per person continues to climb. Surveys among primitive peoples eating less processed and refined foods have shown extremely low caries rates. The high proportion of refined sugars and starches in the U.S. diet combined with our irregular eating habits are important causes of our present high caries rate.

High dietary intakes of refined carbohydrates (sugars, starches, breads and cereals) produce decay in two ways. 1) By displacing more nutritious foods, the general state of nutrition is lowered. During the earliest years when the permanent teeth have erupted, poor nutrition weakens the supporting tissues around the teeth. 2) Refined carbohydrates, if they remain on the surfaces of the teeth, promote conditions favoring decay. The ever-present bacteria in the mouth break down food residues. These bacteria and their metabolic products attack the tooth enamel, allowing the decay processes to begin.

The practice of giving apple juice to babies in their bottles has turned up a new hazard to teeth. Continued exposure of baby's four upper front teeth to the acid and sugar in apple juice may cause severe cavities in these teeth, sometimes completely rotting them away to the gums. Apple juice is an almost "empty calorie" food and when large amounts are fed, it interferes with the appetite for other really useful foods.

What can be done?

All three measures outlined below are important. Any one is definitely not a substitute for the other two.

1. Dietary Control. It is impractical to

remove all refined carbohydrates, but their inclusion in the diet can be judiciously restricted to the times they will do the least damage. There must be a generous selection of foods from all the basic food groups with careful attention to storage and cooking procedures that preserve the original nutritive values. A source of vitamin D must be provided throughout the entire period of the child's growth and development.

2. Dental Hygiene. The control of the decomposition of food particles in the mouth is achieved by 1) thorough brushing of the teeth immediately after eating, and 2) regular visits to the dentist for cleaning the teeth, treatment of cavities, and other corrective and preventive measures.

3. Fluoride Supplementation. The incorporation of small amounts of fluorides in the tooth enamel will reduce cavities. The best results (50-60% reduction in caries rates) are obtained from a fluoridated communal water supply to which the chid is exposed for the first two decades of life. This method has been conclusively demonstrated to be safe and effective. If this is not available in your community, your dentist or pediatrician will prescribe a fluorine supplement and tell you how to use it.

Planning food for children

Sticky, high-carbohydrate foods that adhere to the teeth should be avoided when it is not possible to brush the teeth immediately after eating. Candy or sweet desserts are best fed at the end of the meal. This will satisfy the child's desire for a sweet and will not dull his appetite for more nutritious foods. Snacks can then more easily consist of fresh fruits, raw vegetables, fruit juices or milk. Soft drinks, because they contain little else but sugar, should be used sparingly if at all. Cola type beverages ("diet" or regular) may be harmful because of their high acidity. The

evidence on this point is good but not conclusive.

Uncooked dried fruits, because they are so sticky, are only suitable when the toothbrush is handy. Bread with butter is less sticky than bread with peanut butter. Crackers are better than most cookies; animal crackers or arrowroot cookies are preferable to more compact cookies with icing or sweet fillings. The substitution of brown or raw sugar, honey, or molasses for ordinary white sugar is of no benefit since all these products are very high in sugar.

Encouraging good habits of dental hygiene

Children need to be taught to brush their teeth every time they eat or drink anything. Choice of a dentifrice is less important than proper technique. If the adults in the family brush their teeth after eating using the correct method (ask your dentist to demonstrate it if you are unsure), the children will pick up the habit readily. Electric toothbrushes seem to motivate some children to brush more regularly, but consult your dentist before you invest. If between-meal snacks are given at definite times (mid-morning, mid-afternoon, or before bedtime), brushing the teeth can soon become a part of the total eating pattern.

When a child starts to school, he should be instructed to rinse his mouth after any food eaten away from home. He may use water from a drinking fountain or his last swallow or two of milk. Swishing any liquid about in the mouth and then swallowing it will clear away many food particles. The tongue should also be used to dislodge bits of food. You will need to remind the child many times about this new habit. He will be helped to remember it by seeing you do it when you eat meals away from home. Possibly you can enlist the aid of his first teacher in establishing this pattern.

You may know someone who boasts quite truthfully that in spite of eating all sorts of sweets, he has never had a cavity. There are such people but, unfortunately, most of us are not that lucky. Many people with good dental **heredity have developed cavities because of poor diets and/or poor dental hygiene. Many adults would have fewer fillings and missing teeth if the procedures in this summary had been followed during their period of growth.

Bag lunch blues again *by Helen Balck*

And no new solutions have emerged since this time last year! However, it is customary for home economists everywhere to utter a few clucking sounds to distraught lunch-makers. So I say to you, be comforted; and keep in mind the following:

Your child is mortal

So expect him to trade that egg sandwich-on-whole-wheat for the jelly on balloon bread made by Kevin's mother down the street. Or to leave his lunch on the bus. Or to lug it home, uneaten. Or to eat it before he gets to school. EVERYBODY has the same problems with kids.

Teenagers need Hero sandwiches

Plan for a limitless appetite with twice the normal size or number of sandwiches, plus several sneakable snacks for between classes: pieces of cheese, bags of nuts, beef jerky.

Let your kid have her whims such as

. . . baked beans, cheese, ketchup and pickles on raisin bread

. . . tuna, mayonnaise, chopped walnuts and raisins on any bread

. . . old fashioned crunchy peanut butter, sliced banana and honey on whole wheat

Or fool around with alternatives

It doesn't have to be sandwiches. Some people would rather have a yogurt container of tuna salad, plain bread and butter, and lettuce and tomatoes all separate.

But luncheon meat at $3.35 per pound???

When that sliced meat is 3 oz. for 63¢ — it adds up to a very high price per pound. So watch it! When you buy luncheon meats, don't forget that sliced meats are more expensive than unsliced.

Strange vegetables for clean teeth

Wrap up some raw carrots, cauliflower, zucchini, turnips or celery for crunchy contrast to sandwiches. Great at the end of eating, for cleaning teeth. But don't spring it on your very young child! Especially if the vegetables are strange to him. He needs the comfort of familiar favorites, for his lunches away from home.

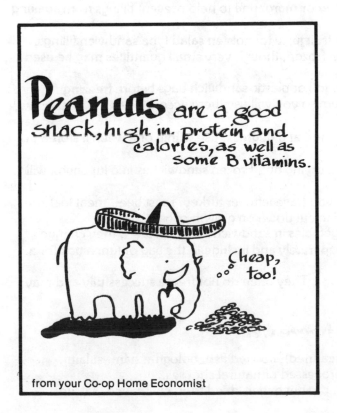

Peanuts are a good snack, high in protein and calories, as well as some B vitamins.

Cheap, too!

from your Co-op Home Economist

Packing a school lunch . . . .

Mary and Johnny can do it

Since lunch should contribute roughly 30% of the daily food intake, it is important that a school lunch, whether bought or brought from home, should be nutritionally sound. Potato chips and a soft drink do not fulfill this need. But there are many foods that do. If you have been in a rut with tuna fish or peanut butter and jelly, here are ideas to get you out of it.

Some protein food should be included in a lunch. Jelly sandwiches—or even cream cheese and jelly—will not answer this need. They are all right occasionally, but not as the everyday choice.

We've divided the sandwich suggestions into freezable and non-freezable varieties, with some specific recipes for fillings that do freeze. It is a great convenience, if you have the room, to make enough sandwiches for one or two weeks at a time (or even for 2 or 3 days). A hurried morning schedule will be more relaxed if you or the children can reach into the freezer for a sandwich. This, supplemented by a piece of fruit, a carrot and a thermos of milk or soup, should surely tempt and satisfy lunchtime appetites.

Freezing hints

DO use fresh ingredients; keep them refrigerated until you use them. Make sandwiches from a variety of fresh or frozen whole grain breads.

DO cover bread slices with small amounts of butter or margarine to help prevent fillings from soaking into the bread.

DO use small quantities of sour cream, yogurt or fruit juice to moisten salad type sandwich fillings. Mayonnaise or salad dressing may separate when frozen, though very small quantities may be used successfully.

DO package sandwiches securely in plastic wrap, foil or plastic sandwich bags before freezing.

DO label sandwiches as to kind of filling; date them so you will use them according to the freezer law, "First in; first out."

DO plan to use sandwiches within two weeks if stored at 0 degrees; use within one week if stored in the freezer compartment of your refrigerator.

DO keep sandwiches wrapped until used to avoid drying out. Frozen sandwiches in a lunchbox will thaw in 3 or 4 hours.

DO make a few sandwiches for the freezer when you have leftover turkey, roast beef, meat loaf, ham or pot roast. Make them soon after the meal to cut down on growth of bacteria.

DO NOT use lettuce, tomatoes, or other raw vegetables in sandwiches to be frozen; they change texture when defrosted. Wrap these vegetables separately and include in the bag or lunch box for a tasty, nutritious additon at lunch time.

DO NOT use sandwich fillings which are very moist. They often do not freeze successfully and may soak into the bread.

Sandwich filling ingredients which freeze well

Cooked chicken, turkey, meats (fresh cooked or canned), cooked fish, bologna, ham, salami.
Cheese such as cream cheese, cheese spreads, processed or natural cheeses.
Hard cooked egg yolk, sour cream, baked beans, peanut butter, dried fruit, chili sauce, catsup.

Ideas for sandwiches that freeze

Egg and Bologna - Mince ¼ lb. bologna with one hard cooked egg yolk. Bind with 2 tablespoons sour cream.

Spicy Devilled Ham - Blend one 3 oz. can devilled ham with 1 tablespoon bottled sweet pickle relish.

Fruity Chicken - Combine 1 cup diced cooked chicken or turkey with one or two tablespoons cranberry-orange relish and dash of salt.

Herbed Sardines - Blend one 3¾ oz. can sardines, drained, with 1 tablespoon minced parsley, ½ teaspoon thyme or marjoram, dash of salt and 1 tablespoon sour cream or unflavored yogurt.

Walnut Cheese - Grate ¼ lb. Swiss or American cheese. Chop ¼ lb. walnut meats fine. Season with salt and paprika, and mix with 3 tablespoons butter, softened.

Egg and Sardine — Use equal quantities of hard cooked egg yolk and sardines. Blend thoroughly until smooth. Add salt, paprika, and prepared mustard to taste. Add a dash of lemon juice and a few drops of salad oil to make a paste.

Baked Bean Spread - Combine 1 cup mashed cold baked beans with 2 tablespoons chili sauce, 1 tablespoon minced onion and salt and pepper to taste.

Lunch box extras and non-sandwich ideas

Fruit Suggestions

1. Peeling an orange seems like a big job to some children. You can peel one and wrap it tightly in a plastic wrap or just start the peeling by taking a little off the top with a paring knife. Be sure to peel your child's apple if you know he or she will not eat the skin and may discard the whole apple if it is left on. Wrap it securely in plastic to retard darkening. However, it is a good idea, nutritionally speaking, to eat the apple skin if your child will go along with this advice.

2. Try a cored and quartered apple spread with peanut butter on the cut surfaces and then put back together.

3. Dried fruit, especially in the winter months, can be a change: **try dates, raisins, apricots, figs, pears or peaches.** Occasionally stuff the dates and figs with peanut butter, cream cheese or cottage cheese.

4. Put a baked apple or stewed fruit in a washed out cottage cheese or yogurt carton.

Nibbles and extras

Hard cooked egg; raw vegetables: carrots, celery, lettuce leaves, turnip chunk, cabbage wedge, tomato; also cold boiled potato or a package of popcorn.

Nuts: peanuts in shell or out; walnuts, cracked not picked.

Treats: Try to keep these infrequent and choose low sugar items, such as a slice of quick bread (banana or pumpkin), a muffin, mixtures of seeds, nuts and dried fruit, or homemade oatmeal cookies.

Lunches without sandwiches

Many foods can be placed in washed out cottage cheese or yogurt containers as a change from the sandwich or for weight-watchers who do not want the 2 slices of bread. Some require refrigeration.

Baked beans, fruit or molded salads, canned or stewed fruits topped with cottage cheese, leftover tamale pie, tuna or sardine salad, hard cooked egg, celery stuffed with cheese, fruit salad, green salad with separate container of salad dressing.

Cold chicken — you can buy an extra chicken when they are on sale. Cook one for dinner, an extra for lunches. Cut chicken in portion size pieces, sprinkle with salt and pepper and one or two herbs such as oregano or rosemary, bake at 350° for one hour or less, until chicken is tender. Surface may be brushed with a little margarine or butter, but this isn't crucial.

Wrap a whole, cooked, cold artichoke in plastic wrap. Include a small container of salad dressing as a dip for the leaves.

Wrap an avocado half in plastic wrap, include a wedge of lemon and a plastic spoon.

Use a bamboo skewer to make a kebob of "things" such as cherry tomatoes, cooked sausage or hot dog pieces, green pepper chunks, cheese chunks or what have you.

For the thermos: milk, chocolate milk, fruit juice, soup, cocoa. (But remember that most children can buy milk at school.)

NOTE: Many children like to buy a hot school lunch part of the time (where it is available). Post the monthly printed menu in the kitchen, so that your child can pick his favorite. A prepaid ticket is a great convenience in schools where it is available.

The calculating lunch packer

by June Kadish

Into the brown bag or Snoopy decorated lunch box go the sandwich, fruit, carrot sticks, potato chips or cookies, etc. You've got the routine down to a science after 1 to 30 years of packing school and/or work lunches. Hopefully, you've given lots of thought to making this midday meal a nutritious one by including a protein food in some form, fruit and vegetable, whole grain bread, milk or cheese, plus extras such as nuts, dried fruit, or oatmeal cookies.

But have you ever calculated the cost of packing this away-from-home meal? Likely not. I did some figuring and have come up with a few statistics.

Here's the cost of a couple of typical lunches:

Bologna sandwich	.38
1 carrot	.06
1 apple	.13
popcorn (about 1 cup)	.05
	$ .62 plus 15¢ for milk

Tuna sandwich	.31
1 small tomato	.12
1 banana	.11
2 oatmeal cookies	.06
	$ .60 plus 15¢ for milk

priced August, 1979

"Food for little people"

When do food habits start? Right away. What can be done to promote good food habits? Lots.

And *Food for Little People* is a booklet about snacks for pre-school children which gives simple directions to carry out some sophisticated ideas about eating. It was prepared jointly by the Berkeley Department of Public Health and the Berkeley Unified School System in 1973. The photographs of small children preparing foods, and the drawings by Brigit Rose, age 5, are charming! But what interests me the most is that the booklet effectively presents other ways to interest children in wholesome foods, instead of simply haranguing about the evils of sweets. The suggestions for snacks, the recipes and the lessons about food are based on a shrewd understanding of the several meanings of food in our lives.

What Makes a Good Snack? It is useful to ponder this question. *Food for Little People* lists seven virtues of the good snack. Then it provides two pages of snack ideas, divided more or less into basic food groups. Recipes are provided, most of which can be made by children or with their help.

Food Lessons, As Well As Music Lessons. Most of us assume the value of teaching children about music. But what about food, in this day of pre-prepared convenience foods? Learning about foods is an important preliminary to the development of good food habits. The section called "Learning About Food" includes several projects which parents or teachers can use at home or at school. One project, called "Feats with Heat," explores such amazing changes in matter as occur when ice cubes are fried, or cookie dough is baked. Observing such natural laws, all too frequently taken for granted by adults, can be the beginning of a child's grasp of scientific concepts.

There are stories about food, very good for reading aloud. The "Story of Stone Soup" intrigued me; there's food for thought there, not just for children's thoughts, either.

More Teaching Aids. This is only a thirty-page booklet. So the list of other places to look for teaching aids on food for small children is important.

Who and Where? Anyone working with pre-school children should find this booklet stimulating and helpful. It is available from the Berkeley Health Department, 2180 Milvia, Berkeley, California 94704 for $2 plus 5% tax.

About Foods
and Buying

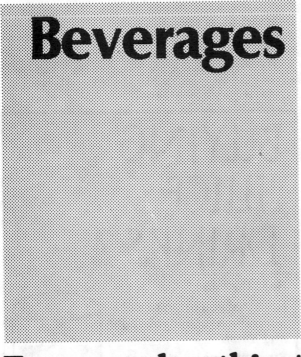

To quench a thirst

by Helen Black

Long ago, people drank water. After a hot sweaty hunt for saber-tooth tigers, they loved the feel of cool, sparkling water in their parched throats. Later, they learned to make wine. How thrifty, to save the grapes for winter use! And what a thirst quencher.

And after the passage of a thousand years, give or take a few, what hath science and industry wrought? Soft drinks! It became possible to get your water nourishment in a sweet, prickly soft drink. Little children blamed their parents if they suffered thirst, when there was no cola in the refrigerator.

Finally came the present, and a great clamor about water pollution. People now worry about phosphates, nitrates and plain old sewage in the water sources. After all, babies' formulas are made with water, fish grow in water, and even soft drinks are made from water. Some people yearn for the good old days, and think about drinking water to quench their thirst. Some even buy bottled water! It may become the fashion to serve water at dinner parties, and to argue the flavor of Mokelume River over Hetch Hetchy water.

Bottled water
by Mary Gullberg

Sales* of bottled water reached $36 million in 1977, a 23% increase over 1976. It is estimated they will increase at least that much again in 1978. (In 1970, the sales were a bare $8.7 million). Bottled water carries one of the highest gross margins of any liquid refreshment.

Perrier, an imported, naturally-carbonated water, is in the lead. For a three-month period in 1978, the Co-op sold 15,952 bottles of the 23-ounce size of Perrier. We sold 11,920 gallons of Black Mountain Spring Water (a natural spring water) and 4,600 gallons of Napa Valley Spring water (a natural mineral water).

What are some of the reasons for this increasing use of bottled water? Some people just like the taste. Others are concerned about possible health hazards from environmental pollutants that may get into municipal water supplies or substances like chlorine and fluoride that may be added to it. Still others prefer not to drink beverages that are colored, flavored or sweetened with compounds they feel may be unsafe to drink in large amounts.

It is essential that we take in the daily equivalent of eight glasses of water (more when the weather is hot). We need it to keep our bodies functioning right, take the nutrients out of the food we eat and excrete the wastes we produce. But bottled water may carry as many questionable minerals as the municipal water supply. Any water that comes up out of the ground as a spring or geyser will carry minerals picked up from the soil it travels through — not to mention pesticides and industrial wastes that may have gotten into the water during its travel to the surface. Some of the minerals dissolved in drinking waters we are now finding out are essential nutrients in tiny amounts but, like fluoride, are toxic in larger amounts.

The dilemma is that we don't know enough about what is needed and what can harm us. And we are continuing to pollute our environment more all the time.

*From CHAIN STORE AGE/SUPERMARKET November 1978.

Apple juice, humph! *by Helen Black*

"Apple juice is a waste of money!" said the wicked, mean, establishment-type Co-op home economist.

And everybody fainted. Their sensibilities were badly bruised. Because, isn't all apple juice unsweetened? True. Isn't it so that apple juice, being pasteurized, never contains preservatives? Oh, yes! Isn't it more wholesome for kids than colas? Indeed, yes. Isn't the loveliest refreshing cool drink on hot days? Yes, yes. Isn't it the fastest moving grocery item of any at the Telegraph Avenue Co-op? So true. Don't Co-op shoppers buy an average of 5,000 gallons a week? Yes, yes, yes it's all true. So how could anyone attack apple juice?

Well, these virtues do not change the fact that in nutritive value, apple juice is forgettable. Apples themselves, though admirable for their crunchy, juicy, tooth-scrubbing, gum-exercising action, are very low in vitamins A and C, for which we usually depend on fruits and vegetables. B vitamins[1] in apples are even lower than in apricots, bananas, cherries, grapefruit, melons, and oranges, most of which are low also. Apples, like most fruits, are also low in iron.[2] Even mildly processed, unfiltered apple juice does not have more nutrients than the apple itself.

Juices that would contribute more nutrients to a meal or snack than apple juice include orange, grapefruit and tomato juices.

This wicked, mean, establishment-type Co-op home economist has quit lugging home gallons of apple juice (regularly) for another reason. I had discovered that one of my offspring would drink **anything** between meals to quench his thirst except water. I should exert my labor and pocketbook to support his extravagant tastes? A pox on such food habits! Anybody drinking apple juice — or soda pop, beer, wine, etc. — **just to quench thirst between meals,** is spending more money than necessary on food.

In these sad days of shocking food prices,

every purchase needs sharp scrutiny. Even, dear friends, apple juice!

1 Thiamine, riboflavin, niacin, pantothenic acid, pyridoxine.

2 However, canned apple juice contains a respectable amount of iron, possibly picked up in part during the canning process or from the can itself.

BUYING JUICE DRINKS?

Read the label.

Note that you often pay a fancy price for a lot of sugar and water.

Straight juice, like orange and tomato, gives you vitamins, minerals and quenches thirst too.

Add your own water if you like.

from your Co-op Home Economist

The "Guess the juice" game *by Helen Black*

With the decline of water as a drink (pity!) there came Kool-Aid, juice drinks, nectars, cocktails, punches and others to quench your thirst. Some, not all, contain certain amounts of juice. Juice, as you know, is the fast, modern way of drinking an apple or orange. To heck with that old tedious biting, chewing and swallowing! The game is to find out how much juice is in these thirst quenchers. Match your wits with the labels on the cans.

The Name is the Tip Off

You can tell a real juice, because by law the label name, with a few exceptions, is "juice." That's all, just "juice." Not juice-drink, not cocktail, not punch and not any other fancy name that sounds juicy. The label of a juice may or may not say "unsweetened" or "100 percent" or "pure," which comforts some people.

A Few Drinks are 50 Percent Juice

The other 50 percent is water, sugar, citric acid, etc. But good news! Some products say "50 percent juice" right there on the front label! Others are 35 percent or 45 percent juice.

Lots are Less

Bunches of products are only 6-12 percent juice. A few say so, right on the front. Others conceal it. Clue: try the INGREDIENT STATEMENT on the back in small print.

Some are No Juice

How can this be? No juice at all? Actually, it's easy, starting with sugar, citric acid, cellulose gum or modified food starch, salt, artificial flavor and color, etc., etc., etc. A few of these products say "Contains No Fruit Juice."

The Bad News

And some products give no information at all about the percent juice. Should there be a law? Well, there is, sort of. A regulation recently finalized by the federal Food and Drug Administration will soon require that products containing no juice must say so on the front panel of the container. Alas, low-juice products can still maintain their mystery. So we'll still be playing games guessing the juice content when we buy.

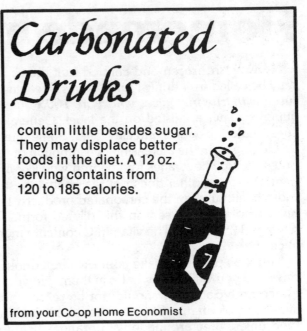

Carbonated Drinks

contain little besides sugar. They may displace better foods in the diet. A 12 oz. serving contains from 120 to 185 calories.

from your Co-op Home Economist

JUICE OR ???

'NECTAR' or 'PUNCH' or 'DRINK' or 'ADE' or 'COCKTAIL' or 'SWEETENED'

means the product can contain sugar, water and other ingredients besides juice.

from your Co-op Home Economist

CALORIES?
per cup

Fruit sodas and collins mix..... 114
Root beer......... 100
Cola................ 96
Gingerale........ 76
Quinine water.... 70
Soda water........ 0

Homemade fruit drinks

Many fresh, frozen and canned fruit drinks have appeared on the market in recent years. They may be called fruit drinks, juice drinks, breakfast drinks, fruit-ades, etc., but *they should not be confused with true fruit juices which are 100% juice.* Fruit drinks contain other ingredients which, as required by law, are listed on the label. Generally, these products are mixtures of water, fruit juice, sugar, coloring agents and citric acid. Some (but not all) contain added vitamin C.

Judging from the increasing consumption of these drinks, they are being substituted for carbonated and cola-type beverages for children who like a between-meal drink. This substitution could be accidental — the mother does not realize that these are not pure fruit juice, or she may think these are more healthful than the carbonated products. In any case, they are expensive in terms of the actual amount of juice present in this diluted form. They are also relatively high in calories, since they average 12% sugar. The vitamin C content ranges from zero to about half the amount in pure orange juice.

You may prefer to make your own fruit drinks, since these are less expensive than the commercial ones and you will know what is in them. However, remember that these homemade drinks, as well as the commercial ones, should not be relied upon to supply very much of the recommended daily allowance of vitamin C. They should not replace the usual good sources of this vitamin in the daily food unless they are made with orange juice, the most concentrated source of ascorbic acid of the usual fruit juices. Three ounces of orange juice supplies the daily allowance of vitamin C for children and adolescents and adults.

To mix a drink comparable to the better commercial recipes, use the following proportions:

Fruit Juice	Water	Sugar	Citric Acid	or	Lemon Juice
2 cups	4 cups	¼-½ cup	¼ teaspoon		1 tablespoon
1 quart	2 quarts	½-1 cup	½ teaspoon		2 tablespoons

Suggested fruit juices might be orange pineapple, grape, grapefruit, tangerine, lemon juice, etc. Fruit nectars are often used in combination with the juices mentioned above for variety and flavor. Pineapple juice particularly may need the addition of some other fruit juice for a more appealing flavor. A little lemon juice added to taste may be used in place of the citric acid. The smaller amount of sugar in the above recipe yields a drink with a 5% sugar content; the larger amount is equivalent to 10% sugar. Since fruit juices vary in sugar content, it is wise to begin with a small amount of sugar and add more if necessary.

The sugar content should be kept as low as is compatible with the "sweet taste" preferences of the children. The aim should be to create a thirst-quencher rather than a high-calorie drink.

Citric acid is the most plentiful acid in citrus fruits and is either extracted from them or prepared by the fermentation of glucose. It adds a tangy flavor to the drink. It may be purchased at most drugstores or may be sold as sour salt in some grocery stores, often with the canning supplies.

Drinks made from this recipe will keep for several days with little loss of quality or nutrients if tightly covered and refrigerated.

Glen's fruit drink

This recipe makes almost a gallon — good for a crowd. The color is a bit muddy, the cost is not as low as that of a homemade orange drink, but this drink has several pluses: An excellent flavor, 50% juice (rather than the 10-33% for commercial drinks), and no added sugar except that in the frozen grape "juice."

One part orange juice — 3 cups (6 ounces frozen plus 3 cans water)
One part grape juice "beverage" — 3 cups (6 ounces frozen plus 3 cans water)
One part unfiltered apple juice — 3 cups (¾ quart)
Two parts water — 6 cups (1½ quarts)

—Glen Kitzenberger

CAFFEINE
in foods and beverages

COLAS, 12 oz, average 45 mg. TEA, 5 oz. cup 45 mg.

COFFEE 5 oz. cup
  Instant 65
  Regular 100-150

BAKING CHOCOLATE, unsweetened, 1 oz. 25

COCOA, 5 oz. cup 15

DECAFFEINATED coffee 5 oz cup 3

from your Co-op Home Economist

When you grind your own Coffee Beans

Whole bean and ground coffee should be kept in a tightly-covered container and stored in a cool, dark place — not in a refrigerator. A storage limit of one month after roasting is recommended for whole beans. After grinding, coffee should be used as soon as possible.

Different kinds of coffee beans owe their special qualities in part to the area of the world in which they are grown. Below are descriptions of some of the important types of coffee beans. We are indebted to the late Jim Hardcastle from Capricorn Coffees, supplier of Co-op Coffee Beans, for preparing this information.

Straight Coffees

Each distinctive coffee is selected and roasted after many samplings, testings and tastings. Checks are made for flavor, taste, body, aroma and acidy quality. Incidentally, the word "acidy" is misunderstood and misused by most people in reference to coffee. In the coffee trade, the term simply means that the flavor is sharp and pleasing to the taste, that the coffee is smooth and rich and has snap and life. It does *not* refer to the actual amount of acid in the cup, nor does it carry the chemical connotations of sour, caustic or bitter. Coffees low in acidy flavor, by comparison, are sweet, heavy and mellow. The range in the list below is from mild and mellow to the very liveliest.

South American
BRAZIL SANTOS: The finest coffee grown there is one developed from Mocha seed — Bourbon Santos. It is smooth, has heavy body and a bittersweet taste that adds to blends, and yet, because its own flavor is "light," it does not detract if richer flavored straights are mixed with it. By itself a most palatable cup, it is essential in blending.

COLOMBIAN: Because of its extensive promotion, Colombian is probably the best-known coffee in the United States. However, there are many varieties and grades, and only the better varieties measure up to the claims of richness, body, flavor and aroma attributed to straight Colombian coffees.

PERUVIAN: Coffee from Peru compares favorably to the coffee from Colombia. This coffee is dark in color, mild in strength.

Central American
COSTA RICAN: This sharply acid coffee with its heavy body is particularly adaptable for use in blends.

NICARAGUAN: These beans are good roasters and have fine acid. Though somewhat like the Mexican, it is difficult to make comparisons because the Nicaraguan stands apart in its own special way.

EL SALVADOR: Noted for its good acidity and body and its mild taste, this coffee is a splendid blender. There is just enough of a winey characteristic to make this a remarkably fine cup by itself.

ANTIGUA: This is a real treat for coffee lovers because it is considered to be one of the choicest coffees grown anywhere in the world. It is grown on table land at an altitude of between five and six thousand feet in a district just west of Guatemala City. The essentials of good coffee — fine acidity, body, flavor and aroma — are indescribably combined in the Antigua.

GUATEMALAN: This mountain-grown coffee makes a wonderful brew with a full, heavy body. As one would expect, this coffee is much like the Mexican in its character. More acidy, its distinction is its nutty flavor, rich and sweet.

MEXICAN: The bean we use is from the west coast area of Mexico and is selected because it is less acidy than some of the current varieties. Mellow, it has wonderful bouquet and rich, full body.

Mexican is the preferred straight coffee of most of our customers. We use this sweet, fragrant coffee extensively in our blends.

African and Mideastern

ETHIOPIAN MOCHA HARRAR: The cup is remarkably spicy and aromatic, quite acid and flavorful with a taste which seems slightly sweeter than the Arabian Mocha coffee from Yemen.

KENYA: This African coffee, one of the world's superior coffees, is grown on beautiful plantations in this east African country that borders the Indian Ocean. Quite strong, it leaves a distinctive *dry* taste on the palate, a quality suggestive of the finest burgundy wines. It has a pleasing caramel-like taste. The kind of Kenya coffee we buy is difficult to obtain since it is almost all consumed in the European market.

ARABIAN MOCHA: Our Mocha coffee comes from Yemen, a district in Arabia along the Red Sea known for its superior grade of coffee. After it is roasted, this coffee has a bouquet much like sun-dried wild berries. But a taste that is reminiscent of bitter chocolate is its real claim to fame. Naturally acidy, this chocolate-like flavor, so easily detected by coffee lovers, enhances the taste and aroma of any blend into which Mocha is added.

Far East and Oceania

CELEBES KALOSSI: A rich, full flavor, slightly acidic with mellow, velvety undertone.

JAVA: Only coffees of the *Coffee Arabica* variety grown upon this island of Indonesia can be labeled "Java" in the United States, although other varieties are grown there. Partly because of this regulation, Java coffee is fast becoming rare in the United States. The fragrance released when the beans are being ground is a remarkable prelude to the spicy bouquet of a coffee in the cup.

SUMATRA MANDHELING: This coffee has a heavy body with a unique "smoky" flavor and aroma. The bean has a dull, flat, brown color when roasted — not at all the appearance one usually associates with good coffee. Yet this Indonesian Arabica bean is one of the world's best and truly unique.

NEW GUINEA: Our high grown New Guinea bean is smooth and mellow, rich in flavor and a great favorite of people who prefer a medium strength coffee.

Roasts

LIGHT FRENCH ROAST: This French Roast is a combination of three coffees, roasted darker than the usual American type so that the natural oils come to the surface. We have blended Brazil for its bittersweet taste and for its body, Mexican for its sweetness, Colombian for its flavor.

DARK FRENCH ROAST: This is the darkest of all coffees. Roasted almost to the burning point, it is quite oily in appearance. Excellent to serve with cheese, fruit, pastries and rich desserts of all kinds, it also makes a superb cafe au lait. Try it with brandy or cognac, or with liqueurs.

ITALIAN ROAST (ESPRESSO): In color it actually lies between the two French Roasts. This is a combination of four coffees, roasted dark and heavy to make a fragrant, thick and creamy cup. Though designed for use in espresso machines, its excellent flavor is maintained when made at home using any method.

BRAZIL NEW ORLEANS TYPE ROAST: This is a darker roast, falling between Light French Roast and Italian Espresso Roast for a New Orleans type coffee which is tasty alone or when used with the addition of chicory imported from France.

Blends

When one coffee is mixed with another, or several others, to achieve a different and desirable taste, the process is called *blending*. We consider blending both an art and a science. Behind the blend that makes a satisfying cup is the specialized knowledge about each coffee used. And just as colors are put together considering tone, intensity, hue, depth, brilliance, etc., so are coffees put together to produce the utmost in fullness, fragrance and flavor. Of the many blends possible, here are two famous ones.

MOCHA-JAVA BLEND: Everyone seems to have heard of the combination of Mocha with Java.

These coffees were available before coffees were produced in many other parts of the world, and it was learned years ago that when these two were combined, the product was a delightful and unforgettable taste experience. Blenders vary their proportions so a Mocha-Java blend can vary in taste considerably from place to place.

NEW ORLEANS BLEND: A tradition in the Mississippi Delta country and extending throughout the Appalachian area. In recent years the substitution of inferior coffee to cut production costs has tended to downgrade this famous old blend. As originally made, chicory imported from France was combined with Bourbon Santos which had been brought up to a French Roast, that is, the beans had been roasted high enough to bring the natural oil of the coffee to the surface. We have turned back to this traditional blend, bringing it back to its old standards, hoping to restore it to a pungent, strong, rich and creamy drink.

Others

FRENCH CHICORY: The root of a plant grown in France, chicory is cured, roasted, ground for export and used as a coffee enhancer. It adds a rich, bittersweet flavor to coffee. Chicory is used for blending only. Use ¼ chicory to ¾ coffee.

Tea, a pleasurable beverage

Tea is the world's most popular beverage next to water. Every day more of the world's population drink tea than any other prepared beverage.

The story of tea is so ancient that its origins are lost in time. It most certainly has been refreshing palates and quenching thirsts for at least 4000 years. Tea is crucial to the economy of many of the countries of the world. India, Ceylon and China, among others, count on tea for a large part of their export income.

A wide variety of tea is available on the market, and a tea drinker must make his or her choice on the basis of flavor, fragrance, color and cost. The following descriptions and glossary of tea terms may help you find your way through the maze of tea choices. If you have always bought only one kind, be daring and try another.

Black, Green and Oolong

BLACK TEA has been allowed to ferment before drying; GREEN TEA is dried immediately after plucking. OOLONG is different; it's between green and black in flavor. It's partially fermented (and sometimes flavored with jasmine blossoms). All come from the same plant. A cup of tea of moderate strength contains about ½ the stimulant, caffeine, in a cup of coffee of moderate strength.

Tea should be stored in an airtight container to preserve its freshness.

Black and Green Teas are classified according to leaf size. The larger the leaf, the "poorer" the quality. About 97% of the tea drunk in the U.S. is black. Black teas in order of increasing size of leaf: Flowery Pekoe, Orange Pekoe, Pekoe, Pekoe-Souchong, Souchong. Very small and broken leaves called Fannings are usually used in tea bags. The word "Pekoe" refers to the downy appearance on the underside of young leaves, and the word "orange" to the color of the tips of still younger leaves.

Some other terms describe the geographic source of the tea. They indicate flavor differences, not quality necessarily.

Assam	These teas from the Assam province of India are "robust." Growing at a relatively low altitude probably contributes to their characteristic flavors.
Ceylon	Teas from this area are grown at 4000 feet or higher; their

strong aroma probably relates to the slower maturation of leaves at this altitude.

Darjeeling   Teas from this area in north-eastern India grow at an altitude of 7000 feet; it is considered by many to be the best of Indian teas.

Keemun   Refers to a tea originally coming from the province of that name in China; its flavor is described as sharp or winey.

"Herb Teas"

There are, of course, dozens of herb teas available. These are not true teas, but are dried herbs which are steeped in boiling water to make a hot drink. Two of the most popular are Peppermint and Camomile. As with tea, herb drink preferences are personal. Experiment until you find your favorites.

A glossary of other tea terms

These terms have come into common use for various reasons:

EARL GREY - this mixture of Indian and Ceylon black teas originally referred to a special blend made up for the private use of a British nobleman, an importer of teas over one hundred years ago. There is no longer a copyright on the name, so any blend of teas can legally be called "Earl Grey." One's choice depends on individual preference.

ENGLISH BREAKFAST - this term usually refers to black tea from China or of the Chinese type. The term is an American term, not used in England.

LAPSANG SOUCHONG - this strong tea has a smoky flavor due to the baking of the tea leaves over smoking fires. It is black tea, usually from Taiwan.

Brewing teas and herbs

Tea is unlike coffee in that there is only one good way to prepare it as far as devoted, orthodox tea drinkers are concerned.

1. Use a preheated pot, preferably earthenware as it retains the heat well.

2. Allow about 1 teaspoon tea leaves per 6 oz. cup of water (¾ of a measuring cup). If you prefer a weaker brew, use less tea.

3. Heat freshly drawn water just to the point of a brisk boil. This is important to prevent the driving off of dissolved air and carbon dioxide.

4. Add the tea to the pot and pour water over leaves; allow to steep for 3-5 minutes.

5. Serve immediately; or pour into heated teapot, removing tea leaves in the process. Longer steeping extracts the tannins in tea which make it bitter and drives off the volatile oils which are responsible for the aroma.

Cost of Tea vs. Coffee

To compare the cost of one cup of tea with the cost of one cup of coffee, figure:

1 oz. loose tea yields about 16 cups of brewed tea - 1 cup tea costs about 1¢.

1 lb. ground coffee yields about 50 cups of brewed coffee - 1 cup coffee costs about 6¢.

September 1979

Carob or cocoa? *by Helen Black*

Carob powder is a brown powder that tastes surprisingly like cocoa. It comes from pods of a large evergreen tree which grows in any climate suitable for orange trees. The pods, which look like a large insect, may have been the "locusts" that St. John the Baptist ate in the wilderness. So, the carob pods are also called St. John's Bread.

Carob versus Cocoa

Carob powder is a welcome substitute for those who are allergic or sensitive to chocolate and cocoa. In addition, since cocoa is one of the sources of caffeine (and a related compound called theobromine) carob can be used by those who wish to avoid these stimulants.

Carob powder is about 1½% fat, while cocoa is from 8-24% fat. Chocolate, from which cocoa comes, is 53% fat.

Carob powder can be used to make a milk drink like cocoa, using the same recipe. I found the carob drink pleasant and quite acceptable, though chocolate freaks may notice differences. Carob is lower in fat than cocoa, but when made into a beverage with milk the difference in calories and fat is slight.

Carob in Junk Foods

Carob used in candies in place of chocolate or cocoa has no nutritional advantage, to my knowledge. In order to make a candy of acceptable texture, fat must be added to make up for the lack of fat in carob. The chocolate-like coating on malt balls and various nuts has hydrogenated vegetable oil as its largest ingredient, followed by sugar, then whey, and finally carob. These products are essentially high fat, high sugar junk food and the shrewd shopper should be wary of them.

Serving wines

By Dr. Karel Popper,
Chemist USDA
Agricultural Research Service

The first reason for drinking wine is that it makes one feel good.

The Spanish peasant will drink wine from the bota and feel good at his artistry of not spilling a drop.

I, on the other hand, will refuse wine from a paper cup.

It is not only the wine one drinks, it is also when, how, and with whom.

To come straight to some of the do's and don'ts:

Temperature

Chilled: white wine, sparkling wine, dry vermouth and flavored wine. An exception — some of the very sweet whites.

Room temperature: red wine. At a picnic, somewhat chilled. (Very good red wine is wasted on that occasion.) Exception - Portuguese Vinho Verde. This is to be always chilled.

Opening

Should be some considerable time before pouring. Great reds are supposed to be opened the day before serving and transferred from the bottle to a decanter. The wine is to remain remote from the kitchen and dining room until serving. So, if you don't have a cellar and a wine steward, forget it and open your wine when you put the roast in the oven. It is a good idea to keep it away from the cooking area since (a) it will absorb odors, and (b) you might feel inclined to nibble. Open your whites for about half an hour, close them again and stick them in the refrigerator for something like five hours. An ice bucket will do the job in about half an hour.

What with What

Whatever you like. The classic rule is red with red, white with white, sweet with sweet.

The function of wine is that of a salad. It restores your taste and lets you savor the food you eat. Do not serve wine with a salad unless the salad is your main dish.

A vinous menu would perhaps be:

Dry Sherry
Soup
Fowl with dry white wine
Salad
Roast with red wine
Cheese with red wine
Pastry with sweet wine
Coffee
Brandy, liqueur, port

Without food or with finger food: champagne, sherry, port, sweet white, aperitifs.

Glassware

Either the classical differentiated stemware which makes for an interesting table and tells the guest what to expect, or the general tulip. The universal, clear, tulip-shaped wine glass is excellent for all wines except champagne. There the suggestion is hollow-stemmed tulip. A silver goblet is also very good. DON'TS: Keep your heavy cut crystal on display where it belongs, or serve ice cream or tomato juice in it. Burn your paper cups and use your colored glass for candle holders.

Pouring

The first little bit into your own glass, just enough to cover the bottom. Next, ladies, and next, men. Then fill your own. Girls are held by the waist, thieves by the throat, and bottles just below the neck. Use a slight rotary motion. Do not try to squeeze out the last drop — you might give someone a mouthful of sediment.

Talk

Unless you know a great deal about it, not about wine. Embarrassment is easy.

Questions and answers on
Cooking with wine

These are questions which shoppers have asked Co-op home economists. We are pleased to have them answered for you by a wine expert, Dr. Karel Popper, a research chemist at the United States Department of Agriculture Western Regional Research Center in Albany, Calif.

1. When wine is added during cooking, how many calories are added?

Answer: Negligible — the alcohol evaporates. Should very sweet wine be used (and that is done but rarely), as in basting lamb with Vermouth, even there the calorie increase is very low.

2. Is it a waste of wine to use it in stew prepared in a pressure cooker? What happens to the flavor at that higher temperature? Does alcohol cook off in the same way?

Answer: It is not a waste, provided the pressure cooker is allowed to cool off to some 170°F before venting. Alcohol cooks off to a somewhat lesser degree than in open pot cooking. The bouquet of the dish is enhanced, thus go easier on herbs.

3. I use wine now and then in cooking but do not drink it. Is there any way to keep the opened bottle from spoiling, other than by refrigeration?

Answer: Refrigeration is your best bet. Keep the bottle closed to avoid refrigerator odor in the wine.

4. Does adding a few drops of olive oil to a bottle of wine for cooking prevent spoilage if the wine is stored at room temperature?

Answer: An edible oil will help to minimize oxidative spoilage. The Greeks and other ancients have done it before. It does not, however, prevent growth of some bacteria and you may have a bottle of hazy but perfectly usable wine as pathogenic bacteria do not grow at those levels of alcohol and acidity. When stored in a warm environment you may develop a sherry flavor — for soups and sauces this may be an advantage.

5. Does wine act as a tenderizer? If so, how does it accomplish tenderizing and does it make any difference in the tenderness of the product if a cheap wine is used? Is the tenderizing effect as great on lean meat as on fat meat?

Answer: Wine acts as a tenderizer since it helps to break down some of the connective tissues and helps in fat distribution. Also the alcohol within the food item acts on heating somewhat like baking powder. Price has nothing to do with it. Taste the wine and if you can stand it, use it.

The tenderizing effect is unfortunately greater on fat meat which needs less tenderizing anyhow. For lean meat you may want to include a commercial meat tenderizer in the wine.

6. Is any red wine o.k. for cooking? How about rose wine? What is the proper wine to use in a fondue?

Answer: Depends on what you cook. By and large you have to like the wine if you are to like the dish. The one exception is Madeira — you may not like it but your sauce will. I would not recommend rose for cooking; its character will be lost and it won't do much for your dish. The one exception would be Chaux d'Eaux. For fondue, any dry white wine and remember the kirsch.

7. What type of American white wine is good to use in cooking? Julia Child says that the "right" white wine for cooking is not easy to find in the U.S. and recommends a dry white vermouth as the best substitute for a proper French wine.

Answer: Dry white vermouth, in small amounts, is fine for martinis. There is a wide range of perfectly good California wines — for Alsatian dishes, use Napa, Sonoma or Livermore riesling other than grey riesling. As to the rest, sauterne from all over the state is fine. For a little bit of sparkle, try Emerald Dry or any of the California champagnes.

8. Is there any advantage to using a wine labeled "Cooking Wine"? Does the salt added to such wines help to keep them after opening?

Answer: No! No! No!

9. Does sherry have to be added to the end of cooking? Why?

Answer: The Spaniards and Portuguese add sherry to soup at the table. I like it. Why? Because you want to taste the sherry and get more volatile aroma during eating, thus you do not want to boil off the alcohol.

10. I ruined a perfectly good recipe by adding a little extra wine. Is there a rule-of-thumb on the proper amount of wine to use per pound of meat?

Answer: The rules of thumb are:
1. If you can taste garlic in your salad, you put in too much.
2. If you wish to use lots of wine as in boeuf bourguignon, use very good wine.
3. In delicate dishes, be stingy. A Dover sole should taste like sole, not like wine — the wine merely removes the "fishiness," and for that you need very little.

Beer

Beer making began in the home long before it became a successful commercial venture. Recently, many have been moving this activity back into the home for several reasons: it's usually cheaper than buying brewery beer (after the basic equipment has been acquired); many beer drinkers claim that good home-made brew is of superior quality to those one can buy — *not* excluding the imports — and, of course, there is the same sense of satisfaction to be gained from making beer as there is from baking bread, canning fruit, putting up preserves, or making a macrame wall hanging. It's all part of the trend among large segments of the population towards do-it-yourself projects to counteract the commercial entrepreneurs who want to do everything for us — at a price! Lastly, the law prohibiting making beer at home without a license was repealed in 1978 by Congress and by the California legislature.

Most of the beer drunk around the world is lager beer. Lager is a German word meaning 'to store' and is a type of beer made from a bottom-fermenting yeast rather than a top-fermenting yeast, such as is used in wine and bread baking. (A few countries such as the British Isles and New Zealand drink a different type of beer which is top fermented.) Lager beer is stored for varying lengths of time to age.

The first lager brewery started in Philadelphia in 1842, but lager production didn't become commercially important until about 1880. Before then, most Americans (excluding Indians) drank English beer and stout, which are much heavier brews.

Of course, the brewing of beer goes back thousands of years and has been done by ancient Babylonians, Egyptians and Chinese using a wide variety of grains such as wheat, millet, barley, and rice. For many, beer was the beverage consumed regularly, since the town water was often not fit to drink. In the colder European countries where the climate was not conducive to grape growing, beer was the substitute for wine. Farley Mowat in *West Viking* relates that when the Vikings reached Greenland, they found that while they could grow hay and other grass crops for their cattle, the climate did not permit the growing of grains. Therefore, the Vikings were unable to brew beer. The end result was that these already contentious, feisty characters became even more hostile and tended to slit everyone down the middle with their swords rather than listen to the other person's side of the question.

Today, American beer is brewed from barley plus corn, rye and hops. In addition, cultured yeast is needed for fermentation to give the sparkle to the pure, filtered water which is 90% of the finished beverage. The alcoholic content of most American beer is 3½% by weight, but is sometimes as much as 5%.

There is no *one* recipe for home brewing of beer, but here is one that has been used successfully. To make 14 gallons of beer:
2 cans (3 lb. size) hop-flavored malt
10 lb. cane or beet sugar
2 pkgs. dry yeast (same as used for baking)
Mix sugar with one gallon water and bring to a full boil stirring until all the sugar is dissolved. Add the hop-flavored malt that has been mixed with enough hot tap water so that it will pour and mix easily. Cool the mixture by adding cold water until the temperature is below 80° F.

Add the yeast that has been dispersed in a small amount of cold water (1 cup). Place mixture in large crock or other container that will hold 14 gallons but do not add all the water or the mix will foam over the top of the container during the first 12 hours of fermentation. Place the crock in an even-temperatured room (about 70°F.) and let it ferment. After two or three days, fill crock to 13 gallon mark.

In 4 to 7 days the beer will be ready to bottle. As the fermentation reaches its end, the color of the mix will change since the yeast cells will settle out. The color change is from a somewhat opaque tan to a somewhat darker and clearer brown. A little foaming around the edges will also occur at this point. You may wish to use a hydrometer to help you determine when the beer is ready to bottle.

Before you bottle the beer, a little sugar is added to produce fermentation in the bottles. Dissolve one to two cups of sugar in about a gallon of water. Bring mixture to boil and add it while hot to the wort. Stir to mix. Let stand for half an hour, then bottle the beer. Store the bottled beer at room temperature for about two weeks before drinking it.

The water used for the above recipe was Berkeley tap water. If your water supply is very hard, you may want to consider other sources.

There are several paperback books available on the market which discuss in more detail the making of beer. One of them is:

A Treatise on Lager Beer, Fred Eckhardt and Jack McCallum, $1.75. Available at Wine and the People, 1140 University Avenue, Berkeley, Calif. 94702.

Also, "Making Beer At Home," free from Wine and the People. Please send stamped self-addressed business-size envelope.

Beans and nuts

Dry beans, ancient and honorable

Since prehistoric times, new bean recipes have been emerging from the kitchens of inspired cooks in every corner of the world. Because their flavor is bland, beans can be agreeable even when combined with the most preposterous ingredients. Consider sweetening with molasses, brown sugar or fruit, adding tartness with vinegar, wine, tomatoes or sour cream; adding pepperiness with mustard, chili or curry; thickening with cornmeal or rice; combining with meat, fish or cheese — to mention only a few! Join the hosts of anonymous cooks of history, and make up your own recipe.

Nutritional value:

Dry beans can be substituted for meat to make an economical meal. Figure about 1½ cups cooked beans as equivalent to 3 oz. cooked meat. To improve the quality of the protein in the beans, include in the same meal a cereal food or a small amount of animal protein food. Many bean recipes include some meat or cheese. A cottage cheese salad or custard for dessert accomplishes the same thing. Beans also provide calcium, iron, and B vitamins.

Varieties of beans:

Cranberry, pinto, pink, red, and kidney beans are similar and can be used interchangeably in recipes. White beans, including Great Northern, small whites, navy or pea beans are similar enough to be interchangeable. Mung beans are similar to split peas. Black beans are whitish inside, cooking up to a gray color if broken. Lima beans, blackeye beans, garbanzos and soybeans have somewhat more distinctive textures or flavors than the others. Soy and mung beans are both commonly used for bean sprouts.

To prepare beans:

Packaged dry beans need only be rinsed and any imperfect beans removed. Beans purchased in bulk many require more careful picking over before rinsing.

To soak dried beans:

Beans may be soaked overnight. Or, boil 1 cup dried beans in 2-3 cups water for 2 minutes. Set aside. Soak 1 hour before cooking. Then proceed with your favorite recipe. Some people like to use the water in which the beans have been soaking to cook the beans. Note: lentils and split peas do not need soaking.

How long to cook:
Blackeye peas, lentils, split peas, lima beans, and whole peas: ½ to 1 hour. All others: 1½ to 2 hours. Do not cook beans at a rapid boil as they tend to break up. Gentle cooking, or simmering, helps prevent this. Beans that have been stored several months take longer to cook.

Adding seasonings:
Do not add acid foods such as tomatoes or vinegar until beans are almost tender, as the acid delays the softening of the beans and so makes longer cooking necessary. Salt may be added at any time after soaking. Figure about 1 teaspoon salt per cup of dry beans if no other salty food is being added such as salt pork. Meats, onions, celery and herbs add more flavor if added during cooking rather than after beans are cooked.

To help prevent foaming during cooking:
Add about 1 tablespoon fat per cup of dry beans. This will not help much to keep large limas from foaming, however.

Using a pressure cooker:
Foaming may clog the cooker vent tube; see above. In addition, fill the cooker no more than ½ full including the water. Follow directions that come with the cooker. Pressure should rise and fall slowly so as to prevent breaking of beans.

At high altitudes or where water is hard:
Increased cooking time is required in both instances.

Freezing bean dishes:
Cooked beans freeze well and will keep 4-6 months in a freezer.

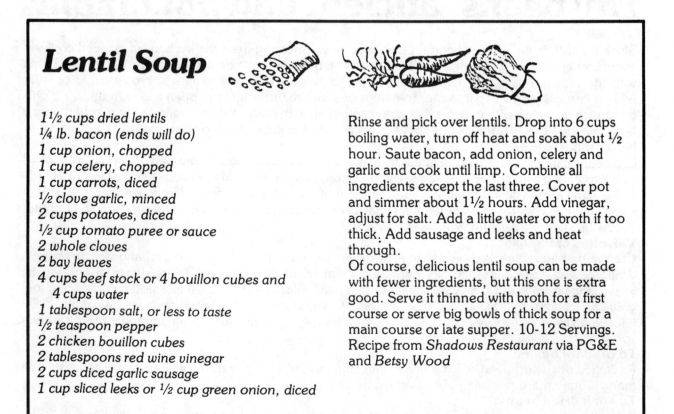

Lentil Soup

1½ cups dried lentils
¼ lb. bacon (ends will do)
1 cup onion, chopped
1 cup celery, chopped
1 cup carrots, diced
½ clove garlic, minced
2 cups potatoes, diced
½ cup tomato puree or sauce
2 whole cloves
2 bay leaves
4 cups beef stock or 4 bouillon cubes and
   4 cups water
1 tablespoon salt, or less to taste
½ teaspoon pepper
2 chicken bouillon cubes
2 tablespoons red wine vinegar
2 cups diced garlic sausage
1 cup sliced leeks or ½ cup green onion, diced

Rinse and pick over lentils. Drop into 6 cups boiling water, turn off heat and soak about ½ hour. Saute bacon, add onion, celery and garlic and cook until limp. Combine all ingredients except the last three. Cover pot and simmer about 1½ hours. Add vinegar, adjust for salt. Add a little water or broth if too thick. Add sausage and leeks and heat through.

Of course, delicious lentil soup can be made with fewer ingredients, but this one is extra good. Serve it thinned with broth for a first course or serve big bowls of thick soup for a main course or late supper. 10-12 Servings. Recipe from *Shadows Restaurant* via PG&E and *Betsy Wood*

More beans: soybeans, black beans and mung beans

Soybeans differ from other dry beans in that they are higher in protein, lower in carbohydrate and higher in fat. The caloric value is only slightly higher than that of other beans, however. Soy protein has the highest quality of any vegetable protein.

Soybeans are an important crop in the United States as animal feed and as a source of many important food products for man, including soy sauce, soybean curd or tofu, miso, soy oil, soy protein, and lecithin. Soy flour, used in the proportion of 1/6 cup with 5/6 cup wheat flour in place of 1 cup of wheat flour, improves the nutritive value of breads and other baked goods. This is because the soy flour has more protein, calcium and certain B vitamins than wheat flour, and because the proteins of the two flours complement each other as well.

Dry soybeans can be cooked as are other dry beans and substituted for them in most recipes. Because of their higher percentage of protein, they tend to foam somewhat more than other beans and take longer to cook. They are firmer than most other beans and have a delicious, nut-like flavor. To make them as tender as other beans, they are best cooked in a pressure cooker.

Black beans are also called turtle beans or turtle soup beans. These small black beans are whitish inside. They are used extensively in South America. They should be soaked and cooked as are most other beans requiring at least two hours cooking after soaking to become tender.

Mung beans are small dark green beans native to India. They are used for bean sprouts or can be cooked into a thick soup or mush. Botanically they are related to the more common beans, such as limas and white beans, and their chemical composition is similar. If mung beans are not available, split peas can be substituted for them in recipes.

Guatemalan Black Bean Soup

2 cups dry black beans
1 lb. ham (ham hocks or leftover meat may be
    used), optional
1 carrot, diced
3 cloves, whole
¼ teaspoon mace
dash tabasco sauce or hot sauce
3 small onions, minced
1 clove garlic, minced
salt to taste
¼ cup sherry
3 hard-cooked eggs, sliced
1 lemon, sliced

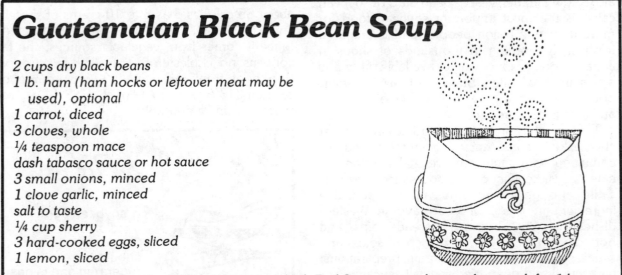

Rinse beans, cover with water and bring to a boil. Boil 2 minutes and set aside to soak for 1 hour. Add meat, carrot, onion and seasonings (except for sherry). Cover and cook slowly at least 3 hours, or until the beans become very soft. Add a little water or broth as needed to prevent dryness. Add salt if needed. If desired, run beans through sieve. Add wine and serve, garnishing each serving with slices of egg and lemon. 5-6 servings.

Fried Soy Curd (Tofu) in Mushroom Sauce

Batter:
1 medium egg
1 tablespoon flour
1 teaspoon water
¼ teaspoon salt
1 cake of tofu, cut into slices 1 x 1 x ¼ inches
3 tablespoons salad oil

Sauce:
1 cup water
1 chicken bouillon cube
4 teaspoons soy sauce
¼ lb. fresh mushrooms, sliced
1 tablespoon cornstarch
¼ cup water

Add flour, 1 teaspoon water and salt to egg. Beat until smooth. Heat oil in frying pan. Dip curd slices in the batter and brown on both sides in hot fat. Remove browned curd slices to a dish. Brown mushrooms lightly in leftover fat. Add water and bouillon cube and bring to a boil. Add soy sauce. Mix cornstarch and ¼ cup water. Stir into sauce and cook until thick. Add browned curd slices to sauce, cover pan and simmer for 1 or 2 minutes. Serve at once. Serves 2-4 depending on what other dishes are served at the meal.

Tofu

This low-cost protein backbone of the East Asian diet [for more than 2,000 years] was discovered by a Chinese prince in 140 B.C. Tofu, also known in the West as bean curd or soybean cake, is the most important soybean food for more than one billion people, and is prepared fresh each morning in thousands of shops in Japan alone. Now widely available in many states in the United States, tofu is becoming popular among a growing number of nutrition and cost-conscious people.

Tofu is white in color, bland tasting, rather cheeselike in consistency. It is added to soup or combined with meat and vegetable dishes or eaten as is, seasoned with soy sauce. It is versatile enough to become an indispensable ingredient in many of your favorite Western dishes including dressings, spreads, dips, and hors d'oeuvres; salads, sandwiches, soups and sauces; egg, vegetable and grain preparations; barbecued and deep-fried specialties; casseroles and even desserts.

Tofu is prepared from soybeans which are soaked overnight, then ground, boiled and strained through a cloth. The addition of either calcium chloride or calcium sulfate to the liquid results in the precipitation of the white curd, which is cut into blocks, covered with water, and sold in cartons in the refrigerated sections of the produce departments in supermarkets. The residue from the preparation of tofu, called kirazu, is also eaten but is not generally available in stores.

Nutrition value. A quarter pound of tofu has about 85 calories, has 8 to 10 grams of protein and 5 grams of fat, most of which is unsaturated. Since it comes from vegetable sources, the fat contains no cholesterol. Tofu is a fairly good source of iron and quite a good source of calcium (13% and 19% of the US RDA, respectively, in ¼ pound).

Bean Cake or Tofu is soybean curd, used in many Oriental recipes. It should be refrigerated and is best used within a day or two. If not used right away, drain the water and replace with fresh water everyday.

from your Co-op Home Economist

Miso What is it?

by Mary Gullberg

Miso might have been used in that tasty soup served to you as a first course in a Japanese restaurant. It is a fermented blend of rice, soybeans and salt. It has the consistency of peanut butter and has a flavor all its own. Because it is so high in salt, it keeps well without refrigeration for long periods of time. Once opened, it should be refrigerated. It comes in several varieties from light colored to almost black. Do not add salt to recipes in which you use miso until you have tasted them — ¼ teaspoon salt equals 1 teaspoon soy sauce or 2 teaspoons miso.

Which foods are improved with miso?

Miso has a pleasant, rather nutty flavor that complements a wide variety of foods. The Japanese use it mainly in soup and as a preservative for pickled vegetables. However, it can be used as a flavoring for fish, shellfish, fresh vegetables (raw or cooked), and meats. Experiment with it, mixing it with cream cheese for a dip or spreading it thinly on raw vegetable slices for a snack or hors d'oeuvre.

Miso Soup

2 cups dashi*
2 or 3 teaspoons miso paste
1 or 2 green onions, chopped (use tops)
1 or 2 stalks bok choy, chopped (use leaves)
¼ cup chopped meat (may use leftover),
  optional

Simmer all ingredients together for 10 to 15 minutes. Strain and serve as a first course. The soup will be cloudy because of the fine particles of bean paste. Garnish with a sprinkling of green onion. 4 servings.

*Dashi is shaved bonito and a special seaweed. The dry ingredients are available in envelopes in the Oriental Food section at the Co-op.

Peanut butter

Does your child demand peanut butter on his toast for breakfast? If so, please keep cool. He is making a most nutritious choice! Peanut butter is a good source of protein, as are other members of the bean or legume family, and can be used as a substitute for meat. Protein quality is improved when bread or other grain is eaten at the same meal, or when small amounts of animal protein food such as milk, eggs or meat are included in the meal. Unlike other legumes, peanuts and peanut butter are very high in fat, about 50%. One tablespoon of peanut butter is almost 100 calories.

Early in the 1900's, peanuts were developed as a crop to enrich depleted soils in the South by the famous Black scientist, George Washington Carver. Of the more than 300 by-products of peanuts developed by Carver and others, peanut butter is certainly one of the best known and loved. Strangely enough, the use of peanut butter has not spread much beyond the United States. Most other countries grow peanuts mainly for the oil.

Peanut butter must be 90% peanuts

Any product called "peanut butter" must

conform to government standards. This means that it contains at least 90% peanuts, with the remaining 10% limited to sweeteners, hardened vegetable oil (stabilizer) and salt. Products containing less than 90% peanuts may call themselves "peanut spreads." Added vitamins, artificial sweeteners or flavorings, etc. are not permitted. If hydrogenated vegetable oil is added, the peanut oil does not separate from the peanut butter. The product spreads easily. Such peanut butters are often called "homogenized."

Another type of peanut butter is on the market which consists of just peanuts and salt or even of peanuts alone. Sometimes called "old fashioned" or "natural," these products have a stronger peanut flavor, and the peanut oil tends to rise to the top of the jar upon standing. They are harder to spread and do not keep quite as well, but true peanut butter fanciers love them. In blind taste tests, people can easily tell one type from the other and tend to have decided preferences. For best quality, stir in the oil and store in the refrigerator. Remove a short time before using to let it soften.

The price of beans

In 1974, the price of dry beans shot up to nearly a dollar a pound. Understandably, grocery shoppers were outraged! An underlying cause was the world need for protein foods which increased the demand for beans. Then the bean crops in the Midwest were damaged by floods in 1973, with 100 million acres of beans under water at one time. The Russians' sunflower crop failed, so they were buying up soybeans to make oil. Suddenly in 1974 beans became extremely scarce and high priced, resulting in some odd situations where dry beans were more expensive than canned, per equivalent serving.

The situation eventually corrected itself.

Nigerian Groundnut Stew

1 lb. boneless lamb shoulder, cut in cubes
2 tablespoons oil
1 cup water
1-2 large onions, sliced
1 teaspoon salt
1 can (8 oz.) tomato sauce

1 tablespoon lemon juice
2 teaspoons chili powder (or to taste)
1/2 cup peanut butter
1 cup beef bouillon
3 cups hot cooked rice (1 cup raw)
3 hard-cooked eggs, shelled

Brown lamb in oil. Add onions and cook until limp. Add water, cover, simmer until meat is tender (about 1 hour). Mix salt, tomato sauce, lemon juice, chili powder, peanut butter and bouillon together and pour over meat. Heat thoroughly. To serve, put a helping of rice on plate, put 1/2 egg in center, and cover with stew. Makes 6 servings, each providing about 20 grams protein.

Browsing among the beans

by Helen Black

In the cheap old days, about two years ago, you could take 10 cents worth of dry beans and make a marvelous old-fashioned toy called a "bean bag." This device for amusing kids and old folks alike could be made into all kinds of shapes, even like a clown, with arms and legs! It could be hurled gloriously into the air, or perched rakishly on top of the bookcase, with one leg dangling over the edge.

But no more. Beanbags can no longer be classed as inexpensive. And it is even urgent to browse among the beans, dry or canned, comparing prices before buying. For food, that is! It's a good idea, too, to compare the cost of beans with meat or other high-protein foods. THEN decide which to buy.

It's a Little Tricky!

When comparing cost of raw food versus cooked food such as canned, consider the changes which take place during cooking. For example, meat shrinks in size and weight when baked or broiled, due to dripping of fat and evaporation of water. The protein is thus more concentrated in cooked meat than in raw. Canned tuna provides more protein per pound, and so more servings per pound, than fresh fish.

On the other hand, beans and rice or other grains take up water during preparation. So the protein in cooked beans or rice is less concentrated than in raw beans or rice. To compare the costs of the amount of raw beans which provide equal amount of protein with that of canned beans, the change in protein content must be taken into account.

It addles my brain to try to remember, when shopping, how much meat shrinks or beans swell on cooking. Therefore, I like to use rules that compare yield, or equivalent protein values such as are listed below.

Dry Beans Versus Canned

This rule-of-thumb takes into consideration the liquid added to the canned beans in processing:
1 POUND DRY BEANS equals about 3½ POUNDS CANNED BEANS (5½ CUPS, COOKED)

Beans, Any Kind, Versus Meats

The easiest way to compare dry or canned beans with meat, fish etc., is by number of servings per pound, with each serving having about the same amount of protein. The servings below each have about 20 grams protein, about one third the recommended daily protein intake for an average size adult:

1 POUND DRY BEANS equals 5 SERVINGS
1 POUND RAW BONELESS LEAN MEAT equals 4 SERVINGS
1 POUND RAW FAT & BONY MEAT equals 1-2 SERVINGS
1 POUND CANNED BEANS equals 1½ SERVINGS

When I Browsed on July 11, 1974

It was most illuminating! By the above rules, dry red beans were more expensive per serving than canned kidney beans, and just about the same as regular ground beef. Try it yourself. You, too, will be amazed!

	Cost per serving*
Spareribs at 98¢ lb	49¢
Regular ground beef at 79¢ lb	20¢
Golden Grain dry red beans at 99¢ lb	20¢
Co-op Canned kidney beans at 15½ oz. at 25¢	17¢
S&W Canned kidney beans at 27 oz. at 45¢	18¢
Golden Grain dry blackeyes at 65¢ lb	13¢

August, 1979 update: Here's the cost per serving of these same items about 5 years later, reflecting the various peculiar economic forces affecting different foods:

Spareribs at 1.39 lb	70¢
Regular ground beef at $1.59 lb	40¢
Golden Grain dry red beans at 60¢ lb	12¢
Co-op Canned kidney beans, 15½ oz at 40¢	28¢
S & W Canned kidney beans, 27 oz. at 70¢	28¢
Golden Grain dry blackeyes at 63¢ lb	13¢

*****Providing 20 grams of protein.**

A gassy subject

by Mary Gullberg

Shoppers keep asking the home economists which beans produce the smallest amount of gas, medically called flatus or flatulence. Well, the scientists are working on this problem and now have a few answers for us. This is important economically in light of the protein shortages worldwide, because beans and legumes are the cheapest sources of protein we have availabale to us.

They know what causes gas

Beans contain some complex carbohydrates. Humans do not have the enzymes needed to digest these compounds. However, when these substances reach the large intestine, some of the millions of bacteria present in this portion of the gut can break them down. The result is that gas is produced — largely hydrogen and carbon dioxide.

Scientists at the USDA Western Regional Research Laboratory in Albany tried to isolate these offensive carbohydrates and breed a silent bean. So far, they have failed.

How much gas is produced?

Dr. Michael Levitt, whose research was done at the University of Minnesota Medical School, has determined that the average person on a normal diet passes between 400 and 1,200 milliliters of gas daily. If one assumes as an average 800 milliliters per person, then 2,800 billion milliliters of wind is broken around the world each day. That's more than enough to fill several Goodyear blimps.

However, Dr. Louis Rockland at Western Regional Research Lab has come up with a "flatulence rating." He says his list is a preliminary one and might prove incorrect after further tests are completed. So take it with a grain of salt. Number one is the gassiest and number 10 the least:

1. Soybeans
2. Pink beans
3. Black beans
4. Pinto beans
5. California small white beans
6. Great northern beans
7. Lima beans, baby
8. Garbanzos
9. Lima beans, large
10. Blackeyes

Dr. Rockland says that cooking soybeans with an equal portion of rice eliminates about two-thirds of their flatulence. Also rumor has it that peppermint will control flatulence, and that is why there is often a dish of peppermint candy next to the cash register in restaurants.

Other suggested remedies for flatus

A San Francisco nurse writing in the American Journal of Nursing recommends headstands on the theory that gas rises. "The methods usually recommended to relieve gas pains proved either inappropriate or ineffective. Walking, though popular with the hospital staff in cases of stubborn and intractable flatulence because it gets the patient out of bed and out of sight and hearing, provides only temporary relief," nurse Ardith Blackwell wrote.

References: The list of beans is from "*The Books of Lists*" by Wallechinsky and Wallace, 1977. The rest is from an article by Donald Zochert in The Calgary Herald for July 2, 1977.

How gassy*are beans?
Listed from most to least:
1. **Soybeans**
2. **Pink beans**
3. **Black beans**
4. **Pintos**
5. **Small whites**
6. **Great Northerns**
7. **Baby Limas**
8. **Garbanzos**
9. **Large Limas**
10. **Black Eyes**

*Based on preliminary evidence.

News about nuts

by June Kadish

A favorite snack in my family is walnuts in the shell. When hunger pangs strike at 9 p.m. after a small dinner, the bowl of walnuts gets attacked by hand, hammer and nutcracker. Every so often, the shelled nut reveals a dark, dried, mysterious lump only remotely resembling a walnut kernel. A fossilized walnut? No, a mistreated one. Nuts have a high oil content and unless they are handled with tender loving care, they tend to get rancid, shrivelled and otherwise unappealing. So, cover them tightly and store in the refrigerator or freezer for the months ahead. Family, friends and neighborhood squirrels will thank you.

Prices and How to Cope

Nuts in the shell are about $1.25 per pound. About half is waste, bringing the cost of the kernels to $2.50. Shelled walnuts are $1.66 for 6½ oz. or $4 per lb. Pecans are $1.63 for 6 oz. or just over $4 per lb. At today's prices they are interchangeable. Normally, pecans are a lot more expensive. In that case, try substituting walnuts. They work in most recipes. And how about some of the soybean products which are similar to nuts? An eight ounce jar of Soy Nuts is 99¢ — half the price of tree nuts. Try grinding toasted ones in a blender or grinder for a few seconds to coarsely chop them and use in cookies and breads. Their flavor is distinctive, so be sure you like it before tossing them into the chocolate chip cookie batter.

The President's Crop

Peanuts, not botanically a nut but a legume, are probably the least expensive "nut" and are good in some cookies, homemade trail mix, or for the evening "quick, my stomach is empty" snack. A 12 oz. bag of peanuts in the shell costs 69¢.

Shopping Around

As noted above, nuts in the shell are generally less expensive then shelled nuts. One pound in the shell will yield approximately one half pound of kernels. Try to avoid nuts with cracks, holes, mold and discoloration or stains. Soft, rubbery or shrivelled kernels indicate a definite lack of that TLC we talked about before. Discard moldy nuts, as they are not safe to eat.

If preservatives are used on packaged nuts, the label will so indicate.

Jan. 22, 1979

Nuts in Shells

1 lb. of English walnuts, almonds, Brazil nuts, or pecans in the shell will yield 1 ½ to 2 cups of nut meats.

from your Co-op Home Economist

Is there a great anti-vegetable-protein-balancing conspiracy?

by Betsy Wood

"Why don't you tell people how to balance vegetable proteins?" "Why do you discourage eating vegetable protein?" "Why?" "Why?" We've gotten many such letters, some quite angry.

Some of these responses were to a line in our ad under beans. "Add a little animal protein for better utilization of bean protein." I'm getting rather defensive on this issue because I see no way that such a sentence indicates an anti-vegetable protein conspiracy.

We haven't said much about balancing of amino acids by mixing vegetable proteins because it doesn't seem to be a practical problem with many people in this country. We do encourage eating vegetable protein: we include vegetable proteins in Lifeline, we publish low-meat and no-meat recipes, and we encourage eating less meat. Here, roughly, is our position: **Americans eat too much meat.** And Americans eat almost double the protein they need. Where does the extra protein go? It becomes calories just like carbohydrate and fat. It is hard not to get enough protein if you eat a varied diet which meets your calorie needs and which includes grains, beans, dairy foods, eggs, and vegetables.

Eating most of our protein and much of our calories in animal form and eating more protein than we "need" is very wasteful of resources. *Diet for a Small Planet* by Frances Lappe is a terribly important book, because it awakened many people to this possibility.

My family's personal response in the last few years (and maybe the response of the Co-op home economists and other nutritionists) has been to cut way down on meat and to increase use of grains and beans but not to cut out meat altogether. Many people are vegetarians for moral, religious, health or ecological reasons. I think the home economists have been supportive of people who've decided to cut out meat completely. From a practical standpoint we probably end up with more "protein saved" by convincing many people to cut down on meat and excess protein than to convince a few to be vegetarians. But I feel: to each his/her own.

Protein balancing should be no problem for vegetarians who eat milk, cheese and eggs. "Having a little animal food at each meal" is good advice. (Example: milk complements protein of oatmeal.)

Strict vegetarians (no dairy products or eggs) may need some advice on balancing proteins. The main thing to remember is that grains and beans (or other legumes such as peanuts) COMPLEMENT EACH OTHER. Also a wide variety of food is important. Protein balancing becomes more important when protein intake is very low. I don't think the detailed balancing advocated by Ms. Lappe is necessary in this country.

Protein may be the least of your problems if you are a vegetarian.

In the average American diet meat, milk and eggs provide 1/3-2/3 of the major vitamins and minerals except vitamin C. Milk is important for calcium and riboflavin. Meat provides iron, niacin, zinc. Vitamin B-12 is found only in animal foods. As we decrease the sources of our food, we decrease the chance that we will meet all our nutrient needs. This doesn't mean it's impossible, but strict vegetarian diets need careful planning for all nutrients, not just protein.

Experimental evidence seems to indicate that it's possible to plan an adequate strict vegetarian diet for healthy adults. I don't think we know enough to say such diets will be adequate for children, pregnant women or people in poor health.

Pinto Bean Fruit Cake

2 cups well-cooked pinto beans
1/4 cup cooking liquid from beans
1/2 cup butter or margarine
1 cup sugar
2 teaspoons vanilla
1 egg, unbeaten
1 cup sifted all-purpose flour
1 teaspoon soda

1/2 teaspoon salt
1 teaspoon cinnamon
1/2 teaspoon ground cloves
1/2 teaspoon allspice
1/2 teaspoon mace
2 cups finely chopped peeled apples
1 cup seedless raisins
1/2 cut walnuts or pecans, chopped

Mash beans with bean liquid thoroughly, using potato masher or electric mixer. Cream butter, add sugar gradually, beating until fluffy. Add vanilla and whole egg. Beat well, then beat in the mashed beans. Mix thoroughly. Sift together flour, soda, salt and spices. Add half the flour to the batter and stir until just mixed. Then add the apples, raisins, nuts and remaining flour mixture. Stir until just mixed. Spoon into buttered 9-inch tube cake pan. Bake at 350° for 1 hour. May be served with a hard sauce if desired, but is very nice served plain.

from the Idaho Bean Commission

Breads and cereal foods

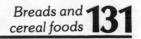

Parboiled White Rice

such as Uncle Ben's and Golden Pearl has been specially treated to retain vitamins.
Whole rice kernels are steeped in hot water before milling. This lets the water soluble vitamins in the bran and germ soak into the kernel.
Nutritive values are better than enriched white rice but not as good as brown.
from your Co-op Home Economist

Grains . . . odd and interesting

by Helen Black and Betsy Wood

Who eats grains? Who eats all that corn, wheat, oats, barley, rye, millet, rice?

Well, everybody. All of us chickens, cows, hogs, and humans eat grains. In fact, 70 percent of what we humans of the world eat is grain! Either we eat it directly, or we eat the chickens, the cows, the hogs who eat it directly.

We're on quite intimate terms with processed grains such as flour, bread, breakfast cereals. But now the Co-op is carrying the whole grain seeds, merely harvested, threshed and cleaned, in the bulk sections of our produce departments. These are strange, unfamiliar. How does one cook these hard kernels of barley, rye, wheat? Searching for answers to this question and others, we stumbled over odd and interesting facts about whole as well as processed grain.

Grains are not fashionable in the U.S.

In some parts of the world people get 60 percent of their calories from grain or grain products, eaten directly. Here we get only 21 percent of our calories from such foods. We used to eat more! In 1969 we each ate 114 pounds of grain foods; 50 years earlier it was 309 pounds per year. Now, we spend only 13 percent of our food dollars for grains, though from grains we get 20-40 percent of our protein, iron and the three major B vitamins.

Grains, processing, nutriton

Some processing, such as refining wheat into white flour, results in loss of important nutrients, which is partly compensated in the enrichment of white flour and rice. Other processing is less damaging:

Parboiled rice is more nutritious than regular white rice. While both are enriched with iron, thiamine and niacin, parboiled rice such as Uncle Ben's Converted Rice contains over twice the vitamin B$_6$ that ordinary white rice contains and almost ¾ of that of brown rice. That's because this process involves steaming the rice before milling, during which some of the water-soluble nutrients are absorbed into the white kernel.

Microflaked wheat or rye are whole grains. They have been briefly heated (5 seconds at 220 degrees) and then rolled to crush them slightly. The nutritive value of these whole but slightly crushed grains should be good, and they are fairly fast cooking. Because they are more tender, too, when cooked, they may be more acceptable to people unaccustomed to the chewiness of relatively hard-to-digest wheat berries.

Cooking guide for whole grains

Start with one cup of grain in two cups of water or broth and ½ teaspoon of salt. Cook until done. Here is a rough guide for time:

About 15-30 minutes: Cracked wheat, bulgur, white rice, buckwheat, microflaked wheat or rye (millet 35 minutes).

About 45-60 minutes, sometimes more: brown rice, barley, whole oats, triticale, rye.

Two hours: wheat berries.

Pressure cooking works well for long-cooking grains; brown rice cooks in eight minutes.

4-19-76

Wheat and wheat products

Wheat is the grain of a grass that probably originated in the Euphrates Valley thousands of years ago. It is the most widely grown of all cereal grains. In the United States, the colonists brought wheat to our country quite early but, because the climate on the east coast was unfavorable, it was not until the middle west was opened to homesteading that wheat became a major crop.

The wheat grain has three main parts: 1) the outer covering, the bran, 2) the inner part, which is largely starch, called the endosperm, and 3) the tiny nucleus within the endosperm, the wheat germ which is responsible for the sprouting of the wheat kernel. If the entire wheat kernel (also called the wheat berry) is ground, we have whole wheat (or graham) flour. If only the endosperm is ground, we have white flour. Hard or soft wheats are used for making various kinds of flour: soft wheat for pastry, cake and all-purpose flours, and hard wheats for bread flours and pasta. Many all-purpose flours are mixtures of hard and soft wheats and so contain enough high-quality gluten (found more abundantly in hard wheat) to make satisfactory bread when well kneaded.

Store flours at cool room temperatures in tightly closed containers. Whole wheat flour should be stored in as cool a place as possible and not kept for more than three months unless refrigerated. The whole wheat products all tend to become rancid due to the presence of fat in the wheat germ. Because the germ is missing in white flour, it can be stored much longer than whole wheat.

In most states, the law requires that all white flour and products made from it must be enriched — the levels of thiamin, riboflavin, niacin and iron are restored to about their original levels in the whole grain. (Nutrients *not* added back include zinc, vitamin B$_6$ and others.) These products must also be nutrition labeled and also have an ingredient statement. You may wonder why malted barley is added to most white flours. It is added to standardize the enzyme level so the yeast action will be more uniform from batch to batch of white flour.

Besides the various types of wheat flours, wheat is marketed as the whole wheat berry, cracked wheat which is the berry coarsely ground, hot and cold breakfast cereals, bulgur (parboiled wheat), wheat flakes, wheat germ and various kinds of crackers.

Wheat Berry Pilaf

Wheat berry pilaf makes a nice substitute for rice with Chinese dishes when prepared like fried rice or pilaf.

¼ cup butter or margarine
1 onion, diced
½ pound mushrooms
½ cup beef or chicken broth
   (or use ½ cup water and 1 bouillon cube)
1 teaspoon basil or other spices
3 cups cooked wheat berries

Sauté onion and mushrooms in butter until onion is transparent. Add broth or water and bouillon cube and spices. Add wheat berries and simmer for 10 minutes or until wheat berries are heated through.

Variations: Top with cheese and heat under the broiler to melt the cheese. Various types of vegetables and cheese can be added to give new flavors and textures. Makes 6 ½-cup servings.

A pasta primer

Simply defined, pasta is a dough made from semolina and water. Semolina is the heart of the durum wheat, high in gluten which contributes the protein to grains. All pastas, of which there are more than one hundred varieties, are made from this basic dough. The different shapes are produced either by forcing the dough through a variety of perforated metal plates, forming in molds, or pressing through rollers before drying. Egg noodles are made from the same basic mixture to which at least 5.5% of egg solids must be added. Vegetable macaroni is pasta to which not less than 3% vegetable solids have been added. These vegetables may include tomato, artichoke, beet, carrot, parsley or spinach, either fresh, canned or dried. It is difficult to analyze the precise nutritive value of these vegetable pastas. Both the egg solids and vegetable solids contribute a small plus to the diet, but probably not of any great significance.

Some of the more imaginative Italian names for pasta include farfalloni (big butterflies), linguini (little tongues), occhi di lupo (wolf's eyes), rigatoni (little fluted ones), vermicelli (little worms), and stelline (little stars). Not all of these are widely available, but many are fun to use as a change.

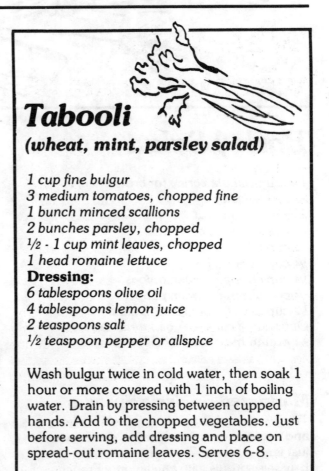

Tabooli
(wheat, mint, parsley salad)

1 cup fine bulgur
3 medium tomatoes, chopped fine
1 bunch minced scallions
2 bunches parsley, chopped
½ - 1 cup mint leaves, chopped
1 head romaine lettuce
Dressing:
6 tablespoons olive oil
4 tablespoons lemon juice
2 teaspoons salt
½ teaspoon pepper or allspice

Wash bulgur twice in cold water, then soak 1 hour or more covered with 1 inch of boiling water. Drain by pressing between cupped hands. Add to the chopped vegetables. Just before serving, add dressing and place on spread-out romaine leaves. Serves 6-8.

-from Fisher Ala package

Delightfully different: Bulgur

Bulgur is a food which may be made from several varieties of wheat. The bulgur is processed by boiling whole grain wheat, drying it, removing some of the outside bran particles and cracking the kernel. For many centuries, bulgur has been produced in various countries of the world where hand methods are used.

Today, modern food technology has provided methods for mass production of bulgur making it widely available. It may be of fine, medium or coarse grain, depending on the need for different granulations for various cooking uses. Bulgur is a versatile, nutritious product roughly comparable to brown rice in nutrients. It may be used as a cereal, an ingredient in soup or salad, a side dish with the main course, or as the main dish when a small amount of meat, fish, poultry or cheese is added. It can be substituted for rice in most menus and recipes. Some people may find that the roughage in bulgur is more than their digestive systems can easily tolerate. If so, we suggest combining bulgur with enriched white rice for a colorful, tasty combination.

Barley Salad

1½ cups whole barley (or brown rice)
2½ cups water
1½ teaspoons salt
¼ cup lemon juice
⅓ cup oil
¼ cup chopped parsley
¼ cup chopped green onions
¼ cup chopped green peppers
½ cup pitted, ripe olives, halved
Optional: 2 cans (6-7 oz.) tuna, drained
¾ pound marinated Brussels sprouts

Bring water and salt to a boil, add barley. When water simmers reduce heat, cover, cook 35 minutes or until barley is just tender and water is absorbed. Toss cooked barley with lemon juice and oil. Chill. Mix remaining ingredients with barley, garnish with marinated Brussels sprouts (see below). If tuna is used, this makes a main dish for 8, each with 17 gms. protein.

Marinated Brussels Sprouts

Trim ¾ pound Brussels sprouts, slice lengthwise and cook in water barely to cover. Cook until just tender, about 7 or 8 minutes. Toss hot Brussels sprouts with any favorite French dressing and chill several hours. Drain; serve as hors d'oeuvre or in salad above.

Questions and answers on bread enrichment

Question: What does enrichment of breads and cereals mean?

Answer: It simply means adding to refined flour, bread and cereals the most important vitamins and minerals lost in the milling. Specifically, this means restoring thiamine, riboflavin, niacin and iron to the level present in the whole grain products.

Q. If extra fat, milk solids, sugar, eggs, etc. are added to give richness, why is it necessary to add vitamins and minerals?

A. While these ingredients improve the flavor, and some of them may improve nutritional qualities somewhat, they do not add thiamine, riboflavin, niacin or iron in sufficient amount.

Q. Why don't you forget about adding things to white bread and promote the use of whole grain cereals only?

A. For years nutritionists have tried to do this. However, the widespread acceptance of white bread and refined cereals makes it imperative that these products be made nutritionally as close as possible to the whole grain products.

Enriched Flour

is refined flour to which thiamine, riboflavin, niacin, and iron have been added in amounts that "restore" these nutrients to about the levels in whole wheat flour.

from your Co-op Home Economist

Q. Do foods made with unbleached flour need to be enriched?

A. Yes. White flour needs enrichment whether it is bleached or unbleached. It is the milling of flour that takes away the B vitamins and iron.

Q. What about white rice? Should it be enriched?

A. Yes. However, enrichment of rice differs in that riboflavin, a yellowish vitamin, is not added because of technical problems. Note: the added vitamins and iron will be washed off.

Flour Power

by Joan Taylor, Home Economist

A question often asked by shoppers:

I see many kinds of flour in the store. What are their basic differences and how can I use them?

1. Whole wheat flour

Made from the whole kernel of wheat and contains the bran as well as the germ. It has more minerals, vitamins and slightly more protein than enriched white flour. Because of higher fat content, whole wheat flour does not keep as well as white flour.

2. All-purpose flour

Usually made from fairly hard wheat and is satisfactorily used for quick breads, raised or fermented breads, and pie crust. It may contain too much gluten to make delicate textured cakes but can make successful cakes that have a high fat or high sugar contant such as butter cakes, pound cakes, fruit cakes and cookies.

3. Cake and pastry flour

These flours are both made from soft wheat and have a low gluten contant. Cake flour is bleached and is the most finely ground of all the flours. It is soft and satiny. Chief use is for cakes and pastries but may be used for quick breads. These flours may be more desirable for waffles than all-purpose flour because they make a more tender product.

4. Bleached and unbleached

Both whole wheat and white flours may be

bleached or unbleached. Bleached is chemically treated to age it and unbleached is aged naturally. Because the "age" of unbleached flour varies, the handling of yeast doughs may not be consistent from batch to batch. Aging improves rising power.

5. Self-rising flour

This is refined bleached flour that contains leavening and salt in proper proportions for home baking. The leavening will lose its potency if stored too long. This is not recommended for making bread or pastry.

Wheat flour is the most extensively used flour because of its high content of the protein gluten. The only other flour that contains much gluten is rye. Gluten is important for its binding and stretching qualities making it possible for yeast breads to have a high volume and a fine texture. It stretches and forms an elastic framework to enclose bubbles of gas produced by the yeast. In other baked products, fat and/or sugar cut the gluten strands, thus making a more tender product.

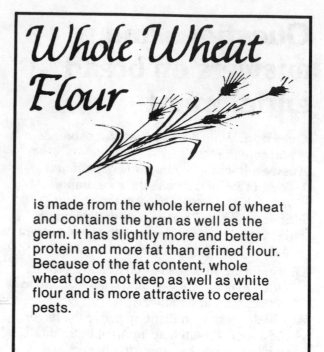

Whole Wheat Flour

is made from the whole kernel of wheat and contains the bran as well as the germ. It has slightly more and better protein and more fat than refined flour. Because of the fat content, whole wheat does not keep as well as white flour and is more attractive to cereal pests.

from your Co-op Home Economist

Whole wheat bread has more: true or false?

1. Whole wheat bread has better protein, more vitamins and more minerals than enriched white bread, other ingredients being equal.

   True. Several essential nutrients in whole flour are largely lost in the milling and are not added back in the enriching, including magnesium, calcium, potassium, phosphorus, manganese, molybdenum, vitamin B_6, pantothenic acid and vitamin E.

2. The darker the color of bread, the more whole wheat flour it contains and the more nutritious it is.

   False. Many breads have caramel color added, including some "wheat" breads and many rye or pumpernickel breads. Some very dark breads have less whole grain wheat or rye than lighter colored breads. Egg breads or rolls frequently have yellow color added. Read the ingredient statement.

3. Breads called "Wheat Bread" and those with fancy names such as "Natural," "Ecology" etc. are just as nutritious as Whole Wheat bread.

   False. We advise you to regard fanciful names with suspicion. The magic in a name doesn't extend to transforming ingredients! "Wheat" breads and breads with seemingly wholesome names often have less whole wheat flour than enriched white flour. They are usually less nutritious than breads made with all whole wheat flour.

4. Cakes and cookies made with whole wheat flour are just about as nutritious as whole wheat bread.

   False. Sorry about this! Whole wheat cookies and cake still have much larger proportions of fat and sugar than bread does and so less whole wheat. Therefore they are lower in vitamins and minerals than just good old whole wheat bread.

Cheese Pretzels

Pre-heat oven to 425° F. — VERY IMPORTANT
1 pkg. active dry yeast
1½ cups warm water
1 teaspoon salt
1 tablespoon sugar

4 cups flour
8 oz. grated sharp cheddar cheese
1 egg, beaten with a fork
2 tablespoons coarse salt (Kosher salt)

In a large bowl dissolve yeast with warm water. Stir in salt and sugar, then flour and cheese — alternating. Save ½ c. of flour in case dough sticks later. Knead dough until smooth. Form a ball. With a sharp knife cut ball into 32 pieces. Roll each piece into a rope 14 inches long and twist into pretzel shape. Place on ungreased cookie sheet. Brush with beaten egg. Sprinkle with coarse salt. Bake immediately — 425°F. oven for 18 minutes.

Note: This yeast containing recipe does not require raising. Also for those who keep a Kosher home, this recipe should be omitted since it contains cheese.

The recipe for these pretzels came from Eugene Bondi and Cindy Grisham, both from Oakland Technical High School.

What do you save by making bread at home? *by Mary Gullberg*

To find the answer to this question, we took recipes for two of our Co-op label breads and costed them out at current, regular prices. When we compared the cost of the homemade breads with their store equivalents, we found:

Co-op Special Formula Bread 1½ pounds
    Store-bought $ .83
    Homemade   .39 Saving of about 53%
Co-op Whole Wheat Bread 1 pound
    Store-bought   .73
    Homemade   .25 Saving of about 66%

Further savings can be achieved if ingredients such as flour and non-fat dry milk were purchased when these were on sale. The yeast, instead of being purchased in individual packets, could be purchased in larger amounts and stored in a closed container in the refrigerator.

How much time does it take to make bread at home? Depending on the amount you make, how long you knead it, the temperature of the proofing arrangement (rising of the dough) and how many times you let it rise, the total time for the entire process will vary a bit. However, it seems reasonable to allow at least four hours. So you need to plan to be home for this length of time. Of course, you can at the same time do the ironing, house cleaning, sewing or whatever.

To make the best use of your bread making time, make three or four loaves at a time and freeze the extra ones. If you have a small family, you might make smaller sized loaves. Larger families or those that take bag lunches with sandwiches will be able to use the larger sized loaves easily.

Co-op News Sept. 25, 1978

Is "Wheat" bread whole wheat? NO!

"Wheat" breads are usually made mostly from white flour. For example, Co-op Wheat Balloon Bread is only 18% whole wheat flour.

MORAL: Read the label!

Try it — you'll like it *by Mary Ruth Nelson*

Working with yeast doughs can be an exhilarating and satisfying experience. This is dedicated to those who exclaim over home baked breads, but have never tried making them.

I can still remember so clearly, and it was long ago, shivering in the hot summertime while making mud pies. How I loved to mix and shape the muddy mixture into "pie shells" which would later be filled with assorted flower petals and leaves. But, how I hated the feeling when the mud dried on my hands and left me shivering!

A decade after mud pies, I discovered yeast doughs. How delightful the dough felt while kneading and what fun it was to make it into various shapes and forms by braiding, tying, twisting, stretching, rolling or cutting. And, if I used a little flour, the dough didn't stick and then dry on my hands. That was even better than mudpies.

You can do it too! And down with the excuses!

EXCUSE No. 1. There's no time to make bread because of the 40-hour work week.

That's a matter of priorities. All you need is to be available for small periods of time when the dough needs attention — it doesn't need to be watched every minute. For instance, on a Saturday morning, you can garden, saw, plant, clean, paint, sew or even run short errands to the store while the dough is rising. And, after a few tries, the whole process will probably take no more than 3½ hours from start to finish.

The time schedule runs like this:

Assembling ingredients and mixing	**20 minutes**
First rising	**45 minutes**
Second rising	**30 minutes**
Shaping dough into loaves	**10 minutes**
Rising of dough in pans	**60 minutes**
(pre-heat oven the last 10 minutes of rising time.)	
Bake at 375 degrees	**15 minutes**
Bake at 325 degrees	**25 minutes**
	————————
Total	**205 minutes**
	(about 3½ hours)

EXCUSE NO. 2 It takes an expert to make good bread.

NO WAY! Experienced bakers accept the fact that the bread will vary from time to time because of the protein content of the flour, the freshness of the yeast, temperature variations while doughs are rising, or just plain differences in mixing techniques from one batch to another. You can do the same.

Helpful suggestions for the beginner:

(1) Keep the dough warm but not too warm. Growing yeast (in the dough) prefers a temperature about 80 degrees — this is slightly warmer than the usual room temperature. However, avoid a temperature above 90 degrees as it will kill the yeast; if that happens, the dough will rise no more and, if baked, will be "as heavy as a ton of lead."

(2) Use unbleached all-purpose white flour or half all-purpose flour and half whole-grain flour. Until you get the "feel" of yeast doughs, it is better not to use only whole-grain flours. The latter, though more tasty in breads and more nutritious, will produce a coarser and heavier product than white flours. And it would be all too easy to equate the "heavy" product with failure.

To this day, I am envious of the potters shaping clay with their hands (likening it to making mud pies), but I revel in the fact that they cannot boast of a wonderful fragrance when "baking" their wares.

Why lime in corn tortillas?

by Mary Gullberg

The ingredient statement on La Tolteca Corn Tortillas is very simple: corn, water and lime (calcium hydroxide). We have had objections from shoppers to the lime which they fear might be harmful.

Let's talk about it. Corn tortillas are the ethnic "bread" from old Mexico using the native corn. It was the "staff of life" for most Indians in Mexico long before the white man introduced his favorite foods. Whole corn is soaked in a weak solution of lime (originally derived from birdlime prepared from holly bark or from limestone) to loosen the outer hull. When this is removed, the germ remains with the kernel and small traces of lime are present in the corn. The corn is then ground, mixed with water, pressed into flat cakes and baked on a flat hot surface. This limed cornmeal has a characteristic flavor.

Nutritionists tell us that the small amounts of calcium from the lime remaining in the corn tortillas contribute appreciable calcium to the Mexican diet when lots of tortillas are eaten and practically no dairy foods. Jack cheese is about the only dairy food eaten by Mexicans even today in sizeable amounts.

Lime (calcium hydroxide) is caustic in concentrated form and can cause skin burns. However, in the small amounts found in the finished tortilla, it is perfectly harmless and probably beneficial.

Scientists have now come up with another "educated guess" as to why the corn tortillas were such a vital part of the traditional Mexican diet. This diet was low in animal protein and corn was one of the main sources of protein. In our southern states pellagra was endemic in the poor population in the early 1900s, eating a diet high in cornmeal and low or lacking in animal protein. This cornmeal was not treated with lime as the Mexican corn was and it did not contain the germ. Unfortunately, corn is rich in an antivitamin that knocks out the vitamin, niacin. Corn is also low in tryptophan, one of the amino acids in proteins that the body cannot make and that therefore must be present in sufficient amounts in our foods. Tryptophan can be converted to niacin if there is enough present in the diet to first meet the protein need. But since the cornmeal was low in tryptophan, this couldn't happen and the poor people developed pellagra.

Native American Indians living in the plains of the United States and Mexico did not develop pellagra because they used wood ashes in their cooking. The ashes added lye which, like lime, produced alkaline conditions in the foods. This, so the present theory goes, inhibited the antivitamin, allowing the niacin present in the corn to be used by the body. Thus the niacin plus the tryptophan was available in sufficient amounts in the Indian diets to prevent the development of the deficiency disease, pellagra.

We need to have respect for native foods. They have been developed over many thousands of years of trial and error. They are, for the most part, beautifully tailored to meet the nutritional needs of the people eating them.

Cereals

Champion of breakfasts?

A report by Co-op Home Economists originally printed in Co-op News December 30, 1974. Revised July 1979.

Question

Is cereal enough breakfast every day?

Answer

It is if you add orange juice and milk and maybe toast—and, if it's a "good" cereal.

Question

So? What's a good cereal?

Answer

One good cereal would be any whole grain, simmered in milk. A poor cereal is a high-sugar cereal such as Sugar Pops (which are up to half their weight in sugar—and sometimes more sugar is added at the table). Also not recommended are those super-fortified cereals with 100% of the Recommended Daily Allowance for vitamins (Kellogg's Concentrate, Total, Product 19 and many others) because you can get TOO MUCH of some vitamins, especially of vitamins A and D.

What you should expect of a cereal

This is hard to decide. Joan Gussow states well the argument for whole grains (see below). Cereal should contain the minerals, vitamins, protein, carbohydrate and fiber of the original grain. And of course it should taste good.

We have been exploring and pondering the criteria for rating cereals. We have finally agreed on these:

• Whole grain cereal is best.

• HOT cereal is generally more nutritious than cold.

• Added sugar is BAD, especially at the levels of 30-35 percent found in the sugared cereals.

• Fortification, if done at all, should be at moderate and uniform levels (about 25 percent of the Recommended Daily allowance).

Joan Gussow, professor of nutrition education at Columbia Teachers College, has this comment on cereal fortification.

"The question is whether it is OK to enrich garbage. We simply don't know enough to keep someone alive on enriched garbage. The fact is that at present we take out of cereal grains all kinds of vitamins and minerals and then we "enrich" them by putting back in only those which science in its infinite wisdom has shown to be 'essential.'

"The obvious answer to what a cereal ought to contain is that it ought to contain those nutrients normally found in cereal grains, i.e., most of the trace minerals, the whole B-vitamin complex, naturally unsaturated oils, iron and protein, leaving it to other foods (e.g., fruit, fruit juices, milk, butter) to supply calcium and vitamins A, C and D at breakfast.

"Moreover, I am waging war on the side of 'natural' foods because we just don't know enough about nutritional requirements — especially where the trace elements are concerned — to take the chance of not eating natural foods."

Whole grains are best

When grains are milled, many of the nutrients are removed in the outer layers and germ. When grains are fortified, some of these nutrients are added back but others are not. With the American diet becoming increasingly refined, these "minor" nutrients may be in more critical supply in our diets.

While it is true that the natural balance of nutrients in a grain has evolved for the growth and reproduction of that grain, not for the benefit of animals and man, we favor the likelihood that whole grains, with their original nutrients, are superior foods to highly refined grains with added nutrients.

"Hot" cereal is generally more nutritious than "Cold" cereal

When cold (ready-to-eat) cereals are manufactured, they are subject to a lot of processing including hot, dry heat to make them crisp. This hot, dry heat is more destructive of nutrients such as thiamin and protein than is the moist heat at which hot cereals are cooked at home. (Some hot cereals such as Wheatena are toasted so we can't make a blanket statement that all hot cereals have been processed in a nutrient-saving manner.)

We suggest that you *cook hot cereals in milk.* We have found that people put much too little milk in a bowl of cooked hot cereal (it's already moist) than they do on a bowl of dry cereal. So, unless everyone is drinking some milk for breakfast, why not simmer the cereal in milk? (Example: Add ⅔ cup dry milk and ½ teaspoon salt to 2 cups water. Then add 1 cup rolled oats and simmer 5 minutes.) Other longer-cooking grains can also be cooked in milk, but you may want to use a double boiler. Another advantage: milk consumed at breakfast sticks with you through the morning so you are less hungry than with a predominantly carbohydrate meal. The protein in the milk also complements the protein in the cereal.

Rolled Oats

Regular rolled oats are made by simply rolling the oat grain flat.

To make quick cooking oats, the kernel is cut into several pieces and then rolled.

Food values of the two are about the same.

Added sugar is bad

Presweetened "cereals" have as much sugar as cookies or cakes

We think that "cereal" is not a proper term for presweetened cereals which contain 30-55% sugar and sometimes more. A serving of cereal is about one ounce, so 50% of this is about a tablespoon (3 teaspoons) of sugar.

While it's possible (but not likely) for someone to add this much sugar at the table to any cereal, it's impossible to separate out the sugar in a high-sugar cereal. Besides, some people add no sugar to cereal, and many add just a little.

How much sugar?

When we first printed *Cereal, Champion of Breakfasts?*, we wrote to every cereal company asking for their product's composition including approximate percent of sugar. Most told us it was a trade secret although testing for sugar is a simple matter for those with a laboratory. Finally, in the spring of 1976, Kellogg's started listing the amount of added sugar and the other cereal companies eventually followed suit. The problem is that sugar is stated as grams per ounce which is less meaningful than percentage of added sugar by weight.

When reading labels keep in mind that 1 ounce of cereal weighs about 28 grams and 1 tablespoon of sugar weighs about 12 grams. So, Cap'n Crunch which lists 12 grams of sucrose and other sugars per ounce contains 1 tablespoon sugar in an average serving or approximately 43% sugar (12 divided by 28). Some consumer groups suggest that any cereal with a sugar content about 25 or 30% should not be called cereal but "sugared breakfast food."

What's so bad about sugar?

The average American eats more than 100 pounds of sugar a year, for which he/she gets no nutritional benefits other than calories. Regular white sugar is 100 percent carbohydrate with NO vitamins or minerals. (Brown sugar, raw sugar and honey aren't much better.) Most nutrition authorities say that 100 pounds of sugar per person is too much. Why? 1) Sugar definitely contributes to cavities, especially in children; 2) high sugar consumption means that there isn't as much room in the diet for better foods; 3) current research has found a relationship between high sugar intake and high blood fat levels, which is suspected of contributing to heart disease.

The high-sugar cereals are mostly low in protein and without fortification they would be low in other nutrients. Sugar simply replaces the grain with its protein, vitamins and minerals.

High sugar cereals are often eaten as snacks. This is even harder on teeth than is sugary cereal eaten with milk for breakfast because the milk and other foods help wash the sugar away from the teeth.

Percent added sugar

There is no added sugar in most hot cereals, and in Shredded Wheat, Puffed Rice and Puffed Wheat.

Sucrose and other sweeteners in 1 ounce cereal (Divide grams sugar by 28, multiply by 100 to get %)

	Grams
1-11%	
Cheerios	1
Corn Flakes	2
Grapenuts	3
Product 19	3
Rice Chex	2
Rice Krispies	3
Wheat Chex	2
Wheaties	3
12-20%	
Life	5
Team	5
21-30%	
All Bran	6
Cinnamon Life	6
Corn Bran	6
C.W. Post	7
Fortified Oat Flakes	6
Granolas	approx. 9
Most	8
40% Bran	7
100% Bran	6
100% Natural	8
30-55%	
Golden Grahams	11
Kellogg's and Post Raisin Bran	9 and 13
All sugar cereals	10-16

Fortification should be moderate

This is a complicated subject. Ideally our diet of food would contain all the nutrients we need. But even on a "good" diet it is hard for some people to get enough of certain nutrients — such as iron. Most ready-to-eat breakfast cereals are fortified with about eight nutrients, added at levels higher than in whole grains. This could be good for those people who are low in these nutrients and a waste for others. When we have listed hot, whole-grain cereals above refined, fortified, ready-to-eat cereals, it is based on our judgment from an accumulation of data rather than on specific research showing one is superior to the other.

You can get too much especially of vitamins A and D, which accumulate in the body. We see no reason for a single bowl of cereal to carry 100 percent of the vitamins and minerals listed as mandatory on nutrient labels. These "cereals" are essentially vitamin pills in a sugar-grain flake, puff or blob. A child of five eating two one-ounce bowls of cereal a day would eat four times his Recommended Daily Allowance of vitamin A just from cereal. When you add vitamin A from milk, other foods and a vitamin pill, the child could be getting a toxic level of vitamin A over a long period.

While the hazard of too much vitamin A or D is well documented there are potential problems with imbalance of other nutrients. Examples: Increased consumption of one mineral may change the need for another mineral. Calcium and phosphorous should be consumed in approximately equal quantities daily, according to the RDA. The need for certain B vitamins is proportional to calories consumed.

Very high protein diets may increase the need for other nutrients. Long-term consumption of high levels of vitamin C may increase the need for that vitamin. These are just some of the examples of why fortification and vitamin supplementation are tricky business.

> **More is not better.**
> We suggest you **avoid** breakfast cereals with 100% of the Recommended Daily Allowance of vitamins A or D.
> High intakes of vitamins A or D from cereals, added to that in milk, other foods and pills, can lead to excessive intakes.
> If cereal does contain vitamins A or D, it is better to have these at low levels (25-33% of the U.S. Recommended Daily Allowance) than at the 100% level.

Some other considerations

Fiber

. . . the forgotten substance

Fiber is the indigestible carbohydrate which does not provide calories but which helps move everything along inside your digestive tract. There has been an increased interest in fiber recently.

Some nutritionists question whether Americans in their highly refined white-sugar-white-flour diets are getting enough fiber. They speculate that lack of fiber may be related to increases in colon cancer, diverticulosis and other intestinal diseases. Whole-grain cereals contain much more fiber than refined cereals. Bran cereals contain the most fiber of all but often they contain added sugar and/or fat.

Recently, eating unprocessed bran has become a popular way of adding extra fiber to the diet. We don't have much information on the long-range effects of this practice but we have been told that eating excess bran is probably not dangerous. Large amounts of bran generally cause gas, diarrhea and discomfort so that a person tends to eat only what he/she can tolerate. We recommend that people get fiber by eating unrefined basic foods such as beans and dried peas, fruits, vegetables and whole grains. These foods provide fiber as well as being good sources of a wide variety of nutrients.

Fat

. . . why add to cereal?

Many cereals are low in fat, containing less than one gram in a one-ounce serving. But that pattern and the type of fat added are changing. Some of the cereals contain coconut or palm oil. Even though these oils are from vegetable sources, they are as saturated as some animal fats. This is a problem because diets high in saturated fats are thought to be one of the causes of heart disease. Granolas contain considerable added fat: about 20 percent or 6 grams per one-ounce serving. While the oil is usually not coconut or palm oil but one of the unsaturated vegetable oils, the fat does add many unnecessary calories and substitutes for the grain. We recommend selecting cereals with little or no added fat.

Additives

Some people want to avoid artificial colors or flavors or other additives such as preservatives or stabilizers. Most hot cereals, most granolas and a few other ready-to-eat cereals do not contain additives. To be sure, read the label.

Premiums

We've seen recommendations NOT to buy cereals with premiums. This is rather hard for a cereal-eating family to do because except for granolas, Co-op cereals and Kellogg's Concentrate, most ready-to-eat cereals have some kind of a "premium" or offer.

Basic Granola—Make it at home!

3 tablespoons margarine or oil
¼-½ cup brown sugar or honey (optional)
¼ teaspoon salt
¼ cup water
3 cups regular (not quick) rolled oats

Melt margarine; add sugar, salt and water. Cool slightly and pour over oats. Toss gently to blend and spread about ¼ inch in a shallow baking pan. Bake at 350 degrees for 15-20 minutes, or at 250 degrees for 25-30 minutes. Stir once or twice during baking period until mixture is a golden brown. Cool and store in covered container in a cool place. Serve with milk and some kind of fruit — fresh, canned or dried.

Variations: Add any of the following before or after toasting the oats mixture, to taste:
   ¼-½ cup wheat germ
   sunflower seeds
   chopped nuts

Consider the cost of cornflakes

One ounce equals one serving; 1 pound equals 16 servings

	PRICE PER LB.
Kellogg's Cornflakes	.84¢
Kellogg's Sugar Frosted Flakes	1.08

(Identical ingredients but Kellogg's Frosted Flakes higher in sugar)

Wheaties	1.11
Total	1.48

(Same ingredients but Total has higher levels of vitamins added.)

Cost per year for family of 5
If cereal eaten daily . . .

	Price Per Lb.	Price Per Year
Rye (Microflaked)	29¢	33.00
Rolled Oats	35¢	40.00
Wheat Chex or Granola	89¢	101.00
Cherrios	1.21	138.00
Snack Pak (6)	1.76	201.00
Apple Jacks	1.82	207.00
Kellogg's Concentrate	2.93	334.00

Priced July 1979

Beware of the OFFER MONSTER

He has an offer on every cereal box. But really the **OFFER MONSTER** just wants your money — on another box of cereal.

from your Co-op Home Economist

The List

Numbered in the order of our recommendation of cereals available at the Co-op (with cost per pound based on June '79 prices)

Recommended cereals

1 WHOLE GRAIN NON-COMMERCIAL
Found at Co-op Natural Food, Basic Food and in bulk sections and rice shelf at Co-op Food Stores.

	PRICE PER POUND
Barley (whole)	26¢
Brown Rice	39¢
Cornmeal (Whole)	27¢
Mixtures 4 Grain	36¢
Mixtures 9 Grain	54¢
Oats (Whole)	33¢
Oats (Steel Cut)	37¢
Oats (rolled)	35¢
Rye (Whole)	33¢
Rye (Microflake)	29¢
Triticale	26¢
Wheatberries	29¢
Wheat (Cracked)	41¢
Wheat (Microflake)	45¢
Wheat (Bulgur)	50¢

2 COMMERCIAL WHOLE GRAIN CEREALS

Instant Ralston	61¢
Roman Meal	59¢
Rolled Oats	38-65¢
Wheatena	65¢
Zoom	61¢

3 WHOLE GRAIN CEREALS
14% Sugar or Less

PRICE PER LB.

Back to Nature	78¢
Familia No Sugar Cereal	2.12
Grapenuts	91¢-1.05
Grapenut Flakes	1.06
Puffed Wheat	83¢
Shredded Wheat	95¢-1.04
Skinner's Raisin Bran	1.13
Uncle Sam Cereal	91¢
Wheat Chex	89¢-99¢
Wheaties	1.11-1.19

OK cereals

4 OTHER HOT CEREALS
Not Whole Grain

Alber's Quick Grits	32-35¢
Cornmeal	21-47¢
Cream of Rice	82¢
Cream of Wheat	53¢
Mix 'N Eat	1.30
Hominy Grits	43-46¢
Wheat Hearts	53¢
Malt-O-Meal	50¢
Maypo	94¢
Oats, Instant (Plain)	1.25-1.50

5 WHOLE GRAIN OK,
but most are fairly high in sugar or fat.

Alpen	1.25
Buckwheats	1.38
C.W. Post	1.12
Familia	1.83-2.12
Fortified Oat Flakes	1.37
40% Bran Flakes	91¢
Granolas (Co-op, Harvest Gold, Lassen)	73¢-1.03
100% Natural	1.00-1.13

6 NOT WHOLE GRAIN
But higher than average protein

Life	1.07-1.16
Special K	1.43-1.59

7 NOT WHOLE GRAIN   PRICE PER LB.

All Bran .... 89¢
Bran Chex 1.06
Cheerios 1.21-1.46
Cinnamon Life 1.14
Corn Bran 1.18
Corn Chex 1.09
Cornflakes .... 92¢
Cracklin' Bran 1.44
Kix 1.58
Puffed Rice 1.01
Rice Chex 1.32-1.42
Rice Krispies 1.36
Team 1.09
Toasty O's .... 94¢
Unprocessed Bran .... 79¢
100% Bran .... 89¢

Not recommended

The cereals below are not recommended because of over-fortification with vitamins A or D or because they have a high sugar content. *Read the label on the cereal box.* As always, ingredients are listed in order of predominance by weight.

These are high in sugar — 30% to 55% more

PRICE PER LB.

Apple Jacks 1.82
Cap'N Crunch 1.40
Froot Loops 1.48
Golden Grahams 1.42
Honeycombs 1.44
Honey Nut Cheerios 1.31
Kellogg's & Post Raisin Bran 1.08-1.21
Oats, Instant, Flavored 1.28
Snack Pak 1.76
Sugar Frosted Flakes 1.16
Sugar Smacks 1.16
Trix 1.67

These are over-fortified with vitamins A or D

Kellogg's Concentrate 2.93
Most 1.27
Product 19 .... 1.42-1.51
Total 1.48

Cereals, and some happy changes

by Betsy Wood

"Aw, people will never change," we are often told. But they do change every day in response to some ughy TV ads. Do Co-op shoppers change in response to the pleadings of nutrition-conscious home economists? At least in the cereal case: YES.

We blasted you with advice and counsel

In December '74 we printed "Cereal, Champion of Breakfasts?" in the Co-op News. Our main points were:

- **Whole grain** cereal is best
- **Hot cereal** is preferred to cold
- **Don't eat** cereals with 100 percent of the Recommended Daily Allowance of vitamins A or D
- **Avoid** added sugar

You read this, digested it, sent it to your in-laws in Oshkosh, and many of you changed your eating habits.

High-sugar cereal sales are down by one-half. In the first half of 1976 our high-sugar cereals sold at 52 percent of the rate in 1974. That's a big change. (We measured cases of cereal sold as a percent of all cases going through our warehouse).

Our grocery buyer has been wonderfully cooperative and we now sell only ten brands of high-sugar cereal compared to twenty-nine brands in '74.

High vitamin A or D cereals down by 21 percent. Not a big change. Many of you are still wedded to these cereals that are like vitamin pills, such as Total, Product 19, Kellogg's Concentrate. (You can get **too much** vitamin A and D). Even so industry figures show that Co-op shoppers buy **more** of these too highly fortified cereals than do others in the Bay Area. Too bad, but we are moving in the right direction.

Hot, whole grain cereals: no change.

(We couldn't measure increase in sales of **bulk** whole grains).

Whole grain, ready-to-eat: a modest 15 percent increase.

Center councils into the act

Several Center Councils have become involved in seeking to influence cereal sales through reshelving and signing. They've experimented with 1) reshelving by group according to our recommendations, 2) hanging large signs over cereals listing Recommended, OK and Not Recommended, 3) putting high-sugar cereals on top shelves, out of easy sight and reach of little kids, 4) facing box ends, not the broad sides (with the bright cartoon characters) toward the shoppers.

We've also continued with shelf cards and we generally don't advertise any of the No-No's.

"Cereal, Champion of Breakfasts" is being reprinted for the fifth time. Maybe it's time to reread it.

9-20-76

Popcorn is peculiar

Popcorn is peculiar because when heated, it explodes. At one time this strange behavior was thought to be due to the presence inside each kernel of a little devil, who got *so mad* when he was put on the fire that he exploded with rage!

This charming theory, alas, has given way to a more sober explanation by scientists. They point out that the small hard kernels of popcorn have an especially large proportion of endosperm. The kernel acts like an airtight jacket surrounding a moist interior. When heated, the moisture turns to steam, expanding and building up pressure until suddenly the jacket bursts, turning the popcorn inside out.

Yellow and white popcorn

These two kinds of popcorn are available on the market. They have the same nutritive value.

Yellow popcorn pops to slightly larger volume than white, looks yellower when popped, and accounts for 85% of the popcorn sold in the United States. It is the type usually sold at theatres, circuses, or baseball games. Its yellowish appearance looks "buttery," and fewer kernels are needed to fill a bag. One-fourth cup, unpopped, yields 4-6 cups popped corn. Incidentally, the "butter" on commercially buttered popcorn is often butter-flavored oil, not melted butter.

White popcorn pops to smaller volume, each kernel being slightly smaller when popped. However, it is more tender than the yellow and some people think it has more flavor. Thus, it has its devoted followers. One-fourth cup, unpopped, yields 3-5 cups popped corn.

Calories and what else?

One cup of popped popcorn, prepared with just enough oil for popping, contains about 40 calories. (A slice of bread has about 60 calories.) Popcorn also has some protein, iron and B vitamins, though in smaller quantities than bread.

When popcorn refuses to pop

Popcorn must be carefully dried after harvesting in order to pop properly. Too much or too little moisture can interfere. Scratches, nicks and cracks in the kernel jacket may cause the

kernel to explode only partially, or not at all. If popcorn doesn't pop, the usual reason is that it is too dry. Rejuvenate by putting in a closed jar with 2 tablespoons of water, shake well and let stand for several days. Or put a sponge moistened with very salty water in the jar and store for several days.

How to store popcorn

Unopened popcorn may be stored in the bag it comes in or transferred to an airtight container. This keeps it in the best condition for popping and also prevents infestation by pantry pests, a troublesome problem for all cereals and dry foods.

Recommended storage limits are:

unpopped corn in airtight container	1 year
popped corn, in plastic bag	2 weeks
popped corn, opened	2 days

Note to mothers:

1. For small children, popcorn balls, and sometimes even just plain popcorn, are just too hard to chew and swallow safely, and so are not recommended for them.

2. Most popcorn snacks are fine for older school age children, barring their eating too much sweetened popcorn.

The awful truth about crackers
by Helen Black

When I grabbed a handful of succulent whole wheat crackers before dinner, a still, small, cynical Voice asked, "Why do you love those crackers?" And I said, "It's the salt, of course!"

Cracking the books to be sure I was right, I found I was wrong. Crackers are salty; they are saltier than bread, but not as much as I expected. But some crackers are obscenely **fat**.

Ritz, Triscuits, Wheat Thins: Fatter than cookies or cheese!

The horrid truth is that the crackers I loved are very high in fat, though virtuous in other ways, such as being whole wheat. Triscuits, Wheat Thins and Ritz Crackers range from 22 to 30 percent fat (that's 40-50 percent of calories from fat). Saltines are much lower, around 12-13 percent fat.

Ry Krisp, Veri Thin Pretzels: low or no fat

A squint at labels in the cracker section of the Co-op reveals plenty of low-fat, or fat-free crackers, too. Wasa Rye Crackers, Finn Crisp and plain or seasoned Ry Krisp have very low or no fat; most are whole rye, too, and so more nutritious than many others. I tried, and liked, Nabisco's pretzels. They are an acceptable substitute for crackers, and at only 2-4 percent fat have about two thirds the calories of Ritz crackers.

Hallelujah!

Feather River Rice Cakes, Wasa Rye Crackers, Finn Crisp and Ry Krisp all have nutrition labels! But Nabisco, Sunshine and Fireside crackers do not have this good information on their labels. To find out the nutritive value of their products you must write to the company. Just use the address on the package. They have the information and will send it to you. And as long as you're writing, ask them to get nutrition labels on their products, too. A little shoving from consumers might do the trick.

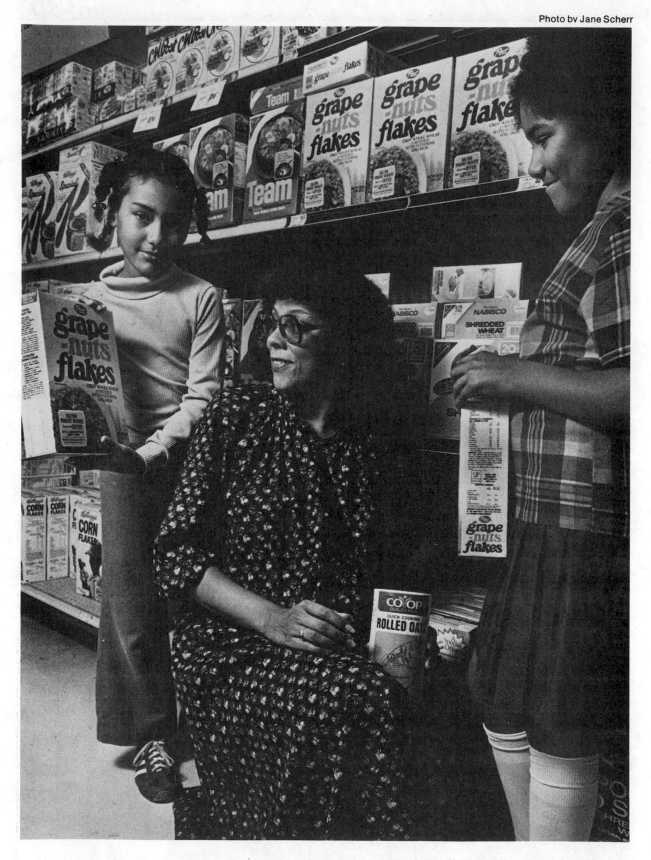

Hot cereals are more nutritious than cold cereals, according to comparisons made by Co-op home economists.

Fruits

The fruit seasonal heartbreak

By Helen Black

You succumb to the glowing peach. Or invest in a melon. You fetch it home, slavering. You cut, you bite it . . . and have nothing. No juiciness. No sweetness. No aroma, flavor, melting texture. It is awful!

It is our misfortune that large scale farming and long-distance marketing make such summer fruit available when it is not really ready to eat. It becomes a matter of skill and forbearance to know, first, when fruit is worth buying, and second, how long to wait before eating it.

Chemists study the ripening of fruit in marvelous detail and still say they don't know the whole of it. One of the important happenings is a COLOR CHANGE. The green banana turns yellow, because its chlorophyll has broken down, letting yellow pigments show through.

SOFTENING is important. As fruit ripens, complex pectins break down to mere pectin and with over-ripeness to pectic acid. For jelly-making it is important to avoid over-ripe fruit, for the whole pectin has become pectic acid.

With SWEETENING, sugar increases, sometimes due to the change of starch to sugar. There may also be a decrease in acids and in puckery or astringent substances.

AROMA, that heady, characteristic fragrance of fruits, develops with ripening. Other gases form. Ethylene gas, present in all plant tissue, builds up in the fruit and at a certain stage of maturity it stimulates ripening. In some fruits this does not happen as long as the fruit is still on the tree.

Avoid seasonal heartbreak with these rules

1. Buy at the peak of the season. Early fruit and late fruit tend to be poorer in quality and higher in price.

2. Learn the signs of ripeness. In general, ripeness is judged by background color, fragrance and changes in texture from hard to firm to soft. Each fruit has its own typical color, odor and texture that must be recognized.

3. Ripen at home at room temperature. Don't eat until fruit is FULLY RIPE, judging by the signs typical to that fruit. Fruits capable of ripening after harvest include peaches, pears, plums, bananas, apricots and melons.

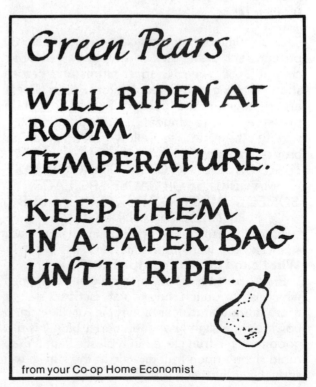

Green Pears WILL RIPEN AT ROOM TEMPERATURE. KEEP THEM IN A PAPER BAG UNTIL RIPE.

from your Co-op Home Economist

Apples in Bags
MAY WEIGH
3 OR 4 POUNDS.

READ
THE LABEL.

from your Co-op Home Economist

How can I tell if the fruit is good unless I taste it?

By Joan Taylor

Look at the background color in muskmelons, peaches and nectarines. It should be yellow or creamy, not green. Grapes, plums and berries should have good, bright, uniform color. Pears are ripe when the flesh will yield to gentle pressure of the fingers. Depending on the variety, they may be yellow-green, green or brown when ripe.

HARD SQUEEZING OR PINCHING OF FRUIT MAY BRUISE OR CAUSE SPOILAGE. SOMEONE MUST PAY FOR FRUIT LOST BY CARELESS HANDLING.

Smell the fruit too. When ripe, many fruits will smell like you want them to taste.

What can I do with unripe fruit?

Fresh fruit in the store may only be "firm ripe" which is not quite ready to eat. Let fruit stay at room temperature for a couple of days in a bowl, or in a slightly opened paper bag. It is not good to leave fruit closed in a plastic bag; it may mold. Don't ripen fruit directly in the sun. It will shrivel, sunburn and rot.

Pancakes with Cottage Cheese and Orange Sauce

1½ cups sifted all purpose flour
2½ teaspoons baking powder
¾ teaspoon salt
3 tablespoons sugar
1 egg, slightly beaten
¼ cup milk
¾ cup orange juice
3 tablespoons melted butter
1 cup cottage cheese

Sift together dry ingredients. Combine egg, milk, orange juice, and melted butter. Stir into dry ingredients. Make 4 large pancakes, baking on a hot griddle one at a time and using about ⅔ cup batter for each pancake. Watch carefully to avoid burning. Stack pancakes, spreading ⅓ cup cottage cheese between each. Cut in wedges, serve with golden orange sauce over each serving. For dessert or breakfast.

Orange Sauce

1 tablespoon cornstarch
½ cup sugar
¼ teaspoon salt
1 cup orange juice
2 tablespoons grated orange
   rind (fresh or dried)
1 tablespoon butter
1 orange, sectioned or
1 - 11 oz. can mandarin
   oranges, well drained

Mix cornstarch, sugar and salt in saucepan. Blend in orange juice, add orange rind. Cook over medium heat until mixture comes to a boil, stirring constantly until thickened. Add butter and orange sections; serve warm.

How to pick a melon

Melons, besides being delicious, are noteworthy for other reasons. They are low in calories — an average slice has about 30. Cantaloupes and other netted varieties are good sources of vitamin C, an average serving (¼ of a 2 lb. melon) providing about ½ of an adult's recommended daily allowance. The same amount of honeydew would provide about ⅓; watermelon and casaba, about ⅕ of the allowance.

Below is a chart which should help you to get a good melon. All of the melons listed, except watermelons, may be ripened at home. Keep them at room temperature out of the direct sunlight until ripe, then store in a plastic bag in the refrigerator until ready to eat. A few melons, such as a very green honeydew, may never ripen.

Softness at the stem or blossom end of a melon may indicate ripeness in a melon which has never been handled, but may also merely mean that many people have been pressing it to see if it is ripe. This is properly a valid test only where the melon is purchased green to be ripened at home. Aroma, while an indication of ripeness, is not necessarily an indication of good flavor. Aroma is not significant in watermelon.

	APPEARANCE	TOUCH
Cantaloupe	Thick, raised netting; yellowish color underneath. Scar should be "full slip" (smooth scar at stem end).	Should not be hard. Heavy for size. Softness around stem end.
Honeyball	Creamy, yellow; thin netting at blossom end. Scar should be full slip.	Slightly soft. Heavy for size.
Honeydew	Larger melons are usually best. Creamy white to pale yellow.	Should not be hard; slight softness at stem end. Heavy for size. Sticky rather than slick.
Persian	Covered with fine netting. Color underneath should be light green or brownish.	Surface yields to slight pressure. Heavy for size.
Cranshaw	Smooth, golden yellow, pointed at end.	Surface yields to slight pressure. Heavy for size. Sticky rather than slick.
Casaba	High ridges. Deep yellow; round rather than pointed.	Heavy for size. Blossom end yields to slight pressure.
Watermelon	Yellow ground color (sometimes white).	Heavy for size; well shaped with rounded ends. Skin peels easily when scraped gently with fingernail. Should be dry rather than moist or oily. Sound when thumped is not always reliable indication.

Cantaloupe scar should be "full slip" - smooth.

Jagged scar means melon picked too green

Pears stuffed with Gorgonzola cheese

4 small firm ripe pears
1 tablespoon lemon juice
2 ounces imported Gorgonzola cheese
(about ¼ cup) at room temperature

2 tablespoons soft unsalted butter
2 tablespoons crushed walnuts or pistachio nuts

With a small sharp knife, peel the pears and cut them in half lengthwise, leaving a stem attached to one of the halves of each pear. Remove the cores using a melon baller and scoop a scant tablespoon of pulp out of each of the pear halves. To prevent the fruit from turning brown, paint each section of pear inside and out with pastry brush dipped in lemon juice.

Cream the Gorgonzola cheese and softened butter together by beating them against the side of a small bowl with a wooden spoon until they are soft and fluffy. Fill the hollows of the pears with 1 tablespoon of cheese and butter mixture and carefully press the two halves of the pear back together again. Roll the pears around in the crushed nuts, then arrange them on a serving plate. Chill for about 2 hours, or until the cheese is firm. 4 servings.

Fruit cocktail

In case anybody thinks canned fruit cocktail has been around forever we hasten to say that this is not quite true! Fruit cocktail required the development of some rather amazing machinery, and only became a reality in the late 1930's when one machine for chopping fruit and one for stemming grapes were invented. Considering that the stemming is done by machine, isn't it remarkable to find so few stems in the finished product?

Standards of Quality. However, when a stem does get through, it is considered a defect. Two grades for quality have been set up by the U.S. Department of Agriculture: Grade A and Grade B. Anything below this is "substandard." Quality is judged by clearness of syrup, number of defects, brightness and uniformity of color, uniformity of size, and firmness of texture. Flavor, unless it is definitely "off," is not considered because it is so hard to evaluate.

Standards of Identity. In addition, Standards of Identity were established by the Food and Drug Administration in 1942, so that any product which is called "fruit cocktail" must meet these standards. The amounts of different kinds of fruit that may be used are specified:

30-50% peaches, diced
25-45% pears, diced
6-20% seedless grapes
6-16% pineapple, diced or sectioned
2-6% cherries, halved

Usually, these fruits are all fresh when canned except for the cherries and pineapple. The standards of identity also state that the sweetner added may be a syrup made with sugar, corn syrup, or dextrose in various combinations. Corn syrup is present in the syrup of practically all canned fruits.

Are Private Label Brands of Fruit Cocktail a Good Buy? Because fruit cocktail is standardized to a degree far beyond that of most canned fruits, there is little difference between brands. When private label brands are priced below the national brands, you save when you buy them and you get about the same quality. In can cuttings performed by our home economists, Co-op fruit cocktail has compared well with Del Monte, Libby, Townhouse, and other brands. All are USDA Grade B; very little Grade A fruit cocktail is on the retail market.

Dried Fruits

Dried fruits, while not cheap, can still be considered a good buy for certain uses. They are easy to store and transport because of their concentrated form. They are a very good dessert for lunches just as they come from the package. Dried fruit stewed with small amounts of sugar or no sugar at all make simple dessert or breakfast fruits and help add variety during months when fresh fruits are not plentiful. Hikers and campers find them almost a necessity where foods need to be carried in concentrated form.

Dried fruits are fully ripened fruits that have about 75% of their moisture removed by dehydration or sun drying. These fruits are allowed to ripen longer in the orchards than those used for other purposes. Therefore, their natural or fruit sugar content is higher.

To appreciate the food value in dried fruits, consider that each one pound is concentrated from several pounds of fresh fruit: apricots represent 6 to 8 pounds, figs about 3 pounds, prunes from 2½ to 3 pounds, and raisins represent 4 pounds of grapes. Naturally, the caloric count has a similar jump in proportion: 1 pound of dried apricots has 1200 calories to 220 per pound of fresh.

During the drying process, light colored fruits are exposed to sulphur dioxide fumes for several hours to preserve the natural color and their vitamin A and C content. When sulphur isn't used, the dried peaches and apricots are brown in color rather than the expected golden orange. These unsulphured fruits are available in our Co-op Natural Food store and many other stores. Whether sulphured or not, they are a good source of vitamin A and a fair source of iron.

Knickerbocker Figs

½ pound dry figs
frozen unsweetened cherries (or raisins)
walnuts, shelled

¼ cup orange juice
3 tablespoons sugar
2 teaspoons lemon juice

Slit figs from stem to blossom end on one side and stuff with one cherry and pieces of walnuts. Combine juices and sugar in saucepan, add the figs, cover and simmer gently until figs are tender (about 30 minutes). Cool, drain, serve in individual paper cases. Nice as dessert with apples and cheese.

Tips on buying and storing dried fruit

Dried fruits come in handy, protective cartons and in bags. Both may be used for storing the fruit, even after opening. Close the box or fold the bag tightly. Dried fruits should be stored in a cool, dry place. On very warm days, keep them in the refrigerator.

Usual Dried Fruit Sizes

Prunes:
Prunes are USDA graded as follows:
Small - not more than 85 prunes per lb.
Medium - not more than 67 prunes per lb.
Large - not more than 53 prunes per lb.
X-Large - not more than 43 prunes per lb.
Sometimes one sees a "jumbo" size prune (20 to 30 per lb.)

Raisins:
1½ oz pkg. "Snac-packs"
15 oz pkg. - 3 cups (approx)
1 lb. bag - 3¼ cups (approx)
2 lb. bag - 6½ cups (approx)
Apricots, Peaches and Mixed Dried Fruits are usually sold in 11 oz. boxes or 8 or 12 oz. bags.

Preparation of dried fruits: Packaged dried fruits are ready for cooking. They do not need to be washed. Soaking shortens the cooking time and tends to give a richer juice, but is not necessary. Time of cooking is approximately ½ hour. If fruit has been soaked, use the same water for cooking. Cook slowly. If sugar is used, add ¼ to ⅓ cup per pound of dried fruit.

Recipe tips with dried fruit

Plump Raisins: If you want your raisins extra moist, you may plump them by covering with boiling water for 5 minutes. Drain thoroughly before adding to recipe.
Flouring: If a recipe calls for floured raisins, shake seedless raisins in a paper bag with a small amount of flour.
Chopping: To chop raisins easily, oil the blade of your chopping knife.
Snipping: Raisins, prunes and apricots may be snipped extra-quickly if you use a bit of cooking oil on the blade of your scissors.

Fruit Soup

½ lb. prunes
1 cup seeded raisins
¼ lb. dried apricots
4 tablespoons tapioca
1 cup sugar

1 stick cinnamon
½ orange, sliced thin
¼ lemon, sliced thin
3 apples, diced and peeled
1 can (1 lb.) cherries, sour, with juice

Soak dried fruits, tapioca, sugar, cinnamon, orange and lemon, in enough water to cover, overnight. In morning add diced apples and cook until fruit is soft. Add canned fruit last. May be served hot or cold.

The absolutely most perfectly wonderful dessert: Fruit

By Helen Black

Fruit is it. Fruit is the most perfectly wonderful dessert! It meets all those very high standards we humans have for dessert, which I have just figured out.

A dessert should be bad for us.

Yes! That's it. A dessert should be bad for us! Nobody says, "Shut up and eat your dessert, it's good for you!"

But is fruit bad for us? Well, no, of course not. Look at it this way, though: most fruits are not **that** nutritious. The same nutrients in better amounts can usually be had in vegetables, cheaper. SO: fruit is not necessary. SO: fruit can be a dessert.

Or else it's rare and costly

That's good. If a food is indecently expensive, we'll be able to forgive any nutritional value! Does fruit fit? Yes! Think of fresh pineapples, and mangoes, from over the seas. Because it takes lots of land for orchards. Because it takes years for trees to reach the fruit-bearing age. Because it takes careful tending, to care for fruit. That's MUCH costlier than growing sugar beets for a cake!

Or it's tricky to fix

That melon with blissful aroma, ripe enough to be sweet and juicy, took skill to choose, and an iron will to wait, wait, wait, for the right moment to cut it. It's tricky! It's a dessert!

Or it's cozy, to eat together

May I peel you an apple? Will you pit me a prune? Or shall we share a pear? A bowl of fruits and a handful of knives is perfect. Everyone peels, pits, slices and talks while eating a rare, wonderful, SOCIABLE dessert!

Melons may need several days more ripening at home after purchase.

OW! you're hurting!

Please be gentle when examining fruit. Bruises lower nutrients and storage time.

Fruit Pudding

*2 pkg. (10 oz.) frozen sweetened raspberries
or 1 pkg. each frozen boysenberries &
raspberries
2 teaspoons grated lemon peel (optional)*

*2 tablespoons lemon juice
2 tablespoons cornstarch
dash of salt*

Thaw berries. Drain syrup into saucepan. Blend together lemon peel, lemon juice, cornstarch and salt and add to syrup. Cook over medium heat, stirring constantly, until mixture thickens and becomes transparent. Gently stir in berries. Pour into glass bowl for serving. Chill. Serve plain or with cream.

Melon Balls with Aloha Sauce

*⅔ cup sugar
⅓ cup water
2 tablespoons orange juice
2 tablespoons lime juice
2 tablespoons lemon juice*

*grated rind of 1 lemon
flesh from one 3 lb. melon cut into bite-
     sized cubes or cut into balls with
     melon cutter*

Place sugar and water in saucepan; boil a few minutes until sugar is dissolved; remove from heat and allow to cool about 5 minutes. Add orange juice, lime juice, lemon juice and lemon rind. Pour over melon balls and chill in refrigerator until ready to serve. This may be prepared several hours in advance. Yield: 5 half-cup servings.

Meat, fish and poultry

PROTEIN

THE AMOUNT OF PROTEIN IS ABOUT THE SAME IN:
- 3 OZ. COOKED BONELESS MEAT, POULTRY, FISH
- 4 OZ. BONELESS LEAN MEAT, POULTRY, FISH (BEFORE COOKING)
- 3 OZ. CHEESE
- ¾ CUP COTTAGE CHEESE
- 2½ CUPS MILK (SKIM OR WHOLE)
- 1½ CUPS COOKED BEANS*

*Protein from beans is better used by your body if some animal food (as a glass of milk) or some cereal food (as a slice of bread) is eaten at the same meal.

The night they stopped eating meat

"That does it!" yelled Ooga the Caveman, throwing down his club in disgust. "It's too blasted much work hunting game for protein every day! If I'm lucky, which isn't often, I get to drag home some huge beast that takes the tribe two days to skin, clean, carve up and hang. Then half of it spoils before we can eat it. I'M SICK SICK SICK OF THE WHOLE LOUSY SYSTEM!"

Ooga was really worked up this time! So Goona the Cavewoman, who was cleaning a jackel for dinner, said:

"And I'm sick of hearing you bitch about it! I keep telling you, we don't have to eat meat, fish or fowl for protein. Why don't we go out and discover agriculture? Maybe we could invent bread, too. We'd get 8 or 10 grams of protein just from four servings of bread and cereal."

Ooga started counting on his fingers. "That's true," he said. "And we could try storing some milk in a goat-stomach bag, to see if it'll make cheese. Three ounces of cheddar would give us 20 or so grams more." He unwrapped his feet and started counting toes. "Let's see, that makes . . ."

"Don't forget beans and nuts," put in Goona. "Two or three handfuls of beans would add another 25 or 30 grams . . ." and she unwrapped her feet too.

Ooga started a second time around on his fingers and toes, saying, "I suppose we'll want some fruits and vegetables, too, and four servings of them will add in 5 or 10 grams . . ."

THAT'S IT!" interrupted Goona joyfully. "EUREKA! That's 55 to 65 grams of protein and that's all we need per day! Ooga, we can do it!"

They were so excited that they couldn't eat the jackal, so they took it out and gave it a decent burial and afterwards Ooga sank down on the bed and said solemnly:

"Goona, this is a great truth that I've discovered. We don't need to eat meat at all! Why didn't I think of it before?" *by Helen Black*

Beef *by Betsy Wood*   *August 3, 1977*

What are needs in beef research? A dry subject perhaps, but I got pretty involved when I was asked to give the consumer view for a symposium last May. After much pondering I settled on three areas: producing beef that is lower in fat, eating less beef, and being sure that the beef we eat is safe.

Lower fat beef is needed. Why? Because Americans on the average eat too much fat, especially saturated fat. Actually, beef marketed today is leaner than a year ago because new federal grades permit the inclusion of more lean beef as "Choice" grade of beef.

How can we move toward eating less beef? Beef consumption has almost doubled in 20 years. Production of beef uses lots of resources — not just grain but energy. Beef is an expensive way to get calories and protein. A modest amount of beef fills a need for many people — for pleasure as well as for protein, iron, etc. But the great amount of meat and animal fat we eat is a suspected contributor to heart disease and maybe to intestinal diseases.

The Senate Select Committee on Nutrition & Human Needs says Americans should get fewer calories from fat and sugar, more calories from complex carbohydrates, and the same calories from protein. If we did this we'd be bound to eat less meat because more of our protein would come from starchy foods. (Senator George McGovern, who chairs the Select Committee, seems to have backed away from the "less meat" suggestion because of pressure from cattle people. Too bad.)

Is there enough thought to safety? Probably not. New food additives get pretty thorough checking. But existing additives or processes are used without enough assurance of safety. Examples: Antibiotics and DES are used to fatten cattle despite serious warnings. Other problems: Use of nitrites, accidental contaminants such as PCBs (polychlorinated biphenyls), use of chlorine, effectiveness of inspection, food poisoning bacteria.

After the symposium I wondered whether maybe we should go slower and not always jump to apply "modern" methods. Today we can bring a steer to maturity in less than 12 months with corn, supplements, hormones, antibiotics. It used to take 4-5 years when cattle just ate grass. When our eye is only on "efficiency" we may not look for long-run ramifications. There is a maxim among ecologists that any change in the ecosystem will have ramifications greater than anyone could have imagined.

Many of our problems and health hazards have surfaced lately because their consideration wasn't on our agenda. I think eating large amounts of meat and other energy-intensive foods is part of our over-consuming society which also uses too much fuel, steel, plastics, medicine, and produces mounds of garbage.

We're all in it — industry, government, consumers. To have a more ecologically balanced and healthier food system, consumers must be willing to eat more grains and smaller portions of meat and to have that meat less marbled and less dripping with fat.

DES and antibiotics are still being used to fatten cattle despite serious warnings.

The Food and Drug Administration has been trying to ban the use of DES (diethylstilbesterol) for several years. A ban to have started July 20, 1979 was postponed to November 1, 1979.

FDA also proposed in January, 1979 to drastically limit the use of penicillin and tetracycline in cattle feeds; hearings have been in progress as of September, 1979.

How to Buy BEEF

Two things are important when you buy beef—the quality grade and the cut.
Different cuts vary in tenderness. But for any one cut—like a rib steak—the higher the U.S. Department of Agriculture (USDA) grade, the more tender, juicy, and flavorful the meat will be. (Meat grading is voluntary — paid for by the processor.)

LOOK FOR THE QUALITY—These marks, stamped on the meat, are a dependable guide to quality. The meat must first be inspected for wholesomeness before it can be graded. (Inspection is mandatory — required by law before meat can be sold.)

Prime grade beef is the best and most expensive. Most cuts of this grade are very tender, juicy, and flavorful.

Choice grade beef is high quality—and this is the grade sold in most stores. It is produced in such large amounts that it is often a very good buy. USDA Choice steaks and roasts will be quite tender and juicy and have a good flavor.

Good grade beef is not as juicy and flavorful as the higher grades—it is somewhat more lean, but it is fairly tender.

LOOK FOR THE CUT—Any cut of beef makes good eating if it is cooked properly. Use dry heat—roasting in the oven, broiling, or pan frying—for the most tender cuts and the higher grades. Use moist heat—pot-roasting or braising—for the less tender cuts and the lower grades.

The **most tender cuts** are rib roasts and steaks and loin cuts, like porterhouse, T-bone, club, and sirloin steaks. These may be cooked with dry heat in any grade. These cuts are the most expensive, but are no more nutritious than less-tender cuts.

Moderately tender cuts, which are usually a good buy, include rump roasts, sirloin tip roasts, blade chuck roasts and steaks, top round roasts and steaks, and shoulder clod roasts. Cook these with dry heat in the Prime and Choice grades; use moist heat for lower grades.

Less-tender cuts are often the best buy. Such cuts include shoulder arm chuck roasts and steaks, flank steaks, bottom round and eye-of-round steaks and roasts, and brisket. Cook these with moist heat in any grade.

 U.S. DEPARTMENT OF AGRICULTURE   CONSUMER AND MARKETING SERVICE
Adapted from How to Buy Beef Steaks, G 145, and
How to Buy Beef Roasts, G 146

Would you flunk this beef quiz?

by Helen Black

The hardest kind of shopping is for meat. It takes both skill and knowledge. Find out how smart you are by trying this quiz:

True or false:

1. Ungraded beef is not SAFE to eat.
2. Ungraded beef is usually cheaper, so it's a good buy.
3. Money spent for meat by most people is so small that it's silly to worry about it.
4. A. U.S. Grade Choice cross rib roast should be tender enough to oven roast.
5. For a nutritious diet, you can't eat too much meat.

Answers:

1. FALSE. Ungraded beef is inspected for wholesomeness just like graded beef and is just as nutritious.
2. FALSE. Ungraded beef may be cheaper, but you don't know whether it comes from a tender young animal or a tough old beast. Grading helps the shopper tell whether he's paying a fair price for meat.
3. FALSE. I KNEW you'd all get this one! Americans spend at least 30% of their food dollars for meat.
4. TRUE, usually. But if you buy an UN-GRADED cross rib roast you'd better pot roast it.
5. FALSE. More meat than you need does not do a thing for you except make you fat.

Babootie

2 lbs. ground lamb
2 onions, grated or chopped
2 cloves garlic, chopped
1 #303 can (16 oz.) tomatoes
1½ tablespoons sugar
2 tablespoons curry powder (more or less to taste)
2 tablespoons vinegar
salt to taste
2 firm bananas, sliced
1 apple, peeled, diced
1 tablespoon apricot jam (or 4 canned apricots, sliced)
¼ cup slivered almonds (optional)
tomato juice as needed for thinning

Variation: Use ground beef or ¾ beef and ¼ pork.

Brown the meat in a large skillet and drain off the fat. Add all the other ingredients. Simmer gently, stirring frequently, for about 30 minutes. Add tomato juice to taste if the mixture is too thick. Serve over steamed rice with sweet chutney. Serves 8.

History: This is a traditional South African national dish.

Ground Beef

Although the lowest priced ground beef has the most fat, it is usually the most economical on the basis of **cost per ounce of protein.**

from your Co-op Home Economist

Four recipes from one round steak *by Catherine Sinnott*

By all the market reports it looks as if beef prices are high and going higher. Here's a couple of ways to enjoy beef and beat some of the cost. One is to buy a large piece and cut it up to make several recipes. The other is to plan smaller servings of beef and make it up with other less expensive protein foods at the same meal.

Check prices and when you see a good buy in a roast or large steak, grab it. Allow yourself time to cut it for cooking, refrigerating or freezing. You can save money and a lot of time this way on later meals. A good, thick chuck roast is a favorite for this, but other roasts, even steaks, can be used with great success.

Here's how

Recently, I tried the cut-up method with a round steak, which has practically no waste. The plan was for four meals for the four people in the family from two pounds of meat. I cut the steak into fourths to prepare for beef stroganoff, stew, stir-fry, and shish-kabob. Half the round steak was cut in quarter-inch strips, browned and simmered until tender with a large sliced onion. Half of this was put in the freezer for stew which would be finished later with vegetables and thickening. To the other half of the cooked meat, I added a can of mushrooms, some sour half and half and served it for dinner over noodles as beef stroganoff. The third section of meat was frozen raw. At a later date, this will be partly thawed, cut paper-thin and cooked as Asian-type stir-fry with tofu and vegetables. The last part of the meat was cut in 1½" squares and put in the refrigerator with meat tenderizer and marinade. Two days later it was broiled on skewers with vegetables, and served as shish-kabob on bulgur wheat.

On protein

You're right, two pounds of meat can't furnish enough protein for four meals for four people. You will have to add other good protein sources, such as tofu in the stir-fry, extra milk, cottage cheese, bean salad, cheese, etc. If you add these high protein foods with your low meat meal, protein needs can be met.

Meat's high *by Betsy Wood*

No, it's not fair to say "Eat Less" when you scream about meat prices. And eating less is no long term solution to drastic inflation. But it's all we can suggest practically. Eating less meat should help your pocketbook, might help your health (because you eat less fat), could help the ecology of our country (by devouring less grain and energy) and might help bring meat prices down a little.

Plenty of protein: We've said it before: Many people in this country eat more meat and more protein than they "need." This gets expensive because extra protein above physical requirements is burned for calories. Protein is probably the best supplied nutrient in the American diet, except for calories.

Mix it up: Getting protein from several sources means that a variety of other nutrients can be provided. Beans, meat, and eggs are good sources of iron. Milk and cheese provide calcium and riboflavin. By **not** counting on meat too much for protein and by eating more beans, tofu, poultry and fish you also eat less fat.

Vegetarian? This is a solution for some, for a variety of reasons. If your primary source of protein is from plant foods (beans, seeds, nuts, grain) the usability of the protein will be improved if you mix several foods, especially grains and beans. Or you can add some animal food such as milk, cheese, eggs, or fish at the same meal.

Cutting down, not cutting meat out altogether is the answer for many. You might have several no-meat dinners a week and use small amounts of meat stretched with vegetables, grains and beans most of the rest of the week.

What else for protein?

by Betsy Wood and Helen Black

What does it cost to get your day's protein? Well, that depends. If you get it from turkey legs, beans and peanut butter it costs about 39¢ per person. If you get it from bologna, T-bone and bacon, it costs about $2.69. Quite a difference. With meat prices high and going higher it's a good time to look for alternative sources of protein.

How much from a pound?

The amount of protein and the number of servings vary with the kind of food, the amount of bone or fat in the meat, etc. The chart below gives you the number of servings per pound, if each serving provides about 20 grams of protein.

EIGHT SERVINGS PER POUND. Includes soybeans (uncooked) and nonfat dry milk.
SIX SERVINGS PER POUND. Peanuts, peanut butter, eggs (per dozen).
FIVE SERVINGS PER POUND. Includes most beans (uncooked), canned fish, cheese.
FOUR SERVINGS PER POUND. Includes lean, boneless, raw meat, fish or poultry.
THREE SERVINGS PER POUND. Whole raw chicken or turkey, chicken breasts and thighs, roasts and chops with some bone or fat, bologna, frankfurters and cottage cheese.
TWO SERVINGS OR LESS PER POUND. Includes meat with much bone or fat such as bacon, spareribs, chicken wings and backs, pork sausage, lamb shanks, etc.; also, fluid milk (per quart)

COST OF PROTEIN

	Cost per pound*	Cost per serving providing 20 grams protein
PINTO BEANS	$ .49	10¢
NONFAT DRY MILK	1.24	16¢
PEANUT BUTTER	.98	16¢
GROUND BEEF, regular	1.64	41¢
CHEDDAR CHEESE	2.15	43¢
CHICKEN BREASTS	1.51	50¢
SPARERIBS	1.19	60¢
BACON	1.89	95¢

*Priced in July 1979

Hams and other cured pork cuts

An old legend tells us that the curing of pork was discovered when an injured pig ran into the ocean and died of its wounds in the briny deep. When its flesh was cooked, the flavor was enthusiastically relished by the ancient Sumerians in whose time this event is alleged to have occurred.

Today a wide variety of hams is available to consumers who want to know, among other things, the differences between smoked hams and fully cooked hams, between shank and butt halves, between picnics and hams.

Curing is one process for preserving fresh meat. To do this a solution of water, salt, sugar and sodium nitrite is pumped into the ham mechanically to preserve the meat, develop the flavor and pink color. After curing it may be smoked.

Smoked Ham is the hind leg of the hog. It has been smoked to an internal temperature of 140°F. This is hot enough to kill trichina but not hot enough to completely cook the meat. These hams need additional cooking.

Fully-Cooked or Ready-to-Eat Ham is heated to an internal temperature of 150°F. in addition to smoking. It does not need further cooking but may be reheated if desired.

Ham, Water Added, may contain up to 10% added moisture. If the finished ham contains more than this amount, it must be labeled "Ham: up to 20% added water" or "Ham: up to 25% added water," etc., as appropriate.

Shank Half is the lower portion of the ham. It is more pointed in shape, has a smaller proportion of meat to bone, and is usually slightly lower in price than Ham Butt.

Butt Half is the upper part of the ham (the part nearest the hog's body). It is more rounded in shape, has a higher proportion of meat to bone, and is higher in price.

NOTE: If the center slices are removed from either half of the ham, the remaining portions must be labeled Butt or Shank End or Portion; these are higher in bone.

Canned Hams are boned and trimmed of most of the fat. They are then properly called "skinless and boneless." They are cured in a brine solution and may or may not be smoked before canning. The label should make this clear. If the label says "smoke flavored," it means just that; the ham has not undergone a true smoking process. If the ham to be canned is not smoked, the cured, raw ham is vacuum sealed with a small amount of dry gelatin, in a can. It is then fully cooked. During this process the ham juices combine with the gelatin. The label must say "Fully Cooked Ham with Natural Juices, Gelatin Added." The juices plus gelatin are edible and are included in the net weight marked on the can.

All canned hams are "fully cooked;" however, not all are "fully processed," meaning that although they are cooked, they are not sterile and must be kept refrigerated at all times. Canned hams weighing less than 3 lbs. are usually sterile and need not be refrigerated. Read the label and follow instructions for refrigeration. All canned hams, of course, should be refrigerated after opening.

Some meat departments will open a canned ham for you, slice it to desired thickness, and tie it back together for convenience in heating. Be careful not to overheat such presliced hams, or the ham will dry out too much.

Smoked Shoulder Butts and **Picnics** are smoked pork cuts with characteristics similar to ham. They are from the shoulder, are somewhat less tender than ham, and are less costly. Smoked shoulder butt, a boneless cut weighing 1 to 4 lbs., should be cooked before eating. It may be baked, simmered in water, or sliced and then pan fried or broiled. Picnics are available as either cook-before-eating or fully-cooked products.

Recommended Baking Times for Cured Pork

	Internal Temperature	Minutes/lb. 325° F. oven
Cook Before Eating		
Whole Ham	160° F.	18-20
Half Ham, Butt or Shank	160° F.	22-25
Rolled, Boned Ham	160° F.	30
Shoulder Butt (boneless), Picnics	170° F.	35-40
Fully-Cooked		
Whole Ham	140° F.	10-15
Half Ham, Picnics	140° F.	14-18
Rolled, Boned Ham	140° F.	12-15
Canned Ham, 6 lbs. or under	140° F.	15-20
Canned Ham, 8-13 lbs.	140° F.	10-15

To bake a ham, place the meat, fat side up, on a rack in a shallow roasting pan. Do not add water or cover, and do not baste. Insert a meat thermometer into the center of the thickest part of the meat, making sure it doesn't touch any bone.
Center slices can be baked, broiled or pan-fried.
Glazing a ham. Half an hour before end of cooking time, stud the ham with cloves and glaze with 1 cup of red jelly mixed with ½ teaspoon dry mustard and 2 teaspoons horseradish. Or use your favorite glaze.

Meat for breakfast — no nitrites
by June Kadish

Bacon and eggs, pancakes and ham. For many, this is the American breakfast. One problem with this meal is that bacon, ham, lunch meats and cured meats like corned beef and pastrami all contain nitrites which, in recent years, have become suspect as carcinogens.

Some consumers would like to avoid nitrites completely. Others would like to cut down on their intake, but not necessarily eliminate them entirely. Based on the best available current information, it is difficult, if not impossible, to set specific limits. Much more nitrite is microbiolically developed in our intestines and saliva than is consumed in foods with added nitrite.

However, if you're eating a lot of foods containing nitrites, it may be prudent to cut down. This is especially important for young children, since they will have more years for the nitrite to be working as a carcinogen, if indeed this proves to be the case. It's probably a good idea for pregnant women as well.

So what meat is there for breakfast?

1. There's fresh and frozen sausage, both in bulk and in links. The bulk is for breakfast patties; the links are already in shape.
2. In the "deli" case, I spied Leo's Breast of Turkey, oven baked, which would be good between two slices of bread, dipped in egg and milk and sauteed for a French toast sandwich.
3. How about bratwurst or bockwurst, uncured veal and pork sausages packed in random weights? Simmer or fry slowly until well cooked and serve with hash browns.
4. Frozen ground turkey and turkey sausage are naturals for the innovative cook. Slice the plain turkey roll into half-inch slices, sauté and season with herbs or spices of your choice. The sausage is already seasoned.
5. The freezer case offers several soy protein "meats" such as breakfast patties, strips and grillers which may be reasonable facsimiles of comparable animal products.
6. There are, of course, several suitable fresh meats such as chicken livers, beef liver, chicken parts or, considering today's prices, a VERY small hamburger patty or cubed round steak.

This is not an exhaustive list. For other choices, read the labels for the ingredients contained in the foods you're considering.

Vary your meals with variety meats

Variety meats is the terms used to designate the following edible portion of meat animals: Liver, heart, kidney, tongue, tripe, brains, and sweetbreads. Liver, heart, and kidney are very flavorful, while brains, sweetbreads and tripe are delicate in flavor. Heart, liver and kidney are much more nutritious than other meats. Iron and B vitamins are much higher; vitamin A is much higher in liver and somewhat higher in kidney. Except for liver, these meats are in less demand than other cuts. This usually means lower cost. There is no bone waste to contend with when figuring costs, and prices do not fluctuate greatly.

Most of the variety meats are slightly more perishable than other meats, and should be used within 2 days after purchase. Liver, heart, kidney, brains and sweetbreads are best purchased fresh. Tongue is sold fresh, pickled, corned or smoked. Tripe may be fresh, pickled or canned. Fresh tripe is partly cooked before selling. Variety meats, like other meats, are cooked according to their tenderness. Liver and kidney from young animals, brains and sweetbreads are tender. Tongue, heart, tripe, beef kidneys are less tender and need longer slow cooking in moisture. An exception is beef heart, which is tender if sliced thinly and stirfried or sauteed quickly. Pork liver also is at its best when braised. Variety meats are usually cooked well done, with the exception of liver, which is more moist when cooked only to the medium stage. Variety meats from pork are always cooked well done.

Sweetbreads are thymus glands of beef, calves and lambs. They are considered great delicacies and are usually quite expensive. To prepare sweetbreads, simmer 15 minutes in salted water to which 1 tablespoon of lemon juice or wine vinegar has been added. Drain, plunge in cold water and remove membranes. They may then be pan-fried in a little butter, or broiled after brushing with melted butter. Served with mushrooms, they are delicious.

Liver is good – BUT TOO MUCH IS NOT !

We suggest you not eat beef or lamb liver more than once a week. Two ounces of cooked beef liver contain 30,000 units of vitamin A (six times the adult Recommended Allowance).

Excessive amounts of any nutrient may be toxic. Vitamin A above daily needs will be stored in the body.

Liver is an excellent source of protein, iron and B vitamins, so eating liver once every week or two **is** a good idea.

from your Co-op Home Economist

Sautéed Chicken Giblets

4 tablespoons butter
1 lb. chicken livers, hearts or
gizzards (or 1/3 lb. each)
1/2 lb. fresh mushrooms or 4 oz canned
1/2 cup chicken broth or dry sherry
1/2 teaspoon salt
1/4 teaspoon coarse ground pepper
2 tablespoons chopped parsley

Melt butter. Add livers, hearts, and/or gizzards. (Precook gizzards by covering with water and simmering for one hour, or until tender.) Trim gristle at ends of gizzards if desired. Brown over low heat. Add mushrooms, cook gently until limp and browned. Add other ingredients and simmer about 10 minutes, or until liquid is gone. Serve as a main dish with buttered French bread and a tossed green salad, or stick with toothpicks and serve as appetizers. 3-4 servings.

Chicken Livers Guillaume

1/2 lb. chicken livers
1/8 lb. butter (1/2 stick)
2 tablespoons soy sauce
1 teaspoon vinegar

Melt the butter and saute the livers in it quickly. Add soy sauce, vingear and 1/4 cup water. Turn the heat high, allow sauce to bubble up, stir thoroughly, and serve. Salt and pepper to taste. Serve with French bread or over toast. (From *Wild in the Kitchen,* by Will Jones.) 2 servings.

Fish

To retain highest quality,
cook all fish the same day you buy it.

If you want to put "frozen" fish in the freezer,
the quality is best if you buy a still-frozen piece
rather than refreezing thawed fish.

There is no health hazard in refreezing thawed fish,
provided it has not been thawed long
and its temperature has not risen above
normal refrigerator temperatures.

from your Co-op Home Economist

Fish Stew

1/2 cup dry vermouth or dry sherry
3 large green onions, chopped
1/2 pound mushrooms, chopped
2 tablespoons butter
3 pounds fish, several kinds of
    firm-fleshed fish fillets
6 to 8 medium-sized raw shrimp
    shucked and cut into quarters; optional
1 10 1/2 ounce can condensed cream of
    shrimp soup
1 cup sour cream
2 tablespoons flour
3/4 cup grated mixed cheeses, parmesan and
    Swiss
salt and pepper to taste

In a heavy pot that will hold 2 quarts, melt the butter and saute the green onions and mushrooms. Add the vermouth or sherry, cover and simmer for 5 minutes. Cut the fish into bite-sized pieces and prepare the shrimp. To the mushrooms and onions add the soup and the sour cream that has had the flour stirred into it. Over moderate heat, bring almost to a boil stirring constantly. Add the fish and shrimp and continue cooking until shrimp turns pink and fish loses its transparent appearance. Add the cheese, stir until just melted and serve at once in soup bowls. Serves 6-8.

Fish: a gift from the sea

Fish is good for you and tastes good too, when properly prepared. It has about the same amount and quality of protein as a serving of meat or poultry. All proteins from animal sources (fish, eggs, milk, as well as meat) are of high biological value, having all the essential amino acids present in the correct proportions for efficient use by the body.

Fish is lower in both calories and fat than most cuts of beef and pork. Even the so called "fat fish" such as salmon, butterfish, herring and mackerel average from 5-16% fat, while a choice grade steak may be 25% fat. Fish is suitable for fat-controlled diets because of the low total fat content and because the fat is relatively unsaturated.

Fish contributes B vitamins to the diet and the fat fish contribute some vitamins A, D and E. Fish also contains iodine, iron and copper. Canned fish eaten with the bones, such as salmon, sardines and mackerel, contributes good amounts of calcium and phosphorus.

Not enough of us rely on fish for its nutritive value, or on the variety available. Ask a cook how he or she prepares fish, and chances are the answer will be, "flour it and fry it." If you fall into this category, consider these cooking methods:

Broiling: Brush fish with melted butter or oil. Baste lean fish several times during broiling. Preheat broiler. Broil 4 inches from heat for about 12 to 15 minutes or until fish flakes and breaks apart easily with a fork. Unless fish is very thick, you will not need to turn it. Use pancake turner to remove fish from broiler pan.

Baking: Bake fish on oiled baking dish or oiled brown paper, either stuffed or unstuffed. Do not fill fish more than 2/3 full of stuffing. Bake in 400° F. oven until fish flakes. Brush fat fish with oil, sprinkle with salt and lemon juice. Baste lean fish several times as it bakes with extra oil or butter or with a sauce. This method is also suitable for slices of fillets.

Steaming or Poaching: Steam or simmer, do not boil. Add lemon juice or vinegar to water to firm and whiten flesh. Part dry white wine or tomato juice may be used as liquid. Onion, garlic and herbs may be added, or fish may be poached in milk, being sure to keep the milk below the boiling point. Thicken remaining milk and use as cream sauce over the fish. For fat fish, tie in cheese cloth so that the fish may be easily removed from kettle. Place on rack over hot water and cover tightly. Steam. Serve with sauce. This method eliminates excess oil.

And of course, Frying: Fry as is or roll fish in seasoned flour or cornmeal or wheat germ, or dip in batter before placing in pan. Fry in butter, oil, bacon or other fat, over moderate heat. Turn only once. Fairly fat fish such as salmon are most suitable for broiling or baking.

General Rule is cook fish **quickly** and for **as short a time as possible.** The protein of fish sets quickly at a temperature much below the boiling point. Cooking too long or at a temperature higher than necessary ruins the texture and flavor of fish.

Storing Fish: Keep fresh fish refrigerated until time to use. Fish loses flavor with any length of storage, therefore, use as soon as possible after purchase, perferably on day you buy it. Keep in the freezing tray or meat compartment of the refrigerator if it is not to be used the day it is bought. Remove store wrapping and rewrap tightly in waxed or parchment paper. Use it within 2 days of purchase. If you want to freeze fish after buying it, it would be advisable to buy frozen, not fresh fish for this purpose. Keep frozen fish frozen until time to use. Do not refreeze after thawing, since the quality will deteroriate rapidly. Cooking may be started before the fish is completely thawed. The most desirable way to thaw fish is in the refrigerator and not at room temperature since a considerable amount of dripping usually results.

Ground Turkey Sausage

1 pound raw ground turkey
½ teaspoon salt
½ teaspoon pepper
1 tablespoon fresh sage chopped OR
   ½ teaspoon powdered sage
½ to 1 teaspoon grated fresh ginger root

1 teaspoon rosemary
¼ teaspoon marjoram
¼ teaspoon thyme
¼ teaspoon freshly ground nutmeg

Grind together sage, rosemary, marjoram, thyme and nutmeg in mortar or mix in small dish. Mix ground turkey lightly with seasonings. Shape into eight patties. (Separate patties with wax paper and freeze, if desired.) Using a little butter, brown on both sides, reduce heat, cover and cook about 5 minutes more until cooked through but not dry. Serve for breakfast (6-8 servings) or for dinner (4 servings).

Squid is delicious
by Catherine Sinnott

figure 1

FIRST CUT

figure 2

SECOND CUT

figure 3

← slit

↑ slit

Nutrients in squid and abalone are similar

Nutrient values per 100 grams (about 3½ ounces)

	Calories	Protein (grams)	Fat (grams)	Carbohydrate (grams)
Squid	84	16	1	1.5
Sirloin	313	17	27	0
Abalone	98	19	.5	3

Cleaning takes skill — so practice

Most cleaning directions are quite complicated. However, there are very simple directions. To prepare, cut the head above the eyes. (Figure 1) Slit body (Figure 2) and remove cartilage and viscera, along with head. Rinse well and drain on absorbent paper.

In addition, the thin outer skin on the remaining flat section can be slipped off easily under running water to leave the edible legs and a lovely piece of light meat very much like abalone. The trick to keep this piece from curling when fried is to make a small slit on the two cut edges (Figure 3). Then pound lightly a few times with a flat object.

Cooking is fast

The simplest frying method is to dip cleaned squid ("legs" and flat pieces) in flour which has been seasoned with salt and pepper. Fry quickly to a golden brown. Drain on absorbent paper. Serve immediately.

If you want to be a little fancier, shake cleaned squid in a bag with flour and a bit of salt. Now dip in beaten egg, than cracker or cornflake crumbs and fry in oil about 30 seconds to the side. Delicious! Two pounds will make six moderate servings.

Let's talk turkey

New, shorter cooking times for turkey — cook stuffed turkeys to an internal temperature of 180-185°F. in 325°F. oven.
These times are approximately 15 minutes per lb.

Ready to Cook Weight	Time In Hours*
6 to 8 lbs.	2 to 2½ hours
8 to 12 lbs.	2½ to 3 hours
12 to 16 lbs.	3 to 4 hours
16 to 20 lbs.	4 to 5 hours
20 to 24 lbs.	5 to 6 hours

*These times are approximate and are for birds covered only with cloth. Using foil, paper or other coverings can also affect cooking time. The most accurate "doneness" test is to use a meat thermometer placed in the thickest part of the breast. Be sure the bulb does not touch a bone. Turkey is done when it registers 180-185 degrees F. For stuffed bird, point of thermometer should be in center of stuffing and register 165 degrees F. (For thawed frozen turkeys, 180 degrees is best and they will be less dry if cooked for the minimum time.) The pop-up "doneness" indicators imbedded in turkeys are not reliable. Double-check using a meat thermometer or the "joint test." This "doneness" test is when leg moves easily in joint. Allow bird to rest about ½ hour before carving.

Cook your turkey completely through at one time

Do not partially cook poultry one day and complete the cooking the following day. The poultry may not be heated enough to kill spoilage bacteria, but may instead have reached just the right temperature (between 40 degrees and 140 degrees F.) to allow growth of harmful bacteria. It is not a wise procedure to use low oven temperature such as 160 degrees - 185 degrees F. and cook the turkey for many hours such as overnight for the same reasons.

Size of bird to choose

Allow ¾ to 1 lb. per serving under 12 lbs.; allow ½ lb. to ¾ lb. for birds over 12 lbs.

How to thaw a turkey

Thaw in original wrapping, on a tray IN REFRIGERATOR for 2-3 days. You may also thaw in original wrapping in cold running water, or in cold water which is changed often.

Preparing and stuffing the turkey

Today's processing methods give consumers turkeys which require very little further cleaning. However stray pinfeathers should be removed and the inside cavity should be well washed to insure that all bits of lung and kidney are also removed.

Care of fresh turkeys

These may be refrigerated at home 1 or 2 days before roasting, making sure that the original wrappings are slit to allow for air circulation. Be sure to loosely wrap the giblets and store separately.

After the meal

As promptly as possible after dinner, remove the stuffing from the bird and refrigerate the turkey meat, the stuffing and the gravy each in its own container. Do not allow any of these foods to stand at room temperature, but refrigerate promptly.

Cooking an unstuffed turkey

For quicker, easier cooking, roast the turkey unstuffed, decreasing the time by 3 minutes per lb. Bake the stuffing in a casserole during the last hour the turkey is in the oven. Baste occasionally with drippings.

Stuffing suggestions

How much stuffing?

Allow approximately ¾ cup of prepared stuffing per lb. of ready to cook turkey. A one lb. loaf of bread will yield about 8 cups of soft bread crumbs. To this, of course, you add other ingredients to produce a wide variety of stuffing.

Basic bread stuffing

½ lb. butter or margarine
½ cup minced onion
2 teaspoons salt
½ teaspoon pepper

2 teaspoons sage, thyme or
poultry seasoning
8 cups soft bread crumbs

Melt shortening; saute onions until they are tender. Add bread crumbs and all seasonings. Toss together lightly. For a more moist stuffing, add a little hot water or broth. Makes enough for a 10 to 12 lb. turkey.

Variations

Seasoning: Instead of the herbs in the basic recipe, add 1 or 2 teaspoons celery seed, marjoram, chopped parsley, Italian seasoning or mixed herbs. One or more of these may be used.

Additions to basic recipe:

1 small can water chestnuts, drained and sliced thin,
½ lb. fresh mushrooms, sliced and sauteed until tender and light brown
1 lb. sausage meat, sauteed until brown; drain off excess fat before adding to bread mixture
1 cup chopped nuts. Almonds, filberts, walnuts, peanuts, or pecans are good choices.
Fruit: 4 cups peeled, diced apples instead of 4 cups of the bread crumbs.
1 cup pitted, cut-up stewed prunes plus 1 cup cut-up stewed apricots may be added to replace 2 cups of the bread crumbs.

Corn bread stuffing

One recipe corn bread, baked in 8 x 8 x 2 pan.

1 teaspoon salt
1 tablespoon poultry seasoning
½ cup chopped onion
1 cup chopped celery
1 can corn, drained

The turkey giblets, cooked
and diced
¼ cup melted butter or margarine
½ cup turkey broth from giblets

Crumble corn bread in a bowl. Add all the other ingredients and mix lightly with a fork.

Chestnut stuffing

2 cups cooked, peeled chestnuts
10 slices bread
¼ cup chopped parsley
½ cup cream or undiluted evap. milk

½ cup sherry
2 teaspoons salt
¼ teaspoon pepper
¼ lb. butter, melted

Cut chestnuts into small pieces. Toast bread. Soak bread in small quantity cold water, until soft; squeeze out the water. Tear bread into pieces; mix with chestnuts and other ingredients. Bake uncovered in greased casserole at 325 degrees for 1 hr.

Whole chickens (not parts) and turkey parts (not whole) are the best buys *by Betsy Wood*

You may have wondered which gives you more cooked meat for your money — whole poultry or parts? At current prices, the headline summarizes it all. I drew these conclusions after cutting and weighing, and looking at prices and other people's tables on chicken and turkey.

Whole chickens are the best buy
(Even whole, cut-up chickens are a good buy)
—You pay extra if you want chicken parts, in fact, 40-60 percent extra.
—If you do want just the fancy pieces — breasts, thighs, and drumsticks for a party meal, you can probably get them from a whole chicken and get the wings, backs and giblets "free," for another meal.
—But if you are making Chicken Kiev, you'll want breasts, no matter what the cost.
—Turkey parts — hindquarters, drumsticks and wings are the best buy, compared to whole turkeys.

—Boneless turkey roasts cost plenty for convenience — about 35 percent more than whole turkey.
—YIELD of MEAT INCREASES from backs to wings to whole bird to drumsticks to thighs to breast. You probably knew this. But did you know that you get only a shade more meat on drumsticks than you get on the whole bird?
—POOREST BUYS of all would be frozen "Gravy with Turkey" which may have only 15 percent turkey meat, and "Turkey with Gravy" which may have only 35 percent turkey meat.

CHICKEN PRICE COMPARISON*

Then you get the same amount of meat for your money when parts cost:

If price per pound of WHOLE CHICKEN is:	BREAST	THIGH	DRUM STICK	WING
49¢	65¢	55¢	50¢	39¢
59¢	78¢	66¢	61¢	48¢
69¢	91¢	77¢	71¢	56¢
79¢	1.04	88¢	81¢	64¢
89¢	1.18	99¢	92¢	72¢
99¢	1.32	1.11	1.02	81¢
1.09	1.45	1.22	1.13	89¢
Actual prices as of 8/30/79:				
79¢	1.49	1.39	1.35	98¢

SO, AT CURRENT PRICES, THE WHOLE CHICKEN IS A BETTER BUY THAN ANY OF THE PARTS.
*Twenty grams of protein is a little more than ⅓ of the recommended daily allowance for adults. Three and one-half ounces of cooked meat contain roughly 20 grams of protein.

TURKEY PRICE COMPARISON

if price per pound of WHOLE TURKEY is:	BREAST	HIND Qtr.	THIGH	DRUM STICK	WING	boneless ROAST
		Then you get the same amount of meat for your money when parts cost:				
59¢	75¢	63¢	72¢	60¢	55¢	1.03
69¢	88¢	74¢	85¢	71¢	64¢	1.21
79¢	1.01	85¢	97¢	81¢	73¢	1.38
89¢	1.13	96¢	1.09	91¢	82¢	1.56
99¢	1.26	1.06	1.21	1.01	92¢	1.73
1.09	1.39	1.17	1.34	1.12	1.01	1.90

Actual prices as of 8/30/79:

	BREAST	HIND Qtr.	THIGH	DRUM STICK	WING	boneless ROAST
89¢	—	69¢	—	59¢	59¢	2.17

SO, THE PARTS WE HAVE AVAILABLE ARE A BETTER BUY THAN WHOLE TURKEYS.

Pansit (a Chinese Noodle Dish of the Phillipines)

½ lb. bean threads (Shiritake)
1 2½-lb. frying chicken, cut-up
8 cups water
1½ lbs. fresh pork, fat trimmed and thinly sliced
2 large cloves garlic, crushed
1 tablespoon oil or more if needed
4 stalks celery, chopped
2 or 3 onions, chopped
1 tablespoon parsley
2 beef bouillon cubes

2 chicken bouillon cubes
½-¾ cups soy sauce or to taste
⅓ cup tomato sauce
1 teaspoon msg, optional
½ lb. sliced fresh mushrooms
  or 8 oz. canned
  or 6-8 dried, cut in pieces
hard cooked eggs, sieved or cut
chopped green onions, with tops

Soak bean threads in hot water for 30 minutes. Simmer chicken in water until almost tender, about 30 minutes. Bone chicken, cut meat into small pieces. Save broth for next step. Sauté pork and garlic in oil until slightly browned. Add celery, onions, parsley, and bouillon cubes. Cook until vegetables are softened but not limp. Transfer to a large kettle with a tight lid, adding soy sauce, tomato sauce, msg, and mushrooms. Cook about 5 minutes, stirring to blend ingredients. Add 8 cups chicken broth; cover and simmer about 20 minutes until pork is thoroughly cooked. Add chicken and drained bean threads, cut to desired length. Simmer 10 minutes. To adjust consistency, add water or bean threads. Mixture should spoon easily but not be soupy. Serve over rice decorated with hard cooked eggs and green onions. May be reheated. Serves 12. (Recipe from Vangie Elkins.)

Morg Masalam *(India)*
(Chicken with happy spices)

2-3 lb. chicken fryer
3 tablespoons butter or margarine
¼ teaspoon ground ginger
½ teaspoon tumeric
8 whole cloves
1-inch stick cinnamon

¼ teaspoon cardamon
2 small onions
½ clove garlic, minced
¼ teaspoon chili powder or cayenne
1 teaspoon salt

Cut up chicken. Melt butter in skillet, fit in chicken, and sprinkle with ginger, tumeric, cloves, cinnamon stick and cardamon. Fry over medium heat until brown, 12-15 minutes. While chicken browns, slice onion thinly and crush garlic. Place on chicken and add chili powder. Cover tightly and cook very slowly for 30 minutes. Give skillet a shake every 10 minutes. DON'T LIFT THE LID! After 40 minutes add salt and check to see whether chicken is done. (Contributed by Mrs. W.D. Sikes)

Milk, dairy products and eggs

Milk

. . . some basic information

Fluid whole milk contains 87% water, not less than 3¼% milk fat (butterfat), and at least 8¼% nonfat milk solids.

Nutritional Value

Milk is a good source of protein, calcium, riboflavin and some other minerals and vitamins.
An 8-ounce cup of whole milk yields the following percentages of the U.S. Recommended Daily Allowance for 6 nutrients:

Protein	20%	Vitamin D	25%
Vitamin A	4%	Calcium	25%
Riboflavin	30%	Phosphorus	25%
(Vitamin B₂)			

Calories:

1 cup whole milk	160
1 cup low-fat milk	140
1 cup nonfat milk	100

Low-fat milk contains 2% fat; nonfat or skim milk contains less than ½% fat. Except for calories their nutritional value is roughly the same as whole milk.

Pasteurization

Most milk sold in the U.S. is pasteurized. This means heating the raw milk to destroy harmful bacteria. A small amount of raw (unpasteurized) milk is sold in some communities. It is labelled as such. It is more expensive. It is more perishable.

Need for Milk in Diet

For the majority of the population milk is a valuable food to be included in the daily diet. For those who cannot tolerate milk or who have allergic reactions to milk, we suggest you consult your physician.
Young children should have 2-3 cups daily.
Children aged 9 through teens need 3-4 cups daily.
Adults need 2 or more.
Pregnant women need 3 or more.
Lactating mothers need 4 or more.
Cheese can be eaten as part of the day's milk intake.

Storage

Get milk home quickly and refrigerate for best quality and storage life. The date on the carton is the date after which the store should not sell the milk. However, if properly cared for, milk will keep up to a week after the pull date.

Nonfat dry milk

Even with recent increases in prices, nonfat dry milk is widely acclaimed for its economy and nutritive value:

consider . . .

. . . a quart of nonfat milk made from the dry powder costs from 3/5 to 3/4 as much as a quart of fresh whole milk, depending on the size package used. A family using 3 quarts of milk per day could save as much as $185 a year by switching from whole to nonfat dry milk.

. . . Nonfat dry milk has all the protein, minerals, and the most important of the water-soluble vitamins of fresh whole milk but only half the calories. In most brands the fat-soluble vitamins A and D have been added. Since many Americans struggle with overweight sooner or later, why not ease the pain by accustoming your palate to less rich foods such as this in anticipation?

How to learn to love to drink it

Can food habits be changed? Advertising, especially TV, does it all the time! Food habits can be changed — but not always quickly. We don't eat the way we did 25 or 30 years ago. In part we've been cajoled by tantalizing advertising. Keep that in mind.

Be positive — expect to appreciate nonfat milk. Nonfat milk has certain qualities which should be appreciated. Don't present it as a substitute for whole milk, because it *is* different. Many people prefer nonfat milk. They like its special "mouth feel," and the very cold sensation it gives on swallowing. They even find the taste of whole milk unpleasantly creamy.

When you make the BIG CHANGE . . . if you decide to change to nonfat milk after years of drinking whole milk, consider either "The Sudden" or "The Gradual" methods.

★ If you choose to use **The Sudden Change**, take the family into your confidence, explaining your reasons for changing to nonfat milk, and acknowledging to them that nonfat *is* different from whole milk. It is important for everyone in the family to understand that the project will take time and patience. Enthusiasm for the project is an essential ingredient for success.

★ **The Gradual Change** may be more acceptable. This can be accomplished by mixing a small amount of nonfat milk with whole, gradually increasing the proportion of nonfat as much and as often as your family will accept. Start with 1/4 or less of nonfat, and 3/4 of whole. Use this proportion for 2 or 3 weeks before increasing the amount of nonfat milk. Even though a complete change from whole to nonfat milk could take several months, it's worth it! If your family balks at some point and refuses to go any further, give in gracefully. Continue with the proportion acceptable to them and congratulate yourself on succeeding to this extent.

Set up signs of success. Which ever method you use, it is a good idea to set up signs of success as a means of encouraging your family. Maybe the money saved by using nonfat dry milk could be set aside daily, in a piggy bank perhaps. Put the bank in a place of honor in the middle of the dining room table. Everyone can watch the fund grow. Then, at some agreed-upon time, spend the money for something special that all of you want.

Non-Fat Dry Milk

For best quality should be stored in a cool dry place and used within 2-3 months. (It **can** be used up to one year.)
Mix at least four hours before serving. After mixing, refrigerate like fresh milk.

from your Co-op Home Economist

Avoid these dangers

Careless preparation of the nonfat milk can get you off to a very bad start. Follow directions on the package. Be sure to *mix up the milk several hours in advance* of the time it is to be used, to give the milk time to thoroughly chill. Warm milk doesn't taste the same, whether it's skim or whole. Many a person has been completely disillusioned by drinking warm, freshly mixed nonfat milk, forgetting that everyone is accustomed to cold milk.

The program can be disrupted if your family drinks nonfat milk at home and whole milk at school, or if you lapse into serving whole milk at home when you're too busy to mix up the nonfat. This latter situation is avoidable. After all, nonfat and low-fat fluid milks are both sold at the market! Keep your program going with them. If children are drinking whole milk at school, maybe low-fat milk is your best bet at home. Mix equal amounts of whole and nonfat to make low-fat milk.

Keep nonfat dry milk powder stored properly in a cool, dry place. Unopened packages may be kept for several months. If temperatures reach 90°F. or more for long periods, flavor changes may occur.* After mixing with water, refrigerate and use within a few days as you would any other fluid milk.

*If the powder becomes lumpy, it has deteriorated in both flavor and quality. Prevent this change by excluding air; close container tightly.

Buttermilk
by Betsy Wood

I thought you should know more about buttermilk, so I asked some experts, friends and relations, and here's what they said:

How do you like it?

Tessa: I love it! I thought I hated it till I drank some at your house. Now I'm a convert.

Jettie: Ugh!

Mal: When I want beer with dinner and there isn't any, buttermilk tastes almost as good.

Fattening? No.

Jack (manager of Valley Gold Dairy): Ours is low-calorie (about 90 per glass) and low fat (about 1% fat compared to 2% for low-fat milk). The thickness doesn't mean it's rich. It's due to adding culture to milk and letting it grow.

Helen: That yummy Bulgarian buttermilk is made from whole milk and has the calories of whole milk.

Salt added? Yes.

My Dad: Alas, no buttermilk on my low-sodium diet, unless it's homemade.

How do you use it?

Nancy: Make blue cheese dressing with buttermilk, crumbled blue cheese, few drops olive oil, small clove garlic, something green like fresh basil or parsley. Blend. Other good, cheap, low-calorie salad dressings: One-third mayonnaise and two-thirds buttermilk OR equal parts commercial dressing and buttermilk.

Anything else?

Cathy: Why the craze for yogurt and kefir while buttermilk is similar and costs half to a quarter as much?

Aunt Jane: It's not like it was when I poured buttermilk off the churn after making butter, warm, with the cat around my feet.

Mary: Dry buttermilk is available and can be used for cooking, but it's not good for drinking.

A very controversial subject: Milk

by Helen Black

The next time you sit tongue-tied at a social gathering, why not throw out a remark on some controversial subject? You could mention religion, politics, or milk. All of these subjects are bound to galvanize the group into heated argument . . . er, discussion. The results, of course, may not be enlightening. It is unclear why milk is so controversial, but plenty of what you hear about it is wrong. Here are some wrong ideas I've heard recently. They range from downright dangerous to merely mild misconceptions.

"Extra nonfat dry milk in baby's bottle is good" . . . **a highly dangerous wrong idea.** Excess protein can have serious, even fatal consequences on young infants. Nonfat dry milk is over 35 percent protein. Neither it nor any other high protein substance should be added to already adequate baby formulas **except under explicit instructions from your doctor.**

"Raw milk is better for you" . . . **also a dangerous wrong idea.** The problem with raw milk is that it often contains very risky bacteria, straight from the cow. The milk heat treatment of pasteurization removes this risk but reduces the levels of two vitamins. One of the vitamins, thiamine, is reduced only slightly; the other, vitamin C, is abundantly available in other foods.

"The reason fresh milk keeps is that preservatives are put in it" . . . **No! No! No!** This is quite untrue. But milk does keep better now than it did 10 years ago. The reason is that milk is handled more carefully now. For example, in California in 1973 a law was passed requiring a temperature-recording device to continuously monitor farm milk. If the record shows excessive storage temperature, the trucker will not pick up the milk.

"Yogurt is more nutritious than milk" . . . **this is not exactly true.** Bacteria consume some of the B vitamins as they convert milk to yogurt. However, commercial yogurt is usually made with more added milk solids than fluid milk, hence has correspondingly increased nutrient content.

"Non-instant dry milk has lower heat processing and is more nutritious" . . . **Wrong again.** This is a very persistent non-truth. The process used to instantize nonfat dry milk does not involve heat at all. In fact, most of the non-instant nonfat dry milk sold is subjected to **higher** heat treatments, in order to improve performance in bread making in commercial bakeries. Instant nonfat dry milk has been quite thoroughly studied in animal feeding experiments and the nutritional losses from the processing are insignificant.

"Buttermilk contains no fat" . . . **Nay, not so.** Buttermilk can be made from nonfat milk, but usually it isn't. Valley Gold Buttermilk is 1.5 percent fat. Tuttles Buttermilk is made from whole milk, and is about 3.8 percent fat.

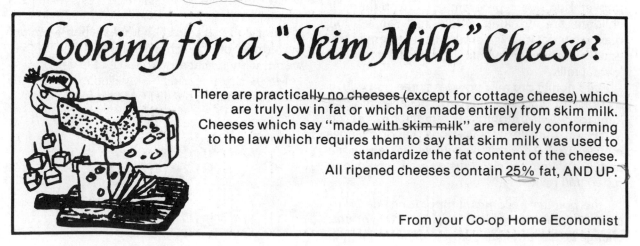

Looking for a "Skim Milk" Cheese?

There are practically no cheeses (except for cottage cheese) which are truly low in fat or which are made entirely from skim milk. Cheeses which say "made with skim milk" are merely conforming to the law which requires them to say that skim milk was used to standardize the fat content of the cheese. All ripened cheeses contain 25% fat, AND UP.

From your Co-op Home Economist

Cheese

Cheese has been a most useful and versatile food for thousands of years. It is made in many countries around the world. Its use in the United States has, until recent years, been limited to casseroles, sandwiches, or snacks. However, in many countries, it is used with breakfast rolls, at tea time, or is served as a dessert.

Technically, natural cheese is classified by the method of producing the curd, the animal source of the milk and its fat content, and the mold or bacteria used in the ripening process. (During ripening the flavor, appearance, and texture characteristics of the *aged* cheese are developed.) However, for convenience the various cheese may be classified as hard, semi-hard, and soft, depending on their moisture content. The term "natural" used with cheese merely distinguishes it from blended or modified cheeses. It does *not* mean that the cheese contains no added color, salt, or other additives.

HARD			SEMI-HARD*		SOFT		
Bacteria Ripened 12-16 mo.	Bacteria Ripened 3-12 mo.	Bacteria Ripened 2-3 mo.	Bacteria Ripened 1-8 mo.	Mold Ripened 2-12 mo.	Bacteria Ripened 1-2 mo.	Mold Ripened 2-5 mo.	Unripened
Cheshire Parmesan Romano	Cheddar Edam Gjetost Gruyere Provolone Sap Sago Swiss	Nokkelost Kumminost	Bel Paese Brick Fontina Gouda Jack Muenster Port du Salut Tilsit	Blue Gorgonzola Roquefort Stilton	Limburger Liederkranz	Brie Camembert	Baker's Cottage Mozzarella Neufchatel Ricotta Teleme

*Some of these cheeses may be fully cured and used for grating.

Besides the natural cheeses, there are other cheeses that have been modified. **Pasteurized process cheese** is made by blending and heating one or more kinds of pulverized natural cheese with an emulsifying agent; acids such as lactic, acetic, phosphoric; salt and flavorings. The heat used in the processing "fixes" the flavor so that no further aging takes place. The flavor will remain unchanged for several months. The composition is essentially the same as the cheese from which it was made.

Process cheese food is made in the same way as process cheese except that certain dairy products (cream, milk, milk solids, cheese whey, whey albumin) are added. It has more water but less protein and less fat than processed cheese. Examples of process cheese food are limited. However, **process cheese spread** widely abounds on the grocery shelves. Cheese spreads differ from cheese foods in that the moisture content is higher (maximum 60%) and the fat content lower (minimum 20%). As a result, the protein content is only about two-thirds as much as in processed cheese.

Cold pack cheese or cheese food merely means that the ground cheese and other ingredients are mixed *without* heat.

NUTRITIVE VALUES. Cheese is an excellent source of animal protein. Equivalent amounts of natural or process cheese can be substituted for boneless meat in the diet. However, the process cheese spreads contain a lesser amount of protein than process cheeses. The protein content of cheese in general varies with the moisture content. It ranges from 8% for cream cheese (soft, unripened) to 36% for the very hard grating cheeses such as Parmesan.

Cheese contributes varying amounts of calcium, riboflavin, and vitamin A to the diet which could be important to the non-milk drinker in terms of better nutrition. The fat content of the cheeses is quite high. For those on a fat-restricted diet, *dry cottage cheese or baker's cheese is the only cheese* with no fat. Creamed cottage cheese has 4% fat, and various natural and process cheeses will range from 20-35%.

Cooking Qualities. Natural cheeses have more distinctive flavors than process cheeses, but some tend to be stringy when melted. For distinctive flavor and better melting qualities, choose a soft, aged, natural cheese. Process cheeses and process cheese spreads melt smoothly and easily in cooking.

Storage. The keeping qualities of cheeses are related to their moisture content. Soft cheeses are perishable and must be refrigerated. The very hard grating cheeses need no refrigeration. While the mold typical of Roquefort cheese is thought to be harmless, it is not known for sure whether cheese that molds in your refrigerator is safe. Prevent cheese from molding by wrapping tightly to exclude air after opening; use up opened packages promptly. If you do trim mold off, cut deeply around moldy spot.

The best protein buy in cheese is cottage cheese, but its calcium content is quite low. Therefore, for the non-milk drinker in particular, the loaf-type cheese spread is a better buy.

CHEESE	Grams Protein per pound	Approximate number servings per pound, each serving providing 20 grams of protein.	Cost per 20 grams protein (⅓ of adult daily protein allowance)*
Cheddar — natural	113	5	43¢-62¢
— process	105	5	59¢
Processed Cheese Spread	73	3.6	55¢
Cottage cheese	62	3	26¢
Cream Cheese	36	2	89¢

Of course, there are factors aside from cost that enter into cheese choices, the most important being the flavor and texture and the intended use. Cheese spread would be acceptable to many in a casserole, but it would be hard to imagine eating it with fresh grapes or a crisp apple for dessert!

Process cheese in large loaves is usually cheaper than its natural counterpart. But if it is unique flavor and texture that one wishes, the natural cheeses, whether domestic or foreign, are a great delight!

*Based on August, 1979 prices.

Curdled milk for lunch?
by Judy Heckman

Sound unappetizing? Well, lots of us seem to like it. At the Co-op we sell about 6,500 quarts of cottage cheese each week.

Cottage cheese production starts with pasteurized skim milk. A culture of lactic acid developing bacteria and heat curdle or coagulate the milk protein into a soft curd. (Rennet, a coagulating agent obtained from the stomach lining of young mammals, is used only for large curd.) The curd is cut, the whey drained off and the cheese washed. One percent salt and a mixture of cream and milk are added to the creamed varieties.

Choose your style

Creamed is available in small or large curd, plain or flavored with chives or pineapple. All are about 4 percent fat and 120 calories per ½ cup. (Pineapple flavored contains 140 calories per ½ cup.) *Low Fat* contains 2 percent fat and 104 calories per ½ cup. *Uncreamed* or *Dry Curd* has no added salt or creaming mixture. Fat content is about ½ percent with 95 calories per ½ cup.

Ricotta Cheese differs from cottage cheese because it's made with whole milk or a mixture of whole milk and skim milk. Fat content is about 8½ percent with 160 calories per ½ cup. It's more expensive than cottage cheese and differs slightly in flavor. Ricotta cheese does not keep well once it's opened so use within two to three days.

Use instead of meat

Cottage cheese is a good source of protein. One-half cup supplies about 17 grams or 1/3 the Recommended Daily Allowance. That's about the same amount of protein as found in 3 ounces of cooked meat, fish or poultry, 2 cups of milk or 3 eggs. Although made from milk, cottage cheese is not a complete substitute for milk because much of the calcium, and some of the other nutrients, remain in the whey which is drained off.

Store cottage cheese tightly covered in the refrigerator. If properly refrigerated, unopened it will keep a week or more beyond the pull date stamped on the bottom of the carton. It spoils more rapidly every time it is opened. Creamed cottage cheese keeps longer than low-fat. Dry curd should be used within 2 or 3 days of purchase.

Cheese

often has color added. The colors are usually either ANNATTO or CAROTENE and are not thought to be harmful. They are vegetable dyes.

from your Co-op Home Economist

Cottage cheese ideas

Combine with spices and seasonings — caraway or poppy seeds, rosemary, tarragon.

Combine with fruit — any kind, but especially good with berries, peaches, melons and stewed dried fruit.

Combine with vegetables — mix with diced vegetables in a salad, with chives or green onions on baked potato. For a quick, delicious lunch try cottage cheese with tomato, sliced onions and sour cream.

For dips — mix with bleu cheese, horseradish, anchovies, chopped onion, clams, fresh, canned or smoked.

Combine with meats — in a casserole such as lasagna made of tomato-meat sauce, cooked noodles, dry curd cottage cheese, mozzarella and parmesan cheeses.

For dessert such as blintzes or cheese cake use one of the dry curd cheeses. Or, just regular or low-fat cottage cheese sweetened with sugar, flavored with vanilla and cinnamon, and topped with cranberry relish or other fruit is easy and delicious. Also try cottage cheese topped with flavored yogurt.

% Fat in cheese

cottage cheese, creamed	4%
ricotta, part skim or whole	8-16%
mozzarella, part skim	17%
camembert, Swiss process, mozzarella	20-26%
provolone, Swiss, American, Edam, blue	27-29%
Meunster, Colby cheddar	30-33%
cream	36%

adapted from the Journal of American Dietetic Association 2/15

from your Co-op Home Economist

Cultured milk products are not all the same

by Mary Gullberg

What is a cultured milk product?

It is a whole, low-fat or nonfat fluid milk which may have nonfat dry milk solids added to give it more body and nutrition. It is pasteurized to destroy unwanted bacteria which might produce off flavors during fermentation. It is then innoculated with the appropriate organisms (lactobacillus bulgaricus and streptococcus thermophilus in the case of yogurts) and incubated at about 100°F. until it is the consistency of junket or custard. It is then refrigerated until used. All ingredients are not yet listed on the labels of all brands, but we are hoping that this will come about in the near future.

There are different nutritive values among cultured milks.

As the percentage of butterfat increases, the total calories go up and the nutrients from the nonfat milk components go down. Comparing sour cream with buttermilk, for instance, sour cream with 20% fat has four times as many calories as buttermilk with 1% but 25% less protein, about 20% less calcium but nearly 20 times more vitamin A. Comparing plain lowfat yogurt with lowfat yogurt containing fruit, we find almost double the calories in the fruit yogurt and a reduction of the vitamin A by about one third. The water soluble vitamins and minerals are reduced, but by a lesser amount (about one-fifth) because nonfat dry milk solids are added to both products. If you think of the fruit yogurts as desserts (they do have added sugar in addition to the sugar in the fruit), then they are very nutritious when compared to most desserts.

Cultured milk products keep longer than non-fermented ones.

Non-fermented dairy foods are the fresh milks — whole, lowfat, nonfat, chocolate, etc. The cultured products keep longer, because the fermentation produces acid which inhibits the growth of spoilage organisms. As the cultured products age (in the refrigerator, naturally) the amount of acid gradually increases, and the whey will tend to separate from the milk curds causing a "weeping" of the product. For this reason, most of these cultured milk products contain either gelatin or a vegetable stabilizer to keep the texture smooth. The stabilizer also helps the delicate product withstand handling and transportation. Most cultured milks will keep quite a while after the date on the carton which is the last day the product should be sold. After this "pull date" most of these products will keep one to two weeks if handled properly. If they should develop mold or an unpleasant taste or smell, they should be thrown out.

What's yogurt?

by Mary Gullberg

What can be learned from comparing the nutrition information on the labels of various yogurts?
And how do these products compare with fluid milk and cream as well as frozen dairy desserts? Below is a table giving the grams of fat and the calories in some of these products:

One Cup	Calories	Grams of Fat
Continental Plain Lowfat Yogurt	130	5
Continental Plain Yogurt	270	15
Valley Gold Strawberry Yogurt	240	4
Lucerne Red Raspberry Frozen Yogurt Dessert	240	3
Ice Milk	200	5
Ice Cream	255	14

Why so MANY CALORIES in Continental Plain Yogurt? If this product were just richer in fat, the calories should be 220. Apparently, however, they have also added nonfat dry milk solids, and this would account for the extra 50 calories. The ingredient statement says: "skim milk, cream, Lactobacillus bulgaricus, agar, natural flavor." Doesn't say anything about added milk solids.

Most of us think of yogurt as a low-fat product. Continental Plain Yogurt has three times the fat of other yogurts, and ice milk is lower both in fat and calories than the Continental product. Personally, I don't think this product should be called "yogurt," since it is a manipulated product with more than double the calories in the Continental Lowfat Yogurt. Perhaps it should be called "Extra Rich Yogurt" to call attention to its distinctly different type of composition.

July 31, 1978

Blue-Veined Cheeses

The name ROQUEFORT may only be used for cheese made from ewe's milk in a certain area of France. Similar cheese may be called "Roquefort-type." GORGONZOLA is a blue-veined cheese from Italy made from either cow's or goat's milk.
Some domestic BLUE cheeses are colored to give the cheese a creamy color. Most domestic blue is made from cow's milk. The blue veining is the mold with which the cheese was innoculated.

MOST
YOGURT
IS NOT HEATED AFTER CULTURING
Therefore most yogurt contains live lactobacillus bacteria and most plain yogurt can be the starter for more yogurt!

ALL yogurt making starts with pasteurized milk.

from your Co-op Home Economist

I scream, you scream, we all scream for ice cream

by Catherine Sinnott

What were Italians doing in the year 1550? Among other things, they were making ice cream, using ice brought down from the mountains. The ice cream business has changed greatly since then.

On checking with the supplier of Valley Gold ice cream, we learned some interesting information about our regular ice cream (sold in the rectangular box) and premium ice cream (sold in a round container).

Basic Mixes

Valley Gold ice cream is made from a basic mix (one for regular, one for premium). Included in the mix are cream, butterfat, condensed skim milk, sugar, corn sugar, and stabilizer (from seaweed). Condensed sweet buttermilk and whey powder also are used. Regular ice cream has 10% butterfat and premium has 12% butterfat. Fruit, nuts, chocolate chips, etc., and flavors are added to the mix to make different varieties. The only color added to these V.G. ice creams is annatto, a natural food coloring from the seed of the annatto tree. No color is added in chocolate, strawberry or vanilla (except extra rich).

Whipping

Before packaging, the ice cream mix is whipped with air to double its volume. This gives the smooth, creamy texture and "mouth feel" we associate with fine ice cream. Valley Gold's premium ice cream, in the round box, has somewhat less air whipped in.

Labelling

Ice cream has not been covered by the labelling laws required for many foods. It will be after July 1979 for ice cream shipped interstate.* However, Valley Gold ice cream has had its ingredients on regular ice cream for many years (premium more recently), in line with Co-op member demand. If you have questions about ingredients, you can answer most of them by just reading the box.

*Although extension may be granted to permit supplies of old labels to be used up.

May 28, 1979

Ice Creams

contain nonfat milk solids, corn syrup, stabilizers, emulsifying agents, colors and flavors, in addition to the sugar, cream, fruits, etc.

★ store at —5° F.
★ never leave out of freezer more than ½ hour.
★ store carton in plastic bag to avoid moisture loss.

from your Co-op Home Economist

Orange Cheesecake

8 oz. cream cheese
¼ cup orange juice
2 eggs, well beaten
¾ cup sugar
1 teaspoon grated orange rind
1 cup crushed vanilla wafers (about 25)
2 tablespoons butter or margarine, melted
1 tablespoon orange juice
1 tablespoon sugar
Orange sections for decoration

Blend cream cheese with orange juice. Beat in eggs and sugar and grated orange rind until fluffy. Pour into vanilla wafer crust, prepared by thoroughly blending wafer crumbs, melted butter, orange juice, and sugar and pressing evenly on the bottom and sides of 9" pie pan. Bake at 350 degrees about 40 minutes, or until knife comes out clean. Cool. Decorate top with orange sections.

Cottage Cheese Pancakes

1 cup whole wheat flour
1 teaspoon baking powder
2 teaspoons sugar
1 teaspoon salt
4 eggs, well beaten
2 cups low fat cottage cheese
¼ cup skim milk

Mix the dry ingredients well; add beaten eggs and cheese. Stir in the milk. Fry on a hot greased griddle until well browned on both sides.

These are good served with fruit preserves and sour cream, or with sliced fruit, applesauce or syrup.

Serves 4.

California Cheese Casserole

1 cup rice
7 oz. can green chiles
4 small zucchini
1 large tomato
1 lb. Monterey Jack cheese
2 cups sour cream
1 teaspoon oregano
1 teaspoon garlic powder or mashed garlic clove
½ green pepper, chopped
2 tablespoons minced green onion or chives
salt and pepper to taste
minced parsley for garnish

Cook rice until barely tender. Slice zucchini thinly and parboil for one minute. Slit chiles; remove seeds. Cut half the cheese into ½ inch strips and place one piece in each chili, folding it over the cheese. Put rice in well-buttered baking dish; cover with layer of chiles and cheese, then with zucchini and sliced tomato. Blend sour cream with spices and green pepper. Spread over all. Cut remaining cheese into very small cubes and sprinkle evenly over the mixture. Sprinkle with parsley. Bake at 350° for about 30 minutes. Serves 8.

The versatile egg

What's oval, white and smooth all over? You're right—an egg! Few of today's convenience foods can beat eggs for packaging, nutrition, low price, versatility and flavor. With eggs as an ingredient, you can be on the way to creating dishes from the world's great cuisines. From France, try a souffle or a quiche; from Italy, zabagalione; from India, curried eggs; from our own shores, don't forget the elegant Baked Alaska. But eggs are worthy of everyday meals as well, from scrambled eggs or omelets, to egg sandwiches, stuffed eggs and custards.

Refrigerated Eggs are "Fresher"

The sooner the egg is removed from the custody of the hen to the refrigerator, the better. Eggs can lose as much quality in a few hours in the hen's nest on a warm day as in a week or two in the refrigerator. Freshness cannot be maintained forever, of course, so plan to use eggs within one or two weeks of purchase. When buying, check the pull date on the end of the carton; the pull date is the date after which the eggs should not be sold. After that date, eggs properly stored should keep at least another week.

How to Tell a Good Egg

Grade AA eggs, purchased at a store where there is rapid turnover and where eggs are refrigerated, should be "upstanding." That is, when broken into a frying pan, the white does not run all over. Rather it stands up thickly around the yolk, which is small and rounded. With age, or improper storage, the thick white becomes watery and the yolk enlarges and flattens, Such eggs are nutritious but not as good looking.

Eating Eggs Safely

Eggs are notoriously contaminated with Salmonella bacteria, one of the nastier bacteria which can cause a miserable bout of nausea, diarrhea, stomach cramps and fever beginning about 8 hours after eating contaminated foods. This is no problem if the eggs are cooked (to a temperature of 140 F., at least). If you wish to use raw eggs in eggnog or beer or meringue, *use only clean eggs with intact, not cracked, shells.*

FIGURE YOUR OWN EGG CHART

When eggs are in this price range:							
Extra Large	1.08	99	90	81	72	63	54
Large	96	88	80	73	65	57	49
Medium	84	77	70	63	56	49	42

*Expect this difference between adjacent sizes for equivalent value: 12¢ 11¢ 10¢ 9¢ 8¢ 7¢ 6¢

*IF THERE IS LESS DIFFERENCE THAN THIS, THE LARGER EGGS ARE A BETTER BUY.

from your Co-op Home Economist

Eggs are not scary
by Helen Black

It is not necessary to be scared of eggs, but some people are. What is terrifying about eggs? Well, the cooking scares some of us. Cholesterol content scares others.

The Tough Egg

The tough, rubbery egg has been overcooked. It's the protein in eggs which gets tough with too high heat, or too long cooking, or both. An egg **boiled** 3 minutes is tougher than one simmered 6 minutes. That perfect fried egg without nasty frizzled edges which is not too brown on the bottom has been cooked gently over **moderate** heat, just long enough.

The Green-Edged Hard-Boiled Egg

A greenish look sometimes afflicts the yolks of hard-boiled eggs. To avoid it, simmer eggs 20 to 30 minutes, then plunge into cold water. The green color is only due to chemical combination of iron from the yolk with sulfur in the white, the result of too high heat or too long cooking. It looks bad, but it's harmless.

The Cholesterol Controversy

Eggs are high in cholesterol, but wait: the question of how dietary cholesterol affects health is **still** controversial. Not all authorities think normal people should cut out eggs. Since eggs have the **highest quality protein of any common food,** plus minerals and vitamins too, don't eliminate them unless your doctor advises it. Remember, even low cholesterol diets can include three eggs per week.

Jan. 30, 1978

Eggs

**Measuring guide—
How many to fill a cup?**

Egg Size	1 cup whites	1 cup yolks
Small	10	18
Medium	8	16
Large	7	14
Extra Large	6	12

Spinach Souffle

3 tablespoons butter or margarine
¼ cup flour
1 teaspoon salt
¼ teaspoon pepper
pinch of nutmeg
1 cup milk
¼ lb. Swiss cheese, grated (about 1 cup)
1 cup well drained, finely chopped, cooked spinach
3 eggs, separated

Melt butter and blend in flour, salt, pepper and nutmeg. Gradually add milk, stirring until well blended. Cook over low heat, stirring constantly, until mixture is thick and smooth. Add cheese and spinach, and cook until cheese is melted. Cool. Beat egg whites until stiff but not dry. Then beat egg yolks until thick and lemon colored. Add yolks to spinach mixture. Fold in whites. Pour into buttered 1½ quart straight-sided casserole. Bake in preheated slow oven (325 degrees) for 45 to 50 minutes, or until firm in center. Serve immediately. Serves 3-4.

The egg . . . and what the hen ate

This question of what the hen ate before she laid those eggs is a tough one, and we had to call up the experts at the University of California and talk to our suppliers to get the answers.

Are pale egg yolks low in vitamin A?

No. It's true that the brighter yellow vegetables or fruits and the very dark green vegetables are usually higher in provitamin A or carotene. But vitamin A itself is almost colorless. Bright-colored egg yolks are caused by the hen's diet of such feeds as corn or alfalfa, which have other pigments in them.

Arsenic is sometimes used in the feed of layers.

Arsenic in trace amounts is sometimes used in the feed of layers. Arsenic is an essential nutrient for chickens, and feeds may be low in this element. The arsenic is added in the organic form, not the highly toxic inorganic form. Many years ago, arsenic was used as a growth stimulent added to the feed of fryers, but this is no longer done.

But no routine antibiotics.

Antibiotics are given layers only when they get sick; antibiotics are not given routinely in their feed. Again, years ago antibiotics were given as growth stimulants; however, the cost of the medication could not be justified for laying hens and the industry dropped the practice.

And no hormones.

There is no reason to use hormones in the feed of laying hens.

Are fertile eggs from happier hens?

Our experts were unable to answer this question. But they did say that the remnants of sperm and the few cells which could grow into an embryo are so small that it is not possible to detect any chemical differences between fertile and infertile eggs. No difference in lecithin, or cholesterol, or in nutritional value.

Will fertile eggs start to grow?

This could happen, if you took them out of the refrigerator and kept them cozy. In some countries, an egg with a well-developed embryo is considered a delicacy! In others, such eggs are not eaten because it is considered to be the taking of life.

Are some eggs low in cholesterol?

Alas, no. And the chicken's diet is very unlikely to make any difference in the cholesterol content of the egg.

DRIED EGGS

FOR use	DRIED EGG +	LUKEWARM WATER
1 Whole Egg	2½ Tablespoons	2½ Tablespoons
6 Whole Eggs	1 Cup	1 Cup
1 Egg White	2 teaspoons	2 Tablespoons
6 Egg Whites	¼ Cup	¾ Cup

Sprinkle egg on water and stir.

from your Co-op Home Economist

Quick Cheese Quiche

½ cup coarsely grated Swiss cheese
9" unbaked pastry shell
1 cup creamed cottage cheese
1 tablespoon cut chives (fresh, frozen, or freeze dried)

4 eggs
¼ cup milk
1 teaspoon salt
1/8 teaspoon pepper

Sprinkle grated Swiss cheese over bottom of unbaked pastry shell. Combine cottage cheese with chives. Add eggs, milk and seasonings; beat until smooth. Pour mixture into pastry shell. (To avoid spillage, pour egg mixture into shell that has been placed on oven rack.) Bake at 350° for 40 to 45 minutes, or until a sharp knife inserted in center of pie comes out clean. Cool slightly before serving. Serve for brunch, as a luncheon dish, or as an appetizer. Yield: 6 to 8 servings.

Hyde Park Co-op

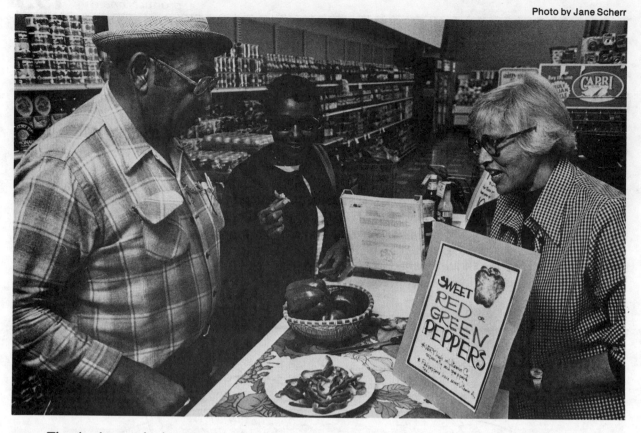

The display on the home economist counter points out that some vegetables are excellent sources of vitamin C.

sesame seed bread — rice + sesame seeds   cheese + garbanzo spread —

Beans, nuts, rice. protein — lacking in amino acids —

$$\frac{wt.}{2.8} = \text{wt in protein} —$$ need to be

D — from milk + the sun .

grains c̄ legumes or nuts
"   milk products

need Folacin in pregnancy —

essential for DNA — cell nuclei

some milk + seeds
"   "   + legumes

megoblastic, macroblastic anemia

3 days storage — can destroy much Folacin

up until 4 years — children need more protein than adults

after 6 mo —
add iron
to a child

children 1 - 3 - 23 gm protein —

Vegetables

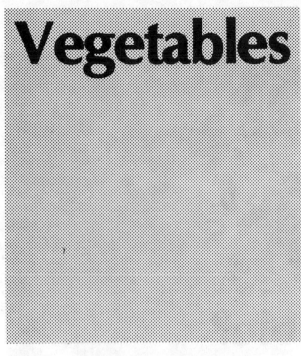

If your body was your car *by Joan Taylor*

How many people do you know who spend more time and money keeping up their cars than they do keeping up their bodies? Just for a minute, think of your body as a car. Cadillac, Rolls-Royce, Volkswagen, or whatever model you like. If you take good care of it and keep it repaired, it will give you good service and performance.

Bad Gas = Junk Food

What happens to a car when you put the wrong kind or bad gas into it? Right. It will give you problems. If you continue to do this your problems may become more serious. Your body works the same way. A continuously poor diet leads to ill health. A poor diet may have a lot of junk foods in it and a lack of nourishing foods your body needs in order to keep running well.

Do You Need a Tune-up?

Do you consume many of your meals in fast food restaurants?

Do you eat sweets for snacks?

Do you omit vegetables from your meals?

Various studies have shown people are eating too few fruits and vegetables. People are eating in restaurants more than ever, which may result in diets high in fat, sugar and salt. Fruits and vegetables, often omitted in restaurant menus, are essential in our diet. They supply us with many vitamins, minerals and the fiber we need to perform necessary body functions.

Tips on Care

At picnics, BBQs and parties include raw vegetables instead of chips and/or crackers to nibble on or dip into your dips. Try raw turnips, carrots, celery, jicama, zucchini, bell pepper, cucumber and tomatoes. This will cut down on your fat and salt intake. For sweet munchies replace pies, cakes, cookies and candy with fresh fruit.

I'd rather eat vegetables than fruit!

One could say this, if vitamin and mineral content is the only consideration. Many vegetables contain several vitamins and minerals in significant amounts in a 1 cup serving. Only a few fruits can make that claim.

A Few Lonely Fruits

While 8 vegetables contain 7 or more nutrients in a single serving, only avocado of the fruits does as well in a fairly reasonable size serving of 1 cup of 1/2" cubes. Such a serving is 260 calories, almost twice the calories of 1 cup of corn.

Dried apricots, peaches and prunes, uncooked, contain from 5 to 7 nutrients in significant amounts in large servings, such as 35 apricot halves or 24 whole prunes.

One cup of orange juice, 120 calories, supplies 4 nutrients at levels at least 10% of the U.S. Recommended Daily Allowance. Like other citrus fruits, it is rich in one nutrient, vitamin C. FRESH orange juice is also quite rich in folacin, a difficult nutrient to include in recommended amounts, especially during pregnancy, and frozen orange juice from concentrate contains good amounts, too. However, vegetables can supply these nutrients in better amounts, plus other nutrients as well, all at much lower caloric levels.

What's a vegetable?

On these pages the word "vegetable" is used in its common, comfortable MENU sense of the term. In this sense, vegetables are the leaves, stems, flowers, roots or tubers and non-sweet fruits of plants. They are extremely important for the minerals and vitamins they contain. In addition, they provide fiber and in a few cases significant amounts of calories.

Leaf Vegetables:

Because leaves do such vital work for the plant, transforming the energy of the sun into sugar, leaves are among the most nutritious vegetables. This process, photosynthesis, requires vitamins and minerals just to happen. Even the protein of green leaves, though small in amount, is high in quality compared to that in other parts of the plant.

Stem Vegetables:

Asparagus and celery are stem or petioles of plants. The stem transports nutrients between leaves and roots and contains the fiber (lignin) which supports the plant. Nutrient content varies. Asparagus is one of the more nutritious stem vegetables, celery is one of the least.

Root Vegetables:

Roots, tubers and bulbs store energy for the plant in the form of sugar and starch. Some are high in calories compared to other vegetables; some contain large amounts of carotene or provitamin A.

Flower Vegetables:

Common vegetables which are truly flowers or buds include broccoli, cauliflower, artichokes and brussels sprouts. They vary in the richness of their nutrient content; broccoli is the richest, while artichokes are the lowest.

Immature Seed Vegetables:

Immature seeds commonly eaten as vegetables are green peas, limas and corn. In contrast, mature dry seeds, such as cereals and legumes, are not included as VEGETABLES as we are using the term.

Fruit Vegetables:

Cucumbers, squash, eggplant, okra and tomatoes are fruits, but in contrast to fruits such as melons, berries and tree fruits are not SWEET. Hence, we think of them and serve them as vegetables, With a few exceptions (okra, winter squash, peppers and tomatoes) their nutritive value is low.

Vegetables

Love 'em, don't leave 'em!
by June Kadish

"Ugh! I hate carrots."

"No vegetable for me, thank you."

Are these the usual comments you hear at the dinner table? If so, maybe a little rethinking on the subject would help change a few minds. It's worth a try.

Why?

Because generally speaking, vegetables are low in calories, high in important nutrients (minerals and vitamins) and when eaten raw OR cooked properly, they taste good. Honest, they do.

Lots of Americans Don't Like Vegetables

Why? Lots of reasons.

Maybe because Daddy won't eat them.

Maybe because brother and sister say they're "rabbit food."

Maybe because Mommy, Uncle Joe or whoever's the cook says they're too much trouble to cook and rarely fixes them.

Maybe because they're often overcooked and mushy.

Maybe because most fast-food places don't serve vegetables, and so lots of Americans are out of the habit of eating them. (French fried potatoes are high in fat and salt and don't really count as a vegetable served this way.)

Maybe because when you were little your parents said "Eat those carrots. They're good for you," so often that you're still rebelling.

Learning to Love Vegetables

It is not as easy to love vegetables as fruits. Fruits, with their natural sugar content, are easily accepted even by babies. It has been suggested that infants, needing more time to learn to love vegetables, might well be introduced to vegetables before fruits. But everybody, young or old, may benefit from learning to eat new vegetables. Here are some ways to make new vegetables acceptable:

- Introduce the new vegetables when hunger is on your side.
- People are more willing to taste when they are hungry.
- Try growing your own. The taste of home-grown vegetables, the suspense that builds as you watch them grow, will coax anyone to eat them.
- Let children help in preparation - shell the peas, peel the cooked beets, tear the lettuce for salad.
- Mix some of the new vegetable, such as jicama or chard, in a stir-fry with familiar vegetables.
- Make it attractive! Mix green, white, red or yellow vegetables to tempt the eye.
- Try herb or spice seasonings.
- Don't get discouraged too soon! It always takes time, plus a few pleasant experiences, to accept a new food.

Fresh vegetable storage tips

Over-buying and long storage should be avoided as much as possible.

Most fresh vegetables should be stored in crisper and/or closed plastic bags in refrigerator at 40°F. Store mature potatoes in a cool, dark place but not in refrigerator. New potatoes may be refrigerated.

Before storing vegetables in refrigerator, remove any bruised or decayed parts, remove tops from root vegetables and wash off any dirt. Drain well before storing.

Ripe fruits should not be mixed with vegetables in crisper. They give off ethylene gas which causes green vegetables to yellow, russet spots on lettuce, toughening of asparagus and a bitter taste in carrots. Members of the cabbage family (cabbage, broccoli, brussels sprouts, cauliflower, kale, kohlrabi, etc.) will give strong odors to other foods, so don't keep them more than a day or two in refrigerator unless they are in closed plastic bags.

Although it's a bit of a nuisance, each vegetable can be stored in its own plastic bag fastened with a twist in the crisper or on the lowest shelf of the refrigerator. These plastic bags can be washed, dried and reused as long as they have no holes in them.

Tomatoes and melons should be stored at room temperature until ripe. Onions and garlic should be stored in open mesh containers at room temperature. (Information from the Dept. of Vegetable Crops, U.C. Davis.)

all about VEGETABLES

or what's in it for you? Check the lists

Super Vegetables

Some vegetables are sources of several vitamins and minerals in a single serving. The vegetables listed here have 4, 5, 6, 7, or 8 vitamins or minerals in amounts of 10% or more of the U.S. Recommended Daily Allowances. The vitamins and minerals evaluated are vitamins A and C, vitamins B_1, B_2 and B_6, folacin and niacin, and the minerals, calcium, iron and magnesium.

Unless otherwise noted, the serving size is one cup, cooked.

The Best
8 Nutrients
Collard Greens
Rich in A and C
Sweet Corn†
Fresh

Second Best
7 Nutrients
Blackeye Peas
Immature*
Kale
Green Peas
Immature*

Turnip Greens
Rich in A and C
Parsley
Raw, rich in A and C
Spinach†
Rich in A

Still Excellent
6 Nutrients
Asparagus
Lima Beans
Immature*
Broccoli
Rich in A and C
Mustard Greens
Rich in A
Okra
Green Peas
Frozen or Canned
Mixed Vegetables
Frozen
Red Peppers, Hot
Rich in A and C

Very Good
5 Nutrients
Brussels Sprouts
Rich in C
Dandelion Greens
Rich in A
New Zealand Spinach
Rich in A
Spinach, Raw†
Rich in A
Peas and Carrots
Soybeans
Immature*
Sweet Corn†
Frozen
Swiss Chard
Rich in A
Tomato Juice
Canned
Watercress, Raw
Rich in A

Good
4 Nutrients
Green Onions
Tops only, raw
Rutabagas
Sweet Corn†
Canned
Sweet Potato
Tomato, Raw
Rich in C

*Immature means young peas, limas, etc. rather than the mature dry veg., such as split peas.

†Nutrient differences between fresh versus cooked, canned or frozen vegetables are due to 1) processing losses or 2) increase in weight of one cup portion on cooking. For example, one cup of cooked spinach weighs about 3 times as much as 1 cup of raw spinach.

Evaluations by Mary Ruth Nelson based on figures from USDA Agric. Handbook #456, 1975; USDA Home Economics Research Report #36, 1969; Jour. Amer. Dietetics Assoc., 2/77, 6/77, 4/75; and Pennington Dietary Nutrient Guide, 1976.

Fresh vegetables . . .
how to choose,
how to cook

What to Look For

Choose vegetables by their fresh, crisp look. Avoid limp, old-looking leaves, stalks and flowers. Avoid those with brown or bruised spots.

Buy local produce when available.

Buy in season. At the peak of picking time, vegetables are least expensive and taste best. For example, when fresh corn appears in April or May, it is expensive and not as flavorful as at the height of the season in June, July or August.

How Much to Buy

Just enough to last a few days. The older the vegetable, the greater the loss of nutrients and the tougher to eat. Serve the more perishable ones like corn and asparagus early in the week. Keep the root types like carrots, turnips and potatoes for later.

How to Cook

The enemies of vegetables are time, water, light, heat, air, bruising and waste. To save nutrients, fight these enemies.

Use the whole vegetable when possible, not cut up. Trim sparingly. Remove only the tough or discolored portions. Use the outer leaves of lettuce and cabbage. Cabbage leaves are good in soups or stuffed with rice and meat mixtures.

Eat vegetables raw sometimes. Most of us think about raw carrots and celery. How about raw turnips, zucchini, broccoli and jicama? These are good dunked in taco sauce or seasoned cottage cheese.

When you do cook them, cook quickly and use the least possible amount of water (or broth). One-fourth cup water is enough for two to three servings. Greens need only the water that clings to the leaves. Root vegetables and corn need just enough to barely cover them.

Instead of boiling, how about steaming? A proper steamer is fine, but you can improvise. Put the vegetables in a sieve or colander over a pot of boiling water. Cover as tightly as possible while they cook. Check regularly to be sure the water doesn't boil away. Time for steaming varies with the size of the pieces. Check every few minutes until the vegetable is barely tender for best flavor. It won't take long.

Another Approach

For variety, how about stir frying? Cut vegetables in small pieces and cook quickly in a tiny bit of oil, water and soy sauce. An excellent method for asparagus, broccoli and green beans among others. Experiment with those your family prefers.

If any liquid is left after cooking, save it for soups, sauces and stews.

Canned and Frozen Vegetables

For canned vegetables, use low heat and a covered pan. Save leftover liquid for other uses.

Defrost them partially in your refrigerator before cooking to save energy due to the shorter cooking time required. Season with a dab of butter or margarine and a sprinkle of seasoned salt or such herbs as oregano, thyme, chervil or rosemary.

Other possibilities are parmesan cheese or a squeeze of fresh lemon or lime juice.

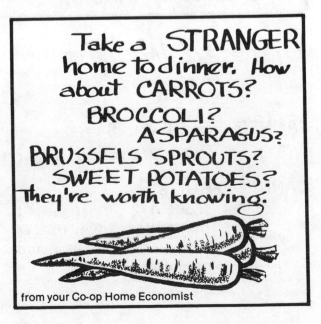

Take a STRANGER home to dinner. How about CARROTS? BROCCOLI? ASPARAGUS? BRUSSELS SPROUTS? SWEET POTATOES? They're worth knowing.

from your Co-op Home Economist

Polybag frozen
VEGETABLES

. . . INDIVIDUALLY FROZEN

Easy to take out amount needed and return the rest to freezer. Boxed vegetables are frozen in the box.

. . . MINIMUM WATER INSTRUCTIONS

These instructions were developed for maximum nutrient retention:

For each cup frozen vegetables put in pan and bring to boil

½-1 tablespoon water

⅛ teaspoon salt

½ tablespoon butter or margarine

Cover tightly, reduce heat and cook according to time listed on labels.

Drained Weight

CANNED VEGETABLES

— about 2/3 of net weight

CANNED FRUITS

— about 1/2 of net weight (more for small pieces such as fruit cocktail and peach slices)

Frozen, canned...
HOW MUCH?

A 10-ounce package of frozen VEGETABLES has **about** the same amount of vegetables as a **drained** one pound can (No. 303).

From your Co-op Home Economist

Let the vegetable be the star!

Plan a menu which features a vegetable as the highlight of the meal.

★★★

Spinach with Sesame Sauce

SPINACH with
SESAME SAUCE
BROWN RICE or BULGUR
BAKED CUSTARD or
FRUIT & CHEESE
MILK or CAPPUCINO

2 - 3 packages frozen chopped spinach
2 - 3 tablespoons soy sauce
2 tablespoons white sesame seeds
Scant 1/2 teaspoon instant chicken
  bouillon powder
1/3 cup boiling water
1 tablespoon sugar
1/8 teaspoon salt

Cook spinach in small amount of water until just thawed. Drain. Add soy sauce to spinach and squeeze lightly to mix.

Toast sesame seeds in a dry frying pan by heating gently; stirring constantly until golden brown. Grind seeds to a paste with mortar and pestle. Mix bouillon with water, add sugar and salt. Add to sesame seed paste.

Serve spinach. Pass sauce separately.

4 - 6 servings.   — *Susan Trower*

★★★

Sweet Red Pepper Winter Salad

SWEET RED PEPPER
WINTER SALAD
CHEESE OMELET
WHOLE GRAIN BREAD
BEVERAGE

1 medium cucumber, sliced
1/2 sweet red pepper, cut in 1/2" pieces
1 cup sliced mushrooms
1 bunch green onion, tops only cut in 1" pieces
2 tablespoons sesame oil

Heat 2 tablespoons of sesame oil on high heat. Add ingredients stirring constantly, until cucumber is wilted and red peppers are slightly soft. Serve immediately. Serves 2. *Helen Gjullin*

★★★

Grandma's Soup

GRANDMA'S SOUP
DEVILED or HARD
COOKED EGGS
CORN MUFFINS or BREAD
SLICED AVOCADO topped
with cottage cheese
BEVERAGE

2-3 tablespoons butter or margarine
2-3 tablespoons chopped onion
1 lb. (2 cups) fresh broccoli (or zucchini or asparagus, etc.)
2-3 cups chicken stock plus water to make 1 quart.
1 cup powdered skim milk
Salt, pepper, fresh herbs or other seasonings to taste

Saute onion in butter until golden. Cook broccoli in small amount of water until just tender. Put half broccoli, onion and 2 cups stock and water in blender and puree. Add 1/2 the milk and "buzz" to blend. Empty in large pan and blend second portion. Heat to boiling, season to taste and serve. A spoon of sherry or dollop of sour cream is nice. 6 small or 4 large servings.

— *Celia Lynd*

Vegetables in a hurry

(None of these vegetables takes more than five minutes.)

How About Canned Ones?

. . . Green beans or limas in a salad or briefly marinated in seasoned oil and vinegar dressing and served on their own.

. . . Canned beets are delicious topped with sour cream or plain yogurt flavored with a dash of black pepper.

. . . The beet juice, flavored the same way, makes a refreshing drink — instant borscht.

How About Frozen Ones?

. . . Heat in briefest time and least amount of water.

. . . Add to soups, canned or homemade.

. . . Cook extra amount to use in a day or two as salad.

. . . Defrost peas in refrigerator. Moisten with mayonnaise. Add a few peanuts for crunch and protein.

How About Fresh?

. . . Wash and slice asparagus, green beans or carrots. Cook in a little water and soy sauce for 3 minutes.

. . . Spinach or Swiss chard can be washed and steamed quickly. Season with sesame seeds or sesame oil.

DO BOTHER

with vegetables. Diets of some Americans are low in the vitamin **FOLACIN**. Vegetables high in folacin include **Beets, Romaine, Spinach and Brussels Sprouts.**

from your Co-op Home Economist

Herb and spice magic for vegetables

The following is a list of suggested spices and herbs that might help you the next time you cook vegetables for the family. One important point is that ½ **tsp. of dried herbs is equal to 2 tsp. of fresh.** Try creaming the butter with the herb or spice and let it melt on the hot vegetables.

ASPARAGUS Nutmeg, curry or turmeric, sesame seeds

BROCCOLI Oregano or celery seeds

BRUSSELS SPROUTS Garlic or sesame seeds

CARROTS Ginger, cinnamon, parsley, tarragon, celery seed or mint

CORN Chives, oregano, parsley

LIMA BEANS Nutmeg, marjoram, sage

SPINACH Nutmeg, garlic, marjoram

TOMATOES Basil, ground cloves, sage, oregano

Cooking vegetables in a microwave

Mystery?

Microwave cooking is not a mystery. The magnetron tube in the oven converts regular electricity into microwaves. The microwaves agitate and vibrate the moisture molecules so rapidly that they cause heat which cooks the food from the inside rather than from the outside as in a regular oven. This method works well with vegetables because of their high water content.

Cookbooks:

There are several microwave cookbooks and of course an instruction book comes with each oven. It's a good idea to attend a class, preferably by someone not selling these ovens, before you invest in a microwave. This method is a completely new way to cook. You may feel more like a juggler than a cook at first!

Timing is Important!

Watch cooking time very carefully. Overcooking destroys texture and nutrients just as with conventional cooking, except that it does it much faster. To convert a favorite recipe to microwave method, find a similar recipe in a cookbook and use that timing. Always use the least amount of time suggested. The food can be returned to the oven if necessary.

Hints to the Happy Homemaker . . . Be it He or She!

Arrange the larger part toward the outside of the pan and smaller or softer parts in the middle. For fresh vegetables a little water is usually needed. Frozen vegetables need no extra liquid. Sometimes it is necessary to rotate the dish of vegetables a time or two during cooking. If you stir them, do it from the inside out. Sometimes it is necessary to let vegetables stand after cooking to get even doneness. Salt should be added after vegetables are cooked because it tends to cause toughness. Add salt to a little water and sprinkle on vegetables after they are cooked. A pump-spray bottle of salted water could be kept for this purpose.

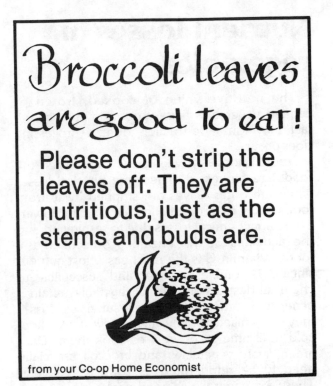

Broccoli leaves are good to eat!

Please don't strip the leaves off. They are nutritious, just as the stems and buds are.

from your Co-op Home Economist

Toasted Pumpkin Seeds

Wash seeds and remove most of the membrane. Spread out in a shallow pan. Sprinkle with salt and add some butter, if desired. Roast in a slow oven — about 250°F. Stir occasionally and take out when light brown — about ½ hour.
Then — Suck, Crack, Nibble and Spit!

from your Co-op Home Economist

Carrot Dill Soup

4 cups carrots, sliced
1 large chopped onion
2 tablespoons butter OR
*   margarine*
6 cups liquid; broth OR
*   water and 3 bouillon cubes*
*   OR powder*
1 teaspoon dried dill weed
1 tablespoon minced parsley
½ teaspoon dried basil
ground black pepper to taste
½ cup yogurt OR sour cream

Saute onions in butter until soft. Stir in carrots, then boiling water or broth, dill weed, basil, and pepper. Partially cover and simmer about 40 minutes, until carrots are soft. Put through food mill or puree in blender. To serve: stir in yogurt or sour cream, heat gently, sprinkle on parsley. Good cold, too. If desired, each bowl may be topped with a dollop of sour cream and the parsley sprinkled on that. Serves six.

Nutrient losses in vegetables

The nutritive value of cooked, frozen or canned vegetables is very good in spite of the fact that some destruction due to processing does occur.

Nutrient losses in vegetables begin when the foods are harvested. There are physical losses when the outer leaves are stripped away from foods such as broccoli, lettuce or cauliflower. There are chemical losses due to respiration and the activities of the enzymes present in the foods. Vitamin C is the most easily lost nutrient since it is soluble in water and susceptible to chemical destruction. Some vegetables retain it better than others, but all will suffer less loss if they are chilled rapidly after harvest and kept cold until time to process or cook them. Dark green, leafy vegetables and broccoli especially need to be refrigerated as soon as possible. These are generally shipped packed in crushed ice. Vegetables that retain their vitamin C well are cabbage, peppers, lima and snap beans, and tomatoes. Tubers keep their vitamin C quite well even when not refrigerated.

Canned foods will show some nutrient losses but newer processes and equipment have improved the quality of canned foods. Canned vegetables stored at 65° or higher will lose 15% to 25% of their thiamin in a year. Don't plan to keep canned foods more than a year because the new crops for processing begin to appear in early summer. This is true for most frozen vegetables also.

FOR COOKED VEGETABLES

you retain more Vitamin C when you
1) start in boiling water
2) use little water
3) cover pan & reduce heat
4) cook a short time
5) serve quickly

from your Co-op Home Economist

Wax on Produce

Some fruits and vegetables are waxed to help them keep longer. The wax or oil may be removed by soaking the product for 2-3 minutes in warm dish-washing detergent suds and then wiping it with a towel followed by thorough rinsing. Some products can be peeled to remove the wax.

from your Co-op Home Economist

The raw vegetable experience

by Helen Black

I submit that any vegetable which is raw, vigorous and wholeheartedly eaten can be a great chewing experience. Keep a sack of raw vegetables in the refrigerator to satisfy this much neglected human need. For superior sound and sensation the following are suggested:

Raw Cauliflower
Broken into flowerlets, it can be eaten as is or with dips. It bursts into a thousand small buds between your grinders. Curl your tongue around and scoop them up.

Raw Celery
What a forthright chewing delight! Its noisiness is part of the pleasure. Do not try to conceal it.

Raw Turnips
The raw turnip is somewhat muted in its percussion, possibly due to its smooth, almost velvety texture.

Raw Carrots
This experience is part of the Puritan ethic. A raw carrot demands diligence and determination from the jaws. It leaves, however, the pleasant exhaustion of a job well done.

Raw Jicama
The ONLY way to eat jicama, in our opinion. Satisfyingly crisp and somewhat juicy, but not enough to run out the corners of your mouth.

Raw Broccoli
Especially lovable is the stem, peeled and cut into chunks; it's a beautiful green, a succulent treat.

Vegetarian Spaghetti Sauce

1 green pepper, finely chopped
1 small onion, finely chopped
1 stalk celery, finely chopped
1 clove garlic, finely chopped
1 teaspoon oregano
1/2 teaspoon sweet basil
1/2 teaspoon red chili
2 tablespoons oil

7 or 8 sliced mushrooms
1 zucchini, chopped
4 or 5 broccoli spears, chopped
3 carrots, grated
11-12 oz. tofu, optional
2 cups tomato sauce
1/4 cup wheat germ

Using a heavy skillet, saute pepper, onion, celery, garlic and spices in oil. Add remaining vegetables and the crumbled tofu if used. Stir fry for 3 minutes. Add tomato sauce and simmer for 5 minutes. Sprinkle wheat germ on top and serve with pasta or rice. 4-6 servings. (The amounts and kinds of vegetables may vary according to the season.)

Devi Doree Chase

New Potatoes   *Late Crop Potatoes*

have thin skins.
They are best for boiling, creaming and salad.
They do not mash well.
New potatoes should be used within a week of purchase.
Keep in a cool, dark place, open to the air.

(OLD POTATOES) have thick skins and keep well. Their mealy flesh is best for baking or mashing.

Store in a cool, dark place, open to the air. Remove sprouts and peel off any green skin before cooking the potatoes.

from your Co-op Home Economist

Raw Spinach with Yogurt Dressing

1 cup plain yogurt
1 teaspoon lemon juice
1 small clove garlic
1/2 teaspoon salt
1/2 teaspoon dry mustard
1 large bunch fresh spinach
6 hard-cooked eggs
6 strips crisp bacon

Crush garlic and add to yogurt, lemon juice, salt and dry mustard. Mix well and chill. To serve, divide spinach into 6 serving bowls. Garnish each with one chopped egg, dressing and one strip of bacon, crumbled. May be served with hot bouillon, crisp wheat crackers and apples with cheese for dessert for a low calorie, high nutrition meal. 6 servings.

Nancy Bratt

Money, money, money . . . Where does it go?

Like everything else you can spend lots or relatively little on vegetables.

Eyeball It . . . Whatever your budget it will help to eyeball what you buy and get a rough idea of what you're paying.

You get about 3 small servings (3½ oz. or ½ cup each) from:

- 11-16 oz. fresh (without a lot of waste)
- 10 oz. frozen package
- 16 oz. can (roughly ⅓ liquid)

For fresh vegetables with moderate waste you get about 3 small servings per pound. If the vegetable costs 30¢ a lb., that's 10¢ a serving. With almost no waste you get 4½ servings a pound. The vegetable could cost 44¢ a lb. and still cost 10¢ a serving. For 10¢ servings the 16 oz. can or the 10 oz. frozen box would need to cost 30¢ or less, a rare occurence. (12¢ servings aren't uncommon.)

Don't Insist on That Out-of-Season Zucchini

At 79¢ a lb. it costs 4 to 8 times what it might be at the height of the season. Some fresh vegetable prices vary wildly, so watch from week to week.

Watch That Enthusiastic Over-Buying

All those fresh vegetables look great, but if you buy too much you may end up with wilted lettuce, ucky broccoli and moldy squash. Some vegetables are high priced most of the year: asparagus, artichokes, chinese pea pods, cauliflower, mushrooms. Consider them special treats.

Weigh the Lettuce

"By-the-each" vegetables prices need a closer look. Tiny heads of butter lettuce weighing ¼ pound cost 6 times as much as a large romaine weighing 1½ lbs. Potatoes in bags may cost ⅓ to ¼ as much as loose potatoes. Maybe you can share a bag with a friend if 10 lbs. is too much.

Buy Co-op Label (or Other Private Labels)

Co-op Quality Pack (Red Label) usually costs several cents less than a national brand and quality is comparable. Economy Pack (Green Label) costs even less.

Is This "Convenience"?

Boil-in-bag frozen vegetables with butter or cream sauce often cost 50-100% more than their plainer cousins. Also the bags take more fuel and cooking time.

What's Cheap?

Prices are for end of August, 1979. Serving size is 3½ oz. or ½ cup.

6¢ a Serving and Under

- fresh potatoes in bags, cabbage, onions
- tomato juice and tomato sauce

7-10¢ a Serving

- fresh carrots
- canned tomatoes, peas (Economy Pack)
- frozen spinach

11-15¢ a Serving

- fresh yams, Brussels sprouts, greens
- canned corn, green beans, potatoes, sweet potatoes, carrots
- frozen corn, peas, broccoli, green beans, limas

Way Up corn on cob (25¢), fancy canned peas (21¢), frozen asparagus (50¢)

Attention to price adds up. For a family of 4 eating 2 small servings of vegetables a day, consider this:

Average cost/serving	Cost per year
8¢ serving	$234
20¢/serving	$584

Is it **BAD** to sprinkle produce?

NO

Water sprinkled on leafy vegetables helps prevent wilting which causes loss of vitamins A and C. (Intact leaves lose nutrients only slightly by leaching.)

Green peppers are easy to freeze!

Wash. Remove stem and seeds. Cut in halves, or slice or dice. Do not blanch. Pack, seal and freeze.

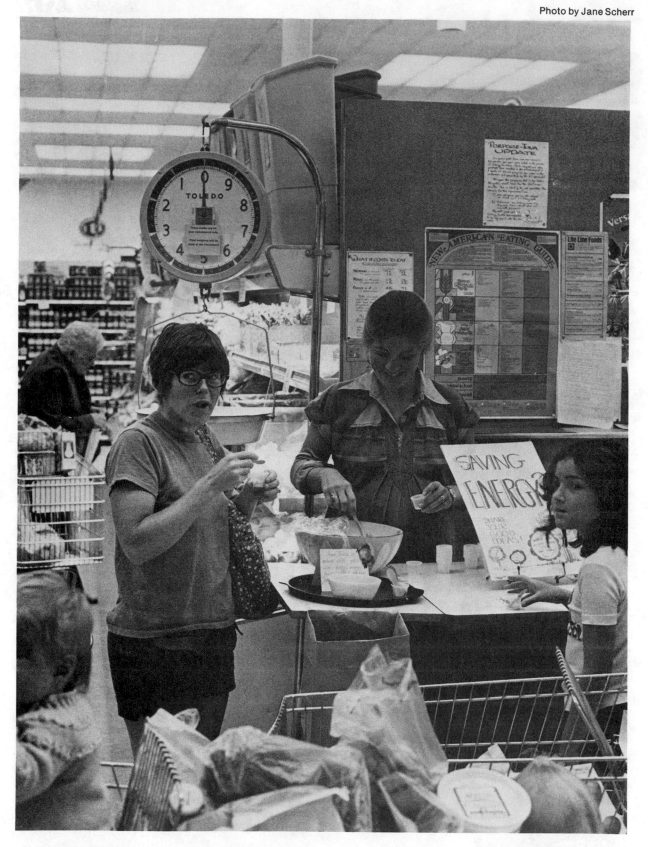

People may be unwilling to try a new food . . . unless someone else fixes it for them.

Canned, frozen or fabricated

Canned, handy and vitamins too! *by Helen Black*

Reckless eaters, snacking here, snacking there, too busy to cook vegetables, might consider the charmingly easy CAN. Are canned vegetables nutritious? Of course. Reports that all vitamins are killed off by canning are exaggerated! Vitamins survive in large numbers!

Canned tomatoes are rich in vitamin C

One cup of canned tomatoes or juice has 60% of the day's recommended vitamin C. Canned sweet potatoes and turnip greens have that much vitamin C, too.

Canned carrots: super source of vitamin A

Only ¼ cup of canned carrots or only ⅓ cup of canned spinach provides all the recommended vitamin A per day.

Canned peas, canned limas

Canned peas have 30% of the day's thiamin; limas have 25% of the iron. QUICK SALAD: toss drained vegetables with french dressing, chopped celery, onion, hard-cooked eggs, bacon bits or you name it. Moisten with mayonnaise, serve.

Even canned peaches have something

The peach, whether fresh or canned, is hardly a vitamin-rich wonder. Yet what it has is retained well in canning: 20% of your vitamin A and 15% of your vitamin C in 1 cup. Try it for dessert sometime.

FROZEN VEGETABLES *in butter sauce*

A 10 ounce package contains about

    8½ ounces vegetables

    1½ ounces sauce
    which averages
    12% butter
    88% water, salt
    and spices

It costs much less to add your own butter and a bouillon cube or herbs.

from your Co-op Home Economist

Easy cooking with Tomato Juice, Puree, Sauce & Paste

Tomatoes have been squeezed, squashed and pummeled into a variety of products which greatly simplify the making of spaghetti sauce. All kinds of people use spaghetti sauce, and not just with ground beef, either. Adventurous cooks find it good with fish instead of meat, or with beans, or nuts, or even tofu. For whatever purpose, it's helpful to know something about the various tomato products that can be used.

The differences between tomato products

All ingredients in tomato products must now be listed on the label in California. In addition, the Food and Drug Administration has standards which provide for the following:

TOMATO JUICE is 5-6% tomato solids.* It is the liquid extracted from tomatoes, with salt added.

CANNED TOMATOES also are 5-6% tomato solids. They must be mature tomatoes, peeled and cored, to which may be added citric acid, calcium salts (to help keep the tomatoes firm), spices, flavoring and salt.

TOMATO PUREE usually contains from 10-12% tomato solids. It must contain not less than 8% or more than 24%. Puree is the extracted and strained liquid from tomatoes; it may be concentrated and it may have salt added. Co-op Label tomato puree is unsalted.

TOMATO SAUCE usually contains from 10-12% tomato solids, like tomato puree. However, there is no standard for percent solids in tomato sauce. Salt, spices, vinegar, sweetening, vegetables such as onions or garlic may be added.

TOMATO PASTE must have not less than 24% tomato solids. It is liquid extracted from tomatoes and concentrated. Pastes may contain salt, spices, flavoring and baking soda. Co-op tomato paste does not contain ingredients other than tomatoes.

In a pinch, switch sauce for paste

However, substituting one tomato product for another recipe may radically alter the flavor or consistency of the finished product. When substituting a seasoned product for an unseasoned one, add the seasonings called for in the recipe in reduced amounts. In a pinch, use these rules:

FOR 1 POUND OF FRESH TOMATOES, SIMMERED AND SEASONED (or 2 cups canned tomatoes) use 1 cup of tomato sauce.

FOR 1 CUP OF TOMATO PUREE, use 1 cup tomato sauce but reduce salt and seasoning in the recipe.

FOR ½ CUP TOMATO PASTE, use 1 cup tomato sauce but subtract ½ cup liquid from recipe and reduce salt and seasonings.

FOR 1 CUP TOMATO JUICE, use ½ cup sauce plus ½ cup other liquid (or ¼ cup paste and ¾ cup liquid); adjust salt and seasonings.

Sauce or paste are usually cheapest

Using tomato sauce or paste in a recipe is cheaper than using tomato puree and may cost only half as much as canned tomatoes or seasoned spaghetti sauces.

Please! Use within 6 months of purchase!

People worry if the inside of a can, when opened, is black and discolored as may happen due to the action of acid foods such as tomatoes on the metal. If the can is not swollen, leaking or badly dented, it is safe to use. But discoloration can be minimized if canned tomato products are used in a

*'Tomato solids' refers to the solid matter left after all water is evaporated from the product. Fresh tomatoes before processing contain about 5-6% solids.

reasonable time after purchase. Keep in a cool place in your home. Rotate the stock to use the oldest first.

After opening, any unused tomato product should be transferred to a glass jar and stored in the refrigerator. Storage in the opened can may cause an unpleasant tinny flavor to develop as well as discoloration of the can lining.

Yes, tomato products add vitamins and minerals

Tomato sauce or puree or paste may contribute important amounts of nutrients to a recipe. They are good sources of vitamin A (carotene) and moderate sources of iron. Vitamin C is present in large amounts but some will be lost in long cooking after opening. Some less familiar nutrients are present. For example, in some spaghetti sauce recipes, more vitamin B_6 (pyridoxine) is provided by the tomato products than by the meat.

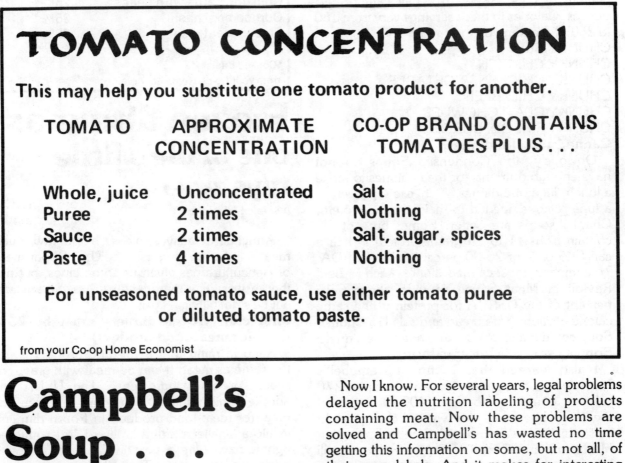

TOMATO CONCENTRATION

This may help you substitute one tomato product for another.

TOMATO	APPROXIMATE CONCENTRATION	CO-OP BRAND CONTAINS TOMATOES PLUS...
Whole, juice	Unconcentrated	Salt
Puree	2 times	Nothing
Sauce	2 times	Salt, sugar, spices
Paste	4 times	Nothing

For unseasoned tomato sauce, use either tomato puree or diluted tomato paste.

from your Co-op Home Economist

Campbell's Soup . . . what's in it?

by Helen Black

Now I know. For several years, legal problems delayed the nutrition labeling of products containing meat. Now these problems are solved and Campbell's has wasted no time getting this information on some, but not all, of their soup labels. And it makes for interesting reading!

Soup or whatever: What's nutritious?

"Nutritious" is a bad word. It is a bad word because nobody has defined it! It may mean one thing to you and another to me. But nutritionists have not been idle; they are trying to define it. One recent definition would call "nutritious" only food which contains at least 4 nutrients in amounts at least 10 percent of the day's recommended intake (USRDA), in a serving large enough to provide 10 percent of a person's caloric requirement for the day.

With such a scheme, I can tell you that most Campbell's Condensed Soups are not "nutritious"! A surprising exception is Chicken Noodle Soup, which barely makes it.

But Campbell's Chunky (Do Not Dilute) Soups mostly are "nutritious." Below are those that meet the criteria, that is, they provide at least four nutrients in amounts equal to 10 percent of the USRDA in a half can, or 9½ ounces. Calories in these servings vary from 160 to 260, depending on the soup.

CHUNKY BEEF
CHUNKY CHICKEN
CHUNKY CHICKEN VEGETABLE
CHUNKY CHILI BEEF
CHUNKY CLAM CHOWDER
CHUNKY SIRLOIN BURGER

Canned soup for dinner?

Obviously, the Condensed Soups do not have enough nutrients for their calories to make a lunch, let alone dinner. A cheese sandwich or a tuna salad is needed to make up the protein. Chunky soups are better. Some, but not all, contain from 11 to 19 grams protein in half a can (9½ oz.), or 20-30 percent of the USRDA. To compare, most canned dinners such as Beef Ravioli in Meat Sauce provide about 6-15 percent of the USRDA for protein in the same calorie portion. With bread and salad, a Chunky Soup could make an easy and adequate dinner.

Soup as sauce is lower calorie

I also learned that 1 cup of Campbell's Mushroom Soup (undiluted) is only 270 calories, compared to about 400 for 1 cup of medium white sauce, for which the soup might be substituted in a casserole. Campbell's Golden Mushroom and Cream of Celery Soups are still lower, or about 180 calories per cup.

All Campbell's Soups have nutrition labels now.

How much meat?

The U.S. Department of Agriculture requires the following minimum amount of meat (based on fresh weight of the meat) in canned or frozen products:

Beef stew	25%
Chili con carne	40%
Chili con carne with beans	25%
Corned beef hash	35% *
Frozen meat pies	25%

*Cooked Basis
from your Co-op Home Economist

Frozen dinners: one of life's little mysteries

by Helen Black

Armchair detectives, please help! How much meat is in frozen dinners? The U.S. Department of Agriculture has given us some clues, but not the answer. The manufacturer has the answer, but he's not telling — yet!

First clue: frozen dinners must be 25% meat (or meat-food-product)

Keep in mind that meat-food-product is not the same as meat. It can be meat with gravy, or sauce, or other ingredients. The USDA has adopted this minimum standard of 25% for meat (or meat-food-product) in frozen dinners. While a smaller portion is illegal, it is quite all right to have a larger portion. You don't know if it's larger, of course. This all means that in a frozen beef dinner (sliced beef with gravy, mashed potatoes and corn, total weight 11 oz.) the meat and gravy together must weigh 2¾ oz.

Second clue: the plot thickens, or throw out the appetizer, bread and dessert

Now it isn't always as simple as the beef dinner, of course. Because the standard says not to count any appetizer, bread or dessert in the dinner when you figure the 25% meat (or meat-food-product). Now here's a frozen ham dinner (ham, with sauce, sweet potatoes, peas and carrots, corn muffin, total weight 10¼ oz.) Just figure 25% of 10¼ minus the weight of the corn muffin, whatever that is.

Third clue: how much meat in a meat-food-product?

Well, now, this depends. There's a LOT of different combinations, you know! And USDA has put out a separate standard for each, like:

. . . in a beef dinner, the beef-with-gravy must be 50% beef. This must be 25% of the total dinner, or 2¾ oz. So now we know there must be at least 1⅜ oz. meat in this dinner! Eureka!

. . . if the meat portion is sweet and sour pork or beef, it must contain 25% meat. So just figure 25% of 25% of total weight to get actual weight of meat. Don't forget to throw out any bread, appetizer or dessert, first.

. . . if the meat portion is Spanish rice with beef or ham, it must contain 20% meat. Figure 20% of 25%, throwing out bread, dessert and appetizer.

Simple solution: nutrition labeling

Most shoppers don't have these wonderful clues. Even if we did, most of us couldn't figure out this puzzle. Isn't it a pity and a shame that nutrition labeling is not on most of these products? The consumer would know at least if the whole dinner contained an adequate amount of protein.

This is breakfast?

by Betsy Wood **May 22, 1972**

Nine years of research and an investment of more than a million dollars produced THIS? Modern science's contribution to breakfast (according to a full-page ad in local newspapers):

"Sugar, shortening, milk protein, flour (bleached), peanut butter, water, soy protein, brown sugar syrup, dried egg, glycerine, salt, oat flour, mono and diglycerides, leavening, calcium carbonate, artificial flavor, dicalcium phosphate, soy lecithin . . . " and on and on through many vitamins and minerals down to "BHA, BHT, citric acid and propylene glycol

added to preserve freshness."

That's General Mills' "Breakfast Squares." Remember that ingredients are listed in descending order of predominance, by weight.

Who is kidding whom? This product is so bad that Co-op managers agreed not to carry it as a regular item. With full-page ads and high-pressure TV commercials (and a high-profit margin to boot), we hope we won't be forced to stock it. (A Co-op center manager has the option to order it just for his store.)

Here are a few of my reasons for saying that "Breakfast Squares" are a bad product:

• They're mostly sugar and fat, the two foods most people already eat too much of. Who needs another dose? Who wants their kids to get addicted to sweet rolls for breakfast?

• The squares undoubtedly contain the vitamins, minerals and protein listed on the box, but they probably don't contain other trace elements present in ordinary, more natural foods.

• The bacon-egg-and-toast breakfast that General Mills chooses to compare its new product with isn't all that good. The egg is okay but the two slices of bacon are high in fat and the two pieces of toast contain more carbohydrates than most of us need. A decent breakfast would include fruit, preferably citrus. It also would be good to have milk — even half a glass.

• The squares aren't cheap. For a family of four the cost would be 79 cents. For that amount everyone can have orange juice, one egg, toast, milk, and coffee too.

Flavor? Try them. Go ahead. All I can say is that everyone I know who tasted them had a mighty peculiar downturn of the mouth.

The development of this kind of "food" bothers me greatly. What happened to the pleasure of eating real food? Where are we all running so fast? I get the feeling that this kind of product isn't just a response to a demand but feeds and encourages our always-on-the-run, ulcer-producing life style.

But you want a fast breakfast? How about a blender job with a glass of milk, two or three tablespoons of frozen juice and a raw egg (wash the shell before cracking)? Or a peanut butter sandwich, milk and an orange? Or last night's salad and meat loaf? Or tomato juice and a quesadillo — a tortilla with cheese heated in a frying pan or broiler?

Boo Berry
General Mills has done it again!

by Mary Gullberg   January 15, 1973

Remember Breakfast Squares from General Mills' line of fabricated foods? In a cookie format, all the nutrients you need for breakfast are offered to consumers. The cookie doesn't taste very good, and the Co-op home economists believe a breakfast of real foods has better nutrition as well as better taste. The Co-op doesn't stock GM's Breakfast Squares (see "This Is Breakfast?" Co-op News, May 22, 1972).

The Buying Committee (two buyers, a store manager and a home economist) screens most of the grocery items that ultimately end up on our shelves. You might think the stuff chosen is not always of the best but you should see what's rejected!

A recent reject was General Mills' new breakfast cereal called "**Boo Berry.**" This product joins **Count Chocula** and **Frankenberry** as the third scary, spooky cereal advertised so as to appeal to children by promising them a 'glo-in-the-dark' sticker inside the boxes of **Boo Berry.** This little play on words is perhaps also intended to make the buyer think the product contains blueberries, although labeling laws require that the fact that the blueberry flavor is artificial be declared on the front of the package. Quite a bit more about the product is also artificial. Sugar is the first ingredient. In fact, there is so much sugar used that the 12 percent protein in the oat flour (second ingredient) has been diluted to 5.4 percent in the finished product. The same fate has overtaken the B-vitamins and iron of the oats, so the sweet mess has been fortified with eight vitamins and iron. To make sure that the product has the most devastating effect possible on kids' teeth, little bits of blue-colored marshmallows have also been added.

Oatmeal served with a small amount of sugar and plenty of milk makes a good breakfast cereal. It is economical, nourishing and low enough in sugar not to pose too much hazard to tooth enamel.

Carnation Breakfast Bar: Second revolution?

by Helen Black   March 3, 1975

Here we go again with another engineered food: Carnation Granola Breakfast Bars in "six delicious flavors!" This amazing product has 38 ingredients. Most of these are isolated or extracted or otherwise tortured out of ordinary food stuffs, then recombined, glorified with vitamins and minerals, packaged, advertised and sold.

The second revolution: snacks?

Some researchers say that we are in the midst of a "Second Revolution,"* the first revolution having been the mass movement of people from country to city in the last century. The first revolution, they say, precipitated the processing of fresh food in order to preserve it in transport from the country where it is raised, to the city where it is eaten. And the "Second Revolution," they say, is the elimination of family meals and the substitution of snacks, fortified with vitamins and minerals, as the normal method of eating.

The hesitation waltz

All this causes a kind of nervous quiver among us Co-op home economists, which I like to think of as The Hesitation Waltz. We hesitate, because we wonder if this Second Revolution is really good, necessary or inevitable. For example, do we truly have the nutritional know-how to go this route? Then, what about the economic effect? Is it any cheaper for our society to do this extreme processing

*Wall Street Journal, Dec. 18, 1974

and reassembling of nutrients, than it would be just to eat foods in simpler forms?

Nutrient fortification is a sticky question

One of the troubling questions about products such as Carnation Breakfast Bars has to do with the addition of vitamins and minerals. Some NEW problems have been brought to light by recent nutrition research:

. . . THE REBOUND EFFECT: a dependency, or a developed deficiency, which may occur after large intakes of vitamins C or B_6 are then decreased to average levels.

. . . UNBALANCED NUTRIENT INTAKE: Large amounts of certain nutrients may create increased need for others. For example, high protein diets have been shown to increase the loss of body calcium, and increased amounts of polyunsaturated fats to increase the need for vitamin E. Trace elements are a particular problem because the range between the level of need and that of toxicity is very narrow.

Carnation Bars are expensive

Carnation Breakfast Bars will be sold at $1.09 per package of six bars. That's about 18¢ per bar. Two slices of bread and two teaspoons of butter, about the same in calories as one Breakfast Bar, only cost 7¢. How about that? The Co-op will be selling this product soon. Buy it if you choose. For the nutritional and economic reasons stated, we don't recommend switching from true meals to snacks such as this. Let the "Second Revolution" wait until we get a few more answers to our questions.

The Twinkies syndrome

by Mary Gullberg   **February 9, 1976**

Are you hooked on this "no taste" product? You're not alone. ITT's Continental Bakery turns out Twinkies at the rate of 50,000 per hour, 3 million a week, for gross retail sales last year of $50 million. Two little oblong sausages of sponge cake filled with some kind of white goop consisting of sugar and grease and selling for 25¢.

Sugar is the most abundant ingredient in Twinkies followed by flour, corn sweetener, water, shortening, eggs, leavening, whey, modified food starch, salt, skim milk, artificial color and flavor, sorbic acid (a preservative). Children eat 80 percent of the Twinkies sold. These famous grease cups are sold in grocery stores, in liquor outlets and from vending machines. They are popular in lunch boxes, for snacks and as dessert.

People concerned about good food habits and about the taste of well-prepared foods are not great admirers of heavily sugared, mass-produced confections. Children accustomed to eating this type of cake may actually come to prefer it to a homemade product with better quality ingredients. These same children will not learn to snack on cheeses, raw vegetables and fruits. They can be observed discarding uneaten an apple or orange found in their lunch bags or served in the school lunch. And they may grow up with a limited interest in buying, preparing and serving good food in their homes.

Mothers should think carefully before using food as a pacifier. It can become a habit to provide the child with a doughnut, a cupcake or a cookie every time the child accompanies the mother to the food store. So let's be sophisticated. Cut out the junk foods and spend those quarters that used to go into ITT's coffers on better tasting, more nutritious foods. You can start today.

Photo by Jane Scherr

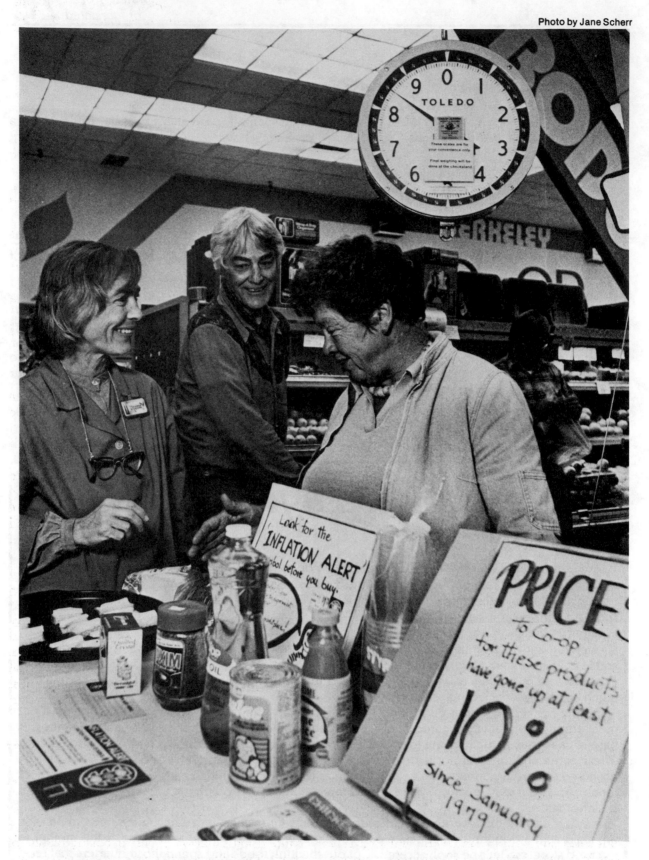

Home economist displays help in comparing prices, a difficult part of food shopping.

Julia, move over, we can be creative too

Take a tip from a gourmet cook

by Mary Gullberg

I'm talking about Julia Child, of course, and I want to encourage you to try creative cookery if you haven't already gotten into it. It's easy once you have some practical experience with recipe cookery.

Plunge right in!

One way to begin is to discover that you're out of cheddar, whole milk and butter — three ingredients needed for twice-baked potatoes. When this happened to me, I rummaged through the refrigerator and found sour cream and Mozzarella. These will do just fine. I mixed up some nonfat dry milk using only half the usual amount of water, stirred in the sour cream, added salt and pepper, and warmed the mixture over low heat. I grated the Mozzarella, mashed the potatoes, creamed them with the milk-sour cream mix, added the cheese, restuffed the potato shells and topped them with paprika. Marvelous!

Sometimes I take two or three recipes for the same dish and select the ingredients from each that I like or can afford. For example, one recipe for a chicken, shellfish and rice casserole will cost too much if I use frozen shrimp and fresh clams, but I notice that rock cod is on special at a good price, so I make a substitution. Another recipe I looked at used canned tomatoes. I realize this ingredient will add flavor, color and moisture to the casserole, so I substitute two cups of tomatoes for half the chicken broth. Maybe this dish could do with a touch of cheese. How about some grated Swiss sprinkled on top just before serving? The whole thing came out quite well; the flavors didn't fight, the guests gobbled it up.

Use your spices and herbs

One day I noted a half head of red cabbage in the crisper. Cole slaw! Don't even need a recipe for this one. Shred the cabbage and moisten it with sour cream and plain yogurt, season with dill weed, celery seed, green onion chopped fine, sugar, salt, pepper and a little lemon juice to taste.

In my herb pot, only three herbs have managed to survive erratic watering, cold weather and stiff breezes — rosemary, a type of sage, and a thyme. Now the main problem I have is to remember that these are growing out on the deck and to make use of them. I like rosemary with fish, with leafy green vegetables and with cheese or egg dishes — but a little goes a long way. The sage can also go with eggs and cheese and fish chowders besides the traditional use in pork and poultry dishes. The thyme complements tomatoes, fish, stews, and most other vegetables. I often use it in a sour cream dip for raw vegetables.

What are the benefits of this type of cooking?

Things never taste exactly the same twice! Variety is achieved by juggling ingredients. It's easier to use up leftovers. You can "stretch" small amounts of meat or fish into a luncheon soup using bouillion cubes or boiling bones for broth and adding a variety of fresh vegetables. And don't forget a complementary herb or spice. It's challenging. It's fun! Try it.

Leavening agents

A leavening agent is a gas incorporated or formed in a batter or dough to make it rise. There are three leavening gases: air, water vapor and carbon dioxide. **Air** can be beaten into the batter or beaten eggs can be folded in. **Water,** when heated in the dough, forms steam which causes the mixture to expand. Popovers and cream puffs are largely leavened by steam and air.

But the majority of products are leavened with **carbon dioxide** gas. Yeast, microscopic single-celled plants, produce carbon dioxide when they multiply in the dough. Recipes made with buttermilk, well-soured milk or molasses need 1/2 teaspoon baking soda for each cup of acid-containing liquid. The acid combines with the baking soda when heated to produce carbon dioxide. Baking powders contain both acid and baking soda. Commercial baking powders also contain a small amount of cornstarch to keep them from caking. Caking causes a loss of leavening power. To test if your baking powder is still effective, mix 1 teaspoon with 1/3 cup hot water. The water should bubble enthusiastically.

Baking powders available in local supermarkets are DOUBLE ACTING, which means that some gas is produced when the liquid is mixed with the dry ingredients but a larger amount of carbon dioxide is formed when the mixture is heated. Therefore, batters and doughs mixed with double-acting powders can sit at room temperature for a while before baking and still make well-leavened products. Check the proportion of baking powder to flour in your recipe before you measure the baking powder. For each cup of flour, use 1 to 1-1/2 teaspoon of a double-acting powder.

Double-acting baking powders contain CALCIUM ACID PHOSPHATE and SODIUM ALUMINUM SULFATE as the two acid ingredients. Some people look upon aluminum as a poison, but actually it poses no health threat in the amount present in baking powder. If you would like to make your own baking powder, here is a recipe from *Joy of Cooking*. For each cup of flour in the recipe, mix 1 teaspoon of cream of tartar, 1 teaspoon of baking soda and 1/2 teaspoon salt. Make it fresh each time you bake, because it doesn't keep very well.

by Mary Gullberg

To cook! Perchance to save some money! *by Helen Black*

A cook's inexperience, nowadays, is sheer extravagence. For example, the mere knowledge of how liquids can be thickened is the open sesame to soups, sauces or souffles. The cook, conniving against penny-waste here or nickel-down there uses up the vegetable cooking water, the scraps of left-over meat, or the egg yolk lurking in the depths of the refrigerator. More, such a skill provides a curious stiffening of the spine in the supermarket! A pox on high beef prices! And alternative eating may even taste better.

A neat trick with fat, flour and liquids

These three are essential to the thickened soup, the sauce, or the souffle. The trick is in the combining:

. . . Melt the fat — it's easy. Most any kind of fat will do — bacon grease, butter, margarine, oil. Use the chart below for proportions.

. . . Adding the flour — it's easy too. The flour is stirred into the melted fat. It seems so easy! Stir and cook the fat and flour together for several minutes over low heat, until well blended.

. . . Adding the liquid is the trick. The liquid must be added slowly, with steady stirring, until a smooth, thick mixture results. Use any kind of liquid. Milk, or broth, or a combination of both is commonly used. Broth or left-over vegetable cooking water can be used to reconstitute canned milk, concentrated milk or dry milk.

Use the trick for clam chowder

Drain 1 can chopped clams or baby clams; reserve liquid. Using proportions for soup, prepare white sauce with the drained liquid plus enough milk to make 1 cup. If desired, saute 1 or 2 tablespoons each of chopped onions and celery in the melted fat before adding flour. Combine white sauce and clams, correct the seasoning, heat thoroughly. Serves two.

Or curry the left-overs

Use proportions for sauce or gravy. When fat is melted, add ½ to 1 teaspoon curry powder. If desired, saute ½ cup chopped onions and celery in the fat. Add flour, stirring and cooking. Add liquid, using broth. When hot and smooth stir in 1½ to 2 cups cooked, boneless meat or fish. Season with lemon juice, salt and pepper to taste. Serve over rice, for two.

Ready for souffle?

Consult a good standard cookbook, for many different kinds of souffles.

Basic Proportions For White Sauce

	soup (or thin sauce)	sauce or gravy	souffle
FAT	1 tablespoon	2 tablespoons	3 tablespoons
FLOUR *	1 tablespoon	2 tablespoons	3-4 tablespoons
LIQUID	1 cup	1 cup	1 cup

* 1 tablespoon of cornstarch, potato or arrowroot starch is equal to 2 tablespoons of flour.

What's with honey, honey?
What it is and how to use it in recipes

Shoppers ask questions about honey — is it cooked, unblended, or organic? Is it better nutritionally than other sweeteners? What does sage or orange blossom mean on a label? How do you substitute honey for sugar in a recipe?

Honey production is a fascinating subject, but let's leave the explanation of how the bees make honey to others better qualified. Commercial honey is a by-product of the beekeeper or apiarist's job. Their bees are essential for the pollination of fifty or more important crops in California, which is why this is a large honey-producing state. The fees for this pollination service are an important part of the beekeeper's income. The bees are moved to wherever they are needed for pollination, or wherever there is a honey crop.

What does organic honey on a label mean? If you define "organic" as meaning no chemical pesticides used and no chemical fertilizers applied, this doesn't fit honey very well. The beekeeper has no control over where the bees go to gather honey except in the rather general sense of choosing the area in which the hives are placed.

Honey production is seasonal but, with the protracted growing season in California, the bees are working most of the year. Sage (which is a wild plant of the mint family growing along the coast in central California) and orange blossom are spring crops. Alfalfa, clover, and wild flowers are summer crops. Honey from eucalyptus and safflower has an unpleasant taste and, if too much is present in the honey, cannot be marketed.

Honey that is sold as "blended" honey means that no one floral flavor predominates. Of course, the beekeeper can't tell the bees which flowers to visit, so, unless it's certain that the product contains at least 60% honey with the flavor designated on the label, it can't be sold as anything but a blend. But, by the same token, honey labeled orange blossom or clover will undoubtedly contain traces of other flavors. Although the law says the label flavor must predominate, there is no laboratory test for particular flavors.

The beekeeper removes the honey from the comb by slicing the caps off an entire section with a knife. The comb in its supporting wooden frame is then spun (centrifuged) to extract the liquid honey. The empty comb can then be replaced in the hive for re-use by the bees.

The extracted honey is allowed to stand in large settling tanks for two or three weeks. Foam, bits of wax, and some of the lighter weight debris rise to the top and are skimmed off. The honey is then put into large, bulk containers and stored until shipped to the packer.

A small amount of honey is sold in the wooden frames — just as the bees stored it. This is comb honey. If it's been taken from the frame, but left in one piece, it's called out-comb honey. Chunk honey is pieces of honey in the comb (sold in the jar) with liquid honey filling up the spaces. This may be especially enjoyable for city slickers who would like the fun of chewing on the comb.

When the packer receives the honey, some of it may have crystallized. In order to label it U.S. Fancy, (U.S. Grade A is another designation that means the same), it must be strained through, at the very least, an eighty-mesh screen. The packer is required to be sure that it contains not more than 18.6% water.

An eighty-mesh screen is fairly coarse. To get honey that is sparkling clear, it must be clarified by filtration through material fine enough to remove all the tiniest specks of pollen and dust. To liquify the honey if it has crystallized and to aid in filtering it, it is heated to about 140°F. for a few hours. Or the packer may "flash heat" it to a higher temperature for a shorter time. Since both color and flavor are damaged by either a high temperature for a short time or a lower one for longer periods, packers use as little heat as possible. Whether these processes produce a "cooked" honey or not, you can decide. It definitely cannot be clarified without some heating, but 140°F. is a long way from boiling (212°F.). Perhaps the only uncooked honey is that in the comb.

Honey should be stored in a dry place at room temperature, since it is more likely to crystallize if it is cold. However, it may crystallize anyhow, because it is a super-saturated solution. Shaking, jarring, or temperature fluctuations may cause crystal formation. Freezing does not impair color or flavor but may hasten granulation. To liquify honey, place the jar in a pan of warm water until the crystals melt.

You wish to replace sugar in a recipe with honey? If more than half the sugar in a cake recipe is replaced with honey, the volume of the baked cake will be less and the cake will brown too much. Half a cup or less of sugar may be replaced with honey without adjusting the liquid in the recipe. If a cup or more of honey is used, often the liquid in the recipe should be decreased by 1/4 cup for each cup of honey used. To minimize burning, lower the oven temperature by 25°F. and bake a little longer. Many baked products except light layer cakes are quite acceptable with less sugar. You may experiment by substituting for the sugar one-half as much honey.

Nutritive value of honey? Honey is mostly sugars. They are simple sugars (monosaccharides) rather than double sugars (disaccharides) such as are found in cane or beet sugar. Double sugars must go through an extra step in digestion — they must be split into simple sugars before they can be absorbed into the blood. However, your digestive juices contain enzymes that do this very readily, so claims that honey is "easy to digest" are technically true but practically unimportant. Honey provides 21 calories per teaspoon, regular sugar has 16. Honey furnishes little except calories. The traces of vitamins and minerals in it are too small to be significant considering the amount that is used in an average person's diet. The best reason for using honey is that you prefer the flavor. Who wants to sprinkle sugar on biscuits when you can use HONEY?

You can do it yourself

Today's "convenience foods" have captured a large part of the consumer dollar. For all of us these can be convenient, occasionally. When the unexpected guest stays for dinner, or when you arrive home exhausted after work or a day's outing with the children, these partially prepared dishes can be life savers. But as a steady diet they are hard on the budget, and often nutritionally deficient. In the same amount of time, or a bit more, the same recipe may be made from basic ingredients you often have on the kitchen shelf. The result is often superior in flavor and nutritional value. Next time you reach for a box of packaged Romanoff or Tetrazini, have a second thought and try one of our recipes.

Chicken Tetrazzini

1 whole 3 lb. fryer
12 oz. thin spaghetti
2 tablespoons butter or margarine
1 medium onion, minced
1 small green pepper, diced
½ lb. fresh mushrooms, chopped
2 tablespoons butter or margarine
1 tablespoon flour
1½ cups chicken stock or broth
¾ cup evaporated milk, undiluted
1 tablespoon sherry, optional
1 cup Parmesan, grated
salt & pepper to taste

Simmer chicken in water seasoned with salt and pepper, until it is tender, about 45 minutes. Cool quickly; reserve broth. Remove skin from chicken; cut meat off bones and cut into small pieces.

Cook spaghetti until barely tender, i.e., al dente. Drain.

Sauté onion, pepper and mushroom in butter for 5 minutes. Save. Melt the other 2 tablespoons butter. Stir in flour. Gradually add broth saved from cooking the chicken, and simmer slowly, stirring constantly for a few minutes until sauce is slightly thickened. Add evaporated milk, sherry and one-half the Parmesan, and simmer for one minute. Add the onion, green pepper, mushroom mixture, and stir until cheese melts. Remove from heat.

Divide sauce in half. Mix one half with diced chicken and other half with the spaghetti. Put spaghetti in casserole, about 3 to 4 qt. size. Cover with chicken mixture. Sprinkle with remaining cheese. Bake uncovered for about 25 minutes at 350 °F. 12 servings, each providing 20 grams of protein.

Noodles Romanoff

1 pkg. (8 oz.) egg noodles
1½ cups cottage cheese (small or large curd)
1 clove garlic, minced
1 teaspoon Worcestershire sauce
½ pint sour cream
3 green onions, finely chopped
1/8 teaspoon cayenne
½ cup Parmesan, grated

Boil noodles in salted water until tender, about 10 minutes; drain well. Combine noodles and all other ingredients except Parmesan. Pour into buttered casserole, about 2 quart size; sprinkle Parmesan over top. Bake at 350 °F. for 20 minutes. 4 servings, each providing 20 grams protein.

Other quick ideas for "gourmet" dishes

Pre-seasoned rices may be made easily by placing 1 cup rice, 2 cups cold water, 1 teaspoon butter and 1 teaspoon, or more, of any spice or herb you fancy such as curry powder, powdered cardamon, oregano, or thyme, into a heavy saucepan with a close-fitting lid. Bring to a boil, lower heat and simmer for 12 to 15 minutes. The rice may also be cooked in a double boiler for 20 to 25 minutes.

An easy fried rice or noodle dish may be prepared by sauteing leftover rice or noodles in oil with a minced onion, green pepper, leftover chicken, beef, pork or seafood until the rice or noodles are lightly browned. Add a beaten egg, salt and pepper and saute another five minutes. This may be served topped with chopped nuts, minced parsley and chives or sesame seeds.

Master mix

This home-made convenience mix may save you time and money when preparing hot breads such as waffles, pancakes, biscuits, muffins or coffee cake.

There are three types of commercial biscuit and pancake mixes on the market now:

1. Biscuit mixes which contain shortening
2. Pancake and waffle mixes which contain NO shortening
3. "Complete" mixes which contain shortening, dry milk in some form and sometimes powdered eggs.

This master mix is similar to the "complete" commercial mixes, but contains no powdered egg. Waffles and biscuits made from a complete mix will be different from those made from scratch. Biscuits, though very acceptable, will not be as flaky, because larger pieces of fat in the flour mixture are necessary to produce the flaky layers which separate easily. Waffles will require a longer baking time and will not be as crisp and tender as those made by the conventional method. In the latter method, the oil or melted fat contained in the liquid ingredients coats the flour particles and therefore produces a more tender product.

Some important facts to know before using master mix:

1. Flours vary in the amount of liquid they will absorb.

Bread and all-purpose flours made from hard wheat of a high protein content will absorb (take up) MORE liquid than cake and pastry flours made from soft wheat with a lower protein content. Unbleached flour takes up MORE liquid than bleached flour, probably because wheat of higher protein content must be used in producing unbleached flour which is aged for several months.

Furthermore, the same *type* of flour may vary from time to time depending upon the quality and type of wheat used in the flour. Therefore, carefully check the amount of liquid used in the recipes *each time flour from a new bag is used.* Excess liquid may result in a soggy and low-volume product.

2. How baking powder works.

Double-acting baking powder (such as Calumet) releases *part* of the carbon dioxide when moistened and the *rest* when the batter is heated.

Most of the thiamine (B_1) in flour can be lost during baking if excess soda or baking powder is used in doughs or batters. Therefore, baking soda has been eliminated from all recipes and a minimum amount of baking powder is used in the mix to insure maximum retention of B_1 in the finished product. However, if you find the volume of the baked products unsatisfactory, add 1 teaspoon more of baking powder per 2 cups mix.

3. Saving energy is folly for quick breads.

Sorry, but the cooking time is so short that the product will be a flop UNLESS you always pre-heat the oven, griddle or waffle iron for quick breads. The initial high temperature causes the batter or dough to expand rapidly and allows the structure to set quickly.

Master Mix

Yield: approximately 13 cups

9 cups whole wheat or unbleached enriched
   flour or a mixture of both
3 tablespoons **double-acting** baking powder

4 teaspoons salt or less
1½ cups instant nonfat dry milk powder
3 sticks margarine (¾ pound)

Measure dry ingredients in large mixing bowl. Cut the margarine in with pastry blender or two sharp knives until the shortening is in pieces the size of small peas. Store it in a tightly closed container such as a cannister or clean 2 or 3 pound coffee can. It will keep for several weeks in a cool cupboard.

For those who like more character, flavor and texture, try:

Higher Protein Master Mix

Yield: approximately 16 cups

9 cups whole wheat or unbleached enriched
   flour or a mixture of both
4 tablespoons **double-acting** baking powder
5 teaspoons salt

2 cups instant nonfat dry milk powder
1 cup soy flour
1 cup wheat germ, raw or toasted
3 sticks margarine (¾ pound)
Mix as directed above.

Recipes using master mix

Biscuits

Yield: 12 biscuits

2 cups master mix   ½ cup water

Carefully add liquid to mix to form a stiff dough that can be removed from mixing bowl in a single lump. Place dough on lightly floured board and knead briefly using extra flour to keep dough from sticking to fingers or board. Pat or roll dough into a ½ inch thickness and cut with a 2 inch biscuit cutter dipped lightly in flour. Place biscuits on ungreased cookie sheet and bake at 425 degrees F. for 10 to 12 minutes, until lightly browned.

Variations:
Buttermilk Biscuits
To 2 cups master mix, add ¾ cup buttermilk instead of water and proceed as above.
Cheese Biscuits
To 2 cups master mix, add ¾ to 1 cup grated sharp cheddar cheese; mix well and follow above directions.
Drop Biscuits
To 2 cups master mix, add ⅔ cup water. Mix until flour is moistened. Spoon batter onto baking sheet. Bake at 425 degrees F. for 10 to 12 minutes.

Muffins

Yield: 12 small muffins

2 cups master mix   ⅔ cup water
2 tablespoons sugar   1 egg

Add water to beaten egg. Add liquid mixture to dry ingredients and mix just enough to moisten.* Fill greased muffin cups ⅔ full. Bake about 15 minutes at 400 degrees F.

* Overbeating muffin batter will result in a tough product with many large holes.

Pancakes

Yield: about 4 servings

2 cups master mix
1 egg, beaten

1 tablespoon sugar (optional)
1⅓ cups water
Margarine or butter for frying

Add water to beaten egg. Add liquid mixture to dry ingredients and stir until moistened. Melt shortening in large skillet or griddle. Pour batter onto hot skillet to form pancakes. Fry until bubbles form all over the surface of the cakes. Turn and brown on other side.

Variation: For two people, 1 cup mix, 1 egg and ½ cup water.

Waffles

Yield: 4 servings

2 cups master mix
2 tablespoons oil or melted margarine

2 eggs, slightly beaten
1⅓ cups water
1 tablespoon sugar (optional)

Add water and oil to beaten eggs. Add this mixture to dry ingredients and blend well. Bake in a hot waffle iron.

Fruit Cobbler

3 - 4 cups fruit (#2½ can including syrup or
   1 pound fresh or frozen fruit)
½-¾ cup sugar, if fruit is unsweetened
1 teaspoon margarine or butter

1 cup master mix
⅓ cup water

Place fruit or fruit-sugar mixture in an 8″ X 8″ shallow pan. Dot with margarine. Add water to master mix and stir until moistened. Spoon batter onto fruit mixture. Bake at 375 degrees F. for 25 to 30 minutes.

Coffee Cake

Batter:

2 cups master mix
⅓ cup sugar
2 eggs, beaten
½ cup water

Topping:

½ cup brown sugar
1 teaspoon cinnamon
2 tablespoons margarine or butter, melted

Stir sugar into master mix. Combine water and beaten egg. Add to dry ingredients and mix until well blended. Place batter in a shallow, greased 8″ X 8″ pan. Combine topping ingredients and sprinkle evenly over batter. Bake at 375 degrees F. for 35 to 40 minutes.

Homemade mixes for baked goods

All of us have had last-minute requests for cookies or cake for a bake sale. All of us have had phone calls announcing the arrival of friends who have just arrived in town for a short visit. Easy-to-make cookies and fragrant gingerbread are yours for serving if you keep a supply of your own basic oatmeal and gingerbread mixes on hand. There may be less expensive commercial mixes on the market, but our recipes may be more nutritious since nonfat dry milk is an ingredient, no preservatives are used, and the homemaker has the satisfaction of baking from "scratch."

Oatmeal Mix *
for cookies and muffins

6 cups sifted unbleached flour *
3½ cups sugar (white or brown)
1½ tablespoon salt
¼ cup baking powder

2 cups dry milk
1 lb. (2 cups) shortening not requiring
　refrigeration
5 cups rolled oats, regular or quick

*Flour may be white enriched or whole wheat or ½ of each. Or use 5 cups wheat flour and ½ cup soy flour and ½ cup wheat germ. (Wheat germ should be added after sifting). If you vary flour used, amount of liquid in recipe may vary somewhat.

Sift flour, sugar and baking powder together 2 times. Cut in shortening until mixture has consistency of cornmeal. Add rolled oats and dry milk and mix well. Store in a covered container. Makes about 20 cups. To measure the mix, pile lightly into measuring cup and level off with spatula.　　　　　*Oatmeal mix adapted from recipe by Christine Groppe.*

Drop Cookies

Spice:		**Hermits:**	
3 cups oatmeal mix	½ cup chopped	3 cups oatmeal mix	¾ cup mixture of
1½ teaspoon	nuts (optional)	½ teaspoon	chopped nuts,
cinnamon	1 egg	cinnamon	raisins, and dates
½ teaspoon nutmeg	¼ cup melted butter	½ teaspoon cloves	1 egg
½ teaspoon allspice	¼ cup water	¼ cup brown sugar	⅓ cup water
Coconut:		**Chocolate Chip:**	
3 cups oatmeal mix	¼ cup melted butter	3 cups oatmeal mix	1 egg
1 cup coconut	or margarine	⅓ cup brown sugar	1 teaspoon vanilla
1 egg	¼ cup water	6 oz. pkg. chocolate	⅓ cup water
		pieces	

Combine all dry ingredients (including nuts, fruit or chocolate.) Beat egg slightly and add to it all liquid ingredients including melted butter, flavorings. Add liquid mixture to dry mixture, and stir until all ingredients are well blended. Drop by teaspoon onto a greased cooky sheet. Bake in a moderate oven (350°) 12-15 minutes. Each recipe makes about 2 dozen large cookies.

Peanut Butter Cookies

¹/₂ cup peanut butter
1 egg
1¹/₂ cup oatmeal mix

Mix peanut butter and slightly beaten egg with oatmeal mix. Shape into balls and put onto a greased baking sheet. Press cookies flat with a fork. Bake in a moderate oven (350°) about 12-15 minutes.

Oatmeal Cupcakes

3 cups oatmeal mix
1 egg
¹/₂ cup water

Beat egg until light. Add water and mix well. Add all at once to oatmeal mix. Stir 40 strokes. (If fruit or nuts are used, add at the end of 30 strokes, then mix 10 more strokes.) Fill well-greased muffin pans ²/₃ full. Bake in a hot oven (425°) about 20 minutes.

Variations:

Add any of the following:
Apple: 3 cups diced apple and 1 teaspoon cinnamon
Cranberry: 1 cup raw cranberries, coarsely chopped and 2 tablespoons sugar
Blueberry: 1 cup drained blueberries
Date-Nut: ¹/₂ cup chopped dates (or raisins) and ¹/₂ cup chopped nuts

Coffee Cake

Cake:
1 egg
¹/₂ cup water
3 cups oatmeal mix

Topping:
¹/₂ cup brown sugar
2 teaspoons cinnamon
2 tablespoons flour
¹/₄ cup melted butter
¹/₂ cup chopped nuts

Beat egg until light. Add water and mix well. Make a well in oatmeal mix and pour all of the egg-mixture into it. Stir 40 strokes. Pour into a well-greased, 8-inch-square cake pan. Mix remaining ingredients and cover coffee-cake batter. Bake in a moderate oven (375°) about 35 minutes.

Gingerbread Mix Makes 11 cups

7¹/₂ cups flour
2¹/₂ cups dried milk
3 tablespoons baking powder
1¹/₄ teaspoon salt

1 cup sugar
1 tablespoon ginger
1 tablespoon cinnamon
1 tablespoon cloves

Sift ingredients together three times, primarily to incorporate dry milk well.

Gingerbread

Makes 12   3″ x 4″ servings
2¹/₂ cups gingerbread mix
¹/₂ cup margarine
³/₄ cup boiling water
¹/₂ cup honey
¹/₂ cup molasses
2 eggs

Sift and measure dry gingerbread mix. Melt margarine in boiling water. Add honey and molasses. Beat eggs and add to liquid ingredients. Add liquid ingredients slowly to dry mix, beating until smooth after each addition. Bake in oiled baking pan, 9 x 13 inches, 350°F. for 25-30 minutes or until gingerbread pulls away from edge of pan.

Fast food at home *by June Kadish*

Can you spare 30 minutes (not counting shopping time) to fix a tasty meal? One which the family will enjoy, be inexpensive and have the bonus of more nutrients and fewer calories than many foods the fast-food outlets offer?

Americans are eating more and more meals outside the home for a variety of reasons. Many of these meals may not provide a vegetable or salad and most are high in fat and calories.

Alternatives? Yes! For example: Very Fast Chicken Dinner and others.

Very fast chicken dinner

Put chicken parts on greased baking sheet. Sprinkle with herbs. Start broiling. Scrub potatoes, slice 1" thick lengthwise and put with chicken. Turn both after 15 minutes. If potatoes get too brown remove for a few minutes. Meantime wash and slice vegetables onto platter; add dressing. Other family members are setting table, putting out bread and beverage, such as milk or juice. Cut up fruit for dessert. Chicken cooks in 30 minutes total. Cost is between $3-$4 for 4 depending on whether you had cut-up or whole chicken you cut yourself. 4 servings.

Quick, almost-pizza dinner

Figure 2-3 English muffin halves per person. Top each with sliced mozzarella or jack cheese, spoonful tomato sauce and sprinkle of oregano, basil, garlic powder and grated parmesan. Bake at 400°F. for 10-15 minutes or broil several inches below heat 'til hot and bubbly. Drain 1 can each green, kidney and garbanzo beans. Add oil and vinegar dressing and toss well. Top sliced fresh fruit with spoonful cottage cheese and/or yogurt. DINNER IS SERVED.

Other quick meals

Baked fish fillets, baked rice, oven-cooked carrots, bread, beverage, fruit and cookies.

or

Canned split pea or bean soup, omelet with mushrooms or sauteed zucchini or tomatoes or all three, bread, beverage and oatmeal cookies.

Dinner in a hurry (half an hour from start to serve)

by June Kadish

You're on the way home from work. It's about 5:15 and you're tired. The temptation to stop at Ye Olde Fish & Chip Shoppe or Hamburger Heaven for the family supper is almost overwhelming. At the traffic light you check your wallet. Five dollars left until next pay day. You resolve to use food already on hand at home for an adequate, if not inspired, family meal. Your fatigued brain develops the menu below since all ingredients are in the family larder.

Menu:
Two-ingredient macaroni and cheese plus bonito
Frozen peas or broccoli
Raw carrots
Whole wheat bread with margarine or butter

Tomato juice and/or milk
Canned peaches and sliced bananas for dessert

Game plan for dinner

Put kettle of water on to boil. Get out the macaroni, Velveeta (yes, Velveeta for this quickie), can of bonito, package of frozen vegetables, carrots, bread from freezer, margarine, fruit for dessert. Add macaroni to boiling water in large pot. While it boils, scrape the carrots. Wrap bread in foil and set to heat in toaster-oven or in a pan set on top of the boiling macaroni pot. Note: You could, of course, use a packaged macaroni and cheese mix, but it does not supply as much protein and takes just as long to prepare, so I question the validity of the term "convenience" food for this kind of product.

Cook the frozen vegetable according to package directions. Drain the macaroni when barely tender. Cut up about four ounces of Velveeta for every 6 ounces of dried macaroni (half a package). Add this cheese food and a drained can of Co-op bonito to the macaroni. Keep on low heat. Add a pinch of dried mustard or speck of cayenne pepper for extra flavor zip. 3 servings.

Another pair of hands

We can assume, I hope, that another member of the household will set the table, put out the beverages, and prepare a bowl of peaches, bananas, and, if available, fresh strawberries for dessert.

This meal, which is suitable for any size family, when you adjust the amounts, uses only two pots. This makes for relatively simple cleanup, a goal I'm constantly striving for.

Other bonuses

The cost of the main dish is about 40c per serving, and it provides about 25 grams of protein per serving, which is more than enough for the main dish for dinner.

Co-op News June 11, 1979

Keeping Food Safely

Food spoilage

As millions cheered

There were just a few thousand of us, jogging along comfortably in the back of the station wagon. Such beautiful surroundings! So moist! And not too sour, either! But I must say, it was uncomfortably chilly, after that long night in the refrigerator. We were all a little dopey with the cold.

But the sun was getting warmer. We squirmed around deliciously in the warmth. We gazed appreciatively at the mounds of potato, egg, mayonnaise, chopped pickles and olives, pimentos and onions. What a wonderful world! We decided to overpopulate it.

Time passed, maybe a half hour. We expanded, stretched, and suddenly there were twice as many of us! A real party! How long would it last?

Another half hour, and we were four times as many. And more time passed. We did our dividing, over and over. We were put out on a table right in the sun, and faster and faster we divided. What a performance it was! What a great day for bacteria! The hilarious thing about it was that nobody could tell we were there! Down the hatch we went!

Well, naturally a lot of people got sick. Not right away. Later. Some got sick the next day. And we didn't feel guilty at all. After all, we have to make the most of our opportunities. We have to live too, you know.

Having a **PICNIC** with just a small ice box?

Then drink warm beer if you must, but **REFRIGERATE** foods susceptible to food poisoning.

from Co-op Home Economist

Don't spoil your summer fun *by Joan Taylor*

Let me remind you of a few safety ideas so you won't get sick from the food you take to the BBQ or picnic.

Keep hot foods hot — cold foods cold

Ice chests or insulated bags with ice, dry ice or reusable cold packs are good for keeping food cold. Chill food before packing.

Hot foods are hot when they are above 140°F.

Harmful bacteria may grow in foods that are lukewarm. It is a good practice not to let food sit around at all at room temperature, especially in warm weather. Chances for foodborne illness are greater if you do.

You may not get sick right away. Symptoms can take as long as 72 hours to develop. Foodborne illness can be a lot like a virus. You may experience any one or all of the following symptoms:

vomiting • diarrhea • stomach cramps

Soap and water

Wash hands with soap and water before PREPARING, SERVING and EATING foods. Bacteria from nose, cuts or not washing after using the bathroom can cause harmful bacteria to multiply in food. Wash the knife after you use it for cutting raw chicken. Don't use the unclean knife to cut up the watermelon. It may pass bacteria from one food to another.

Be extra careful with: Seafood, dishes made with eggs, poultry, soups, cooked meats, foods containing milk, and cream pies. Keep cold until ready to use. Put leftovers in refrigerator or on ice right away.

All fresh fruits and vegetables should be **WASHED** thoroughly in cold water.

Why?
To wash off sprays, bacteria and dirt.

from your Co-op Home Economist.

The most unpopular chore

If there's anything we humans just love to do, it's study each other. Take surveys! It satisfies that old, gossipy curiosity. Lately, some older folks have been scrutinizing the food feelings of younger folks and learned just lots of things.* For example, those kids admit eating is essential and even that it can be fun to fix food, but putting away leftovers is **awful!** You know, those kids may be right, and I think I know why. It's because putting away leftovers is **urgent.** And it takes time, decisions and a good deal of inspiration.

*As reported by Marie Ferree, "Marketing Memos," October 1977

Wash your hands, dearies

by Betsy Wood

Working around food? Just been to the restroom? Wash your hands, dearie. Why? Because not doing so could contribute to making someone sick.

We're not trying to make you into fidgety worriers, scared of every single germ. Germs (bacteria) are everywhere. We take in millions every day — some "good" some "bad." But with careful hand washing and good food handling practices we can cut way down the number of "bad" bacteria we gulp down and thus cut the odds on getting sick.

Bacteria are everywhere but ... those that might make you sick, especially staphylococcus are concentrated around people's noses, and salmonella are concentrated in the intestinal tract of animals, including humans. Many people are regular carriers of these bacteria without knowing it.

Most illness we get from food we get because bacteria reach the food and then multiply to huge numbers. Bacteria divide and two become four, forty become eighty and if conditions are right, millions become billions. (Recently I took a microbiology short course and saw this under the microscope.)

Why dirty hands while preparing food are a no no. Example: Your hands are full of bacteria, you eat cold turkey without washing (not recommended naturally), you ingest a mere hundred thousand bacteria, which your body might fight off. But if you handle the cooked turkey with unwashed hands, let it sit in a warm room while bacteria multiply, and then you feast before bed, everyone might get sick — not right away but hours later. (That's why we say refrigerate leftovers promptly.)

What else goes wrong? It might be CROSS CONTAMINATION. You cut up a chicken. It's full of salmonella. Later you cook the chicken thoroughly so it's okay. You have the wit not to slice the meatloaf for sandwiches on the same board. But you don't wash your hands. The salmonella are carried by your hands to that warm meatloaf. They multiply; your husband saves the sandwich for the end of swing shift — and trouble.

Pity the maligned mayonnaise — You've heard about food poisoning after the political picnic. Everyone blamed the mayonnaise in the potato salad. But mayonnaise by itself is acid and not a good place for bacteria to grow. It's more likely due to all those bacteria from the unwashed hands, hands which cut and mixed the warm potatoes. The bacteria probably incubated to millions and billions for hours on a hot day while everyone played baseball.

Use that soap. Washing your hands thoroughly with soap, even that yukky piece in the public washroom, will get your hands cleaner than just a quick rinse.

Preparing lots of food at a lunch counter or school kitchen? It's good to have a pot with chlorine sanitizer to dip your hands in from time to time. Use one tablespoon chlorine bleach for each quart water. Use this for sponges and cutting boards too.

Besides hand washing, what's good food handling practice?
Briefly: Keep everything clean — utensils, and work surfaces. Keep hot foods hot (above 140 degrees F) and cold foods cold (refrigerated). Most bacteria multiply best at room temperature or slightly warmer. Take care especially with foods that provide a nice place for growth of bacteria: moist meats, soups, vegetables, milk foods. Happy Eating!

Leftovers

Care of leftovers:
Bacteria grow readily in cold meats, poultry, stuffing, gravy, cream sauce and casserole dishes, cream or custard desserts. Foods that cause food poisoning often show no signs of spoilage, so you can't rely completely on taste, smell or appearance.

General Rules: Keep hot food hot, cold food cold; that is, avoid leaving at room temperature.

Refrigerate or freeze leftovers promptly. Food will chill and heat faster in shallow than in deep dishes. Use leftovers as soon as possible. If you don't have a freezer and want to use leftovers a week after preparation, heat thoroughly once or twice in between.

Avoid touching food whenever you can. If you have a cold or skin infection, try to stay away from food preparation. Of course, it is important to wash dishes and silverware thoroughly. However, bacteria have much more chance of growing and being transmitted in leftover food than on your clean utensils.

Be especially careful when cooking for a crowd. Refrigerator and oven space may be inadequate. Do not let food stand long at room temperature.

Meats:

Do not slice until just before serving.

Leftover meat to be served cold should be refrigerated promptly in small packages.

Use in two or three days.

Hams are not cured or smoked as thoroughly as they used to be. Therefore, they need refrigeration — before and after cooking.

Sandwiches for box lunches which will be kept in a warm place all morning should be prepared and refrigerated the night before or at least two hours before being packed in the lunchbox. The safest procedure is to freeze the sandwiches. Avoid using cooked egg whites, tomatoes, green vegetables and jelly in the sandwich fillings.

Gravy: Bring to a boil when reusing.

Stuffing:

Before cooking poultry, wash thoroughly inside and out. Stuff just before roasting, not the day before, because (1) you cannot get the inside cold enough soon enough again to store safely and (2) if bacteria do grow while stored, the stuffing may not get hot enough during the roasting to kill the bacteria. Roast until thermometer inserted in center of stuffing reaches 165° F. Separate leftover stuffing and refrigerate in a covered dish. Heat thoroughly when reusing.

Desserts:

Cream and custard-filled desserts are especially susceptible to food spoilage. Refrigerate until served.

Leftover leftovers:

Many dishes spoil rapidly because of their high moisture, low acid content. Be especially careful of any dish with cream sauce or those made with ground meat, such as meat loaf, hash, croquettes. When reusing, heat to boiling. Meat pies and casseroles should be bubbling. Leftover soup and gravy can be kept indefinitely by bringing to a boil every three days and storing in a clean jar.

Ideas and recipes:

Leftover foods can be used in many ways. Your own cookbook may give you ideas. You can use leftover meat in souffles, croquettes, salad, mixtures with Chinese vegetables, hash, soup, curry, macaroni, bean dishes, meat pies, and of course, sandwiches, hot and cold. An easy dish combines diced meat, gravy or canned cream soup, cooked noodles or rice and green peas or broccoli.

Leftover mashed potatoes can be made into patties and fried, or used as a topping for shepherd's pie. Cranberry sauce keeps well and can be used with many leftover dishes.

So you don't want to poison Cousin John?

Then get the leftover casserole (or roast, or gravy, or vegetables) into the refrigerator right after supper

from your Co-op Home Economist

DO NOT Store Acid Foods in Dinnerware

Do not store acid foods (juices, fruits, tomatoes, salad dressing, wine, carbonated drinks) in dinnerware (pottery, earthenware, stoneware, china).
WHY? Because the acid might leach lead out of improperly fired dishes.
Use glass to store acid foods.

Don't store acid food in dinnerware *by Betsy Wood*

Here we go again. "Don't do this." "Don't do that." We've said it before but now it's time to repeat: DON'T STORE ACID FOOD IN DISHES. WHY? Because sometimes the dish or cup or pitcher contains lead or other toxic metals which may be leachable (dissolvable) by acids. Lead is toxic and it can build up in your body.

What's dinnerware? Any dishes including china, earthenware, stoneware, porcelain — expensive or cheap.

What's acid? Most fruits and fruit juices, wine, vinegar, salad dressings, sauerkraut, tomatoes, pickles.

Sorry, there's no home test to check safety. But if you have a whole set of bright dishes you brought across the border, you might have one or two tested in a commercial lab.

Presence of the metal itself is not the hazard. The dishes become unsafe when a glaze is formulated wrong or applied wrong or fired wrong. Daily use at meals is not as much of a hazard as storing acid foods for a period, which releases the toxic metal.

Actually, most dishes are okay, but since we can't be sure, we still say "DSAF in D." Dishes most suspect are highly colored. White dishes and those commercially produced in this country are generally okay. It's hard to tell about handmade pottery. Many potters are now aware of the hazard and follow careful procedures.

The Food and Drug Administration checks samples of questionable imported dinnerware. They tell me that the percent with leachable toxic metals has gone down in the last few years. FDA also has a domestic surveillance program.

A good law is on the books in California, but even in 1979 there is virtually no enforcement. The bill, passed in 1972, was aimed at protecting consumers through a certification program. Both the Reagan and Brown administrations turned down requests for money to set up the program. This should teach us something about consumer protection bills with no funds.

So where do you store the lemonade till tomorrow? In a glass jar. We used to say glass or plastic. But now some plastics are suspect.

Retraining yourself and your household will take some doing. I suggest that you post this warning on your refrigerator:

Don't store acid foods in dishes

Please don't eat moldy foods *by Betsy Wood*

Years ago we said — "Don't worry about moldy food — it's harmless." No more. Research in the last 15 years has shown that there are dozens of different toxins produced by molds. Sometimes the mold itself may be hazardous to your health. True, there are many useful molds, but since there's no easy way to distinguish these from those that might hurt us, we say don't eat any moldy foods.

What does it do to you?

Different molds produce different toxins, and these do different things in the body. Aflatoxin is the best known toxin and is a potent cancer causer. Most peanuts are inspected for aflatoxin. Aflatoxin may also be produced by mold in grains, beans, nut meats, spices, bread. DO NOT eat these foods if they are moldy.

Don't even sniff mold; it can enter your body through the respiratory tract.

Mold growing on acid food such as pickles may alter the acidity and allow food spoilage, so throw this food out, too.

Throw it out or cut it off?

There's some difference of opinion here among experts, but most conclude it's best to throw out moldy food. Mold spores can imbed themselves below the surface. But if you do cut, on cheese for example, cut deep, don't just wipe the surface.

What about naturally moldy cheese such as roquefort?

The mold that's there to produce cheese is apparently okay.

What to do?

Don't buy moldy food. At home wash and dry your refrigerator and bread box frequently. Keep foods as cool and dry as possible. And don't keep them too long. Cooking will not destroy the toxins produced by mold.

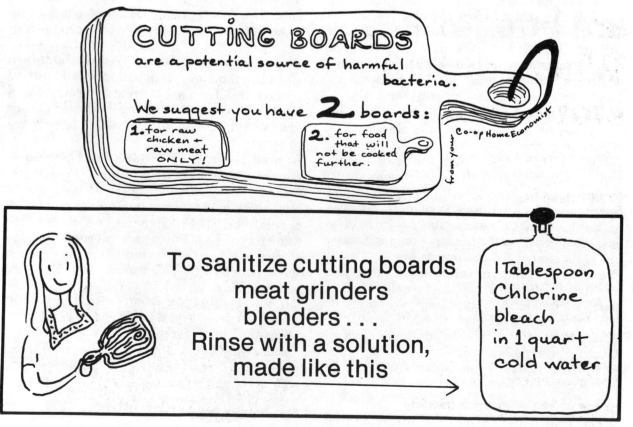

CUTTING BOARDS are a potential source of harmful bacteria.

We suggest you have **2** boards:

1. for raw chicken + raw meat ONLY!

2. for food that will not be cooked further.

from your Co-op Home Economist

To sanitize cutting boards meat grinders blenders . . . Rinse with a solution, made like this →

1 Tablespoon Chlorine bleach in 1 quart cold water

Food storage

The groceries are bought. Where do you store them? *by June Kadish*

Wait a moment! There are two things to consider before you get the groceries home.

In the store buy the non-refrigerated foods first, such as crackers, paper products, canned foods. Get the meat, dairy and frozen items last because thirty to forty minutes in your shopping cart can contribute to a loss of quality.

Head home quickly

Don't do errands while the food is in a warm car. Bacteria and molds love those cozy temperatures and start multiplying at a rapid rate. If you must make a stop or two, bring a picnic chest with you and put the perishables in it so cold foods can keep their cool.

Home at last — unpack quickly

The cold items go into the refrigerator or freezer right away. Meat for the freezer is wrapped tightly in freezer paper and dated so you'll have a record of how old it is. Store vegetables in plastic bags in crisper. Do not wash until ready to use.

Cans, boxes and bags of food under the sink? No way!

Do you put some of them under the sink? Some people do, but it's not recommended. This is a favorite spot for insects and rodents, and it's only a step further into your food supply. There are pipes under the sink which may leak, and moisture is a no-no for safe storage. It can cause rust on cans and molds on grains, cereals and similar foods.

Next to the stove?

Cupboards close to the stove or other heat sources aren't best for food, either. The heat dries up mixes, bread and flour and encourages insect infestation. Use those cupboards for dishes. Use the COOLEST areas for food.

Household cleaners and food are a dangerous combination

Wherever you store cleansers, ammonia and other cleaning compounds, food shouldn't go near them. It's just too easy for a child or babysitter to pick up a bottle of furniture polish and add it to the salad dressing!

Rotate your canned foods frequently

Mark the date of purchase on the can label to remind you to use it before its FIRST BIRTHDAY. If you're suspicious of a food's safety because a can is badly rusted or swollen or shows any sign of leakage. DO NOT TASTE IT. This could be dangerous to your health. Tasting doesn't always tell you food is safe, anyway. **Throw it out.**

No refrigeration?

Cooking without a refrigerator is hard but not impossible. You need to plan carefully, understand what must not be kept at room temperature (so that you won't poison yourself), shop more often and maybe spend a little more, because you can't store leftovers.

You will probably need to shop every day for fresh food, or shop every other day and on alternate nights have dinner from the cupboard — maybe tuna and noodles with cut up fresh celery (a little limp from yesterday) and fresh tomato salad.

Your shelf should include some of your favorite canned items that will make the basis of a quick dinner, and can be finished at one meal — tuna, sardines, beans, corned beef hash, tamales or what have you.

There are many foods which normally are kept in the refrigerator but may be kept a day or two at room temperature. These include:

- **Eggs (in shell or hard cooked)**
- **Hard cheeses such as cheddar and cheese food but not soft cheeses such as cottage cheese, cream cheese, ricotta**
- **Raw vegetables: carrots, turnips, even lettuce or celery (put in plastic bag and closed with a rubber band)**
- **Margarine and butter**
- **Half a grapefruit**
- **Pickles**

A "refrigerator" of your own

A "refrigerator" of your own is possible if you have a good friend nearby with freezer space who is willing to keep a container of water (milk carton, coffee can) frozen for you. Or you can use the "fridgie bags." Put your ice in a foam picnic ice chest and you can keep milk, meat, leftovers and vegetables for a day or two.

For safety's sake if you have no refrigeration

Do not keep any cooked food or leftovers without refrigeration. Certain kinds of spoilage problems are not taken care of by boiling before eating, so just don't keep fresh or cooked meat, cooked vegetables, milk or cooked dishes from one day to the next.

Do not store canned food after it is opened. It is not safe to use half the canned hash for supper and the rest for lunch the next day. Potentially dangerous bacteria may grow. If you want milk in your coffee, use powdered cream or nonfat dry milk, not canned milk.

Milk — Fresh milk and cottage cheese should be used all in one meal. Dry milk can be mixed a glass at a time. A little instant coffee or vanilla improves the flavor for some people or you can try "Milkman" which is more expensive than dry milk but costs less than fresh milk.

KEEP MILK AND OTHER DAIRY FOODS

COLD . . . in the refrigerator, not left out while you watch TV.
CLEAN . . . don't put the licked spoon back in the cottage cheese.
and COVERED . . . so new bacteria, yeasts and molds will not be added.

Storing dairy products

Concentrated Milk. To increase the keeping quality of fresh concentrated milk, it may be quickly frozen and held frozen until ready to use. Like other frozen foods, it must be used soon after defrosting. When defrosted, there may be a texture change to a somewhat grainy consistency. Keep frozen or refrigerated at all times.

Cottage Cheese and other Uncured Cheeses. Cottage cheese is perishable. It needs always to be kept covered in the refrigerator. It should keep five days after the "pull" date on the carton, if handled carefully. It spoils more rapidly every time it is opened and even more quickly if left unrefrigerated. When using these uncured cheeses (cottage cheese, ricotta, baker's or farmer's) be sure to use a clean spoon or knife when removing portions from the remainder. Do not eat cottage cheese directly from the carton for the spoon that has been in your mouth contaminates any product remaining in the carton. Creamed cottage cheese keeps longer than low fat. Baker's, farmer's and ricotta keep after opening for even shorter periods and so are best used within two days of purchase.

Yogurt. Yogurt should be stored in the refrigerator at all times. Most of the storage information for cottage cheese (see above) applies to yogurt. However, because the fermentation process produces acid which inhibits the growth of bacteria other than the innoculating organism, yogurt will keep for a week or more in the refrigerator. However, with longer storage, the whey will tend to separate from the milk curds causing a "weeping" of the product. Should an unpleasant taste or smell develop during storage, discard the product. There are wild bacteria that may grow even at refrigerator temperatures. The innoculating organisms used to make the yogurt also grow slowly in the refrigerator, causing the product to get increasingly acid. This is perfectly all right.

Non-Fat Milk. This product may be purchased as a fresh milk or as a dry powder. Fresh non-fat milk should always be refrigerated. The date on the carton is the "pull" date, the date after which the store should not sell the milk. However, if properly cared for, this product will keep up to a week beyond the pull date.

Non-Fat Dry Milk. For best quality, keep the package tightly closed. Store in a cool, dark, dry place. The quality of the dry milk will be best if kept only 2-3 months after opening the package. If the powder becomes lumpy, it has deteriorated in both flavor and quality. You may want to transfer the powder as the original container becomes empty, to a smaller one with a tight fitting lid, since air in the package hastens deterioration of most food products. If the temperature reaches 90°F. or more for long periods, flavor changes may occur.

   Careless preparation of the non-fat dry milk can cause additional problems. Follow the directions on the package. Use clean utensils and cold water. Mix milk several hours before using and refrigerate to improve flavor. Reliquified dry milk is perishable. Store and use as you would fresh milk. If the same container is used over and over to store nonfat milk, scald occasionally to prevent bacteria build up.

Whole Milk, Extra Rich Milk, Low Fat Milk. All these fresh milks are perishable. Get them home quickly and refrigerate for best quality and longer storage life. These cartons also have a pull date, but if properly stored they should keep at least a week after the pull date.

Shelf Life of Dairy Products can be a guide to their keeping life at home.

   Shelf life is the time between the processing date and the pull date on the carton. Under good conditions and unopened, these products should keep at least a week after the date on the carton. Those with longer shelf lives should keep even longer.

Product	Shelf life
All fluid milks	10 days
Cottage Cheeses	13 days
Sour cream, sour half and half	21 days
Yogurts	30-35 days

Eggs. The carton tells you the size and grade. Grade AA eggs, if refrigerated both in the store and at home, will keep for 2-3 weeks after the pull date on the carton and still retain their AA quality. The pull date on most brands of eggs is 21 days after packing.

You will occasionally find a blood spot in the egg when you crack it, or you may notice that the white has a brownish tinge. Both of these conditions are due to the rupturing of blood vessels in the oviduct of the hen as the egg passes down this tube to the outside world. The brown tinge in the albumin results from a ruptured vessel near the beginning of the egg's trip down the oviduct. The bright red blood spot occured near the end of the journey. There is no need to discard such eggs.

Because of the hen's anatomy, as the egg is laid the egg shell may be contaminated with fecal material containing salmonella, since hens can be carriers of this bacteria. This poses no problem if the egg is broken and then either cooked or refrigerated again immediately. However, a tiny piece of shell in an unrefrigerated eggnog that stood at room temperature for an appreciable length of time could pose a health hazard if consumed. Either eat raw eggs immediately after shelling or refrigerate them again. Cracked eggs should not be used raw.

Eggs provide a nearly perfect medium for the growth of bacteria. Dishes such as custards, quiches, souffles, and other foods containing large amounts of egg in a moist product should be refrigerated if there are any leftovers after the meal. Mayonnaise, while containing eggs, also contains either vinegar or lemon juice, the acid of which inhibits bacterial growth. Therefore, it may safely be stored in a cool place if refrigeration is not available.

Storage of meat, fish, and poultry in the refrigerator and freezer:
How to do it and how long to store

The range in time reflects recommendations for *maximum storage time* from several authorities. Keep prepackaged fresh meats in original wrappers, but loosen to allow good air circulation. Rewrap (using wax paper) fresh meats wrapped in plain market paper; keep wrappings loose.

Storage Time Chart

Type of Meat, Poultry or Fish	Refrigerator 38° to 40°F.	Freezer 0°F. or lower
Roasts		
Beef, veal and lamb	4-6 days	6-9 months
Pork	4-6 days	3-6 months
Steaks and chops		
Beef	3-5 days	6-8 months
Pork, veal and lamb	3 days	3-4 months
Ground meat		
Beef, veal and lamb	1-2 days	3-4 months
Pork	1-2 days	1-3 months
Variety meats	1-2 days	3-4 months
Luncheon meats	1 week	not recommended
Sausage		
Fresh pork	1 week	2 months
Smoked	3-7 days	not recommended
Dry and semi-dry, unsliced	2-3 weeks	not recommended

Frankfurters	4-5 days	not recommended
Bacon	5-7 days	not recommended
Smoked ham		
Whole or half	1 week	2 months
Slices	3-4 days	not recommended
Corned beef	1 week	2 weeks
Leftover cooked meat	2-4 days	2-3 months
Poultry		
Raw	2 days	6 months
Cooked	2-4 days	2-3 months
Fish		
Raw	1 day	2-4 months
Cooked	2-3 days	1 month
Frozen cooked combination foods		
Meat pies		3 months
Swiss steak		3 months
Stews		3-4 months
Meat dinners		3-4 months

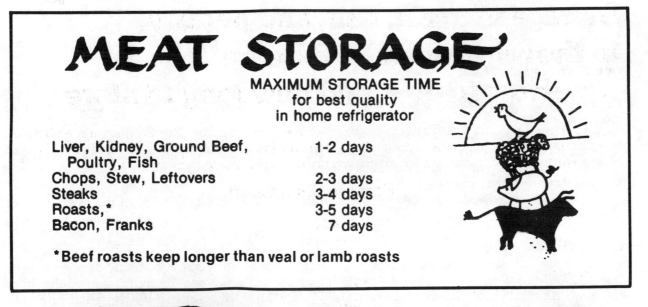

MEAT STORAGE

MAXIMUM STORAGE TIME
for best quality
in home refrigerator

Liver, Kidney, Ground Beef, Poultry, Fish	1-2 days
Chops, Stew, Leftovers	2-3 days
Steaks	3-4 days
Roasts,*	3-5 days
Bacon, Franks	7 days

*Beef roasts keep longer than veal or lamb roasts

Citizen Shopper
Rotate your stock!
Put the oldest cans UP FRONT in your cupboard, the new cans in the back

NEW

OLD

In September, pity the poor can

by Helen Black

In September, it's time to remember those poor old cans in the back of your cupboard. In September, the big canners are busily canning up this year's crop of fruits and vegetables . . . so why are you hanging on to cans from LAST year's crop? Or from the year before last? Food stored at home should be ROTATED! Meaning, use the old first and the new last.

Look in the back, Mack

Cans have a way of getting pushed to the back of your cupboard, where you miss them. What a surprise! Here's that can of berries you bought in '75! and the green beans, from '74! Get 'em out and look 'em over.

Swells and leakers unsafe any time

Swollen or leaking cans are unsafe to use whether you bought them last week or two years ago. CAUTION: discard so no creature can even *taste* the contents!

Dents or rusted cans may be O.K.

A rusted can, not swollen or leaking, is o.k. And a small dent, on the body of the can, does not make the can unsafe. On the other hand, dents on the RIMS or on the SEAM can cause a leak to develop.

Certain foods lose quality

Even if safe, those old canned berries may not taste good. Such acid foods may develop a tinny taste, as well as bad discoloration of the can lining which is unappetizing, though safe enough. Other foods whose quality does not hold up well are CHERRIES, ONIONS, PUMPKIN, SAUERKRAUT and TOMATO PRODUCTS.

But most cans may be stored 18 months

Those green beans from '74 in an intact can are probably excellent eating. But do use them at once. Next year, hopefully, you won't have kept any over a year.

Vitamins are safer at lower temperatures

For example, a vitamin loss which is only 5 percent after 12 months storage at 50 degrees F. may be as high as 25 percent if the storage temperature is 80 degrees F. This is another reason for using up your canned goods promptly. Most home-storage temperatures are higher than in warehouses or even on supermarket shelves.

Last, watch those shopping sprees!

Don't overload on any food. Buy only what you can use in a reasonable time. Especially if the price is very low, it's all too easy to buy too much and end by throwing some away, a truly *awful extravagance!*

September 30, 1976

Food preservation

Freezing is not economical compared to canning
by Mary Gullberg

You need a low cost supply of food:

So you have a home garden, or you're going to the country to pick ripe peaches or apricots, or there are some really good buys in the market. Cost alone is not enough. Bruised, under-ripe or over-ripe foods have a lot of waste. Now, how should you process these foods?

To freeze or not:

Studies by Cornell University Extension nutritionists recently found that food frozen at home costs 19¢ per pound MORE than when fresh food is simply purchased and eaten. This figure assumes that the freezer is full and electric rates are relatively low. When freezer is half empty and operating inefficiently, using high-cost electric current, home freezing can add as much as 53¢ per pound to the cost of food. This cost figure includes the cost of the freezer spread over its life expectancy and cost of electricity to run it. Keep the freezer full, rotate the stock and

use it regularly. Packaging that is rigid with flat tops and bottoms is the most efficient shape, because more can be packed into a given space. Any rigid container that is capable of being sealed to keep oxygen out and moisture in can be used whether made of glass, metal, plastic or cardboard. To prevent breakage of glass, leave sufficient headspace to take care of the expansion of the food during freezing. Do not tighten screw tops until food is frozen.

What about canning?

Canning is much more economical than freezing, but only if your family likes canned fruits and vegetables. Also, choose the right foods to can. Why can carrots if fresh ones are available all year round at reasonable prices? Don't can or freeze more food than you will use within a year. If canning supplies or freezer space is limited, choose foods with high nutritive values.

Tips on freezing
by Mary Gullberg

In August, fresh fruits and vegetables are at or nearing their peaks of ripeness and best prices. Also, backyard produce is nearly ready for harvesting. Perhaps you have questions?

What kinds freeze well? All fresh fruits and most vegetables except those with high water content such as cukes, lettuces, and tomatoes. Tomatoes may be peeled, brought to a rolling boil and then packed in jars or plastic containers and frozen. The flavor is excellent, very similar to fresh.

What to do to produce before freezing? Cantaloupe and most berries can be frozen "as is." No fruits need blanching. However, fruits packed in syrup or sugar keep their colors, shapes and flavors better. Ascorbic acid is usually added to light-colored fruits to retain the color. But they can be steamed quickly to prevent browning and then coated with sugar. The flavor will not be harmed. All vegetables must be blanched before freezing to kill bacteria and stop enzyme action which can cause spoilage.

How long can frozen produce be stored for best quality? Up to one year at 0° F. Check the temperature of your freezer. Date packages with day of processing.

What kinds of packaging to use? Almost any airtight container (glass or plastic) that doesn't give off odors and won't break at freezer temperatures. Plastic wrap, plastic bags and heavy aluminum foil are all right but can be punctured during handling. Recycled plastic cartons (such as cottage cheese containers and milk cartons) are great but you should use freezer bags for liners and seal the cartons with freezer tape (which also makes an excellent label if you write on it with ink).

Does freezing affect nutritive values? Freezing foods quickly, immediately after harvest, reduces nutrient loss. Some loss of water soluble nutrients results from blanching of vegetables.

It's Christmas in in July *by Catherine Sinnott*

Would you believe that July is a great time to prepare many of December's holiday gifts? Well, it's true! With many fruits and vegetables becoming plentiful, the home canning of these foods for presents to friends at Christmas time is a great way to go.

Even though fruits and vegetables may be expensive in the market, when you compare their costs with items like chutney on the fancy foods shelves, you will find making your own a big saving. It's a very special way of giving, since each jar is filled with the labor of your love — and what can beat that? Also, it's fun for your whole family, for everyone can help.

Suit any special taste or diet

Choose a recipe that you would feel pleased to receive as a gift. Examples might be chutney, fruit butter, conserves, marmalade, relish, pickles, spiced fruit, pickled watermelon rind, picalilli, chili, chow chow, or sugarless jam. The list really is endless. The gift should be labeled with the name of the food, the date and your name.

Do it right

It's very important that you have — and follow — good canning directions. These can be found in the Ball or Sunset canning books. Also, free canning booklets can be obtained by calling your county's Cooperative Extension Service. Season's greetings!

As a starter idea, here is one recipe that most folks enjoy:

Peach Butter

4 pounds peaches   2 cups water   Sugar

Wash peaches then quarter, discarding stones, and peeling if desired. Cook with water until tender. Blend in a blender or put through a food press, measure pulp and add half the volume of sugar. Cook until thick, pour into hot, sterilized jars and seal. Makes 3 pints. (One teaspoon of peach butter contains 16 calories, one teaspoon dairy butter — 31 calories.)

Plan and prepare . . . don't panic

Holiday time is busy-time for most homemakers. One partial solution to this problem for those who have freezer space is to use your free hours in the weeks before holidays to prepare and freeze several main dishes plus some baked goods. These can then be used on those days when the seemingly endless round of washing and cleaning leaves little time for meal preparation. Certain basic rules can serve as guides to what will or will not freeze successfully.

Foods that freeze well include:

Combination dishes such as lasagna, spaghetti, meat balls, meat loaf, chicken casseroles, stewed or pot roasted beef, most seafood recipes (in all of these remove excess fat from cooked dish before freezing); baked goods such as bread, rolls, cakes and pies, sandwiches of many varieties (see exceptions below); soups of all types excluding potatoes.

Avoid freezing the following:

1. Fried foods (except french fried potatoes and onion rings), which lose their crispness.

2. Milk sauces, custards, cream fillings, since they may curdle, become watery or lumpy.
3. Potatoes, which do not have a good texture after freezing.
4. Lettuce, other fresh greens, and tomatoes lose their crispness.
5. Cooked egg whites and meringues, since they toughen and get rubbery.

Packaging frozen foods:
1. Pack in amounts to be used in one meal.
2. Exclude as much air as possible before wrapping.
3. Use moisture-resistant containers, bags, or paper. Materials may include glass, metal, plastic, or waxed cartons. All covers should fit tightly, but leave ½ inch headspace for expansion.
4. Casseroles lined with heavy foil may be used. After freezing contents, wrap the foil covered food in freezer wrapping and the empty casserole can then be used for other cooking.

Freezing and storing:
Freeze food rapidly. Place the packages in coldest part of freezer. Allow for cold air circulation. The food temperature must be lowered to below 40° F. within 4 hours to reduce growth of bacteria. Freezer temperature should be kept at 0° F.; for every 5° increase in temperature, the storage time for the food is decreased by half. That is, food that keeps for 6 months at 0° F. will start to deteriorate in quality after 3 months at 5° F.

Thawing and cooking:
Precooked foods may be defrosted in the refrigerator or at room temperature* or by heating. Leave wrapping material on when possible. Uncooked casseroles may be put directly into the oven from the freezer. Add about 20 minutes to the baking time. Unbaked doughs and batters are always defrosted before baking.

Refreezing:
When foods have partially thawed and are refrozen, they will lose some of their quality. Use these refrozen foods as soon as possible. Consider wholly thawed foods perishable and keep them under refrigeration until needed.

The conditions under which the food has thawed will determine if it should be refrozen. You may safely refreeze partially thawed food if it has been thawing for only a brief time (for instance, if it was stored overnight in the refrigerator during a temporary power failure in the freezer), and it still feels cold and contains ice crystals.

On the other hand, if foods have slowly thawed over a period of several days, to a temperature above 40° F., they are not likely to be fit for refreezing. Meats, poultry, most vegetables and some prepared foods may become unsafe to eat. Most fruits and fruit products soon develop an undesirable flavor. Discard any unpleasant looking or smelling food since it may contain microorganisms that make it unsafe.

*This is least desirable since bacteria may grow as the outer layer of food defrosts.

Can Meat Be Refrozen?

Yes, if the meat was thawed properly — in the refrigerator — and was not held for longer than you would keep fresh meat.

Each time meat is frozen and thawed, there is some loss of quality because juices come out as "drip."

from your Co-op Home Economist

Frozen food facts

Frozen foods are sometimes better buys because there is no waste. Orange juice and shelled peas are examples of foods that are almost always cheaper frozen than fresh. Compare and buy wisely. Frozen food saves you labor.

Check your freezer temperature with a thermometer. It should be 0 degrees F. or lower.
Shop for frozen foods last. Put them in your freezer as soon as possible.
Frozen foods kept in the ice-cube compartment should be used within a week.
At temperatures above zero loss of flavor, texture, and nutritive value speeds up.

At zero, maximum storage times for good quality are roughly as follows:

1 year
Fruits, juice concentrates, fruit cake, and large cuts of meat (except pork and veal)
6 months
Vegetables, unbaked fruit pies, large pork and veal cuts
6 months
Pound cake, veal cutlets, cut-up poultry (raw)
3 months
Fish, shell fish, chopped meat rolls, bread, fried chicken, chicken liver, meat pies, small cuts of meat, ground meat.
2 months
Sausage, crabmeat, perch and salmon
1 month
Ice cream and sherbet, shelled oysters, cooked fish

But remember, even at zero temperature quality is going downhill slowly, *and* electricity costs you money, so use *all* frozen foods as soon as possible.

Tips on dealing with household pests

Insect pests in the home need preventive measures before trouble starts. Then, if necessary, proceed to more drastic measures such as the use of relatively mild insecticides. We urge you to try more reasonable approaches to the problem(s) first.

Good housekeeping is essential for controlling pests. Food and garbage (mainly sweets and grease) should be kept covered, out of reach of insects. Dark, damp storage areas filled with odds and ends encourage insects that do not thrive in dry, well-ventilated places. Look for hitch-hiking insects in the packages, bags and other parcels you bring home. Any evidence of insect life, such as webs or excreta, should alert you to return the food package to the store from which it was purchased. The store also wants to know of any insect activity in its merchandise.

Flies and other winged insects can be controlled by screens on both windows and doors. Decaying matter outside the house is a breeding ground for flies. Consider carefully if a compost pile is apt to be a breeding ground for flies. With proper screening, a fly swatter should take care of those that get in. Sticky fly paper in strips or sheets will entrap them. Do not use pest strips — these dispense their active ingredient in a fine mist that falls on anything in the immediate vicinity including food and people. Avoid sprays in the house for the same reason.

Ants: If ants never get started in your house, you've won the battle before it starts. Do not leave food or dirty dishes around the kitchen to attract them. In California, one unwashed jelly spoon can bring an invasion overnight. As soon as the rains start in the fall, ants like to come in where it is dry and warm. Wipe up all food smears on counters, furniture and the outsides of food containers. At the first sign of ants, sprinkle the area where they appear to have gained entrance with a low-hazard insecticide such as powders containing pyrethrum or rotenone, often available as flea powder for pets. Malathion is a broad-spectrum insecticide that is relatively safe for humans and can be used on ants if the following precautions are observed. All three of these are non-persistent and will only be effective for a few days. Place them where they will not be in contact with food and where small children cannot have access to them. If you can find their nests outside or under the house, use ant stakes or syrups containing arsenic if other methods fail. Neither of these products has an environmental pollution potential because there is so little arsenic in them. Still, they should be kept out of reach of small children and pets.

Moths: Moth larvae do not feed very avidly on clean wool. It is the spot of gravy on the coat or dress that they attack first. Therefore, if you wash or dry clean woolens before storage, you should have no problems with moths. If you must use a moth deterrent, naphthalene is safer than paradichlorobenzene. Do not use any product containing dieldrin or other persistent pesticide, particularly on articles that are in intimate contact with the skin. All moth deterrents should be kept out of reach of children — some of them look like candy.

Pantry Pests are a problem, particularly in foods stored in warm places. The problem is that cereals, flours, rice and other dry seeds and grains may have insect eggs in them when purchased or even when packaged. There is no way the processing can completely eliminate them. We have to handle these products in such a way that these eggs do not encounter conditions that allow them to hatch and start eating our food products. There is no health hazard involved if we should eat them, but why let insects eat the goodies that we intend for ourselves?

So focus on prevention: Weevils and cereal mites are not stupid — they know whole grains and flours are better for them than refined ones, so watch temperature and humidity control carefully. Store all dry staples in tightly covered metal, glass or plastic containers (insects can eat through plastic bags and cardboard boxes and thus migrate to other products). If these containers are large, several products in their original packaging can be placed in a single one, thus preserving the cooking and storage directions on the labels. **Do not use any insecticide in food storage areas.**

If an infestation of weevils is discovered, check ALL dry goods, including dog food, bird seed and spices. Dispose of contaminated products. Vacuum with crevice attachment all shelves and cupboards. Dispose of vacuum cleaner bag outside of the house. Wash the area thoroughly with hot detergent solution before restocking. Store these products in the coolest, driest places that your kitchen affords. Whole grain wheat and rice products and wheat germ (because of their fat content) tend to get rancid in fairly short times and may need to be stored in the refrigerator or an unheated area. Insect eggs will not hatch at 40° F. and below. If you want to kill the eggs, place the packages when you bring them home from the store, in the freezer at zero degrees for three or more days. This will kill all but the most resistent food insects.

Cockroaches breed where food and water are available and close to dark hiding places. They are nocturnal and appear on counters and other surfaces at night. *Scrupulous cleanliness is essential in controlling these pests.* Food storage should follow suggestions under "pantry pests." Clean the area thoroughly, stop up all cracks, crevices and holes in woodwork and cupboards, fill or repair cracks around pipes, edges of sinks, and inner and outer walls. Stop all sources of water leaks and keep counters and cupboards bone-dry, especially at night. No food should be left out in any area. This includes pet food and feeding dishes. Cover garbage and waste containers or empty them frequently — especially at night. Dispose of stacked magazines, bric-a-brac, wall hangings or accumulated materials in which cockroaches can hide.

Not only are insecticides hazardous in food areas, but cockroaches tend to develop immunity to them. Boric acid (available in drug stores) is a possible control measure if there are no children or pets around (boric acid is poisonous if eaten in sufficient amounts). Confine the powder to cracks and dark, narrow inaccessible areas. Sprinkle it lightly or dissolve it in water and paint it on (one cup boric acid per gallon of warm water and ¼ cup detergent). Repeat treatment several times because it is slow to act. Do not depend on it if you haven't made every effort to clean up the area.

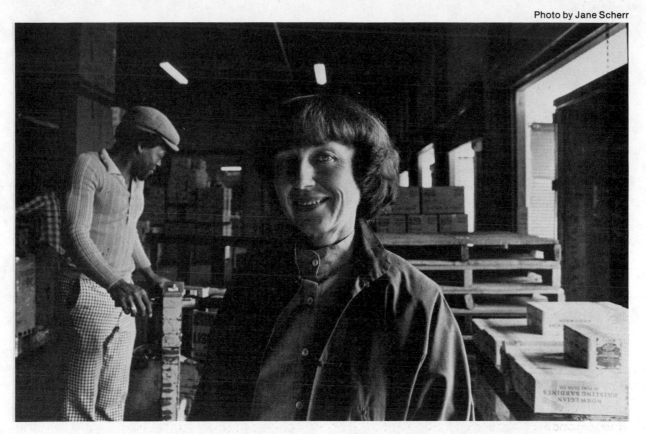

As part of a continuing program of quality control, a home economist regularly goes to the warehouse to select cans for testing.

Appendix

Cost of Food at Home Estimated for Food Plans at Four Cost Levels, October 1979, U.S. Average[1]

Sex-age groups	Cost for 1 week				Cost for 1 month			
	Thrifty plan[2] Dollars	Low-cost plan Dollars	Moderate-cost plan Dollars	Liberal plan Dollars	Thrifty plan[2] Dollars	Low-cost plan Dollars	Moderate-cost plan Dollars	Liberal plan Dollars
FAMILIES								
Family of 2:[3]								
20-54 years..............	28.50	37.30	46.70	56.10	123.40	161.40	202.60	243.00
55 years and over..........	25.60	33.20	41.10	49.20	110.70	143.70	178.10	213.00
Family of 4:								
Couple, 20-54 years and children —								
1-2 and 3-5 years..........	40.20	51.90	64.90	77.80	174.10	224.80	281.00	336.80
6-8 and 9-11 years..........	48.40	62.60	78.60	94.30	209.60	271.10	340.60	408.40
INDIVIDUALS[4]								
Child:								
7 months to 1 year..........	5.70	7.00	8.50	10.10	24.90	30.20	37.00	43.80
1-2 years.................	6.50	8.20	10.20	12.10	28.00	35.60	44.00	52.40
3-5 years.................	7.80	9.80	12.20	14.70	33.90	42.50	52.80	63.50
6-8 years.................	10.00	12.80	16.00	19.20	43.20	55.30	69.40	83.30
9-11 years................	12.50	15.90	20.10	24.10	54.20	69.10	87.00	104.20
Male:								
12-14 years...............	13.30	17.00	21.30	25.50	57.80	73.60	92.30	110.50
15-19 years...............	14.70	18.80	23.60	28.40	63.60	81.60	102.30	123.10
20-54 years...............	14.30	18.70	23.60	28.40	61.80	80.90	102.30	123.10
55 years and over..........	12.70	16.50	20.50	24.70	54.90	71.30	88.80	106.80
Female:								
12-19 years...............	11.90	15.20	18.90	22.50	51.70	66.00	81.80	97.60
20-54 years...............	11.60	15.20	18.90	22.60	50.40	65.80	81.90	97.80
55 years and over..........	10.60	13.70	16.90	20.00	45.70	59.30	73.10	86.80
Pregnant	14.70	18.80	23.10	27.50	63.60	81.30	100.10	119.00
Nursing..................	15.60	19.90	24.80	29.40	67.40	86.30	107.40	127.60

1. Assumes that food for all meals and snacks is purchased at the store and prepared at home. Estimates for each plan were computed from quantities of foods published in the Winter 1976 (thrifty plan) and Winter 1975 (low-cost, moderate-cost, and liberal plans) issues of *Family Economics Review*. The costs of the food plans were first estimated using prices paid in 1965-66 by households from USDA's Household Food Consumption Survey with food costs at four selected levels. USDA updates these survey prices to estimate the costs for the food plans using information from the Bureau of Labor Statistics: "Estimated Retail Food Prices by Cities" from 1965-66 to 1977 and "CPI Detailed Report," tables 3 and 9, after 1977.

2. Coupon allotment in the Food Stamp Program based on this food plan.

3. Ten percent added for family size adjustment. See footnote 4.

4. The costs given are for individuals in 4-person families. For individuals in other size families, the following adjustments are suggested: 1 person — add 20 percent; 2-person — add 10 percent; 3-person — add 5 percent; 5- or 6-person — subtract 5 percent; 7-or-more-person — subtract 10 percent.

U.S. Department of Agriculture
Science and Education Administration
Human Nutrition Center
Consumer and Food Economics Institute
Hyattsville, Maryland 20782

Know your RDA

**Food and Nutrition Board, National Academy of Sciences —
National Research Council
Recommended Daily Dietary Allowances, Revised 1979**

Reproduced from: *Recomended Dietary Allowances*, Ninth Edition (1979), with the permission of the National Academy of Sciences, Washington, D.C.

| | Age | Weight | | Height | | Energy | Protein | Fat-Soluble Vitamins | | | Water- |
								Vitamin A	Vitamin D	Vitamin E	Vitamin C
	(years)	(kg)	(lbs)	(cm)	(in)	(kcal)	(g)	(IU)	(IU)	(mg TE)	(mg)
Infants	0.0-0.5	6	13	60	24	kg x 115	kg x 2.2	1400	400	3	35
	0.5-1.0	9	20	71	28	kg x 105	kg x 2.0	2000	400	4	35
Children	1-3	13	29	90	35	1300	23	2000	400	5	45
	4-6	20	44	112	44	1700	30	2500	400	6	45
	7-10	28	62	132	52	2400	34	3300	400	7	45
Males	11-14	45	99	157	62	2700	45	5000	400	8	50
	15-18	66	145	176	69	2800	56	5000	400	10	60
	19-22	70	154	177	70	2900	56	5000	300	10	60
	23-50	70	154	178	70	2700	56	5000	200	10	60
	51-75	70	154	178	70	2400	56	5000	200	10	60
Females	11-14	46	101	157	62	2200	46	4000	400	8	50
	15-18	55	120	163	64	2100	46	4000	400	8	60
	19-22	55	120	163	64	2100	44	4000	300	8	60
	23-50	55	120	163	64	2000	44	4000	200	8	60
	51-75	55	120	163	64	1800	44	4000	200	8	60
Pregnant						+300	+30	5000	400	+2	+20
Lactating						+500	+30	6000	400	+3	+40
U.S. RDA								5000	400	30	60

NOTE: The 1979 revision includes an additional age group with energy allowances only (which is not shown in the above table), as follows:

Male, 76 years, † 70 kg............................ 2050 kcal.
Female, 76 years, † 55 kg........................... 1600 kcal.

The allowances are intended to provide for individual variations among most normal persons as they live in the United States under usual environmental stresses. The Recommended Allowances can be met by eating a wide variety of common foods; these foods may also provide nutrients that are not listed in the RDA.

The U.S. RDA is taken from the 1968 RDA as a standard for nutrition labeling. These values are the largest amount of a nutrient required by any group in 1968 excluding pregnant and lactating women. The U.S. RDA values for protein have been set at 2 levels for adults. Since nutrition authorities are not agreed on the best method to determine protein quality, FDA has adopted a compromise of 65 grams if the protein efficiency ratio (PER) is less than that of casein (a standard for protein quality). If the PER is equal to or greater than casein the U.S. RDA is set at 45 grams.

niacin equivalent
1 NE = 1 milligram of
niacin or
60 mg of
dietary tryptophane

Soluble Vitamins / Minerals

Thiamin	Riboflavin	Niacin	Vitamin B$_6$	Folacin	Vitamin B$_{12}$	Calcium	Phosphorus	Magnesium	Iron	Zinc	Iodine
(mg)	(mg)	(mg NE)	(mg)	(mcg)	(mcg)	(mg)	(mg)	(mg)	(mg)	(mg)	(mcg)
0.3	0.4	6	0.3	30	0.5	360	240	50	10	3	40
0.5	0.6	8	0.6	45	1.5	540	360	70	15	5	50
0.7	0.8	9	0.9	100	2.0	800	800	150	15	10	70
0.9	1.0	11	1.3	200	2.5	800	800	200	10	10	90
1.2	1.4	16	1.6	300	3.0	800	800	250	10	10	120
1.4	1.6	18	1.8	400	3.0	1200	1200	350	18	15	150
1.4	1.7	18	2.0	400	3.0	1200	1200	400	18	15	150
1.5	1.7	19	2.2	400	3.0	800	800	350	10	15	150
1.4	1.6	18	2.2	400	3.0	800	800	350	10	15	150
1.2	1.4	16	2.2	400	3.0	800	800	350	10	15	150
1.1	1.3	15	1.8	400	3.0	1200	1200	300	18	15	150
1.1	1.3	14	2.0	400	3.0	1200	1200	300	18	15	150
1.1	1.3	14	2.0	400	3.0	800	800	300	18	15	150
1.0	1.2	13	2.0	400	3.0	800	800	300	18	15	150
1.0	1.2	13	2.0	400	3.0	800	800	300	10	15	150
+0.4	+0.3	+2	+0.6	+400	+1.0	+400	+400	+150	h	+5	+25
+0.5	+0.5	+5	+0.5	+100	+1.0	+400	+400	+150	h	+10	+50
1.5	1.7	20	2.0	400	6.0	1000	1000	400	18	15	150

Vit A RE retinol equivalent
1 RE = 1 mg (microgram) of
retinol or
6 mg of beta carotene

**Co-op Home Economists
suggest that you NOT
take vitamins in amounts
exceeding the
Recommended Daily Dietary Allowance**

1 pound - 454 grams
1 gram - 1000 milligrams
1 milligram - 1000 micrograms

3 small, uncooked
dry white beans
weigh about
1 gram.

Estimated Safe and Adequate Daily Dietary Intakes of Additional Selected Vitamins and Minerals[a]

		Vitamins			Trace Elements[b]	
	Age (years)	Vitamin K (mcg)	Biotin (mcg)	Pantothenic Acid (mg)	Copper (mg)	Manganese (mg)
Infants	0 - 0.5	12	35	2	0.5 - 0.7	0.5 - 0.7
	0.5 - 1	10 - 20	50	3	0.7 - 1.0	0.7 - 1.0
Children	1-3	15 - 30	65	3	1.0 - 1.5	1.0 - 1.5
and	4-6	20 - 40	85	3 - 4	1.5 - 2.0	1.5 - 2.0
Adolescents	7-10	30 - 60	120	4 - 5	2.0 - 2.5	2.0 - 3.0
	11 +	50 - 100	100 - 200	4 - 7	2.0 - 3.0	2.5 - 5.0
Adults		70 - 140	100 - 200	4 - 7	2.0 - 3.0	2.5 - 5.0

a Because there is less information on which to base allowances, these figures are not given in the main table of the RDA and are provided here in the form of ranges of recommended intakes.

b Since the toxic levels for many trace elements may be only several times usual intakes, the upper levels for the trace elements given in this table should not be habitually exceeded.

NOTE:

There is a narrow margin between human need and toxic level of some trace minerals (including zinc, copper, manganese, fluoride, chromium, selenium and molybdenum). Co-op Home Economists recommend that the need for these nutrients be met by eating a well balanced diet of varied foods. If mineral supplements are used, we suggest avoiding any pills containing more than recommended daily amounts except under supervision of a doctor.

Reproduced from: *Recommended Dietary Allowances*, Ninth Edition (1979, in press), with the permission of the National Academy of Sciences, Washington, D.C.

		Electrolytes				
Fluoride (mg)	**Chromium** (mg)	**Selenium** (mg)	**Molybdenum** (mg)	**Sodium** (mg)	**Potassium** (mg)	**Chloride** (mg)
0.1 - 0.5	0.01 - 0.04	0.01 - 0.04	0.03 - 0.06	115 - 350	350 - 925	275 - 700
0.2 - 1.0	0.02 - 0.06	0.02 - 0.06	0.04 - 0.08	250 - 750	425 - 1275	400 - 1200
0.5 - 1.5	0.02 - 0.08	0.02 - 0.08	0.05 - 0.1	325 - 975	550 - 1650	500 - 1500
1.0 - 2.5	0.03 - 0.12	0.03 - 0.12	0.06 - 0.15	450 - 1350	775 - 2325	700 - 2100
1.5 - 2.5	0.05 - 0.2	0.05 - 0.2	0.1 - 0.3	600 - 1800	1000 - 3000	925 - 2775
1.5 - 2.5	0.05 - 0.2	0.05 - 0.2	0.15 - 0.5	900 - 2700	1525 - 4575	1400 - 4200
1.5 - 4.0	0.05 - 0.2	0.05 - 0.2	0.15 - 0.5	1100 - 3300	1875 - 5625	1700 - 5100

Nutrient	**Important Food Source**	
Protein	Lean meat, poultry, fish, seafood, eggs, milk, cheese, dry beans, peas and nuts.	
Vitamin A	Liver; dark green leafy vegetables such as broccoli, collards, mustard, beet and turnip greens; red chili peppers and deep yellow or orange vegetables such as carrots, sweet potatoes, winter squash and cantaloupe.	
Vitamin D	Sunlight on contact with skin, fish oils, milk fortified with Vitamin D.	
Vitamin E	Vegetable oils, wheat germ and whole-grain cereals, seeds, nuts, and dark green leafy vegetables.	
Vitamin C	Broccoli, red and green sweet peppers, chili peppers, brussels sprouts, cauliflower, collards, kale, turnip greens, strawberries, citrus fruit, cantaloupe.	
Folacin	Dark green leafy vegetables, raw or slightly cooked; asparagus, liver, legumes, nuts and orange juice.	
Niacin	Lean meat, poultry, fish, nuts, dry beans and peas, whole-grain or enriched cereals and breads, yeast.	
Riboflavin B_2	Liver, kidney, heart, almonds, milk, cheese, broccoli, asparagus, winter squash, dark green leafy vegetables, beef and pork.	
Thiamin B_1	Lean pork, heart, liver, kidney, dry beans and peas, whole-grain or enriched breads and cereals, sunflower seeds and some nuts.	
Pyridoxine	Lean meats, liver, leafy green vegetables, whole-grain cereals, dry peas and beans, nuts, fish and shell fish, poultry and eggs.	
Vitamin B_{12}	Present only in animal protein: Milk, cheese, eggs, meat, poultry and fish.	
Calcium	Milk, cheese, lime-treated tortillas, leafy vegetables such as collards, kale, spinach, mustard, dandelion and turnip greens, nuts (especially almonds), oysters, and sardines, salmon and mackerel if the bones are eaten.	
Phosphorus	Milk, cheese, meat, whole-grain cereals, dry peas and beans, nuts and eggs.	
Iodine	Iodized salt, ocean fish and shell fish.	
Iron	Liver and other organ meats, lean meat, seafood, egg yolk, dried peas and beans, nuts, whole or enriched cereals and grains.	
Magnesium	Nuts, soybeans, whole grains, dried peas and beans, and seafood.	
Zinc	Meat, liver, eggs, seafood (especially oysters), milk, whole grain products, oatmeal, whole corn.	

Supermarket slang and other useful terminology

Some words are for selling

See them in food ads, on food labels. These are words which people react to with a conditioned reflex.

"New"

means to most people that it is also "good." But look sharply. Is that product really just a new smaller size at the same old price?

"Free"

often means, "Try this one free and get hooked on buying forever."

"Pure"

is a word with a double meaning: "faultless, perfect" or "unmixed with anything else." Like "mother," it's a word with emotional appeal.

"Natural"

has no legal meaning. At what point in the journey from farm to market does a food become "unnatural?" On labels, it means nothing.

"Organic"

also has no legal meaning. Sometimes, though, it means "grown without pesticides or chemical fertilizer."

"Less tender"

refers to a cut of meat that is tough. Be sure to cook it with *moist* heat!

"Drink, cocktail, nectar, punch"

all refer to products which are not all juice. Water, sugar, citric acid, etc. are added. Check the ingredient statement.

Some words are highly useful to consumers

They are practices or regulations or concepts that shoppers should understand.

Unit prices

This provides *cost comparisons*. The price per pound, ounce, pint or quart is posted on a small sticker on the edge of the shelf where a product is stocked. Safeway and Co-op provide unit prices, Lucky does not.

Dates

There are different kinds of dates on products: a PULL-date, such as are on dairy products, refers to the date after which a product should not be sold. The product, properly stored, is good for a certain period after the date. PACK-date refers to the date when the product was packaged. EXPIRATION-date is a date after which the product may not be good, as in the case of yeast for baking. CODES instead of dates are used on canned goods embossed in the metal on one end of the can, and also on bread in the form of a colored tie.

Nutrition labels

Nutrition information on labels is voluntary except where nutrition claims are made or foods are fortified. Nutrition information must be expressed in a format determined by the Food and Drug Administration.

Ingredient statement

Ingredients must be listed "in order of decreasing predominance by weight." In other words, the first is most, the last is least. If the label says "Gravy with Meat Slices" it means there is more gravy than meat in the product.

Standard of identity
This means that a product has been legally defined as to ingredients and/or the percentages used.

Imitation
This is a word which has been legally defined from time to time and does not always mean that a product is inferior. For example, "Imitation Ice Cream" in California means that a different kind of fat is used in place of butter fat. Otherwise it is the same, and has the same caloric value. This word is required when a standardized food deviates from its standard.

Item pricing
With universal product codes on most packaged goods, grocery stores with scanning devices at the check-out stands can get along without putting the price on each product. Consumer groups oppose the elimination of item pricing because it would make it harder for shoppers to compare prices.

Trading down
This is a way to save money by choosing a cheaper substitute when a favorite is too high in price. For example, serve meat loaf for dinner instead of stew. Sylvia Porter estimates that shoppers can save 40 to 50% on food bills by "trading down."

Optical illusions
The shape of the bottle or package is such that it *looks* bigger than it is, or the same size as another when it really is smaller.

More supermarket terminology

Some words are for the trade
They are mostly used by sellers in merchandising, or just in the routine handling of goods.

House roll
Beef selected by the "house" meat buyer, not graded by the government. For example, "house" means the store, and "roll" is the gadget that rolls over the carcass leaving a purple stamp.

New crop
See it on produce signs. It's important because the quality of a crop may be different at the beginning of a harvest. New crop potatoes are less apt to have black spots under the skin; new crop broccoli is less apt to be woody, new crop apples are less apt to be mealy. On the other hand, new crop tomatoes are apt to be less juicy than later ones.

Tare
The weight and estimated drip included in meat packaging, which must be subtracted from net weight which appears on the package. For each size of each cut of meat, this tare must be applied. If the County weights-and-measures people find the net weights are too low, the store gets a citation or

gets hauled into court. If they're too high, that's OK, except then the store loses money.

Impulse item
Merchandise strategically located to catch shopper's attention so shopper will buy it "on impulse," such as candy piled near checkstands.

Eye level
What every grocery clerk knows is that merchandise stocked at eye level sells faster than when it is stocked at a higher or lower level.

In and outs
Temporary products which the store has purchased because of special allowance from manufacturer, for example: not regular stock.

Manufacturer's allowance
A special discount on the price which is provided by manufacturer on condition that item is put on the ad, or located in a prominent spot in the store.

Loss leader
Sold at less than 6% gross margin, see definition below.

The heavy stuff — Industry concepts
Supermarketing is getting complicated, and is changing, and there are many issues of interest that we can't cover here, including UCP (Universal Product Code), NCP (National Commission on Productivity), price fixing, fair-trading, executive liability, automated warehousing, etc. But the following are vital:

Gross margins
Difference between what store pays for an item and what the selling price is, expressed as a percent of selling price. For example, we buy at $1.00, and sell at $1.30 so the gross margin is 23%. Must cover all store expenses and allow for small profit.

Net margin
The profit, usually 1 or 2% of the selling price of a product. It's what's left after all expenses are paid.

And who watches out?
Certain government agencies have specific authority over food. Here is a brief rundown. Federal agencies have jurisdiction over products which travel in inter-state commerce. State agencies have authority over products produced and sold within the state.

U.S.D.A.
U.S. Department of Agriculture inspects meat and poultry for wholesomeness, grades for quality (meaning size, defects or amount of fat in meat as related to tenderness), has control of labels for products containing 2% or more of meat and poultry and establishes identity standards for meat and poultry. (Meat grading is voluntary, paid for by slaughterhouse.)

F.D.A.
Food and Drug Administration is responsible for safety of all domestic foods (except meat and poultry) plus ALL IMPORTED FOODS. F.D.A. inspects food processing plants except for meat and poultry. They establish identity standards and label regulations for all foods except meat and poultry.

F.T.C.
Federal Trade Commission has jurisdiction over advertising of all products that F.D.A. supervises. This is because F.T.C. was set up originally under the Pure Food Law, but Congress created a separate agency to keep F.D.A. from being too powerful.

State food and agriculture departments and state health departments
Perform general functions of USDA and FDA within state.

Seasons for fruits and vegetables

These tables give a rough idea of when the major fruits and vegetables are in season. The seasons will vary some each year. Small amounts may be available outside of the "season." The tables are based on supply (not price) data for at least four years.

In general, at the "peak" of the season, the quality will be good and the price low.

If you are planning to can or freeze, look for the fruit or vegetable in the months listed under "peak." It is wise to watch produce department prices and to ask the clerks about the best time for each item. Flats or crates are often available.

Fruits	Season	Peak
Apples	Year round, mostly Sept.-April	Oct.-Dec.
Apricots	June-July	June
Avocados	Year round	---
Bananas	Year round	---
Berries: Black & Olallie	June-Aug.	same
Boysen, Young, Logan	May-July	June
Raspberries	June-Nov.	June-July
Strawberries	April-Oct.	May-June
Cherries	May-July	June
Cranberries	Oct.-Dec.	Oct.-Nov.
Figs	June-Oct.	June
Grapefruit	Year round	Nov. May
Grapes	June-Feb.	Aug.-Oct.
Lemons & Limes	Year round	June-Aug.
Melons: Cantaloupe	May-Oct.	June-Aug.
Casaba	June-Nov.	Sept.-Oct.
Crenshaw	June-Oct.	Aug.-Sept.
Honeydew	June-Oct.	Aug.-Sept.
Persian	July-Oct.	Sept.-Oct.
Watermelon	May-Sept.	June-Aug.
Mangoes	May-June	same
Nectarines	June-Sept.	July-Aug.
Oranges	Year round	Dec.-May
Papayas	Year round	---
Peaches	June-Sept.	July-Aug.
Pears	July-April	Aug.-Oct.
Persimmons	Oct.-Nov.	same
Pineapples	Year round	---
Plums & fresh Prunes	June-Sept.	July
Pomegranates	Sept.-Oct.	Oct.
Rhubarb	Jan.-June	Feb.-May
Tangerines	Nov.-Feb.	Dec.
Artichokes	Year round, mostly Sept.-May	---
Asparagus	March-June	April

These tables were prepared from *Unloads of Fresh Fruits and Vegetables, Oakland 1953-1958,* compiled by the Federal-State Market News Service

Vegetables	Season	Peak
Beans, green	Year round, mostly May-Nov.	June-Sept.
Beets	Year round	---
Broccoli	Year round	Oct.-April
Brussels sprouts	Aug.-Feb.	Oct.-Jan.
Cabbage	Year round	---
Carrots	Year round	---
Cauliflower	Year round	Oct.-March
Celery	Year round	Nov.-Dec.
Celery Root	Oct.-March	same
Chinese cabbage	Oct.-March	same
Corn	May-Nov.	June-Aug.
Cucumbers	Year round	May-Sept.
Eggplant	Year round	June-Nov.
Greens	Year round	---
Lettuce	Year round	April-Dec.
Mushrooms	Year round	---
Okra	June-Oct.	July-Sept.
Onions, dry	Year round	May-Nov.
Onions, green	Year round	---
Parsnips	Oct.-March	same
Peas, green	March-Sept.	April-May
Peppers	Year round	June-Nov.
Potatoes, Calif. mostly white or boiling	Year round	May-Oct.
Oregon, mostly baking		Oct.-April
Idaho, mostly Russets or baking		Aug.-March
Radishes	Year round	---
Rutabagas	Sept.-March	same
Spinach	Year round	---
Squash, winter	Sept.-April	Oct.-Jan.
summer	Year round	April-Oct.
Sweet Potatoes	Year round	Sept.-Dec.
Tomatoes	Year round	June-Sept.
Turnips	Year round	---

Nutrition information resources

Practical information on nutrition can be obtained from a wide variety of sources. However, it is often difficult to distinguish between accurate and inaccurate information. The following books and publications are suggested as reliable sources on nutrition and related food topics. Most have been recommended by the Society for Nutrition Education with some additions made by the Home Economists of the Consumers Cooperative of Berkeley.

Basic nutrition books

The following books are often used in introductory college courses and can be read without an extensive background in science.

Arlin, M.T. *The Science of Nutrition*, 2nd ed., Macmillan Publishing Co., 886 3rd Ave., New York, N.Y. 10022, 1977, 462 pp. A physiological approach to nutrition is emphasized; chapters on food supply and safety are included.

Bogert, L.J., G.M. Briggs and D.H. Calloway. *Nutrition and Physical Fitness*, 9th ed. (revision due 1978), W.B. Saunders Co., West Washington Square, Philadelphia, Pa 19105, 1973. A comprehensive basic nutrition text, chapters on food habits and beliefs and food processing are included.

Deutsch, R.M. *Realities of Nutrition*, Bull Publishing Co., P.O. Box 208, Palo Alto, Ca 94302, 1976, 405 pp. A popularized approach exposes facts and fallacies and discusses the basis of present nutrition knowledge.

Guthrie, H.A. *Introductory Nutrition*, 4th Ed., The C.V. Mosby Co., 11830 Westline Industrial Dr., St. Louis, MO 63141, 1979. The comprehensive coverage of basic nutrition also includes a discussion of contemporary concerns.

Runyan, T.J. *Nutrition for Today*, Harper and Row, 10 E. 53rd St., New York, NY 10022, 1976, 472 pp. Health, nutrition and contemporary issues are stressed.

Whitney, E. and M. Hamilton. *Understanding Nutrition*, West Publishing Co., 50 W. Kellogg Blvd., P.O. Box 3526, St. Paul, MN 55165, 1977, 607 pp. Understanding is stressed through explorations of contemporary issues related to the basic concepts of nutrition.

Periodicals for the general public

Consumer Reports, Consumers Union of the United States, Inc., 256 Washington St., Mount Vernon, NY 10550, monthly.

Consumer Information, A Catalog of Selected Federal Publications of Consumer Interest, Consumer Information Center, Pueblo, CO 81009, quarterly, free.

Family Health, Family Health Magazine, 149 5th Ave., New York, NY 10010, monthly.

Nutrition Action, Center for Sciences in the Public Interest, 1755 S St., N.W., Washington, DC 20009, monthly.

Basic references

Handbook of Food Preparation, 7th ed., American Home Economics Association, 2010 Massachusetts Ave., N.W., Washington, DC 20036, 1975.

National Nutrition Consortium, Inc., with R.M. Deutsch. *Nutrition Labeling: How It Can Work For You*, Nutrition Labeling, P.O. Box 4110, Kankakee, IL 60901, 1975, 134 pp., softcover.

Nutritive Value of American Foods in Common Units, Agriculture Handbook No. 456, Superintendent of Documents, U.S. Government Printing Office, Washington, DC 20402, 1975.

Food for the family

The following books cover a wide variety of nutrition issues — food additives, vegetarian diets, child and pet nutrition, nutrition during pregnancy and food for athletes.

Food for Little People, City of Berkeley Department of Public Health and the Berkeley Unified School District, 2180 Milvia St., Berkeley, CA 94704. Suggestions and recipes for snacks for young children.

Goodwin, M.T. and Pollen, G. *Creative Food Experiences for Children,* Center for Science in the Public Interest, 1755 S St., N.W., Washington, DC 20009, 1974, softcover. Numerous suggestions of food activities, games and recipes for teaching children about food and nutrition.

Hatfield, A.D. and P.S. Stanton, *Help! My Child Won't Eat Right: A Guide to Better Nutrition,* Acropolis Books, Std., 2400 17th St., N.W., Washington, DC 20009, 1973. Suggestions for dealing with problem eaters.

Jacobson, M. *Eater's Digest, The Consumer's Factbook of Food Additives, Are They Safe?* Doubleday and Co., Inc., Garden City, NY, 1976. A guide to food additives commonly used in foods. Discusses history of use, why used in foods and whether the additive poses a threat to health.

Kienholz, E. *Pet Nutrition,* Interstate Printers and Publishers, Inc., Danville, IL 61832, 1977, 247 pp. Common and not-so-common questions about feeding pet animals are answered. Nutrition, diet and pet food composition are discussed.

Lambert-Lagace, L. *Feeding Your Child,* Collier-Macmillan Canada, Ltd., 539 Collier-Macmillan Dr., Cambridge (Galt), Ontario, NIR 5W9, Canada, 1976, 274 pp., softcover. Nutrition during pregnancy, the value of breast feeding, and food and nutrition for the baby and toddler are discussed.

Nutrition and social concern

From the Ground Up: A Grassroots Food Policy, Center for Science in the Public Interest, 1755 S St., N.W., Washington, DC 20009, 1975. A manual for local organizing around food issues.

Hightower, J. *Eat Your Heart Out: How Food Profiteers Victimize the Consumer,* Crown Publishers, Inc., 419 Park Ave. South, New York, N.Y. 10016, 1975, 259 pp. Discusses how the American consumer is victimized by huge conglomerates that control our food supply.

Katz, D. and Goodwin, M. *Food: Where Nutrition, Politics and Culture Meet,* Center for Science in the Public Interest, 1755 S. St., N.W., Washington, DC 20009. A guide for high school and college teachers featuring activities to help students and teachers learn about world food problems.

Lappe, F., Collins, J., and Fowler, C. *Food First,* Houghton Mifflin Co., One Beacon St., Boston, MA 02107, 1977, 460 pp. Discusses food and the politics of hunger worldwide.

School Lunch Action Guide, Center for Science in the Public Interest, 1755 S St., N.W., Washington, DC 20009, 1976. A step-by-step action guide for improving school lunches.

Lappe, F.M., *Diet for a Small Planet,* Ballantine Books, Westminster, MD 21157, 1975, 411 pp. Alternatives to eating animal protein are discussed, and useful information is given on complementing plant proteins to assure a balanced essential amino acid intake.

Levy, J. and P. Bach-y-rita. *Vitamins: Their Use and Abuse,* Liveright, New York, NY, 1976, 116 pp. Basic information about vitamins; discusses common myths and vitamin needs for special circumstances such as pregnancy. Written by an M.D. and Pharmacologist.

McWilliams, M. *Nutrition for the Growing Years,* 2nd ed., John Wiley & Sons, Inc., 605 Third Ave., New York, NY 10016, 1975, 452 pp. Basic nutrition and physical and mental development from conception through maturity is covered as well as the special nutritional requirements of pregnancy, lactation and the growing years.

Mayer, J. *A Diet for Living,* Pocket Books, a division of Simon and Schuster, Inc., 1 West 39th St., New York, NY 10018, 267 pp., 1977. Numerous consumer questions about basic nutrition, weight problems, "healthy" foods, and buying and preparing foods are answered.

Robertson, L., C. Flinders and B. Godfrey, *Laurel's Kitchen: A Handbook for Vegetarian Cookery and Nutrition*, Nilgiri Press, Box 477, Petaluma, CA 94952, 1976, 508 pp. Nutrition basics, the nutrient content of foods, recipes and menus for the vegetarian are discussed.

Special diets

Eshelman, R. and M. Winston, *The American Heart Association Cook Book*, David McKay Co., Inc., 750 Third Ave., New York, NY 10017, 1973.

Katch, F.I. and W.D. McArdle, *Nutrition, Weight Control and Exercise*, Houghton Mifflin Co., One Beacon St., Boston, MA 02107, 1977, 365 pp., softcover.

Osman, J.D. *Thin From Within*, Hart Publishing Co., Inc., 15 W 4th St., New York, N.Y. 10012, 1976, 400 pp. The relationship of foods, energy intake and expenditure, and weight are discussed as well as behavior modification techniques. A food composition table listing calories and nutrients is included.

Shattuck, R.R., *Creative Cooking without Wheat, Milk and Eggs*, A.S. Barnes and Co., Inc., Box 421, Cranbury, NJ 18512, 1974.

Low Calorie Cookbooks:

Jones, J. *Calculating Cook*, 101 Productions of Berkeley, hardcover, soft cover. Includes exchange information for diabetics as well as information for dieters.

Nidetch, J., *The Weight Watcher's Program Cook Book*, New American Library.

For Athletes

Smith, N.J., *Food for Sport*, Bull Publishing Co., P.O. Box 208, Palo Alto, CA 94302, 1976, 188 pp., softcover. Basic nutrition and special topics of interest to athletes of all ages are discussed, e.g., pre-game meals, fluid intake and glycogen loading.

Contacts for Reliable Nutrition Information

For general questions, contact a nutritionist at one of the following:

1. Your city, county or state health department.
2. The U.S. Department of Agriculture - County Cooperative Extension Service
3. The home economist at your neighborhood Co-op
4. The gas and/or electric company

For questions on special diets, contact a registered dietitian or nutritionist associated with one of the following:

1. Your local or state volunteer health organizations - heart association, diabetes, etc.
2. Your local or state public health department.
3. Your local hospital or clinic

Index

Recipe Index